Outside In

Outside In

The Transnational Circuitry
of US History

Edited by
ANDREW PRESTON
AND
DOUG ROSSINOW

OXFORD
UNIVERSITY PRESS

OXFORD
UNIVERSITY PRESS

Oxford University Press is a department of the University of Oxford. It furthers the University's objective of excellence in research, scholarship, and education by publishing worldwide. Oxford is a registered trade mark of Oxford University Press in the UK and certain other countries.

Published in the United States of America by Oxford University Press
198 Madison Avenue, New York, NY 10016, United States of America.

Library of Congress Cataloging-in-Publication Data
Names: Preston, Andrew, 1973– editor of compilation. | Rossinow, Douglas C.
    (Douglas Charles), editor of compilation.
Title: Outside in : the transnational circuitry of US history / edited by
    Andrew Preston and Doug Rossinow.
Description: New York, NY : Oxford University Press, [2016] | Includes
    bibliographical references and index.
Identifiers: LCCN 2016024416 (print) | LCCN 2016038133 (ebook) |
    ISBN 9780190459857 (paperback : acid-free paper) | ISBN 9780190459840
    (hardcover : acid-free paper) | ISBN 9780190459864 (Updf) |
    ISBN 9780190459871 (Epub)
Subjects: LCSH: United States—Relations. | United States—Foreign relations. |
    United States—History—1865– | Transnationalism—Political
    aspects—United States—History. | Social networks—Political
    aspects—United States—History. | Political culture—United
    States—History. | Internationalism—Social aspects—United
    States—History. | United States—Social conditions.
Classification: LCC E183.7 .O88 2016 (print) | LCC E183.7 (ebook) | DDC
    327.73—dc23
LC record available at https://lccn.loc.gov/2016024416

9 8 7 6 5 4 3 2 1

Hardback printed by Webcom, Inc., Canada
Paperback printed by Bridgeport National Bindery, Inc., United States of America

Contents

Acknowledgments

This volume is a true product of collaboration in the best sense. Our thanks must begin with Tony Badger, Bruce Schulman, and Julian Zelizer, the three luminaries who established and led an annual conference dedicated to American political history—an enterprise that, since 2006, has helped set the agenda for the field. Each year, the conference rotated among their home institutions—Cambridge, Boston, and Princeton universities, respectively—and featured a different theme with a wide variety of speakers from the United Kingdom and the United States. The conference not only has contributed to the field of American political history but also has forged enduring transatlantic links of scholarship and friendship. On one occasion when it was his turn to host, Tony invited the editors to come up with a theme and organize the proceedings. That was the beginning of a journey. The end, after numerous changes and with several splendid additions to our caravan along the way, is this volume. We are incredibly grateful to Tony for his faith in us, and for generously funding the conference.

Under Tony's leadership, the staff at Clare College, University of Cambridge, kindly and tirelessly devoted themselves to making the conference a great success. To all who participated in that meeting, we give heartfelt thanks. To all our brilliant volume contributors, we stand in awe of your learning, your accomplishments, and your patience as we reworked the conference proceedings into a more coherent and cohesive book. Finally, Susan Ferber, of Oxford University Press, has displayed remarkable measures of faith, wisdom, and good humor in helping us to get this work to print and to make it the book we envisioned. There would be no book without her support.

Contributors

Leslie A. Butler is associate professor of history at Dartmouth College. She is the author of *Critical Americans: Victorian Intellectuals and Transatlantic Liberal Reform* (Chapel Hill: University of North Carolina Press, 2007).

Darren Dochuk is associate professor of history at the University of Notre Dame. He is the author of *From Bible Belt to Sunbelt: Plain-folk Religion, Grassroots Politics, and the Rise of Evangelical Conservatism* (New York: W. W. Norton & Co., 2011) and co-editor of *Faith in the New Millennium: The Future of Religion and American Politics* (New York: Oxford University Press, 2016). His forthcoming book examines the politics of religion and oil in America's long twentieth century.

Marilyn Lake is Australian Research Council Professorial Fellow and professor in history at the University of Melbourne. Her books include the prize-winning *Drawing the Global Colour Line: White Men's Countries and the International Challenge of Racial Equality* (Cambridge: Cambridge University Press, 2008).

Minkah Makalani is associate professor in the African and African diaspora studies department at the University of Texas at Austin. He is the author of *In the Cause of Freedom: Radical Black Internationalism from Harlem to London, 1917–1939* (Chapel Hill: University of North Carolina Press, 2011), and co-editor (with Davarian Baldwin) of *Escape* *from New York: The New Negro Renaissance beyond Harlem* (Minneapolis: University of Minnesota Press, 2013).

Melani McAlister is associate professor of American studies, international affairs, and media & public affairs at the George Washington University. She is the author of *Our God in the World: The Global Visions of American Evangelicals* (New York: Oxford University Press, forthcoming).

Andrew Preston is professor of American history and a Fellow of Clare College at Cambridge University. He is currently writing a book on the idea of national security in American history as well as editing Volume 2 of *The Cambridge History of the Vietnam War.*

Doug Rossinow teaches in the faculty of history at the University of Oslo. He is the author of *The Reagan Era: A History of the 1980s* (New York: Columbia University Press, 2015), and is currently writing a history of American Zionism since 1948.

Daniel Sargent is associate professor of history at the University of California, Berkeley. He is the author of *A Superpower Transformed: The Remaking of American Foreign Relations in the 1970s* (New York: Oxford University Press, 2015) and a co-editor of *The Shock of the Global: The 1970s in Perspective* (Cambridge, MA: Harvard University Press, 2010).

Jay Sexton is the Kinder Institute Chair in Constitutional Democracy and professor of history at the University of Missouri. He is author of *Debtor Diplomacy: Finance and American Foreign Relations in the Civil War Era, 1837–1873* (New York: Oxford University Press, 2014) and *The Monroe Doctrine: Empire and Nation in Nineteenth-Century America* (New York: Hill and Wang, 2011).

Elizabeth Tandy Shermer is assistant professor of history at Loyola University in Chicago. She has published opinion pieces, journal articles, literature reviews, edited collections, and the monograph *Sunbelt Capitalism: Phoenix and the Transformation of American Politics* (Philadelphia: University of Pennsylvania Press, 2013). Her current project, *The Business of Education*, explores the twentieth-century transformation of American colleges and universities.

Moshik Temkin is associate professor of history and public policy at Harvard University's Kennedy School of Government. His publications include *The Sacco-Vanzetti Affair: America on Trial* (New Haven: Yale University Press, 2011).

Ian Tyrrell is emeritus professor of history at the University of New South Wales, Sydney, Australia. He is the author of *Crisis of the Wasteful Nation: Empire and Conservation in Theodore Roosevelt's America* (Chicago: University of Chicago Press, 2015), and many other books.

Outside In

Introduction

America within the World

Andrew Preston and Doug Rossinow

Although historians do not often like to admit it, their concerns are shaped by the world around us. They try to avoid the dangers of teleology and "presentism" but are naturally drawn to subjects that have contemporary resonance. The once-neglected but now-popular histories of human rights, humanitarianism, and globalization are three prime examples of how historians have shed significant light on human history, but it is no coincidence that these three subjects are major concerns in the contemporary world. This is not necessarily a criticism. Historical research continues to evolve alongside humanity itself, and as societies and cultures develop so does our understanding of the past. As it turns out, people of the past were indeed concerned with human rights and global interconnectedness, an insight that might have eluded historians had they not been alert to the world around them. Sometimes a "presentist" approach allows for the recovery of historical worlds that have been unjustly forgotten.

A good example is the "transnational turn," which emerged out of the acute awareness of globalization that surged in the 1990s and has enabled historians to write global social histories. With their emphases on nonstate actors, works using transnationalism as a dimension of analysis have led historians to uncover globalist sensibilities from an earlier age. In many ways, our current era, it now appears, has more in common with the period between 1870 and 1910 than it does with the nationalism, state-building initiatives, and obsession with sovereignty and self-determination that characterized the world wars and the Cold War. The period betw een 1930 and 1970 marked what some have called a moment of "de-globalization," framed by preceding and succeeding eras of intense and enthusiastic globalization.[1] This mid-twentieth century period of high nationalism, which once shaped our view of all the history that came before, now begins to look anomalous.

Historians have become much less respectful of national sovereignties and much more aware of their own "methodological nationalism" for the simple reason that people, ideas, goods, and institutions have often disregarded national borders and state prerogatives.[2] It is also a reminder that other political forms are in fact much older and more enduring than the nation-state, whether larger (in conception if not always in geographic area), such as an empire, or smaller, such as a tribe.[3] With these basic premises in mind, it is clear that nation-states as we have known them are not static, unchanging, or impermeable. They are shaped and reshaped, over and over, by the world around them.

Yet the nation-state is not about to disappear. It has been buffeted, and weakened in some ways, by the simultaneous integrative and fragmentary forces of globalization, but it remains the single dominant political unit in the world today. Corporate giants like Google adapt themselves to the demands of national governments, and if a small developing nation decides to seize and nationalize privately held oil fields there may be surprisingly little Exxon-Mobil or BP can do about it—indeed, their main recourse may be to turn to another nation-state and co-opt its military power or legal system for redress. International organizations such as the World Bank and the International Monetary Fund are only as effective as the ability of their individual members to cooperate, and even supranational bodies that have managed to dilute national sovereignty, such as the European Union, can be frustrated by the recalcitrance of a single member state. Although the nation-state is only a few centuries old, and although it has only been the global political norm for approximately sixty years, it is firmly entrenched in the modern world system.

This is also true historiographically.[4] The historical discipline professionalized around the same time, in the nineteenth century, when the industrialized nation-state proliferated throughout Europe, North America, and Japan. As a result, history departments around the world are still organized along national lines even for periods when there was no nation-state to speak of. US survey courses, for example, are usually labeled as such even for the period before the United States existed. Easily identified, the problem is still difficult to avoid; even definitions of what is international or transnational intrinsically use the nation as their benchmark. Perceiving American history within a larger framework does not negate the importance of the nation-state; it simply places nations within a different context that can reveal perspectives not normally available to national historiographies.

Thus, while the shortcomings of national histories are clear, so too is a solution. In addition to—and not instead of—national history, a wider variety of historical accounts that are both larger and smaller than the nation are needed. By expanding the geographical scale, the relatively recent fields of world history and global history have gone larger. They have superseded the nation-state in many ways and revealed completely new historical vantage points in the process. They do not ignore the nation-state, but instead enfold nations within wider analyses—usually on topics, such as demographic or climatic change, that are inherently transnational[5]—that are not bound by the strictures of national sovereignty.

The offerings in this book reflect a desire to opt for a larger frame. They are not world or global histories, although they share common traits with both. They are not comparative histories, either, although they prioritize sources and perspectives from other nations, cultures, and societies. Neither are they examples of foreign relations history—a field that is now known, as Thomas Zeiler and Thomas Borstelmann have pointed out, as "the U.S. and the World" due largely to the transnational and cultural turns[6]—although some of them would fall comfortably under that rubric. Instead, the aim of *Outside In* is to demonstrate the ways in which the history of the modern United States can be reconceived internationally and transnationally.

There are no firmly established definitions of these terms—one analysis describes transnationalism as a perspective, not a method[7]—but some disciplinary understandings have emerged. At their most fundamental level, both international history and transnational history focus on topics that both cross and transcend national borders. The key difference between them is that, while international history privileges relations among states, transnational history examines relations among peoples below the state level. One way of thinking of the difference is that international history follows a more traditional historiographical path by examining the state, its officials, and its structures, usually on the basis of research in state archives. Transnational history does not ignore the nation-state—that would be nearly impossible for topics going back to the early modern period—but it focuses on interactions between people who do not wield state power. Whereas international history tends to focus on top-down topics of politics, economics, diplomacy, and war, transnationalism more often provides a bottom-up, social history of the world. Transnational history may incorporate topics such as politics, economics, and foreign relations, but primarily by tracing the stories of nongovernmental institutions and individuals. Unsurprisingly, while international history was one of the founding fields in the discipline of professional, academic history (it was one of Leopold von Ranke's specialties), transnational history is newer, at least conceived as such.[8] *Outside In* does not favor either of them. As with distinctions between state and society and between "inside" and "outside" particular nation-states, the opposition of international to transnational history can be easier to make in theory than in practice. Some of this volume's contributors focus on international history and others on transnational history, but some bring the stories of state and nonstate actors together.

This is, of course, far from the first book to do this. Over the past two decades, historians have powerfully contextualized the American past globally. In 1999, David Thelen assembled a breakout issue on "Transnational Perspectives on United States History" in the flagship journal of American history, the *Journal of American History*.[9] Two subsequent efforts also stand out for their efforts to pioneer a new, internationalized approach to the study of US history. To Ian Tyrrell, the United States is a "transnational nation"—the title he chose for his 2007 overview of the topic—that has been produced over time by successive waves of various foreign influences. In this sense, American history did not develop in isolation but as an inextricable part of world history. "Localism," Tyrrell rightly observes, "was globally produced."[10] Sensing that both the American public and professional historians had become too insular, Thomas Bender launched his own major initiative. "America is 'here,' and the international is 'over there,'" he points out in the introduction to *Rethinking American History in a Global Age*, which provided, collectively, something akin to the mission statement of a movement. "If there is a practical aim in this enterprise of rethinking and de-provincializing the narrative of American history, it is to integrate the stories of American history with other, larger stories from which, with a kind of continental self-sufficiency, the United States has isolated itself."[11] Bender followed the multiplicity of voices in *Rethinking American History in a Global Age* with his own synthesis that reinterpreted American history as an aspect of world history. In this sweeping overview, the United States was no longer a superpower or a New World colossus forging its own way, but "a nation among nations." His two primary objectives were mutually reinforcing: first, to show that "global history commenced when American history began"; and second, to demonstrate that "American history cannot be adequately understood unless it is incorporated into that global context." No more than any other country, the United States "cannot be its own context."[12]

As Bender argues, while American history is an aspect of modern world history, modern world history cannot be fully comprehended without reference to the United States, a conclusion to which world historians themselves have been alert. In their accounts of the emergence of a modern world system since the late eighteenth century, historians such as C. A. Bayly and Jürgen Osterhammel have treated the United States very much as a nation among nations with causal flows running in both directions: as a nation that has been shaped by global phenomena and other nations, but one that has also contributed a great deal to creating those global phenomena and those other nations.[13] In David Reynolds's telling, global currents helped forge the United States in the eighteenth and nineteenth centuries, and in turn the United States became the primary driver of globalization in the twentieth century.[14]

Yet the extent to which the United States was deeply enmeshed in the modern world system was not always appreciated—probably not by world historians, certainly not by American historians, and definitely not by the wider American public. As the novelist Marilynne Robinson has observed, "Americans are astonished to realize that Karl Marx and Abraham Lincoln were contemporaries," that Marx wrote about Lincoln and that Lincoln read Marx. "This is only one illustration of the great fact that we have little sense of American history in the context of world history. Given our power and influence," she concludes, "it seems a sad failure that we have not done more to make the world intelligible to ourselves, and ourselves to the world."[15] That may no longer be the case, as recently seen in the wonderful recent global histories of US icons such as the Declaration of Independence and Abraham Lincoln, though there is much more yet to be done.[16] Change is finally filtering down into the classroom, too, in high schools as well as universities.[17]

Beyond the level of world history, regional and interregional histories have provided models for how to internationalize and transnationalize US history. The largest field in this genre is undoubtedly "the Atlantic World." Consisting of the eastern side of the Americas, western Europe, and the western coasts of Africa, as well as the crucially important oceanic island environments, the Atlantic World is an imagined space in which the fluid interactions of goods, people, and ideas pulls together disparate geographical parts into a coherent political, cultural, and social whole. This is not to say that the features of the Atlantic World were constant or uncontested; nor is it to say that the Atlantic World was a fixed entity or place. Instead, reconceiving the rimlands of the Atlantic Ocean as sites of exchange allows us to appreciate the extent to which cultures interacted and, in the process, transcended the strictures of their national or imperial sovereignties.[18] Imperial and migration histories had to a large extent always been about the Atlantic World, but the new approach has opened the door to innovative transnational social analyses[19] and histories of racial politics[20] as well. A parallel initiative makes a compelling case for the analytic utility of "Pacific worlds."[21] Related fields (albeit ones that have, like the Atlantic World, built upon older historiographical foundations), such as borderlands history,[22] the history of international thought,[23] and American imperial history,[24] hold similar promise.

Comparative history, which has a long and distinguished pedigree in the historiography of the United States, offers similar benefits. Subjects that are inarguably central to the American experience, such as racial ideologies or slavery and emancipation, have been shown, in comparative context, to be regional or global phenomena and not uniquely American.[25] In his massive, four-volume history of the world from ancient Mesopotamia to the year 2011, for example, the historical sociologist Michael Mann places the United States squarely at the center of the development of modernity, yet merely as one of several major actors (be they nations, states, empires, or classes). Doing so enables Mann to highlight what was distinctive and consequential about the US contribution to world history—such as, in the nineteenth century, an unusual disparity between its internal repression of class struggle and an equally unusual weakness on the world stage—without portraying the United States as somehow exceptional and set apart.[26]

Comparative histories, however, have not always been able to avoid exceptionalism. By its very nature, exceptionalism needs, at least implicitly, a comparative framework: if the United States is different and/or better than other nations and societies, it is essential to know something about them in order to judge the United States. The debate over exceptionalism is long-standing, fraught, and nearly impossible to resolve. But without denying that the United States and the American people have been different in some respects, it is our view that perceptions of the United States as exceptional are problematic and, for the most part, unhelpful and unproductive.[27] As Tyrrell argued in a seminal article over two decades ago, international and transnational approaches to American history can unsettle exceptionalist assumptions.[28]

As the chapters in this book demonstrate, many of the political and economic values, culture, institutions, and ideologies that lie at the center of US history are not always intrinsically, organically, or completely "American." This is not an entirely new approach. James Kloppenberg and Daniel Rodgers have shown how transatlantic links, and especially the sharing of ideas and theories about social democracy, shaped American progressivism in the late nineteenth and early twentieth centuries; Tyrrell has done likewise for women's activism on suffrage and temperance in the same era.[29] Economic historians have usually assumed their subject to have important dimensions crossing national borders. Nonetheless, the transnational framework is very much in the minority of US historiography; the work just referenced is still considered exemplary for this very reason. Moreover, recent calls by historians such as Tyrrell and Bender to internationalize and transnationalize US history have taken the form of programmatic and diagnostic syntheses.[30] While they have provided important blueprints for an architecture of historical scholarship, it is now up to historians to provide the bricks and mortar, through detailed empirical and historiographical work, and to move from a blueprint to a usable structure.

Instead of offering another theoretical or programmatic statement of what transnational or international history of the United States ought to be, this book presents an array of detailed, careful examples of this kind of scholarship, with particular focus on the ways in which the transnational flow and recirculation of people, ideas, goods, and actions have shaped the United States. Much of the scholarship on the international and transnational dimensions of American history has paid detailed attention to how the United States interacted with the world by projecting Americans and their ideas and culture outward; this is certainly true of the "U.S. and the World," the established subfield of American history that is most inherently international and transnational. Not coincidentally, one of the first topics to be thoroughly internationalized was the export of US culture and other societies' reception of it.[31] This is a productive approach, and the contributors deploy it to varying extents, but it only covers a small part of the story. For one thing, in much of the Americanist historiography, there is still an assumption that the United States shapes the world but not the other way around, particularly in the twentieth century. But the title of this book, *Outside In*, emphasizes how the rest of the world has shaped US history. One fine example of such an approach is Brooke Blower's account of how expatriate Americans in interwar Paris embraced different political ideologies and formed a new political and social consciousness in the process, one that was scarcely "American" in origin at all.[32] John Fabian Witt has similarly probed the extent to which American legal history was affected by foreign influences.[33] Something similar is happening among labor historians.[34] And in political science, Ira Katznelson and Martin Shefter have made a similar plea for attention to external pressures on American political development.[35] This is a perspective *Outside In* intends to help widen.

Beyond the question of "inside out" or "outside in" directions of influence, however, is the reality that many transnational forces circulated through, across, and between national spaces. This "circuitry," as the book's subtitle indicates, in which currents of action and thought by Americans and others zoomed around the globe, helped make the American world a global world.[36] Some of the actors discussed in the essays seemed to operate in spaces not dominated by nation-states. But even the notion of such "in between" spaces suggests a mutual insulation of state and nonstate realms that much of the work here reveals as unrealistic and artificial. In the largest sense, the term "outside in" denotes not the incursion of external forces into a neatly defined American space, but rather the historical reality that the lived experience of

North Americans took shape within, and was constituted by, a circulatory system that was intrinsically transnational—a circulatory system that interacted with, rather than transcending or overriding, the international system of sovereign states.

There is a good reason historians have not focused as much on the international influences on recent American history: in political, economic, cultural, and military terms, the United States has been disproportionately powerful and influential. It is easy to conceive of the United States, in the past century, exporting power; it is more unusual to think of it importing formative influences. This is especially true of history since 1945, if not 1917, which is perhaps why most internationalized perspectives on US history—be they Atlantic World, borderlands, or programmatic syntheses such as Bender's *A Nation among Nations*—cover periods before World War II. Tyrrell's synthesis does examine the period after 1945 in some detail, but he also argues that by World War I "the nation's balance sheet eventually tipped in favour of outward flows" and, as a result, "the American people became ... more insular than in the nineteenth century."[37] Thus, the international and transnational aspects of US historiography are tilted heavily to the centuries before 1900. There are some exceptions—notably Thomas Borstelmann's incisive account of America in the global 1970s[38]—but overall, more recent eras have not been as thoroughly integrated into the field's international and transnational turns. The essays gathered here, taken together, make a strong case for the relevance of international and transnational history throughout modern US history. They begin their story in the late nineteenth century and then pay a great deal of attention to the twentieth century, dealing with events both before and after World War II.

Outside In's first two essays, by Jay Sexton and Daniel Sargent, provide very different but comparably sweeping big-picture perspectives, offering the view "from 30,000 feet" in terms of, respectively, diplomacy—or "statecraft," as Sexton terms his subject—and political economy at a transnational level. Sexton provides a genealogy of the "Monroe Doctrine" in US history from the 1820s to the 1900s, explaining that there were plural meanings to this constructed and continually reconstructed "doctrine." Never simply an untroubled statement of US hegemonic aspirations in the Western Hemisphere, Sexton shows, the famous doctrine was, in its various incarnations, the product of a transnational and international force field, as US elites responded to both internal North American tensions and the imperial system, in which Britain occupied prime position. Sexton persuasively illustrates how the international history of the United States has to account both for "inside out" and "outside in" dynamics.

Daniel Sargent powerfully juxtaposes what he terms a transnational economic order of trade and investment with the international order of political economy from the 1860s through the 1970s. Taking the long view and deploying a mass of data, he finds an inverse correlation between the economic interdependence of the United States with the outside world and the US willingness to provide leadership in international economic management. Seeing American leadership crest between 1945 and 1970, when the US enjoyed relative economic autonomy, and then falter afterward, when such leadership was, perhaps, badly needed, Sargent ends by suggesting that political dynamics within the United States overcame the objective demands of the international system. In this way he also authoritatively asserts the importance of the national state in fully explaining the course of a globalizing economy.

The next two essays, by Leslie Butler and Marilyn Lake, extend and deepen the study of overseas Anglophone political reform, exploring both Atlantic and Pacific "crossings" over a seventy-five-year period.[39] Butler probes the edges of the internationalist reform discourse of the nineteenth century by describing the retreat of elite thinkers from the Anglophone demand for women's political equality during the decade following the conclusion of the US Civil War. Taking the bounding optimism for US citizenship expansion in the immediate aftermath of the war, in the mid-1860s, and J. S. Mill's famous advocacy of woman suffrage in 1869 as her points of departure, Butler charts the increasingly unwelcome reception of gender egalitarianism on both American and British shores as the 1870s proceeded. Some labeled this moment in Anglophone politics and culture an era of "advanced" thinking. Others, however, feared such changes in gender relations as drastic and radical, and Butler shows that a broad transatlantic current of social thought moved in a conservative direction.

Marilyn Lake follows the pathways of the Australian jurist H. B. Higgins as he made a direct impact on the American debate over the idea of a "living wage" from the 1910s to the 1930s. The Fair Labor Standards Act (FLSA) of 1938, which produced the federal minimum wage in the United States—at least for many workers, as others were pointedly omitted—is still largely interpreted, as Lake stresses, in terms of the forces and limitations of domestic American politics. She makes the broader context of the American debate, and its ultimate resolution in law, inescapable. Lake also points out the reciprocal influences between, in this case, Australia and the United States, and concludes by noting the acute awareness, after 1938, of the discrepancy between Australian and American law's treatment of female workers, with Australian feminist activists facing a continued struggle to gain the equal—at least in theory—standing that women workers gained in the FLSA.

The following three essays—by Ian Tyrrell, Melani McAlister, and Darren Dochuk—all focus on religious institutions, actors, and beliefs as these circulated energetically in transnational networks. The work of these three historians convincingly demonstrates the signal relevance of religious history as a site for transnational studies. Tyrrell's essay closes a circle of a kind, as a pioneer in transnational history offers a masterly account of current scholarship in the rapidly growing field of missionary history. He wryly describes the old view of US "expansion" in the 1890s as a soda-can vision of internal pressure causing an outward explosion. Instead, Tyrrell pushes America's outward thrust back to the 1870s, as technical changes enabled preexisting missionary impulses to migrate abroad. He then follows the globe-trotting paths of missionaries as they responded to inspirations and challenges from both European colleagues and indigenous religious revivals in India and elsewhere. Refraining from easy indictments of missionaries as agents of cultural imperialism, Tyrrell follows the field that he helped found by depicting these Christian internationalists as pulled and pushed within a complex, many-sided moral geography.

Melani McAlister, who employs the term "moral geographies" in her essay, delves into the political and moral conflicts that were always characteristic of missionary work, and that reached a new pitch amid the drama of decolonization and the shifting demographics of global evangelicalism after 1960. By focusing specifically on the controversy over Congolese independence and the embroilment of (largely white) US missionaries in that country between 1960 and 1965, McAlister deeply examines the quandaries of a US-centered evangelicalism at that moment, and achieves a wonderfully multivocal account of this inflection point in the history of relations between the global North and South. She shows what white US evangelical Protestants, their African American counterparts, and Congolese Christians thought about these world events, all of them aware of the transnational environment in which they worked. Unwilling to settle for easy answers to the political questions her story raises, McAlister spotlights the problematic, if earnest, striving for a postcolonial, postracial identity among white evangelicals who saw their worlds undergoing transformation.

Darren Dochuk's essay shifts the focus from grassroots transnational activists to the heights of economic and political power, showcasing the nexus of religion, politics, and international business as it came clear amid the tar sands of Canadian oil. The populist and evangelical political leader Ernest Manning and the redoubtable (and American) J. Howard Pew, chairman of Sun Oil, stand at this story's center, as they advance both revivalist Protestantism and individualist social doctrine, cheerfully celebrating the exploitation of natural resources for profit and social betterment. Yet Pew and the other US-based conservatives, like Billy Graham, never compromised their stout nationalism even as they made deals across borders and forged transnational business and religious circuitry in the post-1945 decades. Another role of the nation-state in the field of transnational history begins to emerge with Dochuk's complex tale of oil and God: neoliberal believers used the state—sometimes more than one state—for their own purposes, among them the promotion of a laissez-faire agenda.[40]

Minkah Makalani advances a vital tendency within diasporic studies with his history of radical black diaspora activists whose horizons and aims were not defined by the nation-state. Determined to take his protagonists on their own terms, Makalani staunchly resists the sometimes unspoken assumptions of what he calls the nation-state's "teleology." He shows the tireless activists of the International Congress against Imperialism criss-crossing the globe throughout the era between the two world wars, endlessly negotiating the international system of state power, and ultimately left only with themselves fully, without qualification committed to their cause. Makalani's essay recreates an era in the internationalism of the disinherited, and it serves as a reminder that even when these black radicals did their best to make use of state power to advance their own agenda—in many instances linking up with the Soviet state, then arguably at the height of its global credibility with colonized peoples—such a fateful alliance brought only a partway, fractured, ultimately ambiguous result.

Elizabeth Tandy Shermer, with her detailed study of the career of Luther Hodges, a North Carolina business leader who became governor of his state, presents a dramatically different kind of internationalism, one that obtained from the 1940s through to the 1950s and far beyond, a neoliberal developmentalism carried around the world in the transnational circuitry of businessmen. Shermer shows how Hodges's post–World War II crusade to bring European capital investment to an economically peripheral zone of the United States was embedded in a preexisting vision of a world economy without borders and set free from meddling by state bureaucrats—a kind of "anti–New Deal for the world" that Hodges promoted even as he worked for the New Deal state during the war years. Here is another neoliberal internationalist who made pragmatic use of the state, at both the national and regional levels, for his own purposes—ones that helped create the contemporary world of economic interdependence and political disaffection from economic management that Daniel Sargent describes.

The internationalism of the far right is the subject of Doug Rossinow's essay. His survey of the transfer of counterinsurgency expertise from late-imperial warfare to US Cold War policy, and his outline of global rightist networks of unconventional-warfare thought and practice as deployed against the global left during the Cold War era, both point toward the surprisingly long roots of recent doctrines of the "war on terror." The left-versus-right narrative of the Cold War is superimposed here upon the broader history of great-power struggles against disruptive threats from below. Rossinow, following his story from the United States to Europe and then to Latin America and the Western Pacific, highlights the frank advocacy of fearsome violence by rightists, both in and outside of state structures, who saw themselves as allies fighting a world war without end.

Finally, Moshik Temkin, in his study of Americans abroad in France during the era of the US–Vietnam War, shows competing internationalisms squaring off against each other, even as he depicts the French state trying to monitor and control internationalist dissidents. To American eyes, Temkin's story of the French national-security state working to seal supposedly polluting foreign—American—political elements out of French national politics may seem eerily familiar, with the French state paralleling similar efforts by the US government in these same years. Temkin concludes with a bracing reminder of the power of the nation-state, even in an era of accelerating circulation of persons across borders, to "contain," as he puts it, internationalist political forces. At the same time, he identifies the international system of cooperating national states as an alternative, implicitly authoritarian internationalism that sought to repress the (perhaps more familiar) internationalism of the Left.

All of these rich and thought-provoking essays offer original and arresting insights, far too many to summarize here. But three recurrent themes, each representing an emerging emphasis in new work on the transnational dimension of US political history, demand at least a brief word. First is the basic importance of studying networks or circuits. In some ways, the "network society" may have existed long before the contemporary world in which, some claim, it has only recently emerged.[41] By documenting the cross-border institutions, informal groupings, conversations, and migrations that specific political actors forged and followed, historians are writing transnational history in the most concrete way. Second, much of transnational history is also international history and national history. This means that the most compelling and complete work in transnational history does not simply exalt nonstate and cross-border actors and downplay state power. Instead, this emerging work arranges a complex matrix of narration and analysis that locates people amid a dense array of forces—institutional and cultural, official and unofficial. A key part of this approach is taking state power seriously, but within the context of transnational history. Third is the evident plurality of internationalisms at work in the modern world. The importance of studying internationalism, meaning a consciousness or identity that takes meaning from, and gives fealty to, something broader than the nation-state, has been recognized by scholars of international and transnational history for many years.[42] Multiple varieties of internationalist identity appear in the essays collected here: the internationalism of statecraft, the internationalism of economic management, the internationalism of Christians, the internationalism of neoliberalism, the internationalism of racial cosmopolitans, the internationalism of warfare—and even, paradoxical though it seems, the internationalism of nationalisms. The history of the United States, it now appears, is shot through with contending international and transnational forces of all kinds, which related to one another and to the nation-state in a multitude of ways. There is no simple way to account for all these forces. Rather than a grand solution to these historical problems, then, *Outside In* offers starting points for new inquiries into American history.

NOTES

1. Ronald Findlay and Kevin H. O'Rourke, *Power and Plenty: Trade, War, and the World Economy in the Second Millennium* (Princeton: Princeton University Press, 2007), 429–76.

2. For "methodological nationalism," see Kenneth Pomeranz, "Histories for a Less National Age," *American Historical Review* 119, no. 1 (February 2014): 2. Such calls to transcend methodological nationalism, which have become increasingly frequent over the last two decades, have a normative element—a call for cosmopolitanism—in addition to an analytical one. While we confine ourselves to the analytical dimension here, we recognize the validity of a normative, even political, meaning to an anti-nationalist interpretive agenda. "People, ideas, goods, and institutions" are Ian Tyrrell's four categories of transnational agents. See his *Reforming the World: The Creation of America's Moral Empire* (Princeton: Princeton University Press, 2010), 6.

3. Jane Burbank and Frederick Cooper, *Empires in World History: Power and the Politics of Difference* (Princeton: Princeton University Press, 2011), 8–11.

4. A point made compellingly by David A. Hollinger, "The Historian's Use of the United States and Vice Versa," in *Rethinking American History in a Global Age*, ed. Thomas Bender (Berkeley: University of California Press, 2002), 381–95.

5. For demography, see Alison Bashford, *Global Population: History, Geopolitics, and Life on Earth* (New York: Columbia University Press, 2014). For climate, see J. R. McNeill, *Something New under the Sun: An Environmental History of the Twentieth-Century World* (New York: W. W. Norton & Co., 2000); and Edmund Burke III and Kenneth Pomeranz, eds., *The Environment and World History* (Berkeley: University of California Press, 2009).

6. Thomas W. Zeiler, "The Diplomatic History Bandwagon: A State of the Field," *Journal of American History* 95, no. 4 (March 2009): 1053–73; Thomas ("Tim")

Borstelmann, "Global Influences on the Historiography of U.S. Foreign Relations," in *America in the World: The Historiography of American Foreign Relations since 1941*, ed. Frank Costigliola and Michael J. Hogan (Cambridge: Cambridge University Press, 2013), 338–60.

7. Bernhard Struck, Kate Ferris, and Jacques Revel, "Space and Scale in Transnational History," *International History Review* 33, no. 4 (December 2011): 574.

8. Akira Iriye, a founder of both these approaches, observes concisely: "Whereas 'international' implies a relationship among nations, 'transnational' suggests various types of interactions across national boundaries. Extraterritorial movements of individuals, goods, capital, and even ideas would seem to be less international than transnational phenomena." Akira Iriye, "Internationalizing International History," in *Rethinking American History in a Global Age*, 51. See also Akira Iriye, *Global and Transnational History: The Past, Present, and Future* (New York: Palgrave Macmillan, 2012); and Pierre-Yves Saunier, *Transnational History* (New York: Palgrave Macmillan, 2013). As early as 1971, the international relations theorists Robert O. Keohane and Joseph S. Nye Jr. stressed the importance of studying not only states but also nonstate actors—the heart of transnational history as it stands today—in their essay "Transnational Relations and World Politics: An Introduction," *International Organization* 25, no. 3 (Summer 1971): 329–49. For further methodological reflections among historians, see C. A. Bayly et al., "AHR Conversation: On Transnational History," *American Historical Review* 111, no. 5 (December 2006): 1441–64.

9. *Journal of American History* 86, no. 3 (December 1999). See the introduction to the issue, David Thelen, "The Nation and Beyond: Transnational Perspectives on United States History," ibid., 965–76.

10. Ian Tyrrell, *Transnational Nation: United States History in Global Perspective since 1789* (New York: Palgrave Macmillan, 2007), 6.

11. Thomas Bender, "Historians, the Nation, and the Plenitude of Narratives," in *Rethinking American History in a Global Age*, 5–6.

12. Thomas Bender, *A Nation among Nations: America's Place in World History* (New York: Hill and Wang, 2006), 6–7.

13. C. A. Bayly, *The Birth of the Modern World, 1780–1914* (Malden, MA: Blackwell, 2004); Jürgen Osterhammel, *The Transformation of the World: A Global History of the Nineteenth Century*, trans. Patrick Camiller (Princeton: Princeton University Press, 2014).

14. David Reynolds, "American Globalism: Mass, Motion and the Multiplier Effect," in *Globalization in World History*, ed. A. G. Hopkins (New York: W. W. Norton & Co., 2002), 243–60.

15. Marilynne Robinson, *The Death of Adam: Essays on Modern Thought* (Boston: Houghton Mifflin, 1998), 10.

16. David Armitage, *The Declaration of Independence: A Global History* (Cambridge, MA: Harvard University Press, 2007); Richard Carwardine and Jay Sexton, eds., *The Global Lincoln* (New York: Oxford University Press, 2011).

17. Carl Guarneri and James Davis, eds., *Teaching American History in a Global Context* (Armonk, NY: M. E. Sharpe, 2008); David C. Engerman et al., "Internationalizing American History," *American Historian* 3 (February 2015): 28–42.

18. For a brilliant analysis of the field's evolution, see William O'Reilly, "Genealogies of Atlantic History," *Atlantic Studies* 1, no. 1 (April 2004): 66–84. For historiographical and programmatic overviews, see Bernard Bailyn, *Atlantic History: Concept and Contours* (Cambridge, MA: Harvard University Press, 2005); Jack P. Greene and Philip D. Morgan, eds., *Atlantic History: A Critical Appraisal* (New York: Oxford University Press, 2008); and David Armitage and Michael J. Braddick, eds., *The British Atlantic World, 1500–1800*, 2d ed. (New York: Palgrave Macmillan, 2009).

19. For a superb example, see Sarah Pearsall, *Atlantic Families: Lives and Letters in the Later Eighteenth Century* (New York: Oxford University Press, 2009).

20. Paul Gilroy, *The Black Atlantic: Modernity and Double Consciousness* (Cambridge, MA: Harvard University Press, 1993); Stephen Tuck, *The Night Malcolm X Spoke at the Oxford Union: A Transatlantic Story of Antiracist Protest* (Berkeley: University of California Press, 2014); Adam Ewing, *The Age of Garvey: How a Jamaican Activist Created a Mass Movement and Changed Global Black Politics* (Princeton: Princeton University Press, 2014). This framework for Americans' involvement in transnational racial politics can, of course, be extended beyond the Atlantic World. See, e.g., Penny M. Von Eschen, *Race against Empire: Black Americans and Anticolonialism, 1937–1957* (Ithaca, NY: Cornell University Press, 1997); Nico Slate, *Colored Cosmopolitanism: The Shared Struggle for Freedom in the United States and India* (Cambridge, MA: Harvard University Press, 2012); and Brenda Gayle Plummer, *In Search of Power: African Americans in the Era of Decolonization, 1956–1974* (Cambridge: Cambridge University Press, 2012). For an essential overview, see Robin D. G. Kelley, "How the West Was One: The African Diaspora and the Re-Mapping of U.S. History," in *Rethinking American History in a Global Age*, 123–47.

21. For overviews, see Nicholas Thomas, *Islanders: The Pacific in the Age of Empire* (New Haven: Yale University Press, 2010); Matt K. Matsuda, *Pacific Worlds: A History of Seas, Peoples, and Cultures* (Cambridge: Cambridge University Press, 2012); Camilla Fojas and Rudy P. Guevarra Jr., eds., *Transnational Crossroads: Remapping the Americas and the Pacific* (Lincoln: University of Nebraska Press, 2012); David Igler, *The Great Ocean: Pacific Worlds from Captain Cook to the Gold Rush* (New York: Oxford University Press, 2013); and David Armitage and Alison Bashford, eds., *Pacific Histories: Ocean, Land, People* (New York: Palgrave Macmillan, 2014). For examples that aim specifically to situate the history of the United States within the histories of the Pacific Ocean, see Evelyn Hu-Dehart, ed., *Across the Pacific: Asian Americans and Globalization* (Philadelphia: Temple University Press, 1999); and Bruce Cumings, *Dominion from Sea to Sea: Pacific Ascendancy and American Power* (New Haven: Yale University Press, 2009).

22. For overviews of borderlands as a discipline, see Jeremy Adelman and Stephen Aron, "From Borderlands to Borders: Empires, Nation-States, and the

Peoples in between in North American History," *American Historical Review* 104, no. 3 (June 1999): 814–84; Nathan J. Citino, "The Global Frontier: Comparative History and the Frontier-Borderlands Approach in American Foreign Relations," *Diplomatic History* 25, no. 4 (Fall 2001): 677–94; and Pekka Hämäläinen and Samuel Truett, "On Borderlands," *Journal of American History* 98, no. 2 (September 2011): 338–61. For examples of North American borderlands history that problematize the fixedness of national boundaries and sovereignties, see Samuel Truett and Elliott Young, eds., *Continental Crossroads: Remapping U.S.–Mexico Borderlands History* (Durham, NC: Duke University Press, 2004); Pekka Hämäläinen, *The Comanche Empire* (New Haven: Yale University Press, 2008); Brian DeLay, *War of a Thousand Deserts: Indian Raids and the U.S.–Mexican War* (New Haven: Yale University Press, 2008); Benjamin Johnson and Andrew R. Graybill, eds., *Bridging National Borders in North America: Transnational and Comparative Histories* (Durham, NC: Duke University Press, 2010); and Rachel St. John, *Line in the Sand: A History of the Western U.S.–Mexico Border* (Princeton: Princeton University Press, 2011). More broadly, see Michiel Baud and Willem Van Schendel, "Toward a Comparative History of Borderlands," *Journal of World History* 8, no. 2 (Fall 1997): 211–42.

23. David Armitage, *Foundations of Modern International Thought* (Cambridge: Cambridge University Press, 2013), 1–32; Duncan Bell, "Making and Taking Worlds," in *Global Intellectual History*, ed. Samuel Moyn and Andrew Sartori (New York: Columbia University Press, 2013).

24. Amy Kaplan and Donald E. Pease, eds., *Cultures of United States Imperialism* (Durham, NC: Duke University Press, 1993); Amy Kaplan, *The Anarchy of Empire in the Making of U.S. Culture* (Cambridge, MA: Harvard University Press, 2002); Paul A. Kramer, *The Blood of Government: Race, Empire, the United States, and the Philippines* (Chapel Hill: University of North Carolina Press, 2006); Alfred W. McCoy, *Policing America's Empire: The United States, the Philippines, and the Rise of the Surveillance State* (Madison: University of Wisconsin Press, 2009); Alfred W. McCoy and Francisco A. Scarano, eds., *Colonial Crucible: Empire in the Making of the Modern American State* (Madison: University of Wisconsin Press, 2009); Paul Kramer, "Power and Connection: Imperial Histories of the United States in the World," *American Historical Review* 116, no. 5 (December 2011), esp. 1357, 1363–65, 1383–87; Julian Go, *Patterns of Empire: The British and American Empires, 1688 to the Present* (Cambridge: Cambridge University Press, 2011); Jason M. Colby, *The Business of Empire: United Fruit, Race, and U.S. Expansion in Central America* (Ithaca, NY: Cornell University Press, 2011); Noel Maurer, *The Empire Trap: The Rise and Fall of U.S. Intervention to Protect American Property Overseas, 1893–2013* (Princeton: Princeton University Press, 2013).

25. On race, see George M. Fredrickson, *White Supremacy: A Comparative Study of American and South African History* (New York: Oxford University Press, 1981); and George M. Fredrickson, *Black Liberation: A Comparative History of Black Ideologies in the United States and South Africa* (New York: Oxford University Press, 1995). On slavery and emancipation, the comparative literature has a long pedigree and is therefore enormous, but for some recent examples, see Thomas C. Holt, *The Problem of Freedom: Race, Labor, and Politics in Jamaica and Britain,*

1832–1938 (Baltimore: The Johns Hopkins University Press, 1991); Seymour Drescher, *From Slavery to Freedom: Comparative Studies in the Rise and Fall of Atlantic Slavery* (New York: New York University Press, 1999); Rebecca J. Scott, *Degrees of Freedom: Louisiana and Cuba after Slavery* (Cambridge, MA: Harvard University Press, 2005); Laird Bergad, *The Comparative Histories of Slavery in Brazil, Cuba, and the United States* (Cambridge: Cambridge University Press, 2007); and Robin Blackburn, *The American Crucible: Slavery, Emancipation, and Human Rights* (London: Verso, 2011).

26. Michael Mann, *The Sources of Social Power*, vol. 2: *The Rise of Classes and Nation-States, 1760–1914* (Cambridge: Cambridge University Press, 1993).

27. It is impossible to do justice to the literature analyzing exceptionalism in this limited space, but for an incisive overview and critique, see Daniel T. Rodgers, "Exceptionalism," in *Imagined Histories: American Historians Interpret the Past*, ed. Anthony Molho and Gordon S. Wood (Princeton: Princeton University Press, 1998), 21–40.

28. Ian Tyrrell, "American Exceptionalism in an Age of International History," *American Historical Review* 96, no. 4 (October 1991): 1031–55. For an example of this approach, see Michael Adas, "From Settler Colony to Global Hegemon: Integrating the Exceptionalist Narrative of the American Experience into World History," *American Historical Review* 106, no. 5 (December 2001): 1692–1720.

29. James T. Kloppenberg, *Uncertain Victory: Social Democracy and Progressivism in European and American Thought, 1870–1920* (New York: Oxford University Press, 1986); Daniel T. Rodgers, *Atlantic Crossings: Social Politics in a Progressive Age* (Cambridge, MA: Harvard University Press, 1998); Ian Tyrrell, *Woman's World/Woman's Empire: The Woman's Christian Temperance Union in International Perspective, 1880–1930* (Chapel Hill: University of North Carolina Press, 1991).

30. See also "The Nation and Beyond"; David J. Russo, *American History from a Global Perspective: An Interpretation* (Westport, CT: Praeger, 2000); David Ryan, *US Foreign Policy in World History* (New York: Routledge, 2000); and Gary Reichard and Ted Dickson, eds., *America on the World Stage: A Global Approach to U.S. History* (Urbana: University of Illinois Press, 2008).

31. For exemplary overviews of how American culture has been exported to and adapted in Europe, see Rob Kroes, *If You've Seen One, You've Seen the Mall: Europeans and American Mass Culture* (Urbana: University of Illinois Press, 1996); Richard Pells, *Not Like Us: How Europeans Have Loved, Hated, And Transformed American Culture since World War II* (New York: Basic Books, 1997); Reinhold Wagnleitner and Elaine Tyler May, eds., *"Here, There and Everywhere": The Foreign Politics of American Popular Culture* (Salzburg: Salzburg, 2000); Victoria de Grazia, *Irresistible Empire: America's Advance through Twentieth-Century Europe* (Cambridge, MA: Harvard University Press, 2006).

32. Brooke L. Blower, *Becoming Americans in Paris: Transatlantic Politics and Culture between the World Wars* (New York: Oxford University Press, 2011).

33. John Fabian Witt, *Patriots and Cosmopolitans: Hidden Histories of American Law* (Cambridge, MA: Harvard University Press, 2007).

34. See, e.g., Leon Fink, ed., *Workers across the Americas: The Transnational Turn in Labor History* (New York: Oxford University Press, 2011).

35. Ira Katznelson and Martin Shefter, eds., *Shaped by War and Trade: International Influences on American Political Development* (Princeton: Princeton University Press, 2002).

36. This metaphor of transnational circuitry may be relatively new for twentieth-century Americanists, but it is more familiar in early modern and Atlantic history. For one very recent example see *The Caribbean and the Atlantic World Economy: Circuits of Trade, Money and Knowledge, 1650–1914*, ed. Adrian Leonard and David Pretel (Basingstoke: Palgrave Macmillan, 2015).

37. Tyrrell, *Transnational Nation*, 8.

38. Thomas Borstelmann, *The 1970s: A New Global History from Civil Rights to Economic Inequality* (Princeton: Princeton University Press, 2012). See also Niall Ferguson et al., eds., *The Shock of the Global: The 1970s in Perspective* (Cambridge, MA: Harvard University Press, 2010).

39. The monument in this field is, of course, Rodgers, *Atlantic Crossings* (which features some coverage of the Pacific as well).

40. The observation is not new, but bears repeating. For the classic account, see Karl Polanyi, *The Great Transformation: The Political and Economic Origins of Our Time* (Boston: Beacon Press, 1944).

41. Manuel Castells, *The Information Age: Economy, Society, and Culture*, vol. 1: *The Rise of the Network Society*, 2d ed. (Malden, MA: Wiley-Blackwell, 2010).

42. See Akira Iriye, "The Internationalization of History," *American Historical Review* 94, no. 1 (February 1989): 6–7, for an early statement.

1

The Monroe Doctrine in the Nineteenth Century

Jay Sexton

The theme of this volume is one in which common ground can be found among historians of the early republic and those of more recent eras. The interplay of the foreign and domestic was as central to nineteenth-century America as it was to the globalizing world of the late twentieth century. Indeed, it could be argued that the imperative of taking such an approach is greater for historians of the early republic on the grounds that the very categories of "foreign" and "domestic" were themselves not clearly demarcated in the early nineteenth century.[1] It was an age in which peoples, goods, and ideas passed relatively freely across porous, ill-defined, and often contested national borders. Furthermore, many Americans at the time viewed their union itself as an experiment in international organization.

The relationship between the internal dynamics of the union and its engagement with the outside world has been the topic of much recent scholarship. This "unionist paradigm," as David Hendrickson has called it, examines the early United States not as the singular nation that it would one day become, but as the decentralized and factious union that it was.[2] The recent scholarship seeks to avoid the anachronistic assumption of an inviolable American nation, which has led no few scholars to project the power of late nineteenth-century America back onto the early republic. This is not to deny the salience of early American nationalism—of which the Monroe Doctrine, the subject of this essay, both reflected and helped to construct—but rather to call for its proper historicization.

When nineteenth-century US statesmen looked beyond their frequently changing borders, they did so through a lens colored by the shifting and often unstable relations among the different states, sections, and social, racial, and political groups within their union. The foreign and domestic objectives of nationalists in the early republic could be symbiotic and mutually reinforcing: the advancement of international ambitions and the internal objective of consolidating the union at home often went hand in hand. Yet US statesmen also were presented with dangers: their republic's vulnerabilities in the international realm, as well as the overzealous pursuit of interests beyond their borders, could deepen internal divisions, perhaps even threatening the union itself. Furthermore, it must be kept in mind that nineteenth-century US statesmen operated in a world conditioned by British power. The British Empire often shaped the policy options available to the statesmen of the young American republic, as well as provided imperialist models that they could follow, particularly in Latin America. Mimicking the successful tactics of the British, however, carried with it domestic political risks in the deeply Anglophobic culture of the early republic.

For all of these reasons, it is impossible to isolate foreign policymaking from domestic politics in the nineteenth century. Indeed, this essay employs the rather old-fashioned term "statecraft" (rather than "foreign relations") on the grounds that it encompasses policies that looked both inward and outward, as did the statesmen of the time.[3] The Monroe Doctrine provides ample evidence of how nineteenth-century statecraft was the product of both internal and external processes. This essay will proceed in two parts. First, we will position ourselves within the union and look out at the wider world through the prism of the Monroe Doctrine. The picture that emerges here is one in which internal forces and anxieties conditioned the worldview and policymaking of US statesmen. Second, we will step outside of the United States and look at the Monroe Doctrine. This perspective reveals how international contexts and forms of diplomacy profoundly shaped what erroneously has been assumed to be a uniquely American doctrine of foreign policy. The essay then follows the circulation of the doctrine around the globe, showing how it took on a transnational life of its own.

The View from the Inside-Out

Historians traditionally interpret the nineteenth-century Monroe Doctrine in relation to expansionist foreign policies and the rising American empire. But if we listen to our historical actors and documents, what we hear is much anxious talk about foreign threats and the security of the union. Although Monroe's 1823 message to Congress came to serve as a blueprint for hemispheric hegemony, it was initially framed as a statement of the perceived security requirements of the American union. "There never was a period since the establishment of our Revolution," stated the opening paragraph of the message, "when . . . there was greater necessity for . . . patriotism and union."[4]

What exactly, one might ask, was the Monroe cabinet worried about when they collectively drafted the 1823 message that warned Old World powers not to recolonize Spain's crumbling New World empire? The drafting of the message is a complex story, but the point to emphasize here is that when the Monroe cabinet discussed the international situation their thoughts returned time and again to the perceived insecurity of their union at home. The statesmen of 1823 certainly viewed foreign affairs through an ideological lens that presupposed the incompatibility of monarchical and republican forms of government and presumed that a single intervention in Spanish America would trigger an all-out imperial scramble in the Western Hemisphere. But though US statesmen spoke in ideological terms—and remained certain of the eventual triumph of republicanism—ideology cannot alone explain the Monroe administration's perception of threat.[5]

The perceived danger in 1823 was not simply external monarchical menace, but the potential for foreign threats to exacerbate preexisting internal divisions. Historians normally frame the 1823 message in relation to the apogee of the early republic "era of good feelings."[6] But for as much as the message reflected this nationalist high tide, it also was the product of internal anxieties concerning the viability of the union, which remained acute in an era in the shadow of the threat of Western separatism, the Hartford Convention, and the recent Missouri crisis. Even an ardent nationalist like Henry Clay, who normally spoke of the rising power of the United States, feared "that within five years from this time [1820], the Union would be divided into three distinct confederacies."[7]

Such concerns shaped the formulation of what later became known as the Monroe Doctrine. The statesmen of 1823 feared that the presence of European puppet monarchies in Spanish America, particularly in neighboring Mexico, would inflame domestic conflict and threaten the union from within. Old concerns about Western separatism resurfaced during the Monroe cabinet's discussions. Secretary of State John Quincy Adams feared that the French still "had a strong party" in Louisiana, which might turn against the United States in the event of a conflict with the Holy Allies. Confronted with such a foreign threat, US statesmen would have no choice but to levy high taxes, create a standing army, and centralize political power. But these actions would in themselves endanger the union by contravening established political practices, perhaps even leading disillusioned Americans into the arms of Old World powers. "Violent parties would arise in this country," Secretary of War John C. Calhoun prophesized during the drafting of the 1823 message, "one for and one against them, and we should have to fight upon our own shores for our own institutions." Although Adams parted from Calhoun on the likely success of a Holy Alliance invasion of Spanish America, he similarly argued that the greatest danger of a European intervention in the Western Hemisphere was that it might trigger a scenario that would place "different portions of the Union in conflict with each other, and thereby endangering the Union itself."[8]

The anxieties of 1823 cast an illuminating light upon the nineteenth-century conception of what we now call "national security." The insecurity of the early republic was twofold: it was weak relative to the Old World powers that dominated international affairs, and it was internally vulnerable, its union in danger of dissolution. The greatest fear of US statesmen was that these internal and external vulnerabilities would merge, transforming their independent union into fractious colonial dependencies, virtual western pawns of the European balance of power. Although most famously articulated in 1823, this fear had its roots in the Revolutionary era, when American statesmen linked independence to union. Such thinking shaped the 1787 Constitution, which sought to create a union powerful enough to maintain its independence in the international realm, but with enough constraints placed upon central authority to avoid internal, anticolonial resistance of the 1776 mold.[9] This logic also lay behind the early diplomatic practice of standing aloof, so far as possible, from conflicts that occurred in Europe. The two most famous articulations of this theme—Washington's Farewell Address (1796) and Jefferson's first inaugural (1801)—argued that a foreign policy of non-entanglement should be pursued not out of some dogma of isolationism, but in order to mitigate internal divisions. Washington's address dealt primarily with the menace of separatist movements in the American West and the entrenchment of ideologically opposed political parties. His "great rule" of diplomatic non-entanglement was a means of preempting these internal threats to the union, not an end in itself. Similarly, Jefferson's call for "entangling alliances with none" was made in the context of an address that called for national unity—albeit one premised upon his political triumph in the election of 1800—after the divisive politics of the 1790s.[10]

The most dangerous moment for the fusion of internal and external threats, of course, occurred during the Civil War when Confederate diplomats crossed the Atlantic in search of an alliance with the British. It is no coincidence that the "Monroe Doctrine" became a nationally recognized phrase and concept during the Civil War era. The invention of this newly imagined "doctrine" was a result not only of the French intervention in Mexico in the

1860s but also of the potential foreign recognition or even support of the Confederacy. Republicans viewed the two threats to the Monroe Doctrine as interlinked: "The French invasion of Mexico," Union General Phillip Sheridan asserted, "was so closely related to the Rebellion as to be essentially part of it."[11] Long treated in isolation by diplomatic historians, the Civil War was in this sense a climactic moment in nineteenth-century statecraft. And as Union leaders intervened in the seceded states of the South, they contemplated newly assertive and interventionist policies to achieve their objectives in Mexico.[12]

Proponents of the Monroe Doctrine advanced a series of nationalist principles of statecraft to preempt the feared overlap of external and internal threats. It is here where the historian can see the relationship between internal politics and assertive foreign policies. The framers of the 1823 message, as well as later proponents of the Monroe Doctrine, concluded that only by controlling the entire Western Hemisphere—and, consequently, the new states of Latin America—would the United States be able to survive, develop, and ultimately replace the empires of the Old World. One should be careful, however, to avoid the temptation to imagine some kind of an American "official mind" of foreign policymaking, for the implementation of the goals of 1823 proved contentious at home.[13] The Monroe administration framed the 1823 message in negative terms: it stated what European powers could not do, but did not prescribe policy for the United States.

The first attempt to translate the 1823 message into a proactive foreign policy triggered great domestic debate. John Quincy Adams and Henry Clay, now operating, respectively, as president and secretary of state, viewed the 1823 message as a call to take the lead in the 1826 Panama Congress, where they hoped to advance US commercial interests, counter British power, and foster republicanism in Spanish America. These objectives, Adams and Clay argued, would enhance the security and union of the United States by establishing its hemispheric primacy. "It is in our power to create a system of which we shall be the centre," Clay asserted, "and in which all South America will act with us."[14] Yet not all in the United States viewed the Panama Congress in this light. The "American system" triggered much opposition, particularly from pro-slavery Southerners who viewed it as a threat to their "peculiar institution" by in some way extending legitimacy to the Haitian slave rebellion. Southern slavers feared that the administration's active foreign policy would extend new powers to the federal government on the slavery issue and, more alarmingly, might embolden slaves at home to take matters into their own hands. In time, southern statesmen would develop their own pro-slavery interpretation of what Calhoun called in 1848 "Monroe's declaration."[15] If the objective of this imagined "declaration" was specific to the South, it drew from the national tradition of thwarting the potential overlap of foreign and domestic threats (manifested in this case in the transatlantic antislavery campaign).

The very nationalism embodied in the 1823 message made it a symbol that rival political groupings sought to claim as their own to provide cover for partisan or even sectional policies. Indeed, it is misleading to refer to the Monroe Doctrine in the singular for there were as many Monroe Doctrines as there were perspectives on nineteenth-century statecraft: an isolationist one and an internationalist one; pro- and antislavery interpretations; expansionist and anti-annexationist ones; interventionist and noninterventionist; one concerned exclusively with ideology and another interested only with interests; an "Anglo-Saxonist" Monroe Doctrine existed, as did one that celebrated "pan-Americanism."

Americans spilled much ink on the Monroe Doctrine. Yet the instances in the nineteenth century when they directed it at foreign governments were few and far between—not to mention largely counterproductive in diplomatic regards. A remarkable feature of the Monroe Doctrine in the nineteenth century is that Americans most often invoked it against one another. They wrote pamphlets to establish their Monrovian credentials; they placed Monroe Doctrine planks in party platforms during election years; they questioned their political opponents' devotion to the dogma of 1823. Monroe did not create a "doctrine." That job would be done by later Americans who competed with one another to lay claim to the mantle of 1823. One should interpret James K. Polk's 1845 invention of what he called "Mr. Monroe's doctrine" in this light, for in reviving what was then a largely forgotten episode from an imagined era of good feelings, Polk sought to provide anticolonial and bipartisan cover for his controversial program of imperial expansion.[16]

The domestic politicking over the Monroe Doctrine sought short-term objectives such as the winning of elections or the consolidation of public support for specific foreign policies. In the long term, however, it had consequences for the ways in which those in the United States conceived of their relationship with Latin Americans. The jockeying between rival politicians and parties to become the most ardent defender of the Monroe Doctrine established a process in which US statesmen competed not only with foreign powers to establish hemispheric supremacy but also with one another to win the confidence of voters that they best could achieve this objective. In their race to demonstrate their fidelity to the Monroe Doctrine, politicians did not emphasize their ideological solidarity with their neighbors, a tactic which had blown-up in the face of John Quincy Adams when he advocated participation in the Panama Congress back in the 1820s. Rather, they competed to become the strongest defender of national security and the most assertive promoter of national interests. Their appeals condemned not only Old World monarchies but also Latin Americans, particularly those in the Caribbean and Central America, who, as the century progressed, increasingly became the targets of racist and anti-Catholic diatribes.[17] The scramble for votes under the banner of the anticolonial Monroe Doctrine paradoxically contributed to the emergence of the imperialist mindset of the late nineteenth century.

The Monroe Doctrine thus was an ever-evolving, contested, and politicized symbol. Its construction owed as much to the internal dynamics and politics of the union as it did to grand strategy and imperial rivalry. Of course, as the nineteenth century progressed and the union became more secure, particularly after 1865, the meaning of the 1823 shibboleth changed. The Monroe Doctrine, Republican John Kasson asserted in 1881, "is no longer for us a question of despotism extending its sphere of supremacy to America. It is a question now of commercial rivalry and commercial advantages."[18] But even in the late nineteenth century, conceptions of the doctrine owed much to domestic politics and, indeed, the successful integration of the union itself. The Pan-Americanism of the 1880s, for example, sought to apply at a hemispheric level the measures that had so successfully integrated and rationalized the US economy. A commercial bureau and inter-American bank would stabilize the hemispheric banking system much as the National Bank Act of 1863 had done at the national level; a common unit of exchange would regulate transactions as had the "greenbacks"; the hemispheric customs union would limit European commercial penetration similar to the high tariffs of the 1860s; a Pan-American railroad would bring the same benefits to the hemisphere that the Pacific Railroad Act of 1862 had brought to the nation. Many Americans also pointed to the development of their own South and West as a model for how to bring Latin America within its economic orbit. US railroad financiers spoke about "Americanizing" Latin America and superimposed maps of Argentina on top of the US West to demonstrate the viability of proposed rail lines.[19]

The View from the Outside-In

Americans imagined the Monroe Doctrine as a proclamation of national exceptionalism. By the early twentieth century, it had become a national myth that stood alongside the other foundational symbols of US history. The "statesmen of 1823" became the diplomatic counterparts to the "Founding Fathers" of the 1787 Constitution. "I believe strictly in the Monroe Doctrine, in our Constitution, and in the laws of God," asserted Mary Baker Eddy on the occasion of the centenary of the 1823 message.[20] Yet this nationalist mythology masked the many and fundamental ways in which the doctrine was the product of transnational currents of statecraft and empire.

When viewed from the outside-in, the Monroe Doctrine first should be seen in relation to the dominant international structure of the nineteenth century, the British Empire. Although the thirteen colonies achieved their political independence during the Revolution, "postcolonial" America long remained within the webs of an expanding and increasingly powerful British Empire. The young American republic continued to be an economic satellite of Britain; British literature and ideas dominated its culture; Britain threatened the union itself, as the 1812 conflict made clear. Yet British power also served the interests of the United States: it provided the largest market for American exports; it served as an exporter of peoples, capital, technologies, and ideas; and, for all of its menace, its naval might, wealth, and statecraft could advance American interests—after all, Americans did not "win the West" on their own nor with their own money. Time and again, when nineteenth-century Americans wrote or spoke about the Monroe Doctrine, their thoughts drifted into a discussion of their ambivalent attitudes toward Britain. Americans desperately sought to escape the shadow of their former colonial master, yet they recognized their continued reliance upon the hated British. The Monroe Doctrine became American shorthand for a hemisphere (and, ultimately, world) cleared of the British Empire. Yet American statesmen would look to that very Empire as a model when devising policies to uphold the Monroe Doctrine and establish their own hemispheric supremacy.[21]

The context surrounding the articulation of the 1823 message serves as a useful illustration of the centrality of British power to the realization of US objectives. The prohibition the Monroe administration placed upon European intervention required the cooperation of the British. Indeed, it was Lord Canning in London, not Monroe in Washington, who deterred the French from venturing into Spanish America. The Monroe cabinet could thump their chests about republican government and the principle of nonintervention only because the Royal Navy sheltered Spanish America from the Holy Allies. Historians often overstate the unilateralism of Monroe's message: it was written within the context of a warming of relations between the two nations and did not constitute a categorical rejection of Canning's earlier offer of joint Anglo-American action on the Spanish American issue. Indeed, Monroe would seek to further Anglo-American cooperation in regard to Spanish America in the weeks after delivering his famous message to Congress.[22] Upon receiving Monroe's message in early 1824, the London *Times* applauded it on the grounds that it articulated "a policy so directly British." Later, the London *Economist* contended that "the Monroe doctrine might quite as fairly be called the Canning doctrine."[23]

Yet scholars have been correct to point out that the message of 1823 also reflected Anglo-American rivalry. Although Canning read with pleasure the two paragraphs dealing with nonintervention in Latin America, his blood boiled when he read the paragraph on non-colonization, which John Quincy Adams crafted with the British Empire in mind.[24] If the United States and Britain agreed on preventing the European powers from intervening in Latin America, they both had their own objectives of acquiring new markets, if not, particularly in the case of the United States, new territory. Monroe's message should be seen in relation to a similar pronouncement of Canning's, the Polignac Memorandum, which was the record of a secret agreement in which the French pledged not to intervene in Spanish America.[25] Both diplomatic documents aimed at currying favor in the new states of Spanish America, where the two English-speaking powers would engage in a century-long struggle for supremacy. Monroe's message and the Polignac Memorandum in this regard were early manifestations of what we now call "public diplomacy." Upon learning of the favorable reception of Monroe's message in Latin America, Canning ordered the mass reproduction of the hitherto confidential Polignac Memorandum through the new technology of the lithograph. "Its date is most important," the Foreign Secretary wrote of the Polignac Memo, "in reference to the American speech which it so long preceded."[26]

The oxymoron of "collaborative competition" best describes this dynamic of the Anglo-American relationship. Despite all of the talk at the time about the ideological divide between the United States and Britain, the two powers pursued similar policies in Latin America. Their rivalry was collaborative in that both (generally) opposed the formal reconquest of Latin America, sought to profit from the economic development and exploitation of the new states, and their merchants and traders worked closely together (indeed, American traders relied upon the British Barings for credit in Latin American port cities deep into the nineteenth century). Yet the two English-speaking states simultaneously competed for market supremacy, strategic superiority, and to establish clients and allies within the new Latin American states. Over time, of course, American politicians would rail against any formal collaboration with the hated British. The 1850 Clayton-Bulwer Treaty, which pledged the two powers to cooperate on the isthmian canal issue, came to be seen by American nationalists in the late nineteenth century as a repudiation of the Monroe Doctrine. They eventually achieved its abrogation in 1901.

The US eclipse of Britain in the Caribbean in the second half of the nineteenth century should not obscure the continued salience of the British Empire to the history of the Monroe Doctrine. The "Americanization" of the Caribbean was a process that entailed not just a shift in the balance of power but also the transfer and appropriation of imperialist methods and tactics. The study of inter-imperial exchange, in terms of both elite statecraft and at the imperial vanguard on the ground, remains in its infancy, but it is already clear that the American empire emerged in relation to its interactions with, and appropriations of, the imperial projects of the Old World powers.[27] Many of the American policies that promoted the Monroe Doctrine were modeled after those employed by British imperialists. Commercial measures to promote US exports in Latin America, for example, drew from the successful tactics of the British. American statesmen looked to Britain's imperial policy in the Suez as an example when formulating their own canal policy in Panama and imperial strategy in Cuba in the early twentieth century. Calls for a Chile to Canada railroad were inspired not only by the US transcontinental line built in the 1860s but also Cecil Rhodes's late nineteenth-century Cape to Cairo railway scheme in Africa.[28] If American statesmen before the late 1890s generally retained a prejudice against formal colonial expansion, they nonetheless came to conceive of their relationship with Latin Americans in the terms of Old World colonialism. "While the great powers of Europe are steadily enlarging their colonial domination in Asia and Africa," James Blaine asserted, "it is the especial province of this country to improve and expand its trade with the nations of America."[29]

In other words, the Monroe Doctrine was not the proclamation of national exceptionalism imagined at the time, as it emerged and evolved in relation to the programs of other expansionist powers—indeed, the national exceptionalism of the doctrine was in part the invention of shrewd US statesmen who sought to disguise the ways in which their policies mimicked those of their former colonial master. Britain, of course, was not the only foreign power that shaped the construction of the Monroe Doctrine. In its form, style, and propagation, the 1823 message shared traits of the circulars and manifestoes of the Holy Allies.[30] Indeed, Monroe's message can be viewed as a rejoinder to the Holy Allies' 1820 Troppau Circular: just as the continental monarchies articulated their right to oppose revolutionary forces in Europe, the Monroe administration declared that European colonization and political intervention in the New World constituted a threat to the United States. The 1823 message and its "American system" interpretation during the subsequent Adams administration also should be seen in relation to Spanish American statecraft. After all, the Panama Congress was the brainchild of Simon Bolívar, who hoped to consolidate Spanish American independence through the establishment of a regional federation. The English-speaking power that Bolívar hoped to ally with was not the United States. As late as 1826, Bolívar called for a "union of the new states with the British Empire."[31] The hemispheric policy of

Adams and Clay sought to contain and counter the initiatives taken by Spanish Americans.

As the nineteenth century progressed, Latin Americans became ever more adept at harnessing the Yankee doctrine toward their own ends. One recurrent strategy was to seek US assistance during violations of the 1823 message: Buenos Aires called for enforcement of Monroe's message during the British seizure of the Falklands; Mexican liberals spoke more of the Monroe Doctrine during the French intervention of the 1860s than did Lincoln and Seward, who feared that its invocation might provoke the French into further aggression in North America; Venezuelan politicians masterfully played their hand in the 1890s by employing American William Scruggs to propagate in Washington their hitherto ignored border dispute with British Guiana. In other instances, foreign diplomats overstated the European threat or even invited foreign intervention as a means of coaxing the United States into certain actions: the politicians of independent Texas shrewdly flirted with the British in part to prompt the United States into annexation; Yucatecan separatists warned the Polk administration that if US support was not forthcoming in their civil war then they would seek help from European powers; Chilean leader José Manuel Balmaceda deftly played upon the Anglophobia of US minister Patrick Egan to enlist American support for his beleaguered government in the early 1890s. It was because of such maneuvers that US statesmen felt the need to assert ownership over the Monroe Doctrine. "In an application of the Monroe doctrine," Grover Cleveland explained during the 1895 Venezuela crisis, "though another country may give the occasion, we are I suppose not looking after its interest but our own."[32]

As the global recognition of the Monroe Doctrine increased with the rising power of the United States, the American shibboleth became a universal symbol and transferable language of international relations. Foreign critics condemned the United States for not living up to the "true" Monroe Doctrine of 1823. Other nations declared Monroe Doctrines of their own: there was talk of a Japanese Monroe Doctrine in the early twentieth century; anticolonial nationalists in South Asia called for a "Monroe Doctrine for India"[33]; Nazis depicted their expansionist policies in Europe as a German version of the Monroe Doctrine; John Vorster in South Africa proclaimed "a Monroe Doctrine for Southern Africa" in the 1960s[34]; and commentators today predict the emergence of a Chinese Monroe Doctrine.[35] US leaders conferred joint ownership of the doctrine to those they deemed reliable allies that had achieved "civilized" status. Theodore Roosevelt decided that Argentina, Brazil, and Chile were "guarantors of the doctrine so far as America south of the Equator is concerned" (in contrast, Roosevelt contended that to ask the same of states in the Caribbean and Central America "would be about like asking the Apaches and Utes to guarantee it").[36]

Another sign of the international reach of the Monroe Doctrine can be seen in the establishment of competing foreign policy "doctrines." During the 1902 Venezuela debt crisis, Argentine Foreign Minister Luís Maria Drago proposed a hemispheric policy of prohibiting the forcible collection of debts by European powers. Initially presented as a complement to the 1823 message, in time the "Drago Doctrine" became an alternative to the unilateral interventionism of the Roosevelt Corollary.[37] In Mexico Porfirio Díaz similarly called for a "Díaz Doctrine" in which the states of the Americas would collectively enforce the 1823 prohibition of European colonization and intervention.[38] In later times, the Soviet Union's "Brezhnev Doctrine" asserted the right of intervention in communist countries (though this was eventually superseded by Gorbachev's so-called "Sinatra Doctrine," which enabled Eastern Europeans to follow the singer's advice from "My Way").

The proliferation of such "doctrines" reshaped the rhetorical style and political salesmanship employed by US statesmen. Nineteenth-century presidents and secretaries of state sought the cover of tradition by invoking Monroe. As late as 1917, Woodrow Wilson chose not to create a "Wilson Doctrine," but rather to present his internationalist vision as an outgrowth of the Monroe Doctrine.[39] By the mid-twentieth century, however, American presidents began to pronounce their own foreign policy doctrines. Indeed, most presidents since Truman have one named after them, even if they did not actually formulate a new or coherent diplomatic strategy. Here we have come full-circle, for the purpose of presidential foreign policy doctrines in recent times has been as much for a president or his partisans to communicate a position to a domestic audience as it has been to proclaim a new diplomatic approach or objective.[40]

All of these themes can be seen not only in the original articulation of the 1823 message but also in the formulation of the Roosevelt Corollary to the Monroe Doctrine in 1904. Viewed from the outside-in, the corollary was the product of specific geopolitical contingencies in the Caribbean. Yet, more than this, it was also the US response to competing plans for how to bring order and financial stability to unstable Caribbean states such as the Dominican Republic, where the corollary was first applied. The Roosevelt administration appears to have had some sympathy for the Drago Doctrine, but preferred the flexible unilateralism of the corollary that would later bear the president's name. Less appealing was a multilateral plan floated by European governments in which the burden of assuming control of Dominican customs houses would be shared by a consortium of imperial powers, as recently had occurred in

Greece and Turkey. But if the unilateral course pursued by Roosevelt reflected traditional suspicion of European diplomacy, its logic of advancing "civilization" upon the "uncivilized" drew from currents of imperial thought popular across the Atlantic.[41] In assuming a share of the burden of the expansion of "civilization," the Roosevelt Corollary linked the Monroe Doctrine to the broader project of Old World imperialism. It also helped European creditors recover defaulted debts in the Caribbean and relieved some of the burden from the Royal Navy in the Caribbean. "The process indicated by the President," the London *Times* wrote of the Roosevelt Corollary, "is one that has been carried out again and again—in Turkey, in Egypt, in China, in Cuba, in Asia by ourselves and others."[42]

Yet it is impossible to understand the Roosevelt Corollary without also viewing it from the inside-out. Much like Polk had done back in the 1840s, Roosevelt deployed an imagined symbol of anticolonialism to justify a nakedly imperialist policy. The move appears even shrewder when placed in its immediate historical context. The Monroe Doctrine had long been the favored symbol of nationalist statesmen like James Blaine and the young Theodore Roosevelt, who authored an important essay on the topic in 1895.[43] But in the late 1890s, those on the opposite side of the foreign policy spectrum, beginning with the Cleveland administration during the 1895–1896 Venezuela crisis, appropriated the doctrine for very different purposes. It was the anti-imperialists, not the Rooseveltian "large policy men," who most often invoked the Monroe Doctrine during the great debates of 1898.[44] In 1904 the Roosevelt team shrewdly seized the language of their opponents, initially announcing their interventionist policy at a May 1904 dinner celebrating Cuba's 1902 independence. Secretary of State Elihu Root later proclaimed that the Roosevelt Corollary was less imperialist than the foreign policy of the Cleveland administration.[45]

The domestic context shaped the substance, as well as the style, of the Roosevelt Corollary. Historians tend to present the corollary as the climax of the evolution of the Monroe Doctrine and US imperialism. Yet it represented a retreat from the position that Roosevelt had occupied just a few years earlier. Rather than advocate formal colonial expansion of the 1898 type, the failings and unpopularity of the "large policy," made clear by the bloody and costly anticolonial rebellion in the Philippines, now led Roosevelt to formulate a hybrid imperial policy that constituted something of a compromise between those on either side of the great debate of 1898. Constrained by domestic opponents and its commitments in the Philippines and Cuba, the Roosevelt administration limited the number and scope of its ventures in the Caribbean, not least by outsourcing the details of debt repayment to private Wall Street banks, without abandoning its overall goal of establishing hegemony.[46]

If the Roosevelt Corollary in these ways embodied the broad themes of the nineteenth-century Monroe Doctrine, it also revealed how much had changed since Monroe's message back in 1823. Roosevelt's Monroe Doctrine was a statement of a self-confident nation concerned more with the great game of imperial rivalry than with the internal dynamics of its once fragile union of states. "We have become a great nation," he stated in his inaugural address in 1905, "and we must behave as beseems a people with such responsibilities."[47] The Roosevelt Corollary differed in this regard from the message of 1823. Even Richard Olney's 1895 "corollary" to the doctrine, despite its bombast, was a deeply anxious document. In contrast to previous major statements on the Monroe Doctrine, Roosevelt's 1904 message did not mention the threat of European monarchy, which was no longer the glue holding the American nation together.[48] With the nation now a given, Roosevelt was free to go about building an empire in a way that would have been impossible for the statesmen of 1823 to imagine.

NOTES

1. The classic exploration of this point is Amy Kaplan, *The Anarchy of Empire in the Making of U.S. Culture* (Cambridge, MA: Harvard University Press, 2005).

2. See, e.g., Kenneth M. Stampp, "The Concept of a Perpetual Union," *Journal of American History* 65, no. 1 (June 1978): 5–33; Peter Onuf and Nicholas G. Onuf, *Federal Union, Modern World: The Law of Nations in an Age of Revolution, 1776–1814* (Madison, WI: Madison House Publishers, 1993); Peter Onuf, "A Declaration of Independence for Diplomatic Historians," *Diplomatic History* 22, no. 1 (January 1998): 71–83; David Hendrickson, *Peace Pact: The Lost World of the American Founding* (Lawrence: University Press of Kansas, 2003) and *Union, Nation, or Empire: The American Debate over International Relations, 1789–1941* (Lawrence: University Press of Kansas, 2009); James E. Lewis Jr., *The American Union and the Problem of Neighborhood: The United States and the Collapse of the Spanish Empire, 1783–1829* (Chapel Hill: University of North Carolina Press, 1998); William Earl Weeks, *John Quincy Adams and American Global Empire* (Lexington: University of Kentucky Press, 1992); John Craig Hammond, *Slavery, Freedom, and Expansion in the Early American West* (Charlottesville: University of Virginia Press, 2008); Brian Schoen, *The Fragile Fabric of Union: Cotton, Federal Politics, and the Global Origins of the Civil War* (Baltimore: Johns Hopkins University Press, 2009).

3. For more on the vocabulary of the internal and external in the nineteenth century, see Hendrickson, *Union, Nation or Empire*, esp. 130. This approach is applied to the Monroe Doctrine more fully in Jay Sexton, *The Monroe Doctrine: Empire and Nation in Nineteenth-Century America* (New York: Hill and Wang, 2011).

4. James Monroe, "Seventh Annual Message to Congress," December 2, 1823.

5. For a recent work that emphasizes ideology, see Robert Kagan, *Dangerous Nation: America and the World, 1600–1898* (London: Atlantic Books, 2006).

6. See, e.g., George Dangerfield, *The Era of Good Feelings* (New York: Harcourt, Brace, 1952).

7. Clay, "Toast and Response at Public Dinner," May 19, 1821, in *Papers of Henry Clay*, ed. James F. Hopkins (Lexington: University Press of Kentucky, 1963), 3:79–82; Hendrickson, *Union, Nation or Empire*, 118–23.

8. Quotes from JQA diary, in *Memoirs of John Quincy Adams*, ed. Charles Francis Adams (Philadelphia: J. B. Lippincott, 1874–1877), 6:197, 206, 223–5.

9. Hendrickson, *Peace Pact*.

10. George Washington, "Farewell Address," September 17, 1796; Thomas Jefferson, "Inaugural Address," March 4, 1801.

11. Quoted in D. P. Crook, *The North, the South and the Powers, 1861–1865* (London: John Wiley, 1974), 262.

12. Thomas D. Schoonover, *Dollars Over Dominion: The Triumph of Liberalism in Mexican–United States Relations, 1861–1867* (Baton Rouge: Louisiana State University Press, 1978).

13. For the "official mind" concept, see Ronald Robinson and John Gallagher, *Africa and the Victorians: The Official Mind of Imperialism* (London: Macmillan, 1961).

14. Quoted in Randolph Campbell, "The Spanish American Aspect of Henry Clay's American System," *The Americas* 24, no. 1 (July 1967): 8; Lewis, *The American Union and the Problem of Neighborhood*.

15. For Calhoun's speech, see *The Papers of John C. Calhoun*, ed. Robert Meriwether (Columbia: University of South Carolina Press, 1959–2003), 25:401–21.

16. Polk, "First Annual Message to Congress," December 2, 1845; Polk diary, October 21 and 24, 1845, in *Diary of James K. Polk during His Presidency, 1845 to 1849*, ed. Milo Milton Quaife, (Chicago: A. C. McClurg & Co., 1910), 1:67–72.

17. For an illustration of anti-Catholicism and the Monroe Doctrine, see Joshua Leavitt, *The Monroe Doctrine* (New York: Sinclair Tousey, 1863).

18. John Kasson, "The Monroe Declaration" and "The Monroe Doctrine in 1881," *North American Review* (September and October 1881).

19. Thomas Schoonover, *The United States in Central America, 1860–1911: Episodes in Social Imperialism and International Rivalry in the World System* (Durham, NC: Duke University Press, 1991), 78; J. Valerie Fifer, *United States Perceptions of Latin America, 1850–1930: A "New West" South of Capricorn?* (Manchester: Manchester University Press, 1991).

20. Quoted in Dexter Perkins, *A History of the Monroe Doctrine* (Boston: Little, Brown, 1963), p. ix.

21. For the importance of British power to nineteenth-century America, see Sam W. Haynes, *Unfinished Revolution: The Early American Republic in a British World* (Charlottesville: University of Virginia Press, 2010); Kariann Yokota, *Unbecoming British: How Revolutionary America Became a Postcolonial Nation* (New York: Oxford University Press, 2011); A. G. Hopkins, "The United States, 1783–1861: Britain's Honorary Dominion?" *Britain and the World* 4, no. 2 (2011): 232–46; Jay Sexton, "The United States in the British Empire," in *The Oxford History of the British Empire, Companion Volume on the American Colonies*, ed. Stephen Foster (Oxford: Oxford University Press, 2013), 318–48.

22. These points are explored in an underappreciated article, Gale W. McGee, "The Monroe Doctrine—A Stopgap Measure," *Mississippi Valley Historical Review* 38, no. 2 (September 1951): 233–50.

23. *Times*, January 6, 1824; *Economist*, November 14, 1863.

24. Edward Crapol, "John Quincy Adams and the Monroe Doctrine: Some New Evidence," *Pacific Historical Review* 48 (August 1979): 413–18.

25. "Polignac Memorandum," in *Foundations of British Foreign Policy: From Pitt to Salisbury*, ed. Howard Temperley and Lillian Penson (Cambridge: Cambridge University Press, 1938), 70–6.

26. Wendy Hinde, *George Canning* (London: Collins, 1973), 355; Harold Temperley, *The Foreign Policy of Canning, 1822–1827* (London: G. Bell and Sons, 1925), 127–9; *Britain and the Independence of Latin America, 1812–1830: Selected Documents from the Foreign Office*, (London: Oxford University Press, 1938), ed. C. K. Webster, 50.

27. For model studies of this sort, see Ian Tyrrell, *Reforming the World: The Creation of America's Moral Empire* (Princeton: Princeton University Press, 2010); Kinley Brauer, "The United States and British Imperial Expansion, 1815–1860," *Diplomatic History* 12 (Winter 1988): 19–37; Paul A. Kramer, "Empires, Exceptions, and Anglo-Saxons: Race and Rule between the British and United States Empires, 1880–1910," *Journal of American History* 88, no. 4 (March 2002): 1315–53.

28. These and related examples are pursued in Sexton, *Monroe Doctrine*.

29. Quoted in Walter LaFeber, *The New Empire: An Interpretation of American Expansion, 1860–1898*, (Ithaca, NY: Cornell University Press, 1963), 105.

30. Just as Washington's farewell address drew from the European tradition of the "political testament." See Felix Gilbert, *To the Farewell Address: Ideas of Early American Foreign Policy* (Princeton: Princeton University Press, 1961).

31. John Lynch, *Simón Bolívar: A Life* (New Haven: Yale University Press, 2006), 216–17; Bolívar, "Views of General Simón Bolívar on the Congress of Panama," in *The Monroe Doctrine: Its Importance in the International Life of the States of the New World*, by Alejandro Alvarez (New York: Oxford University Press, 1924), 154–5.

32. Cleveland to Bayard, December 29, 1895, Olney Papers, reel 14.

33. Erez Manela, *The Wilsonian Moment: Self-Determination and the International Origins of Anticolonial Nationalism* (New York: Oxford University Press, 2007), 90, 164.

34. Robert C. Good, *UDI: The International Politics of the Rhodesian Rebellion* (London: Faber and Faber, 1973), 239.

35. Paul Giarra and Patrick Cronin, "China's Dangerous Arrogance," *The Diplomat*, July 23, 2010.

36. TR to Archibald Bulloch Roosevelt, December 2, 1914, in *Letters of Theodore Roosevelt*, ed. Elting E. Morrison (Cambridge, MA: Harvard University Press, 1954), 8:851–2.

37. Arthur P. Whitaker, *The Western Hemisphere Idea: Its Rise and Decline* (Ithaca, NY: Cornell University Press, 1954), 86–107.

38. Paul Garner, *Porfirio Díaz* (London: Pearson Education, 2001), 149–53.

39. Woodrow Wilson, "Peace without Victory," January 22, 1917.

40. See, for instance, "Is There an Obama Doctrine?" *New York Times*, March 30, 2011.

41. Frank Ninkovich, "Theodore Roosevelt: Civilization as Ideology," *Diplomatic History* 10 (Summer 1986): 221–45.

42. *Economist*, December 10, 1904; London *Times*, May 26, 1904.

43. TR, "The Monroe Doctrine," March 1896, in *The Works of Theodore Roosevelt*, by Theodore Roosevelt (New York: Charles Scribner's Sons, 1926), 13:168–81.

44. For the "large policy men," see Julius W. Pratt, "The 'Large Policy' of 1898," *Mississippi Valley Historical Review* 19 (September 1932): 219–42.

45. John M. Thompson, "The Impact of Public Opinion on Theodore Roosevelt's Foreign Policy" (PhD diss., Cambridge, 2010); *New York Times*, December 23, 1904.

46. Emily Rosenberg, *Financial Missionaries to the World: The Politics and Culture of Dollar Diplomacy, 1900–1930* (Durham, NC: Duke University Press, 2003), 31–60.

47. Theodore Roosevelt, "First Inaugural Address," March 4, 1905.

48. As late as 1895, Olney's "corollary" emphasized the ideological difference between America and the Old World.

2

Globalization's Paradox

Economic Interdependence and Global Governance

Daniel Sargent

"The world economy has become interdependent."[1] So declared President Gerald Ford in 1975, but what did he mean by it? As Ford used the term, interdependence was a consequence of thickening and accelerating transnational economic relations between nation-states. In such diverse areas as agriculture, finance, and energy, Ford explained, national economies were being drawn into an integrated, interdependent web. This affected governance, for policy could no longer be made as if the nation-state were an economy unto itself. The shock of interdependence was inscribed in recent events. Turmoil on the international money markets had forced the United States off the gold standard in 1971. The oil crisis of 1973–1974 had brought price hikes, gasoline lines, and a sharp recession, alerting Americans to the vulnerabilities that energy interdependence entailed. Although Ford's instincts in economics were classically liberal, oriented toward free markets, he argued that interdependence required a globalization of governance commensurate to the transnational reach of economic globalization. It was imperative, Ford explained, that the United States and its allies build "an organized world society that makes the maximum effective use of the world's resources."

Ford was not alone in presuming that interdependence mandated management. The leaders of the other advanced industrial countries concurred, and the annual economic summits—what became the G-7 summits—that began in November 1975 represented one response to the conundrum of governance amid interdependence. In a similar spirit, David Rockefeller created the Trilateral Commission in 1973. He sought to build dialogue among political, economic, and intellectual elites from across the advanced industrial countries, hopeful that doing so would bolster transnational cooperation on common policy dilemmas. Still, the problem in the mid-1970s was not only that interdependence was thickening but also that the United States no longer dominated the international system as it had in the early postwar era. Indeed, an era of US hegemony looked in the 1970s to be passing. On this point, the economist Charles Kindleberger sounded an influential warning, by way of a sustained historical analogy.[2]

Returning to the 1930s, Kindleberger attributed the severity and longevity of the Great Depression to London's inability and Washington's unwillingness to play the hegemonic role. An effective hegemon, Kindleberger argued, presumes responsibility for the world economy, establishing guiding rules and institutions and serving in crises as a lender of last resort and a market for distress goods. The United States had played this hegemonic role for a quarter century, Kindleberger argued, but its ability to do so in the future appeared uncertain. Others concurred in this bleak diagnosis, but there was debate as to where the future might lead. Robert Keohane, a political scientist, offered a hopeful prognosis.[3] While Keohane concurred that the heyday of American hegemony had passed, he hoped that the United States would now collaborate with like-minded nations to build a multilateral governing regime for an interdependent international economy. This was more or less what Rockefeller's Trilateralists favored: a reinvigoration of the postwar hegemonic regime through the incorporation of core US allies as fully-fledged partners, not just the clients and beneficiaries of American largesse. The United States, Keohane and the Trilateralists urged, should remake the postwar international order through a self-conscious assimilation of its allies to the responsibilities of hegemonic leadership. The problem was that reinvigorating the international order required volition as well as capacity—much as Kindleberger argued. Whether this could be mustered was in the 1970s an open question.

This essay develops a panoramic overview of US encounters with the challenges of international economic governance—what Kindleberger called hegemony. Following Kindleberger, the essay presumes that the willingness of great powers to assume managerial responsibilities for the world economy depends upon both capability and will—upon both power and politics, that is. To these variables, it adds a third, which is the intensity of interdependence with the broader world economy. Interdependence, as the word is used here, connotes something subtly distinct from globalization. Globalization is the process that integrates markets that borders and distance have heretofore kept apart.[4] Interdependence is the condition that exists once globalization has entwined nation-states in webs of mutual dependence and vulnerability from which they cannot extricate themselves, except at considerable cost.[5] Crucially, globalization is not a linear process. Globalization has advanced since the 1860s, but it has also retreated, with the effect that interdependence has waxed and waned over time. Focusing on the United States, this essay posits a historical pattern in three parts. From the 1860s through to the 1920s, globalization produced thickening interdependencies, especially within the North Atlantic world. The Great Depression disrupted and reversed globalization, inaugurating a forty-year phase in which the United States was relatively autonomous from the larger world economy. From the 1960s, globalization resumed: the growth of international trade and financial flows outpaced US GDP growth, producing new relationships of complex economic interdependence between the United States and the world. These patterns are illustrated in figures 2.1 and 2.2, which use balance of payments data to construct indices of American interdependence in trade and finance since 1840.

Globalization's paradox, as this essay presents it, is that the United States has taken greatest responsibility for international economic governance when actual interdependence with the larger global economy has been least. It is the mid-twentieth-century phase that stands out—not only for the preponderance of military and political power that American leaders exercised but also for the freedom of maneuver that relative economic autonomy conferred. It was in the

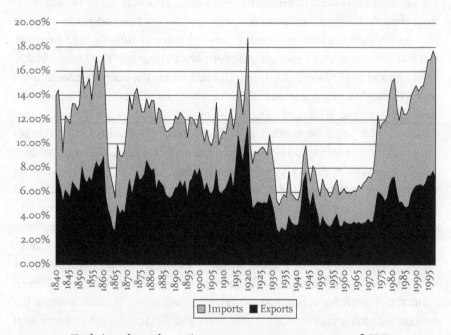

FIGURE 2.1 Trade interdependence (imports + exports as percentage of GDP)

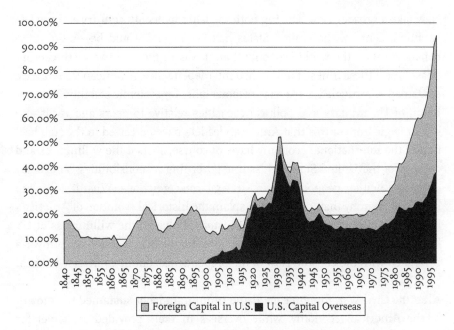

FIGURE 2.2 Financial interdependence (capital imports + exports, total stocks)

shadow of the de-globalization of the 1930s that American leaders in the 1940s constructed a hegemonic regime for the international economy centered upon the United States and the US dollar. This constructive act involved strategic and historical assumptions as well as economic circumstances; believing that their predecessors had forsaken the responsibilities of leadership, American leaders during World War II sought to correct their errors. This is a familiar point. To claim that the reconstruction of the international economic order proceeded at a time when the United States was relatively autonomous in economic affairs is, on the other hand, somewhat counterintuitive. Taking a larger historical view nonetheless bears out the argument.

With its vast internal market, the United States through the early 1930s into the 1970s was substantially self-sufficient. Americans in this phase imported and exported less than they had done in the past—and would again do in the future. Situated comparatively, the United States ranked among the least export-oriented economies on earth. In 1960, Japan exported twice as much, relative to the size of its national economy, as did the United States. France exported three times and Great Britain four times as much as did the United States.[6] Overseas markets were less integral to US prosperity than they were to the prosperity of other capitalist economies. Yet it was the United States that assumed singular responsibility for the international economy as a whole.

Now take a broader view. During both the late nineteenth century and the late twentieth century, the United States had been—and would be—more interdependent with the world economy than it was in the mid-twentieth-century phase. Yet at these times of intensified interdependence, American leaders have disdained or struggled to exercise responsibility for systemic stability. The evolution of US military and political capacities relative to peers and rivals and the strategic imperatives that American leaders have perceived in the stabilization of the international economy have, of course, shaped the willingness and capacity of the United States to assume governing responsibilities. This essay dismisses neither geopolitical nor strategic interpretations. What it does is to highlight an irony that may help to explain the historical evolution of America's hegemonic role: across three distinct historical phases, the willingness of US leaders to assume hegemonic responsibilities for the international economy has correlated with the ebb and flow of interdependence, but in an inverse pattern.

After the Civil War, foreign capital and immigrant labor sustained the growth of the American economy, while overseas markets provided an outlet for US manufactures. While the importance of foreign capital varied from sector to sector, it amounted to nearly 16 percent of overall capital formation in the 1860s and 9 percent in the 1870s—not as much as in the late antebellum period but still consequential.[7] Nowhere was American dependence upon foreign economic inputs more vivid than at Ellis Island in New York and Angel Island in San Francisco. Through these harbor gateways, millions of immigrants arrived in the New World. By 1900, the foreign-born constituted 14.7% of the US population.[8] So great was this demographic movement that its effects were felt far beyond the United States. Migration loosened labor markets in North America and tightened them in Western Europe, producing a convergence trend in wages.[9] The value of American exports, meanwhile, averaged 6.4 percent of US GDP in the 1880s and 6.7 percent of GDP in the 1890s. This by no means made the United States an export-oriented economy, but annual exports in these decades averaged twice what they would be in the 1950s. Thus, even as Americans defined their relationship to globalization on their own terms, deploying tariffs to protect US industries, the world economy nurtured the growth of the United States.

Globalization was a blessing for American economic development, as the historian Eric Rauchway has argued, but it nonetheless stirred a backlash.[10] Immigration proved a particular flashpoint and the subject of legislative actions that peaked in the early 1920s, with legislation that limited immigration on the basis of national origins. While the history of immigration restriction is often told as a story of cultural xenophobia, its economic rationale was the logic of anti-globalization. Workers favored restrictions on immigrants who pushed down the price of labor. So too did a long decline in commodity prices from the early 1870s to the early 1890s bolster political support for tariff protection.[11] The tariff was popular in the North, and efforts to reduce it, which reflected sectional interests, mostly failed. On the gold standard, the positions of the Republican and Democratic parties were reversed. As the basis for international monetary stability, the gold standard was an institutional foundation of nineteenth-century globalization. Its deflationary bias nonetheless exacerbated the downward pressure on wages and prices during the recessions of the 1870s and 1880s. Critics including Democratic presidential contender William Jennings Bryan argued that gold enriched capital at labor's expense. The controversy, which climaxed in Bryan's defeat in the election of 1896, was in a very real sense an argument about whether the costs of globalization were worth paying.[12] While Bryan lost, the vigor of the debate revealed an entrenched domestic skepticism about the virtues of adhesion to global rules.

While Bryan spoke for the worker and the frontier, elites of the Atlantic seaboard embraced the idea of American global mission. Invoking the republic's rising economic capacities as a rationale for American imperialism, strategists like Alfred Thayer Mahan and Brooks Adams called on their countrymen to take up the cudgels of international leadership. What American leaders ended up articulating was a global vision with a liberal accent. Confronted by a European scramble for China, Secretary of State John Hay in 1899–1900 issued two famous notes. They endorsed Chinese territorial independence while insisting that the China trade must be open to all comers. The historian William Appleman Williams saw these notes as the proclamation of a distinctive "Open Door imperialism," but Alfred Eckes and Thomas Zeiler are more persuasive when they describe Hay's dispatches as formalizing an American globalization doctrine, emphasizing free trade, multilateralism, and international law.[13] The formulation of doctrine did not, however, make America willing—or able—to shoulder actual burdens. The hegemonic role, as Charles Kindleberger defines it, was a part that the United States, for the time being, remained both unable and unwilling to play.

Looking back at the pre-1914 era, it is striking how little responsibility the United States took for the management of the liberal world economy from which it benefited. Instead of opening its borders to foreign goods, as a would-be hegemon should have done, the United States embraced protectionism. Other deficiencies were no less debilitating. Where the Bank of England guaranteed Britain's public credit and underwrote the stability of the world monetary system, the United States had no central bank until 1913, when Congress chartered the Federal Reserve System. Until then, American businesses had to finance international transactions in foreign currency, drawn on foreign banks.[14] It was in exasperation at this state of affairs that Paul Warburg and other leading financiers moved, with the support of pro-business Republicans, to create the Federal Reserve System. Only thereafter could the United States play an active role in international economic leadership. While Wall Street helped to build the institutional foundations, it fell to a Democratic president to articulate an ideological vision for American leadership.

When he took the United States into World War I, Woodrow Wilson spoke of a world made safe for democracy. He also conjured visions of economic interdependence in which the seas would be open to the commerce of all nations. A Democrat who shared his party's long-standing commitments to free trade, Wilson conjured a sense of historical mission. It was, he insisted, the responsibility of the United States to foster a new international society: one even more open and interdependent than the world already was. His major innovation was his elaboration of a geopolitical rationale for American internationalism. Without US intervention in World War I, Wilson argued, the world's future might not be liberal and lawful. Instead, militarism, aggression, and authoritarianism would predominate. Wilson's caricature of German militarism was cartoonish, and his association of Britain and France with the liberal future that he sought was naïve. But Wilson was deadly serious when he argued that the United States could not be both aloof and safe. Assuming responsibility, Wilson argued, was essential if the United States wished to enjoy physical security and the benefits of globalization. To this end, he persuaded the Congress to support American intervention in World War I.[15]

Wilson nonetheless struggled to persuade his countrymen to accept the cudgels of world leadership. Thereafter, Americans continued to participate in the affairs of the world even as the US government eschewed hegemonic responsibilities. It was a private citizen and banker, Charles Dawes, who in 1924 tried to negotiate a resolution to Europe's postwar debt imbroglio. The basic idea was that New York would lend to funds to Germany, which would pay its reparations to Britain and France, who would repay their war debts to the United States. In fact, Germany avoided repaying reparations, and American capital fueled Germany's postwar renaissance.[16] Still, New York's centrality in the Dawes concept showed how World War I had transformed American capacities: the world's greatest debtor before 1914, the United States was now the world's leading creditor. But there was still little volition to lead. Republican administrations in the 1920s refused to forgive British and French war debts, and their stubbornness precluded more permanent resolution of the debt issue. New York stepped into the breach in the mid-1920s and out of it shortly thereafter, leaving Europe with a credit crunch. At this point, Owen

Young, another American businessman, devised a plan to establish a temporary moratorium on debt repayments. It did not survive the Great Depression. The interventions of the 1920s were well intentioned, but whether they created a half-decade of European stability or a Rube Goldberg credit machine that broke apart in the early 1930s remains open to debate.[17]

The Great Depression fractured the globalization system that cohered in the nineteenth century.[18] Great Britain abandoned the gold standard in September 1931. The US Congress played its own part in the fragmentation of the global economy, approving the notorious Smoot-Hawley tariff of 1930.[19] Reflecting the depth of public support for tariff protection and the susceptibility of congressmen to their constituents' interests, Smoot-Hawley raised tariffs on a broad variety of goods, prompting retaliation, and confirming the fragmentation of the world economy. Trade plummeted, as figure 2.1 illustrates. Two years after it passed the Smoot-Hawley tariff, the United States elected as president a man who promised bold and creative solutions to the Great Depression. Franklin Roosevelt was a Wilsonian Democrat and, in principle, a proponent of free trade, but his first moves as president suggested a nationalistic, even autarkic agenda. Within months of taking office, Roosevelt had pulled the United States off gold and torpedoed the London World Economic Conference, which had convened in a bid to repair the international monetary system. "Old fetishes of the so-called international bankers," thundered FDR's telegram to London, "are being replaced by efforts to plan national currencies."[20]

After his brusque entrance to the world of financial diplomacy, it was ironic that President Roosevelt laid the foundations for an era of international economic governance in which the United States would play the leading role. At the urging of his idealistic Secretary of State Cordell Hull, he secured from Congress the Reciprocal Trade Agreements Act (RTAA) of 1934. The measure gave the president (renewable) authorization to negotiate tariff reductions with foreign countries, shifting the contentious issue of trade protection out of the legislature, where protectionist politics abounded, and into the executive branch, where trade relations could be related to larger strategic purposes. Coming so soon after Smoot-Hawley, the RTAA marked the beginning of a historic, liberal shift in US trade policy. The assumptions that underpinned it were strategic as much as economic. Trade for both Hull and Roosevelt was a salve of international tensions, and the RTAA pointed toward a world bound together by economic interdependence.[21]

If the New Dealers sought to renew globalization, they also tried, as historian Elizabeth Borgwardt argues, to transform the world in the New Deal's image.[22] Nowhere was this clearer than in their reconstruction of the international monetary order. Restoring monetary stability was a precondition for the revival of world trade, and the Roosevelt administration worked hard to achieve it. As early as 1937, Washington reached out to Paris and London to forge the Tripartite Agreement, which aimed to prevent competitive devaluations and to promote monetary stability. It was not until late 1944, however, that the United States and its wartime allies devised a blueprint for postwar monetary relations. The Bretton Woods System rested upon two institutional pillars: the International Monetary Fund (IMF) and the International Bank for Reconstruction and Development (also known as the World Bank). While the World Bank was to loan money for development, the IMF was to provide for the stable operation of international monetary relations. It innovated upon the gold standard in important ways. Whereas the gold standard had required quick adjustment when countries ran trade imbalances, the IMF supplied temporary financing for deficits. Exchange stability was to be preserved through a system of adjustable pegs, by which foreign countries would fix the values of their currencies against the US dollar. This offered stability while permitting adjustment where prudent. The dollar resided at the center of the entire system. It was to be both the *numéraire* (the unit of value in which other units are valued) and, as a system-wide reserve asset, a source of liquidity for the world economy.[23] The Bretton Woods settlement thus marks the moment when the United States assumed responsibility for the liberal world economy as a whole, a turning point toward hegemony as Charles Kindleberger defined it.

Still, this does not answer the question: Why did the United States in the 1940s accept a hegemonic role after forsaking it for a generation? The answers are both strategic and economic. Put simply, the United States assumed the burdens of world leadership because it could afford them and because its leaders feared the consequences of irresolution. The lessons of the past weighed upon the Roosevelt administration, as Ernest May has argued.[24] Capacities also mattered. By 1945, the United States produced more than 50 percent of the world's industrial output, maintained the greater part of its gold reserves, and held most of its debt. It was the New Dealers' desire to remake the world and their capacity to do so that made the United States hegemonic. The Cold War followed the initial acts of hegemonic creation.[25] The Soviet–American estrangement nonetheless galvanized and transformed American hegemony. Fearing that Eurppe's despair might create inroads for Communism, the Truman administration in 1947–1948 created a massive financial assistance program, Marshall Aid.[26] While the policies that the United States followed in the Cold War were often shortsighted and sometimes brutal, especially in the developing world, American hegemony benefited the advanced industrial countries. Absent the Cold War, the United States would have been far less disposed than it was to subordinate parochial American interests to the promotion of the West's common prosperity.

Yet the irony of America's mid-century hegemonic project is that its formation occurred when US interdependence with the world economy was, by historical standards, surprisingly limited. After the breakdown of the globalized world economy in the 1930s, the United States was relatively self-sufficient in the 1940s and the 1950s. World War II had provided a vast economic stimulus, securing recovery from the Great Depression, but foreign trade lagged behind domestic consumption as a motor of growth. The value of US exports averaged just 3.5 percent of GDP in the 1950s. As figure 2.1 indicates, this was a historic lull. Only in the 1930s had the United States exported so little. Domestic markets sustained US economic expansion in the early postwar decades, contrary to the expectations of State Department planners who feared that domestic demand would not suffice to keep the wheels of commerce turning. Mid-century Americans also imported surprisingly little: annual imports averaged just 2.9 percent of GDP between 1950 and 1970. International capital mobility was also low by comparison with the late nineteenth and late twentieth centuries. None of this is to say that the external world did not depend upon the United States: it did. Rather, the point is that the United States dominated the making of international economic rules and institutions during a phase when US interdependence with the larger world was less than it had been in the past and—and less than it would again be in the future. If we are to understand why the United States so willingly accepted the burdens of hegemony, this relative disengagement is a crucial part of the context.

Hegemony confers benefits, but it also carries costs. The United States after 1945 enjoyed the exorbitant privilege (as French critics put it) of being able to print currency to finance its trade deficits, but it also carried the burdens of an overvalued dollar. Military power conferred superpower status, but the United States made significant contributions to the defense of its allies. In the absence of NATO and the US–Japan Security Treaty, the costs of self-defense in an era of rising Soviet power would have exerted a drag on economic growth in Western Europe and Japan. If military dependency created unequal relationships, the United States did not seize the opportunity to force its allies' markets open to American exports. On the contrary, allied leaders proved adept at leveraging the American market open, as Japanese Prime Minister Hayato Ikeda did when he played upon John F. Kennedy's fears of geopolitical destabilization to secure for Japan privileged access to the American market.[27] Unequal trade barriers, as the political scientist Robert Gilpin lamented in the mid-1970s, bore heavy consequences for the United

States: foreign protectionism encouraged American firms to set up affiliates behind foreign tariff walls, which drained capital from the US economy and diffused American know-how.[28] The United States lost economic ground to its allies fast, its share of the West's total economic production declined from 46 percent in 1950 to 38 percent in 1970.[29]

Cold War fears help to explain why Americans tolerated this relative economic decline, but they are only part of the story. The economic context also matters. So long as American prosperity remained largely self-sufficient and the domestic economy continued to flourish, the costs of hegemony remained tolerable. By the 1960s, however, the United States was again becoming increasingly interdependent with the larger world economy. As jobs came increasingly to depend upon exports and as foreign imports became more commonplace in the domestic market, the politics of trade protectionism resurged.[30] Financial interdependence also became a source of instability. By the end of the 1960s, the dollar's predominant role in the international monetary system was hanging by a thread that currency speculators stood poised to slice.[31] The Johnson administration in 1968 adopted a package of defensive measures intended to cool an overheating domestic economy and defend the dollar, but whether Americans would be prepared to accept economic retrenchment at home in order to preserve their currency's global role was unclear. Thickening interdependence, ironically, thrust the hegemonic vocation into question.

"The foreigners," declared John Connally, "are out to screw us, and it's our job to screw them first."[32] As Secretary of the Treasury from early 1971 through early 1973, Connally grappled with the consequences of hegemonic decline. He and Richard Nixon, the president he served, believed that the United States had borne a disproportionate share of the West's common burdens for a generation and that the time for recalibration had come. They were especially concerned by the dwindling competitiveness of American industry, which they attributed to the dollar's role in the architecture of international monetary order. While other countries were free to devalue their currencies, the dollar could not be devalued unless Congress authorized a change in its gold parity. Even then, US trading partners could easily match the dollar's depreciation by devaluing their currencies against it. The result, after a quarter-century, was an overvalued dollar that priced US exporters out of foreign markets, an effect that trade discrimination compounded.

After years of slippage in the international balance of payments, the United States in 1971 suffered its first trade deficit since 1893. This grim landmark confirmed for Nixon and Connally that fundamental rethinking was overdue. The rapid growth of short-term international capital markets from the mid-1960s, meanwhile, left the dollar (and other currencies) vulnerable to speculation. What happened in the spring and summer of 1971 was that a flight from the dollar precipitated a major financial crisis. For Nixon and Connally, this was also an opportunity. They ended gold-dollar convertibility and imposed an emergency tariff, which they used as a bludgeon to compel US trading partners to revalue their currencies against the dollar. The so-called Nixon Shock was a foreign policy upset, but the episode's real significance was even greater than the diplomatic chill it caused. The United States, Nixon and Connally had declared, would no longer subordinate its own economic interests to the prosperity and stability of the West. The move thus reversed the patterns of twenty-five years and heralded a new era.[33]

Still, it was the oil crisis that began in the fall of 1973 that provided the most dramatic exhibition of American vulnerability. That year's October War exacerbated the crisis, triggering an embargo on Arab (not OPEC) oil exports to the United States, but its deeper origins resided in the West's growing dependence on imported oil. This enabled the Organization of Petroleum Exporting Countries (OPEC) to orchestrate a fourfold increase in the price of oil, announced as the Arab–Israeli War was commencing. The oil crisis inflicted serious damage to Western prosperity. It precipitated a sharp recession and divided the West. While the United States took a belligerent line with the oil exporters, its allies embraced the diplomacy of appeasement. It was true, as European and Japanese diplomats pointed out, that the United States was less dependent on foreign oil than they were, but it was America's relationship to the world oil market that changed most dramatically in recent years. Until the late 1960s, the United States had been the world's greatest oil power and the "swing" producer to the world markets. US oil production peaked in the early 1970s, and the United States became increasingly dependent on imports thereafter, becoming a net importer in 1977. Interdependence came fast, and the oil crisis showed how difficult it could be to mitigate its consequences. When he proclaimed the world economy "interdependent" in 1975, Gerald Ford had affirmed the need to regain energy independence. His efforts to do so soon ran afoul of congressional opposition. In 1975, Ford presented to Congress a serious energy program that sought to reduce consumption and incentivize the development of alternative fuels by raising the domestic price of oil. Republicans and Democrats in Congress balked. Their reluctance to take unpopular steps in order to reduce vulnerabilities over the long term ensured that the vulnerabilities interdependence brought would be unabated.[34]

The decade's energy crises symbolize but will not suffice to explain the economic malaise that gripped the advanced industrial countries during the 1970s. Economists at the time and since have proffered an array of explanations, from cyclical downturns to oil shocks and policy errors to labor militancy. For leaders at the time, the transnational scope of the crisis, which combined sluggish growth and stubborn inflation, was striking. "This is the first global business cycle," exclaimed West German Chancellor Helmut Schmidt in 1975.[35] The point seemed to mandate collaborative action. "The interdependence of all our economies," Henry Kissinger declared in November 1975, "emphasizes the necessity of cooperative solutions."[36] The annual G-7 summits provided a forum in which such solutions might be devised. In practice, the annual meetings of the summit countries produced more dialogue than decision.[37] If the G-7's exertions were incommensurate to the West's problems, it was because interdependence made the global economic management even more difficult than in the past.[38] At the same time, no single government possessed the combination of capacity and volition that enabled the United States to reorder the international monetary system during World War II.

The failures of world monetary reform provide stark illustrations of the indecisiveness that seemed in the mid-1970s to be overwhelming the industrialized countries. The collapse of Bretton Woods in 1971–1973 brought down the curtain on a particular set of monetary arrangements but not on the idea of an ordered international monetary system. Indeed, the IMF in 1972 created a task force, the Committee of Twenty, to redesign the international monetary system for the next quarter century. Its report ended up a dead letter. Trade imbalances that the oil crisis exacerbated and divisions between the United States and its allies over such substantive issues as the role of gold in the international monetary system inhibited accord. The most that the industrialized countries could agree upon, it seemed, was to leave the determination of exchange rates to the markets. This was a solution, but ceding responsibilities to markets did not amount to a reconstruction of international governance. National governments would continue to intervene to influence exchange rates, but there would be no generalized restoration of exchange stability. Financial markets also provided a stopgap solution to the payments deficits that many countries suffered after the oil crisis: they "recycled" funds deposited by the OPEC countries to countries that found themselves unable to balance their payments. This solution worked, but it was prone to instability and crises, as the Latin American debt crisis of the early 1980s would affirm.[39]

If the world economy became less governable during the 1970s, domestic politics also inhibited the tasks of global governance. On this point, the Carter administration's experience is instructive. Carter sought a coordinated stimulus in which the strong economies–the United States, West Germany, and Japan–would pull the rest out of recession. This so-called "locomotive strategy" projected Keynesian solutions upon a transnational scale; it sought to accomplish through coordinated action what could not be achieved within national economies that had grown too interdependent for traditional stimulus techniques to work. The problem was that stimulus was unpopular in West Germany, whose economy remained relatively buoyant and whose voters, harboring memories of the 1920s, feared inflation more than they feared recession. Although Carter managed in 1978 to extract a German commitment to economic stimulus in return for a US commitment to decontrol oil prices, delivering on the agreement proved difficult to accomplish. Amidst political opposition in Germany, Schmidt's stimulus package did not go so far as Carter's advisers hoped. Although Carter overcame Senate opposition to decontrol domestic oil prices in 1979, his complex energy plan became a political millstone. Before long, the dollar thwarted Carter's locomotive. Efforts to stimulate the economy precipitated a dollar crisis, which led the Treasury to issue "Carter Bonds" denominated in Swiss francs and Deutschmarks. Sensitive to the international implications of the dollar's turmoil, Carter in late 1979 appointed Paul Volcker to chair the Federal Reserve Bank. Volcker raised interest rates, stabilized the US dollar, and vanquished the long inflation of the 1970s.[40] His triumph came at a cost, including to President Carter. Volcker's move precipitated a sharp recession, and Carter lost his reelection bid in 1980. Still, the consequences of the Volcker shock were severest for those developing countries that found themselves starved of capital, as high interest rates attracted short-term funds back to the United States in the early 1980s. Interdependence, it seemed, did not equal systemic stability.

From the 1970s, relationships of complex interdependence enveloped the United States. Mass immigration, which resumed in the mid-1960s after a forty-year hiatus, brought cheap labor and foreign talent to American shores. This reaped considerable dividends. Recent research suggests that immigrants to the United States have established almost 20 percent of the Fortune 500 companies founded since 1985.[41] By the twentieth century's end, immigration again reached levels that it last achieved in the late nineteenth century. As in the past, rising immigration faced a backlash that fused economic resentment and cultural nativism. More impressive, even, than the flood of immigrants are the quantities of foreign capital that have penetrated the American economy since the 1970s. As figure 2.2 indicates, both foreign investments in the United States and US investments overseas have surged since the 1970s. Inbound and outbound investments have not moved in tandem, however. The United States became an international debtor in the mid-1980s. This massive influx of foreign capital that it has received since then has transformed the American political economy. During the 1980s, foreign capital permitted the Reagan administration to cut taxes while increasing military spending. Channeled into mortgage-backed securities, foreign capital fueled the property bubble that transformed housing markets from the 1990s and went bust in 2007.[42] Suppressing interest rates, this international deficit still nurtures US government deficits, which now approach levels last recorded during World War II. One difference, of course, is that US public debt in the 1940s was held mainly in the hands of American citizens. In 2012, by contrast, foreign creditors owned almost half of the US national debt.[43] Whether this debt nurtures growth and prosperity, as foreign funds did in the nineteenth century, or is a dangerous liability, even a national security threat, may be a matter of perspective.

Enmeshment in global movements of people, capital, and goods since the 1970s has not compelled the United States to undertake the work of responsible international governance. By comparison with the achievements of the 1940s, when American leaders positioned the United States at the center of a stable international monetary system and assisted economic reconstruction in Western Europe and Japan, the record of the late twentieth century has been flimsy. The failures of international monetary reform in the 1970s set the pattern for what came next. Rather than collaborate with its trading partners to rebuild stable governing institutions, the United States has reacted to crises in real time. Crisis management has sometimes served stability, as in 1994 when the Clinton administration provided Mexico with $20 billion of emergency assistance. The United States has supported IMF stabilization efforts, as during the 1997 East Asian financial crisis. Still, recurrent crisis management does not amount to governance. The sorry record of international financial regulation illustrates this point. After concluding in the mid-1970s that financial globalization required at least some regulatory oversight, the members of the G-10 (distinct from but overlapping with the G-7) participated in the so-called Basel Process, which has devised regulatory guidelines and reserve requirements intended to stabilize the world financial system. Its guidelines, which national governments interpret and apply, nonetheless failed to prevent the global financial crisis that began in 2007. The obstacles to the effective management of a decentralized global financial system are, of course, tremendous. Still, the financial crisis that began in 2007 affirmed that market actors sometimes make poor bets and, crucially, that market-led globalization does not manage itself.[44]

Why has economic globalization since the 1970s not produced a parallel globalization of governance? This is a vast question, and the easiest answer is that globalization abjures governance. This is correct but insufficient. The inherent difficulties are obvious: the disjoint between global economics and national politics has impeded effective governance in the past and will continue to do so. Still, the broad historical panorama affirms that disconnections between territorial politics and transnational economics need not impede the construction of governing international regimes. In the nineteenth century, the British Empire presided over a global settlement whose stability depended on the gold standard, the Bank of England's ability to provide assistance to debtors, and Britain's willingness to be the world's consumer of last resort. In the mid-twentieth century, the United States constructed a more progressive governing order that accommodated the growth of international trade while permitting governments the policy tools and financial support necessary to avoid the deflationary adjustments that the gold standard had required. The historic achievement of the 1940s was to make globalization safe for the welfare state. In the 1970s, however, Bretton Woods collapsed, and no successor regime emerged to take its place. Since the 1970s, the rule of the markets increasingly has supplanted responsible international governance. Explanations for this change may stress the decline of American power, the growing complexity of globalization, and the political failures of US (and non-US) leaders. Each of these factors bears some responsibility. Still, the failures of the 1970s were not the result of ignorance or indifference. American political leaders and policy intellectuals in the 1970s diagnosed interdependence as a novel reality, and they aspired to manage it, envisaging that collaboration among like-minded nation-states could substitute for waning American capabilities. Yet they faced practical and political obstacles that became only daunting as interdependence with the broader world economy increased. As a result, the authority of the United States over the international economy has diminished in an era of renewed globalization, with destabilizing implications for the United States and the international society that it once presumed to lead.

NOTES

1. Gerald Ford, "Address at Tulane University," April 23, 1975, American Presidency Project (APP), http://www.presidency.ucsb.edu.

2. Charles Kindleberger, *The World in Depression, 1929–1939* (Berkeley: University of California Press, 1973).

3. Robert Keohane, *After Hegemony: Cooperation and Discord in the World Political Economy* (Princeton: Princeton University Press, 1984).

4. Anthony Hopkins, ed., *Globalization in World History* (New York: Norton, 2002), 48–9.

5. The literature on interdependence from the 1970s is substantive. Key contributions include Richard Cooper, *The Economics of Interdependence: Economic Policy in the Atlantic Community* (New York: Council on Foreign Relations, 1968);

Robert Keohane and Joseph Nye, *Transnational Relations and World Politics* (Cambridge, MA: Harvard University Press, 1972); and Robert Keohane and Joseph Nye, *Power and Interdependence: World Politics in Transition* (Boston, MA: Little, 1977).

6. United Nations Conference on Trade and Development (UNCTAD), UNCTAD Stat., http://unctadstat.unctad.org.

7. Lance Davis and Robert Cull, *International Capital Markets and American Economic Growth, 1820–1914* (New York: Cambridge University Press, 2002), 3.

8. *Historical Statistics of the United States* (New York: Cambridge University Press, 2006), Series Aa1896-1921.

9. Kevin O'Rourke and Jeffrey Williamson, *Globalization and History* (Cambridge, MA: MIT University Press, 1999).

10. Eric Rauchway, *Blessed among Nations: How the World Made America* (New York: Hill & Wang, 2006).

11. Alfred Eckes Jr., *Opening America's Market: U.S. Foreign Trade Policy since 1776* (Chapel Hill: University of North Carolina Press, 1995), 28–55.

12. Jeffry Frieden, *Global Capitalism: Its Fall and Rise in the Twentieth Century* (New York: W. W. Norton, 2006), ch. 1.

13. Alfred Eckes and Thomas Zeiler, *Globalization and the American Century* (New York: Cambridge University Press, 2003), 14; and William A. Williams, *The Tragedy of American Diplomacy* (New York: W. W. Norton, 1972), ch. 1.

14. Barry J. Eichengreen, *Exorbitant Privilege: The Rise and Fall of the Dollar and the Future of the International Monetary System* (New York: Oxford University Press, 2011), ch. 2.

15. I will not try to summarize the vast literature on Wilson here. Instead I will just mention Frank Ninkovich, *Modernity and Power: A History of the Domino Theory in the Twentieth Century* (Chicago: University of Chicago Press, 1994), as an interpretation that has especially influenced my reading of him. For a more optimistic counterpoint, see Thomas Knock, *To End All Wars: Woodrow Wilson and the Quest for a New World Order* (Princeton: Princeton University Press, 1995).

16. C. H. Feinstein, Peter Temin, and Gianni Toniolo, *The World Economy between the World Wars* (New York: Oxford University Press, 2008), ch. 5.

17. For more positive interpretations, see Barry Eichengreen, *Golden Fetters: The Gold Standard and the Great Depression* (New York: Oxford University Press, 1992), 150–2; and Charles S. Maier, *Recasting Bourgeois Europe* (Princeton: Princeton University Press, 1988). A more critical view, recapitulating contemporary complaints, can be found in Stephen A. Schuker, *American "Reparations" to Germany, 1919–33: Implications for the Third World Debt Crisis*, Princeton Studies in International Finance, No. 61 (Princeton: Department of Economics, Princeton University, 1988).

18. Harold James, *The End of Globalization: Lessons from the Great Depression* (Cambridge, MA: Harvard University Press, 2001).

19. Douglas Irwin, *Peddling Protectionism: Smoot-Hawley and the Great Depression* (Princeton: Princeton University Press, 2011).

20. Franklin Roosevelt, "Wireless to the London Conference," July 3, 1933, American Presidency Project.

21. Ivan Destler, *American Trade Politics* (Washington, DC: Peterson Institute, 2005), ch. 2; and Eckes, *Opening America's Market*, ch. 5.

22. Elizabeth Borgwardt, *A New Deal for the World: America's Vision for Human Rights* (Cambridge, MA: Harvard University Press, 2005).

23. The literature on Bretton Woods is vast. For a venerable introduction, see Alfred Eckes, *A Search for Solvency: Bretton Woods and the International Monetary System, 1941–1971* (Austin: University of Texas Press, 1975).

24. Ernest May, *"Lessons" of the Past: The Use and Misuse of History in American Foreign Policy* (New York: Oxford University Press, 1973), ch. 1.

25. This point is familiar from the revisionist scholarship on the Cold War's origins. See, e.g., Franz Schurmann, *The Logic of World Power: An Inquiry into the Origins, Currents, and Contradictions of World Politics* (New York: Pantheon, 1974); and Thomas J. McCormick, *America's Half-Century: United States Foreign Policy in the Cold War and After* (Baltimore, MD: Johns Hopkins University Press, 1995).

26. Michael J. Hogan, *The Marshall Plan: America, Britain, and the Reconstruction of Western Europe, 1947–1952* (New York: Cambridge University Press, 1987).

27. Timothy Maga, *Hands across the Sea?* (Athens: University of Ohio Press, 1997).

28. Robert Gilpin, *U.S. Power and the Multinational Corporation: The Political Economy of Foreign Direct Investment* (New York: Basic Books, 1975).

29. Calculated from Angus Maddison, "Statistics on World Population, GDP, and per capita GDP, 1-2008 AD," http://www.ggdc.net/maddison/Maddison.htm.

30. Eckes, *Opening America's Market*, 209–14.

31. On the travails of the dollar in the 1960s, see Francis J. Gavin, *Gold, Dollars, and Power: The Politics of International Monetary Relations, 1958–1971* (Chapel Hill: University of North Carolina Press, 2004).

32. John S. Odell, *U.S. International Monetary Policy: Markets, Power, and Ideas as Sources of Change* (Princeton: Princeton University Press, 1982), 263.

33. On the Nixon Shock and the end of Bretton Woods, see Joanne Gowa, *Closing the Gold Window: Domestic Politics and the End of Bretton Woods* (Ithaca, NY: Cornell University Press, 1983); Allen J. Matusow, *Nixon's Economy: Booms, Busts, Dollars, and Votes* (Lawrence: University of Kansas Press, 1998), 149–81; and Odell, *U.S. International Monetary Policy*.

34. On the oil crisis, see Fiona Venn, *The Oil Crisis* (London: Longman, 2002); and Daniel Yergin, *The Prize: The Epic Quest for Oil, Money, and Power* (New York: Free Press, 1993), chs. 28–31. For a sympathetic treatment of Ford's energy proposals, see Yanek Mieczkowski, *Gerald Ford and the Challenges of the 1970s* (Lexington: University of Kentucky Press, 2005), chs. 12–15.

35. Memorandum of Conversation between Gerald Ford, Helmut Schmidt, and Henry Kissinger, May 29, 1975. National Security Adviser Files, Memoranda of Conversations (Box 12), Gerald Ford Presidential Library, Ann Arbor, Michigan.

36. "The Industrial Countries and the Future," Address at the Pittsburgh World Affairs Council, November 11, 1975. In *Department of State Bulletin* 73 (December 1, 1975): 757–64.

37. On the economic summits, see Robert Putman and Nicholas Bayne, *Hanging Together: The Seven Power Summits* (Cambridge, MA: Harvard University Press, 1984).

38. Michael C. Webb, *The Political Economy of Policy Coordination: International Adjustment since 1945* (Ithaca, NY: Cornell University Press, 1995).

39. On the failures of international monetary reform in the 1970s, see Margaret De Vries, *The International Monetary Fund, 1972–1978: Cooperation on Trial*, 2 vols. (Washington, DC: IMF, 1985); and Harold James, *International Monetary Cooperation since Bretton Woods* (Washington, DC: International Monetary Fund; and New York: Oxford University Press, 1996); and John Williamson, *The Failure of World Monetary Reform, 1971–74* (New York: New York University Press, 1977).

40. W. Carl Biven, *Jimmy Carter's Economy: Policy in an Age of Limits* (Chapel Hill: University of North Carolina Press, 2002); and William L. Silber, *Volcker: The Triumph of Persistence* (New York: Bloomsbury Press, 2012), 147–77.

41. Partnership for a New American Economy, "The 'New American' Fortune 500" (2011), http://www.renewoureconomy.org.

42. On the role of foreign debt in the US housing crisis, see Jeffry Frieden and Menzie Chinn, *Lost Decades: The Making of America's Debt Crisis and the Long Recovery* (New York: W. W. Norton, 2011).

43. US Treasury, "Major Foreign Holders of Treasury Securities," http://www. treasury.gov/resource-center/data-chart-center/tic/Documents/mfh.txt.

44. For an analysis of the instability that economic globalization breeds, see Susan Strange, *Casino Capitalism* (Oxford: Basil Blackwell, 1986).

3

A "Badge of Advanced Liberalism"

Woman Suffrage at the High Tide
of Anglo-American Reform

Leslie A. Butler

July 4th found John Stuart Mill in a celebratory mood. Writing to the New Hampshire abolitionist Parker Pillsbury in 1867, Mill expressed satisfaction with recent efforts on behalf of women's rights in both the United States and Britain. The formation of an Equal Rights Association in the United States, serious debate in state constitutional conventions and in the British House of Commons, petitions, and other measures had helped excite "thought and discussion" about woman suffrage "in quarters where the subject had never been thought of before." On this anniversary of national independence, he praised his American friends who, in seeking to rectify the "disabilities of women," were about to remove "the only remaining national violation of the principles of your immortal Declaration of Independence."[1]

Suffrage reformers had more than national consistency as their objective in 1867, as they attempted to "reconstruct" the entire republic, and thus expand upon the bold effort to extend political power to former slaves within the defeated Confederacy. Mill himself had been one of the key forces pushing suffrage expansion at home and had helped finally move what had long been a philosophical interest into a series of political initiatives. These efforts had given "an immense impulse" to woman suffrage and had earned the movement scores of new adherents. Indeed, Mill noted with pride, agreement with woman suffrage was "rapidly becoming a badge of advanced liberalism" across national borders.[2]

It would be more than another half century till women won the vote in either Britain or the United States, though limited victories dotted the last decades of the nineteenth century. British women began to vote in municipal elections and for school boards in the 1870s, while a handful of newly admitted states in the American West fully enfranchised women. But in spite of persistent campaigning and lobbying by women (and some men), the issue made relatively little progress in these decades. How then do we account for Mill's optimism in his 1867 letter to Pillsbury? Had women's enfranchisement in fact excited "thought and discussion" in new quarters in the 1860s? And, if so, had this new attention actually translated into support? If "advanced" liberals took up the issue as a badge, were there non-advanced liberals, as well as conservatives, who resisted it?

Mill's remarks to Pillsbury can serve as a point of entry into the broader Anglo-American interactions over this early push for woman suffrage. While many nineteenth-century reform movements, including the woman suffrage movement, have been identified as transatlantic phenomena this essay offers something different.[3] Rather than focusing exclusively on movement actors or organizations, it recreates the ways in which discussions of woman suffrage emerged and circulated through print and, in doing so, treats advocacy, opposition, and analysis within a shared discursive space. The debate over women voters in the 1860s participated in a transatlantic or, more precisely, an Anglo-American dynamic. English-speaking observers and commentators in Europe and the United States followed developments in each other's countries, corresponded with one another, and read the same newspapers, periodicals, and books. Broader transatlantic influences existed to be sure, but in addition to sharing a language, British and American observers recognized a similar political culture as well, often distinguishing that culture from different continental European cultures. Yet that supposedly shared political culture had come under enormous pressure in the 1860s, as the two countries nearly went to war during the American Civil War. Indeed, this crisis in Anglo-American relations sparked Mill's relationship with Pillsbury, and other northern American correspondents: Mill had emerged as one of the earliest and most outspoken supporters of the Union cause amidst a larger climate of misunderstanding and even hostility.[4]

This essay begins by recapping the events that inspired Mill with such confidence and by exploring his view, widely shared among Anglo-American writers and reformers, that the decade of the American Civil War represented something of a watershed moment for liberal causes, including woman suffrage. It then investigates the crucial role Mill's 1869 *Subjection of Women* played in exciting "thought and discussion," if not necessarily assent, among American writers. Mill may have been correct that woman suffrage was a badge of advanced liberalism in 1867 but by the 1870s, this badge had become in many circles more a burden than an honor.

That Mill could imagine women's political disabilities as the only "remaining" violation of America's founding ideals in 1867 helps to explain his optimism. Passage of the Thirteenth Amendment put a decisive end to the system of slavery that had since the country's founding been considered, by foreign and domestic critics alike, the grossest violation of the Declaration's egalitarian principles. Emancipation of four million slaves had been the fruit of a war that many observers understood as crucial to the fate of liberal democratic principles the world over. This understanding of the war's global significance could be found across the pages of Union newspapers, periodicals, and pamphlets and represented a central theme of President Lincoln's oratory. When Lincoln framed the war as a conflict "testing" whether America or "any nation" dedicated to the principles of the Declaration could "endure," he gave powerful voice to the sentiments of Union advocates on both sides of the Atlantic.

The vindication those Britons felt in having backed the Union cause poured forth in bold predictions of the transnational impact of American emancipation. The Union struggle, as the Oxford historian Goldwin Smith wrote an American correspondent in 1863, was the "most momentous perhaps in the issues it involves, for which the blood of man was ever shed." Victory, he predicted, would "expel from American society the poison of Slavery and that worst of all aristocracies which Slavery brings in its train," but it would do even more. It would check "the reactionary influence of European governments," and thereby make America, "in deed and truth, a new world, the scene of new hopes for man."[5]

With Union victory and emancipation came a fundamental reconsideration of citizenship and political belonging. Abolitionists, freedmen, and Radical Republicans viewed suffrage as an indispensable aspect of citizenship in the American nation. "Slavery is not abolished," insisted Frederick Douglass at the end of the war, "until the black man has the ballot." In other countries, Douglass explained, freedom may not require the vote, but in democratic America, where "universal suffrage is the rule," there was no full citizenship short of voting rights. The popular Congregationalist minister Henry Ward Beecher agreed: "Voting with us is like breathing," he explained. The *North American Review*—the old New England quarterly that had begun to reveal new energy and liberal democratic commitments in the 1860s—argued that the war had been "carried on for the principles of democracy," a cardinal point of which was that the "only way in which to fit men for freedom is to make them free" and the only way to "teach them to use political power is to give it to them." This belief undergirded congressional efforts in the late 1860s: requiring former Confederate states to grant to all men the vote (part of the First Reconstruction Act in 1867); enfranchising all men in Washington, DC (1867, over President Johnson's veto); and finally, passing the Fifteenth Amendment (in 1869), which prohibited the use of race or prior condition of servitude as criteria for the vote.[6]

The 1860s were also a decade of fundamental electoral reform in Britain, the first since the so-called Great Reform Act of 1832. Universal manhood suffrage had been one of the key six reforms in the People's Charter of 1838. Although Chartism had generally faded after 1848, agitation for a more popular suffrage re-emerged in 1865, peaking (at least in the middle-class imagination) with a demonstration in July 1866 in Hyde Park. A series of parliamentary maneuvers ensued, whereby the Conservative and Liberal parties sought to gain political advantage in a newly reformed electorate. The eventual Second Reform Act, passed in 1867, extended the vote to most male householders and nearly doubled the electorate from roughly one to two million out of nearly seven million adult males in England and Wales. While only one in three adult males voted on the other side of 1867, the Second Reform Act ushered in a democratic logic that led to further reforms (in 1884, 1918, and, ultimately, universal adult suffrage in 1928).[7]

Observers were well aware that these major reconsiderations in the United Kingdom and the United States occurred in tandem. To interpret them as related merely continued wartime perspectives, which in turn had built on a dynamic established earlier, in the decades after the French Revolution when waves of reform and reaction seemed to ebb and flow across the Atlantic. The newly founded weekly magazine, the New York *Nation*, had predicted in 1865 that "the effects of the revolution through which we are now passing upon European politics will be still more marked than the effects of the revolution of 1776." Those who pushed for reform and those who resisted it alike pointed to the influence of the United States on the Second Reform Bill.[8]

Reform energies did not simply move back and forth across the Atlantic, they seemed to spread from issue to issue. Indeed the "most certain consequence" of the crises of the 1860s, Mill assured Ralph Waldo Emerson in 1867, was "that all the fundamental problems of politics and society, so long smothered by general indolence and apathy, will surge up and demand better solutions than they have ever yet obtained." In such a context, questions about the political status of women emerged as part of the larger debates over citizenship and suffrage, especially since agitation for women's rights had begun in both Britain and America two decades earlier. A resigned Catherine Beecher, the American educational reformer and domestic advice guru, anticipated the pattern: "Now that negro suffrage is accomplished, the next political struggle that will agitate this country, as well as Europe, will be that of labor and capital, and, connected with it, the question of woman suffrage."[9]

In the United States, where women's rights had emerged within the radical Garrisonian wing of abolition, activists banded together to form the American Equal Rights Association after the war. This organization, founded by abolitionists including Lucretia Mott, Lucy Stone, Frederick Douglass, and others, dedicated itself to securing "Equal Rights to all American citizens, especially the right of suffrage, irrespective of race, color or sex." They held meetings, disseminated pamphlets, and worked to win black and woman suffrage in two major campaigns: a constitutional convention in New York and a referendum campaign in Kansas. These efforts failed, and the movement fractured over the passage of a narrow, minimalist version of the Fifteenth Amendment that said nothing about universal suffrage or woman suffrage. Indeed the question of woman suffrage was more than once mobilized as a sort of *reductio ad absurdum* in order to thwart efforts to extend voting rights to African American men.[10]

In Britain, woman suffrage was also spurred on by the larger reform agitation. Women's rights reformers collected 1,500 signatures on a woman suffrage petition in 1866, which Mill himself (elected MP in 1865) presented to Parliament. The next year saw the emergence of the first national organizations, such as the National Society for Women's Suffrage in 1867, specifically dedicated to the issue. As the Second Reform Bill was debated in the House of Commons, Mill proposed an amendment that would strike "male" from the bill and replace it with "person," thus enfranchising women who otherwise met the criteria established (i.e., propertied single or widowed women). Although the amendment was defeated in the House of Commons by 196 opponents, it garnered a surprisingly robust 73 votes in support. By the decade's end women ratepayers had won the right to vote in municipal and school board elections.[11]

The transatlantic simultaneity of these efforts was not lost on participants or observers. Reformers drew strength and support from the efforts of their colleagues abroad. Mill's "amendment speech" in Parliament (delivered on May 20, 1867) quickly became a canonical tract among suffragists; it was reprinted as a pamphlet and circulated in both Britain and American for decades (even excerpted in the mammoth six-volume *History of Woman Suffrage* edited by Elizabeth Cady Stanton and Susan B. Anthony in the 1880s). The suffragist George William Curtis relied heavily on Mill's May 20 speech, as well as his

Considerations on Representative Government, in presenting his own amendment for woman suffrage to the New York Constitutional Convention in 1867. Curtis invoked Mill for both intellectual and political reasons, hoping the stature of Britain's preeminent political philosopher (and well-known champion of the Union cause) would lend legitimacy and force to his own efforts. "When Mr. Mill unrolls his petition in Parliament to secure the political equality of women," Curtis contended, "it bears the names of those English men and women whose thoughts foretell the course of civilization." While members of the New York constitutional convention may find woman suffrage "to be radically revolutionary and perilous to the very functions of sex," Curtis assured them that "the most sagacious of living political philosophers" considered it "reasonable, conservative, necessary, and inevitable." The rhetorical strategy at work extended the mobilization of shame and national one-upsmanship pioneered by abolitionists.[12]

But these transatlantic connections could also be mobilized to different ends. British opponents of reform, Tory and Liberal alike, worked to taint reform at home with the brush of American radicalism. Speeches in the House of Commons and articles in periodicals invoked the mediocrity, vulgarity, and corruption of democratic American politics as a cautionary tale. The famed illustrated weekly *Punch* enlisted Reconstruction America in its effort to discredit Mill's woman suffrage amendment. Exploiting a complicated set of gender and racial inversions, the magazine ran a satirical letter from Punch's wife Judy to Mill, assuring him that women already ruled the world and simply allowed men to keep themselves busy with politics. Politics, according to Judy, was actually "the natural occupation of the inferior or slavish sex, whom we have admitted to the suffrage, as I see it is now proposed to admit the Negroes in the Southern States." The humor depended on the reader finding a whole series of claims preposterous: that British women actually ruled, that British men were "inferior," that political life was exclusively for inferior beings, and of course that former slaves in the United States might be enfranchised.[13]

Given the rapid pace and extensive reach of change, observers could be excused for feeling that they were living in a new era. For Mill, the 1860s offered a watershed moment, when all the "old prejudices" had been "shaken up and dislocated" and "stagnant waters" had begun "flowing." It is no wonder that the generation of reformers living through this moment believed, as Alexander Keyssar has observed, that "profound ideological and political changes could not only happen, but happen quickly." They had witnessed black suffrage move from being an "idea supported only by those on the fringes of politics" to a proposition that "had acquired the backing of the Republican Party and then been embedded in the Constitution." Commentators on both sides of the Atlantic repeated some version of this sentiment again and again, even when they found it unnerving rather than exciting. One critic in the United States warned that, in this climate of accelerated change, "no custom is likely to be spared, unless it has a better plea for existence than that of age." A conservative writer in *Blackwood's* despairingly agreed, noting in 1869 the "widespread tendency to look with suspicion on the customs and opinions of former generations, and to call in question principles and institutions which were once fondly imagined to be settled on a firm and abiding basis." Such a sensibility had indeed become one of the most "remarkable" characteristics of the present era.[14]

Much as in earlier periods—the international excitement of 1848, for example—this sense of the era's momentum depended on transatlantic developments. The fact that progress seemed to spread from one nation to the other like a contagion raised the stakes and heightened the perception of change. Ocean metaphors worked especially well in this transalantic narrative: observers wrote of historical tides and waves of reform. The "tide is turning in favor of liberalism with resistless force," the *Nation* had insisted after the war. Yet whether this was a positive or worrisome development depended on one's perspective.

Those who dreaded, or at least distrusted, the new reform energies no less than those who embraced them sensed the turning tide. Thomas Carlyle offered perhaps the best-remembered articulation of this sense of "progress" running amuck. He abandoned the "turning tide" metaphor in favor of another well-known, and still watery, image: shooting the rapids at Niagara. Although he wrote in the midst of the Second Reform Bill debates in Britain, it was appropriate that the image Carlyle chose came from the other side of Atlantic, a place he himself had never visited but about which any reader of nineteenth-century print would be familiar. Like Mill, Smith, and the transatlantic liberals, Carlyle linked the zeal for suffrage reform at home to developments abroad, particularly "the late American War, with Settlement of the Nigger Question for result," which Carlyle considered "by far the notablest result of Swarmery" (his Anglicization of the German word for excessive enthusiasm). He found it "strange how prepossessions and delusions seize upon whole communities of men," with no support or basis. Suddenly, with "everybody adopting" them and "everybody finding the whole world agree with him," these delusions come to be "universally" repeated until they are accepted as "axiom[s] of Euclid" and tolerate no contradictions. Carlyle did not mention woman suffrage in *Shooting Niagara*, but the issue certainly aggravated his feeling of unease. In a private letter in 1871 he acknowledged that the whole subject of "female emancipation" had been "for five-and-twenty years past, especially for the last three or four . . .

a mere sorrow to me, one of the most afflicting proofs of the miserable anarchy that prevails in human society." He hoped his 1867 pamphlet, to borrow from a later century, might stand athwart history and yell Stop.[15]

Mill had drafted what would become *The Subjection of Women* in a different moment, before the Civil War had even begun let alone had resulted in Union victory and emancipation, but he hesitated to publish it till the time was ripe for such a discussion. That moment came in 1869, three years after woman suffrage had first been seriously discussed in Parliament and amidst continual agitation on the issue. The "little book," as Mill always called it, would become a touchstone of liberal feminist thought thereafter, hailed in the twentieth century as a "veritable bible" of the woman's movement.[16]

While *Subjection of Women* built on earlier works going back to Mary Wollstonecraft's 1792 *A Vindication of the Rights of Woman*, a more immediate precursor was the article Mill's wife had authored in 1851 and published anonymously in the *Westminster Review*. This article, "The Enfranchisement of Women," demonstrated the power of Anglo-American dynamics to frame questions. Its impetus was the 1850 woman's rights convention in Worcester, Massachusetts, that Mill encountered via the European edition of the *New York Tribune* and urged his soon-to-be wife Harriet Taylor to review. In large measure because of the transatlantic legitimacy it bestowed on the fledgling movement, Taylor Mill's *Westminster* article became an enormously influential text, reprinted continually as one of the best-selling tracts of the American woman's rights movement. The late historian Evelyn Pugh even claimed that this earlier essay had a far more significant and widespread impact on nineteenth-century American suffragists than did Mill's *Subjection* of 1869.[17]

But 1869 was worlds away from 1851, and the changed context affected the latter work's reception. Further, Mill published the book under his own name, which by 1869 was recognizable across the United States and Britain. A book written by "no less a personage than John Stuart Mill," as the *New York Evangelist* put it, guaranteed notice. An advertisement for the book in *Appleton's Journal* predicted that because of "Mr. Mill's high position both as a thinker and a representative of advanced ideas," the book would be "looked for with interest, and widely read." His stature gave "influence and authority to his views, such as no other living man could exert." According to *Putnam's Magazine*, the "woman question," having long been "confined to revolutionary journals" had now only in 1869 "risen to the dignity of Literature, in the person of Mr. John Stuart Mill." A book by Mill assured that discussion of the topic would extend far outside radical or movement circles. The *absurdum* to which some had tried to reduce efforts at suffrage expansion seemed suddenly to have become a lot less absurd.[18]

Unsurprisingly the book did in fact meet with an immediate and extensive response upon its appearance in the summer of 1869. Reviews appeared in dozens of periodicals, from highbrow organs like the *Nation* and *Edinburgh Review* to more popular magazines such as *Harper's*. Indeed, the *Fortnightly Review* declared it "*the* book of the past month." In addition to the many newspaper and magazine reviews, multiple book-length responses appeared in the United States: Horace Bushnell, *Women Suffrage: Reform Against Nature* (1869); L. P. Brockett, *Woman: Her Rights, Wrongs, Privileges, and Responsibilities* (1869); Donald McCaig, *A Reply to John Stuart Mill* (1870); and Carlos White, *Ecce Femina: An Attempt to Solve the Woman Question* (1870).[19]

The book-length reviews of *Subjection of Women* in turn garnered their own reviews, thus extending the discussion of woman suffrage, in ripple-like fashion, across the Anglo-American print sphere, in journals as distinct as the *Contemporary Review*, the *North American Review*, the *New England Farmer and Horticultural Register*, the *Catholic World*, and the *Zion Herald*. Few may have loved it, but none could ignore it, and it is undoubtedly true that the work generated discussion outside the movement, "in quarters," as Mill had written Parker Pillsbury in 1867, "where the subject had never been thought of before." The topic so saturated print culture in these years that by 1870 one periodical greeted with exhaustion the publication of yet another book "upon the interminable 'Woman' question."[20]

So just what were the central arguments of *Subjection of Women* that generated such a spirited response? Mill's central premise, stated on the opening page, made his view clear: "the principle which regulates the existing social relations between the two sexes—the legal subordination of one sex to the other—is wrong itself, and now one of the chief hindrances to human improvement; and that it ought to be replaced by a principle of perfect equality, admitting no power or privilege on the one side, nor disability on the other." To support this view, Mill traced women's customary subordination to an age of brute force out of which society had passed only relatively recently. In what was probably the most controversial aspect of the book, Mill argued that marriage as presently constituted was an unjust, even tyrannical, institution, little different from slavery in its legal aspects. Like Wollstonecraft before him, Mill pointed to the social—rather than biological—factors shaping women's existence, and he dismantled tautological arguments about women's natural sphere or capacities, arguing that we cannot possibly know what's "natural" for women until we give their capacities free rein. The book argued for women's emancipation on both liberal and utilitarian grounds: women, as individuals, were entitled to equal rights, but society as a whole would also benefit from their emancipation and inclusion into public life as full and equal as citizens.[21]

Figures within the movement unsurprisingly lauded the book, writing letters to Mill or his stepdaughter Helen Taylor, reviewing the book in movement organs such as the *Revolution*, and passing resolutions of gratitude to Mill at various conventions. There were also several outright hostile reviews, especially from the religious press. But most reviewers disagreed with Mill rather politely and respectfully. They acknowledged his stature, expressed admiration for his "genius and character," and in some cases offered reluctant demurrals. E. L. Godkin, editor of the *Nation*, granted that the case for women's rights "has never been so ably stated as in this little volume before us," before finding fault with the way Mill emphasized culture and education over biology. William James, writing in the *North American Review*, conceded that Mill had "justice" on his side and was quite possibly "more farseeing than the majority" on the issue. *Subjection of Women*, he admitted, may well "hereafter be quoted as a landmark signalizing one distinct step in the progress of the total evolution." It was simply not a step James himself was keen to take.[22]

An interesting set of responses suggests that the subject might not have received nearly as much attention had a prominent British figure such as Mill not published a book at this particularly fervid moment. One critic began his book by declaring he would never have bothered to write on the subject at all absent the appearance of *Subjection of Women*. He had ignored questions of women's rights for years but felt compelled to offer "this public expression as to their merits" only because he was "certain that the recently-published essay of Mr. Mill will create a strong public sentiment in favor of the reform therein advocated." Several critics shared this anxiety, and Mill's intellectual nimbleness and even rhetorical savvy came in for much backward praise. *Blackwood's* commended his "cleverness" and "ingenuity," while the *Catholic World* deemed him "that arch sophist."[23]

It was not simply the prestige of the author but the fact that a serious book appeared at a moment of such transatlantic enthusiasm that elicited a response. Was it not "rather a striking coincidence," asked the Canadian writer Donald McCaig, that Mr. Mill and Dr. Bushnell should each publish a treatise "almost at the same moment, in different countries, and discussing the same subject?". Even more striking, he observed, was that "in go-ahead republican America, one of her ablest writers should take the conservative side" of the issue, while "in aristocratic Old England, the most radical opinions are put forth as the exponents of changes considered necessary to the well-being and good government of society." While such a phenomenon surely spoke to the right-thinking and good moral sense of the American Congregationalist minister Horace

Bushnell, this curious transatlantic dynamic was cause for concern. The New Hampshire native and one-time abolitionist Carlos White sensed that the pendulum of public opinion had swung hard toward reform after the war. Now in 1870, White worried that the example of Britain would push Americans in an even more radical direction. Americans, he explained, were naturally "anxious to keep in advance of the rest of mankind" and, not wanting to be in the rearguard behind the Old World on any reform, they watched "with jealous eye any European innovation." McCaig agreed, "[Q]uestions of social and political reform" arising in the so-called mother country can "never be treated with indifference." He feared that any question "agitated amongst" the British, so long as it have "any bearing whatever on the present or possible conditions of society," will "easily gain numerous adherents and strenuous advocates."[24]

This sense that the Anglo-American discussion might intensify and accelerate an already pronounced trend led several critics to offer a sober second thought about the suffrage generally. L. P. Brockett, author of several books on the Civil War, seized on the woman suffrage issue as a way to warn Americans about their indiscriminate approach to the ballot generally. Beginning with the "fit of democratic generosity" that had enfranchised all white men back in the 1820s and 1830s, Americans had been "extending the privilege of suffrage" so rampantly that now nearly everyone had it. Under the "pending (fifteenth) amendment," Brockett noted, "negroes and persons of African descent will gain the right of suffrage," and possibly soon enough even the Chinese and Japanese would as well. Woman suffrage became his proverbial line in the sand, and the appearance of Mill's volume, amidst ongoing agitation on the topic, offered the perfect time to reassess. With any suggestion that, having swallowed every inch of the suffrage camel, the United States should hardly now strain at the gnat, Brockett strenuously disagreed. That Americans had been foolish in the past was hardly a reason to "continue to err in the same or any other direction." Drawing the line at woman suffrage might seem a little measure but "that little, if right, should be as valiantly defended as if it were more, since it is *all* that we can retain."[25]

To these critics, Mill's badge of advanced liberalism had become something more like a badge of extreme liberalism: extreme, because it sought to extend right-sounding principles in absurd directions. The evangelical Anglican *Christian Observer* admitted that "like everything that bears the 'liberté, égalite, et fraternité' stamp, there is something at first sight somewhat fascinating in the picture which Mr. Mill has unfolded to our view." But first sight had to be supplemented by a more careful second sight, which would reveal the folly of Mill's position on the equality of the sexes. The major American critics—Bushnell, Brockett, and White—objected that Mill's view took the liberal principle of individual rights too literally. American governance was representative, not individual; voters represented the family unit, not simply themselves. To introduce what Brockett called "individual suffrage," where each "voter represent[ed] only himself or herself" would dangerously "loosen the bond which holds society together." Such thinking smacked of "French" abstraction and was quite far removed from common-sense American practice. Even the relatively sympathetic *Contemporary Review* worried that "the side taken by Mr. Mill is going ahead too fast for its own interests." What the situation called for was calm reflection and a more deliberate response to a proposed major social change, rather than simply giving in to the impulse of the moment.[26]

In providing this calm reflection, Mill's critics contributed to a much larger process of rethinking the suffrage and democratic citizenship in Reconstruction America. Voting, in this rethinking, must be understood as a particular privilege or right, and therefore not one of the "absolute rights of citizenship." This was the position the Supreme Court ultimately took in *Minor v. Happersett* (1875), the woman suffrage case that contributed to the narrowing construal of the Fourteenth Amendment in the 1870s. For those uneasy about the major social changes Reconstruction and democratic expansion promised, woman suffrage provided a way to arrest the momentum, a sort of resting ledge on a slippery slope.[27]

Evidence for how much things had changed since the heady days of 1867 can be found in a public exchange between two Britons who qualified as "advanced liberals" in the mid-1860s. Goldwin Smith, the former Regius professor of history at Oxford, had since transplanted to North America and to a career as a journalist. He had once been a supporter of woman suffrage, had "always been for enlarging the number of active citizens as much as possible, and widening the basis of government," and had even signed the petition Mill had presented to Parliament in 1866. But he had undergone his own second thoughts on the subject, induced both by what he saw of the "public life of American women" and by his own reassessment of Mill after the philosopher's death in 1873. He published his revised view in an essay for *Macmillan's* in 1874, which was reprinted in various American periodicals. Now Smith found himself alarmed that political figures in Britain, as well as the United States, would even consider tampering with "the very foundations of Society" by transforming relations between the sexes. While Smith laid out several reasons for his opposition, he took personal aim at Mill, "the real father of the whole movement." That Mill had been "biassed [*sic*]" by his devotion to his wife and his overestimation of her "political genius" seemed clear to Smith and that bias had undoubtedly clouded his judgment.[28]

So shocking was Smith's liberal apostasy that one of Mill's most loyal disciples rallied from his sick bed to write a response, also published in *Macmillan's* and also reprinted in various American periodicals. John Elliott Cairnes, the Irish political economist, found it sad and strange that a voice so often raised "on behalf of liberal principles, should suddenly be heard issuing from the Conservative camp, in opposition to a measure which many Liberals regard as amongst the most important of pending reforms." He took Smith to task for dragging "Mr. Mill's relations with his wife" into the discussion, rebutted each of his points, and reiterated the "advanced liberal" position on women's equality. But the damage had been done.[29] Opponents of woman suffrage seized on Smith's de-conversion and gleefully publicized it. The *Spectator* noted that Smith "was originally an advocate for the Revolution," but now "disapproves the proposal with a vehemence which once or twice carries him somewhat too far." The *Saturday Review* welcomed Smith's "weighty declaration of opinion against a party with which on other questions the writer has been, and perhaps still is, allied." To this journal, Smith's change of mind about John Stuart Mill carried a good deal of weight. "If Mr. Mill's authority is taken away from the movement for female suffrage," gloated the *Review*, "there is no substantial support left to it."[30]

If Mill's advocacy had enhanced the allure of women's suffrage in 1867, his success in exciting "thought and discussion in new quarters" thus had unintended consequences. During the decade that followed his optimistic interchange with Parker Pillsbury, there were a handful of meaningful achievements, to be sure. Municipal and school board suffrage was extended to women in the United Kingdom, while woman suffrage was established in Wyoming and Utah Territories. But an organized woman's movement in both countries entered, in subsequent years, a dispiriting period of infighting and setbacks that dulled the sense of global excitement that marked the immediate post–Civil War period. The cause would toil with few victories for decades, as it operated in a hostile rhetorical context infused with the sense that reform had been stymied for the foreseeable future.

This is certainly not to suggest that Mill's "little book" had itself set the cause back. There were many and powerful forces working against the enfranchisement of women, not least an ambivalence over democratic expansion in both countries—an ambivalence that had only become more pronounced on the other side of the Second Reform Bill and the Fifteenth Amendment. But Mill's book had focused mainstream attention on the issue, allowing—or even requiring—neutral observers, skeptics, and opponents alike to voice their unease. The rhetorical ripostes to *Subjection of Women* thus played a role in articulating and emboldening reaction, furnishing a series of withering critiques against the basic premise of female political equality. What had been a badge of advanced thinking became a target, and across the realm of Anglo-American public opinion, support for woman suffrage was all too often remade into a badge of foolish excess.

NOTES

1. John Stuart Mill to Parker Pillsbury, July 4, 1867, in Francis E. Mineka and Dwight N. Lindley, eds., *Collected Works of John Stuart Mill* [hereinafter *CWJSM*] (Toronto: University of Toronto Press, 1972), 16:1290. This letter was printed in the *New York Times*, July 27, 1867.

2. Although Mill supported extending the franchise, he was never an advocate of unrestricted universal suffrage. As he explained in *Considerations on Representative Government* (1861), he believed all voters should possess the basic ability to read and write. He did, however, urge the enfranchisement of women and African Americans on equal terms with white men. See his letter to Moncure Conway, where he insisted that "the securing of equal political rights to the negro is paramount to all other considerations respecting the suffrage," JSM to Moncure Daniel Conway, October 23, 1865, *CWJSM*, 16:1106.

3. Historiography on transatlantic reform dates back at least as far as Frank Thistlethwaite's pioneering *The Anglo-American Connection in the Early Nineteenth Century* (Philadelphia: University of Pennsylvania Press, 1959). Antislavery and abolition represents the most developed and extensive literature. For some exemplary monographs, see David Brion Davis, *The Problem of Slavery in the Age of Revolution, 1770–1823* (New York: Oxford University Press, 1975); R. J. M. Blackett, *Building an Antislavery Wall: Black Americans in the Atlantic Abolitionist Movement, 1830–1860* (Baton Rouge: Louisiana State University Press, 1983); Caleb McDaniel, *The Problem of Democracy in the Age of Slavery* (Baton Rouge: Louisiana State University Press, 2013). On the woman's rights movement, see Jane Rendall, *The Origins of Modern Feminism: Women in Britain, France, and the United States, 1780–1860* (New York: Schocken Books, 1984); Christine Bolt, *The Women's Movements in the United States and Britain, from the 1790s to the 1920s* (Amherst, MA: University of Massachusetts Press, 1993); Margaret H. McFadden, *The Golden Cables of Sympathy: Transatlantic Sources of Nineteenth-Century Feminism* (Lexington: University Press of Kentucky, 1999); Bonnie S. Anderson, *Joyous Greetings: The First International Woman's Movement, 1830–1860* (New York: Oxford University Press, 2000); Kathryn Kish Sklar and James Brewer Stewart, eds., *Women's Rights and Transatlantic Slavery in the Era of Emancipation* (New Haven: Yale University Press, 2007). Transatlantic studies of other nineteenth-century reform movements include James Turner, *Reckoning with the Beast: Animals, Pain, and Humanity in the Victorian Mind* (Baltimore: The Johns Hopkins University Press, 1980); Ian Tyrrell, *Woman's World/Woman's Empire: The Woman's Christian Temperance Union in International Perspective, 1880–1930* (Chapel Hill: University of North Carolina Press, 1991); Leslie Butler, *Critical Americans: Victorian Intellectuals*

and Transatlantic Liberal Reform (Chapel Hill: University of North Carolina Press, 2007).

4. The subject of British–American relations during the Civil War has generated an enormous literature (beginning, it might be said, in the 1860s). On this vast topic, see, e.g., Howard Jones, *Union in Peril: The Crisis over British Intervention in the Civil War* (Chapel Hill: University of North Carolina Press, 1992); R. J. M. Blackett, *Divided Hearts: Britain and the American Civil War* (Baton Rouge: Louisiana State University Press, 2001); and Amanda Foreman, *A World on Fire: The Epic History of the British in the American Civil War* (London: Allen Lane, 2010). On Mill during the Civil War, see Butler, *Critical Americans*, chs. 2 and 3.

5. Goldwin Smith to Charles Eliot Norton, November 7, 1863, in "Letters of Goldwin Smith to Charles Eliot Norton," *Proceedings of the Massachusetts Historical Society* 49 (October 1915–June 1916): 106–7.

6. Frederick Douglass, "The Need for Continuing Antislavery Work," speech at the Thirty-Second Annual Meeting of the American Antislavery Society, May 9, 1865, in Philip S. Foner, ed., *Life and Writing of Frederick Douglass* (New York: International Publishers, 1950–1955), 4:166–9; Henry Ward Beecher, *Woman's Duty to Vote* (New York, 1867), 9; "Reconstruction," *North American Review* 100 (April 1865): 554. On the expansion of voting rights during Reconstruction, see Eric Foner, *Reconstruction: America's Unfinished Revolution, 1863–1877* (New York: Harper and Row, 1988); Xi Wang, *The Trial of Democracy: Black Suffrage and Northern Republicans* (Athens: University of Georgia Press, 1997); Alexander Keyssar, *The Right to Vote: The Contested History of Democracy in the United States* (New York: Basic Books, 2000); Kate Masur, *An Example for All the Land: Emancipation and the Struggle over Equality in Washington, D.C.* (Chapel Hill: University of North Carolina Press, 2010); Stephen Kantrowitz, *More Than Freedom: Fighting for Black Citizenship in a White Republic* (New York: Penguin Press, 2012).

7. As with Reconstruction, the Second Reform Act has generated an enormous literature. For starters, see Catherine Hall, Keith McClellan, and Jane Rendall, *Defining the Victorian Nation: Class, Race, Gender, and the British Reform Act of 1867* (Cambridge: Cambridge University Press, 2000); Eugenio F. Biagini, *Liberty, Retrenchment, and Reform*; J. P. Parry, *The Rise and Fall of Liberal Government* (New Haven: Yale University Press, 1993). On Mill's role, see Ann Robson, "The Founding of the National Society for Women's Suffrage, 1866–67," *Canadian Historical Journal* 8 (March 1973): 1–22; Evelyn L. Pugh, "John Stuart Mill and the Women's Question in Parliament, 1865–1868," *The Historian* 42 (May 1980): 399–418; Barbara Caine, "John Stuart Mill and the English Women's Movement," *Australian Historical Studies* 18 (1982): 52–67; Ben Griffin, *The Politics of Gender in Victorian Britain: Masculinity, Political Culture and the Struggle for Women's Rights* (Cambridge: Cambridge University Press, 2012).

8. "Eighteen Hundred and Sixty-Five," *Nation*, January 5, 1866, 4. Butler, *Critical Americans*, 87–109; Robert Saunders, *Democracy and the Vote in British Politics, 1848–1867* (London: Ashgate, 2011); Brent E. Kinser, *The American Civil War in the Shaping of British Democracy* (London: Routledge, 2011).

9. Catherine E. Beecher, "Something for Women Better than the Ballot," *Appleton's Journal of Popular Literature, Science, and Art*, September 4, 1869, 81.

10. *Proceedings of the First Anniversary of the American Equal Rights Association* (New York, 1867), 3. The classic work here is Ellen Carol Dubois, *Feminism and Suffrage: The Emergence of an Independent Women's Movement in America, 1848–1869* (Ithaca, NY: Cornell University Press, 1978), but see also Faye E. Dudden, *Fighting Chance: The Struggle over Woman Suffrage and Black Suffrage in Reconstruction America* (New York: Oxford University Press, 2011). Kate Masur discusses the effort by conservatives in Congress to use woman suffrage to thwart black enfranchisement in Washington, DC, in *An Example for All the Land*. Faye Dudden does the same for the 1867 referenda in Kansas in *Fighting Chance*.

11. On the woman's movement in the United Kingdom, in addition to the citations in note 4, see Barbara Caine, *Victorian Feminists* (Oxford: Oxford University Press, 1992).

12. George William Curtis, "The Right of Suffrage" (1867), reprinted in *Orations and Addresses of George William Curtis*, ed. Charles Eliot Norton (New York: Harper and Brothers, 1894). Curtis's speech itself was also circulated among British feminists, with Helen Taylor (Mill's stepdaughter) forwarding a newspaper clipping of it to Jessie Boucherett, a colleague in the movement ("Thank you for 'the American' newspaper. Mr. Curtis's speech is of much interest.") Jessie Boucherett to Helen Taylor, November 11, [no year], in Mill-Taylor Collection, LSE. Curtis complained of the relative mockery the question met in the United States as opposed to England, where he envied how "manfully" the topic was discussed and "how tranquilly Mill holds his own." Curtis to Caroline Dall, March 27, 1867, in Caroline H. Dall Papers, Massachusetts Historical Society. On the "mobilization of shame," see McDaniel, *The Problem of Democracy in the Age of Slavery*.

13. "A Certain 'Person' to Mr. Mill," *Punch, or the London Charivari*, June 1, 1867, 224–5. On the visual response to reform, see Janice Carlisle, *Picturing Reform in Victorian Britain* (Cambridge: Cambridge University Press, 2012).

14. Keyssar, *The Right to Vote*, 147; Carlos White, *Ecce Femina: An Attempt to Solve the Woman Question* (Boston, 1870); Anne Mozley, "Mill on the Condition of Women," *Blackwood's Edinburgh Magazine Journal* 106 (August 1869): 218. Dudden's *Fighting Chance* develops this view by taking seriously the activists' optimism and excitement after the war.

15. Thomas Carlyle, *Shooting Niagara—And After?* (London, 1867). The work was published as a pamphlet, but originally appeared, anonymously, as an article in *Macmillan's* for April 1867. It was reprinted in numerous American publications — including the *New York Tribune* and *Littell's Living Age*—and also in pamphlet form. Carlyle's 1871 letter (written "only on the strict condition that whatever I say shall be private, and nothing of it gets into newspapers," was reprinted in Scottish and Australian newspapers after his death in 1881). See "Carlyle on the Woman Question," *Sydney Mail*, April 23, 1881, reprinted from the *Glasgow Weekly Herald*, https://news.google.com/newspapers?nid=1302&dat=18810423&id=mbhPAAAAIBAJ &sjid=RpMDAAAAIBAJ&pg=5539,3431057&hl=en.

16. On the composition of *Subjection* and delay in publication, see Alice S. Rossi, "Sentiment and Intellect: The Story of John Stuart Mill and Harriet Taylor Mill," in John Stuart Mill and Harriet Taylor Mill, *Essays on Sex Equality*, ed. Alice S. Rossi (Chicago: University of Chicago Press, 1970), 3–5. "In the contest to free women from a long list of common-law disabilities and attain enfranchisement," Mary Beard wrote in *Woman as a Force in History* (New York: Macmillan, 1946), "feminists used **The Subjection of Women** as a veritable bible."

17. Evelyn L. Pugh, "John Stuart Mill, Harriet Taylor, and Women's Rights in America, 1850–1873," Canadian Journal of History 13, no. 3 (December 1978): 426. For the intellectual continuities between Wollstonecraft's world and Harriet Taylor's, see Kathryn Gleadle, *The Early Feminists: Radical Unitarians and the Emergence of the Woman's Rights Movement, 1831–1851* (London: Palgrave Macmillan, 1998). Pugh noted "an almost absolute silence" about *Subjection* from "the very people it should have appealed to most," citing, for example, the absence of any meaningful commentary on the book by Lucy Stone, Susan B. Anthony, or *The Woman's Journal*. Elizabeth Cady Stanton, one of the more radical and more intellectually inclined of nineteenth-century suffragists, seems to have been the exception. See the excellent essay by Barbara Caine, "Elizabeth Cady Stanton, John Stuart Mill, and the Nature of Feminist Thought," in *Elizabeth Cady Stanton, Feminist as Thinker: A Reader in Documents and Essays*, ed. Ellen Carol DuBois and Richard Cándida Smith (New York: New York University Press, 2007), 50–65. Elizabeth Blackwell, the first woman doctor in the United States (and, incidentally, the sister-in-law of Lucy Stone) provides anecdotal evidence supporting Pugh's claim. She wrote Mill's stepdaughter Helen Taylor in 1896, urging her to allow a new, cheap edition of Mill's book. "I am ashamed to say that I have never read that classical work," she admitted, "and as it is out of print, I know not where to attain a copy." Interestingly, though she had not read the work, she still referred to Mill as "our venerated champion." Elizabeth Blackwell to Helen Taylor, October 1, 1896, in Mill-Taylor Collection, LSE.

18. *New York Evangelist*, July 22, 1869; *Appleton's Journal of Popular Literature, Science, and Art*, August 21, 1869; "Literature—At Home," *Putnam's Magazine* 4 (October 1869): 503. The legitimacy that Mill's stature lent the topic can be seen in private correspondence as well. As William James's friend, the scientist Henry Bowditch, wrote him: "I have not yet seen Mill's book on the woman question but I shall get it & read it at the first opportunity. The question is really *the* great problem of the present day & anything which such a man as Mill has to say on the subject is of great importance," in Ignas K. Skrupskelis and Elizabeth M. Berkeley, eds., *The Correspondence of William James* (Charlottesville: University of Virginia Press, 1992), 386–7.

19. "Critical Notices," *Fortnightly Review*, July 1869, 119. Of the book-length responses, two were direct replies: McCaig's anonymously published *A Reply to John Stuart Mill on the Subjection of Women* (Philadelphia, 1870) and Carlos White, *Ecce Femina* (1870), the subtitle to which was "*Being an Examination of Arguments in Favor of Female Suffrage by John Stuart Mill and Others, and a Presentation of Arguments Against the Proposed Change in the Constitution of Society.*" Horace Bushnell's

Women's Suffrage: The Reform Against Nature (New York: Scribner, 1869) appeared simultaneously with *Subjection*, but Bushnell was aware of and referred explicitly to Mill's book and earlier writings, in his own ("I have been hoping, partly waiting, for the forthcoming book promised by Mr. Mill. . . . It is understood that he takes the side of the proposed reform, as he naturally enough would under his particular bent of philosophy," 164). The scope of Linus Pierpont Brockett's, *Woman: Her Rights, Wrong, Privileges, Responsibilities* (Cincinnati, OH, 1869) was quite large (the subtitle describing it as a "sketch of her condition in all ages and countries, from her creation and fall in Eden to the present time") but Mill loomed over the entire book as Brockett's major interlocutor and antagonist.

20. Review of White, *Ecce Femina* in "Book Notices," *Christian Advocate* 45 (April 7, 1870): 106. McCaig apparently kept a scrapbook of the notices of his book, which includes favorable quotations from newspapers in Philadelphia, Cincinnati, Charleston, and Chicago. *Copies of Certificates, Testimonials, &c. Obtained During a Course of Fourteen Years' teaching: also, Literary Notices on a Work Written in Reply to John Stuart Mill on the Subjection of Women* (Microfilm, from copy held at University of Guelph).

21. Given the importance of this text to the origins and development of liberal feminism, historians and political theorists have generated an enormous body of scholarship. The classic works include: Julia M. Annas, "Mill and the *Subjection of Women*," *Philosophy* 52 (1977): 179–94; Susan Moller Okin, "John Stuart Mill, Liberal Feminist," in *Women in Western Political Thought* (Princeton: Princeton University Press, 1979), 197–232; Susan Hekman, "John Stuart Mill's *The Subjection of Women*: The Foundations of Liberal Feminism," *History of European Ideas* 15 (1992): 681–6.

22. *Revolution*, September 9, 1869; "Mr. Mill's Plea for Women," *Nation*, July 22, 1869, 72–3; William James, "Women's Suffrage," *North American Review*, 109 (October 1869): 556–65. For a fuller discussion of James's response, see Leslie Butler, "Encountering the Smashing Projectile: William James on John Stuart Mill and the Woman Question," in *William James and the Transatlantic Conversation: Pragmatism, Pluralism, and the Philosophy of Religion*, ed. Martin Halliwell and Joel Rasmussen (Oxford: Oxford University Press, 2014), 115–30.

23. White, *Ecce Femina*, 10; *A Reply to John Stuart Mill*, 1; Anne Mozley, "Mr. Mill on the Subjection of Women," *Blackwood's*, 321; "New Publications," *The Catholic World: A Monthly Magazine of General Literature and Science* (March 1870).

24. [McCaig], *A Reply to John Stuart*, 7; White, *Ecce Femina*, 10.

25. L. P. Brockett, *Woman: Her Rights, Wrongs, Responsibilities, and Privileges* (Hartford, CT, 1869), 265, 252.

26. "Mr. Mill on the Condition of Women," *Christian Observer*, August 1869, 622; Brockett, *Woman*, 272, Matthew Browne, "Mr. Mill on the Subjection of Women," *Contemporary Review*, April 1, 1870, 274.

27. In *Minor v. Happersett*, the Supreme Court granted that women were citizens but contended that the right to vote was not among the constitutionally protected privileges of citizenship. This case followed two earlier decisions that sought to

narrow the scope of the Fourteenth Amendment: the *Slaughterhouse* Cases (1873) and *Bradwell v. Illinois* (1873). Ellen Carol Dubois has persuasively argued that the link between the judicial dismissal of women's rights and the repudiation of the Reconstruction amendments has been underappreciated. See her "Taking the Law into Our Own Hands: *Bradwell, Minor,* and Suffrage Militancy in the 1870s," in *Woman Suffrage and Women's Rights* (New York: New York University Press, 1998) and Gretchen Ritter, *The Constitution as Social Design: Gender and Civic Membership in the American Constitutional Order* (Stanford, CA: Stanford University Press, 2006).

28. Goldwin Smith, "Female Suffrage," *Macmillan's Magazine,* June 1874, 139–50. Smith wrote in response to renewed efforts to pass woman suffrage (for single or widowed women) in Parliament in 1874. He claimed that Mill's posthumously published *Autobiography* forced him to reconsider Mill's character and influence, as he found himself put off by the "peculiarities" of Mill's education as well as his embarrassing obeisance to his wife. The question of Harriet's influence on Mill is an enormous and contentious one in Mill scholarship. See Pugh, "John Stuart Mill, Harriet Taylor" for a summary. Donald McCaig, the author of *A Reply to John Stuart Mill,* included compliments on the book from Smith in a scrapbook he kept. In this (undated) blurb, Smith supposedly wrote McCaig: "I entirely agree with you as to the fallacious character of Mr. Mill's teaching in the volume to which you so ably reply," in *Copies of Certificates.*

29. J. E. Cairnes, "Woman Suffrage—A Reply to Goldwin Smith," *Macmillan's Magazine,* September 1874. Cairnes article was reprinted in full in the *New York Times,* September 23, 1874, as well as *The Eclectic Magazine of Foreign Literature* and *Every Saturday.* Cairnes died in July 1875.

30. "Mr. Goldwin Smith on Female Suffrage," *The Spectator,* June 6, 1874, 12; "Female Suffrage," *The Saturday Review of Politics, Literature, Science, and Art,* June 6, 1874, 711. See also "Goldwin Smith v. Fair Play," in *Victoria Magazine,* August 1874, which offers a summary of the reviews of Smith's article.

4

White Men's Wages

*The Australian/American Campaign
for a Legislated Living Wage*

Marilyn Lake

Who Wants a Living Wage?

The long campaign for a national minimum wage law in the United States, on the part of a changing combination of labor reformers, Progressives, judicial activists, feminists, and some trade unionists, finally culminated in victory in 1938, when President Franklin D. Roosevelt signed the Fair Labor Standards Act. It was an important and long-awaited achievement, if limited in its outcome. The prescribed wage was low and the coverage of workers limited.[1] Nevertheless key groups such as the National Consumers League viewed it as a "victory of principle." After a long series of setbacks and reverses, in the state and federal courts, came "the evolution of federal power to the point where it could regulate wages and hours."[2]

American historians have usually presented the campaign for a minimum wage as a national story of Progressive reformers battling judicial obstruction in the courts; or a struggle between labor men's investment in "manly independence" and women social reformers' commitment to "protection"; or as a "consumerist turn" away from "producerism."[3] Here I suggest that the achievement of a legislated national minimum wage in the United States is best understood from a transnational perspective that illuminates the influence of the Australian conception of a minimum wage as a "living wage" based in claims that workers' rights were human rights, as Ohio State sociologist M.B. Hammond noted in his account of "the theory underlying the minimum wage" in 1913.[4] Or in the words of Alice Henry, Australian editor of *Life and Labor*, the Chicago-based journal of the National Women's Trade Union League: "It is a noble, a dignified demand, something at least worthy of humanity. For it means more than life, it means the right at last for all to be human, to be their best selves, to develop who knows what capacities, what un-guessed of powers."[5]

The achievement of a legislated minimum wage is best understood as the product of a transnational discursive space created by the circulation of ideas and publications through activist networks in which conversations between Australian and American labor reformers played a key role. Recent historiography on transnational Progressivism has tended to focus on the North Atlantic world, but here I point to the significance of trans-Pacific and especially Australian inspiration for legislative labor reform. The American campaign for a legal minimum wage derived much of its dynamic and rationale from the example of Australian "state experiments" that translated "ideals into institutions" as Felix Frankfurter put it in a letter to H. B. Higgins in 1918.[6]

In a widely quoted article in *Collier's* magazine, in 1922, called "Who Wants a Living Wage?" that decried the expectations unleashed by the wartime promotion of a minimum wage led by Frankfurter, in his capacity as chairman of the War Labor Policies Board, the business journalist Samuel Crowther waxed indignant: "The American workman having enjoyed high wages during the war now wants a 'living wage' not only defined by law, but granted by law."[7] The use of quote marks was significant as became clear when he referred to Australian experience to illustrate the peril of such developments. In Australia, he was amazed to find, "the living wage is based, not on the value of a man's work but on his requirements as a man in a civilized society." The results, he said, were disastrous: wages very high, prices very high and taxation ruinous.[8]

Crowther was referring to the idea of a living wage as defined by H. B. Higgins, President of the Australian Commonwealth and Arbitration Court, whom Frankfurter had met at Harvard in 1914. Higgins had offered his definition of a living wage as one that would meet the needs of "an average employee, regarded as a human being living in a civilized community" in his famous Harvester judgment of 1907. He had elaborated his arguments in an article commissioned, at Frankfurter's suggestion, by the *Harvard Law Review* called "A New Province for Law and Order: Industrial Peace through the Minimum Wage and Arbitration" that was reprinted by the National Consumers' League in its series on the Minimum Wage edited by Josephine Goldmark. Her study of *Fatigue and Efficiency* was quoted in turn by Higgins in Court judgments in support of a shorter working week and the Australian practice of the "smoko" (a work break taken to smoke a pipe or cigarette).[9]

Higgins had been called upon to determine the meaning of the concept of "fair and reasonable" wages under the Excise Tariff Act, that specified if Australian manufacturers were to enjoy the benefit of tariff protection, they had to show that they paid their workers "fair and reasonable" wages.[10] In response to this legislation, a number of manufacturers, including H. V. McKay at the Sunshine Harvester Factory, an agricultural machinery firm in competition with North American manufacturers, applied for exemption from the excise duty on the ground that he did indeed pay "fair and reasonable" wages. The Implement Makers Union prepared to contest this claim in the Commonwealth Conciliation and Arbitration Court. They employed a new secretary, E. F. Russell, a member of the Socialist Party and a lawyer, J. Woolfe to prepare their case.[11] But what was a fair and reasonable wage?

According to Higgins:

The provision for fair and reasonable remuneration is obviously
designed for the benefit of the employees in the industry, and it must
be meant to secure to them something which they cannot get by the
ordinary system of individual bargaining with employers. ... The
remuneration could safely have been left to the usual, but unequal
contest, the "higgling of the market" for labour, with the pressure
for bread on one side, and the pressure for profits on the other.
The standard of fair and reasonable must, therefore, be something
else; and I cannot think of any other standard appropriate than the
normal needs of the average employee, regarded as a human being
living in a civilized community.[12]

To determine the amount necessary to meet the needs of a human being living in a civilized community, Higgins collected a range of evidence on the cost of living and household budgets from workers and their wives and other witnesses such as real estate agents. Needs would normally include "light, clothes, boots, furniture, utensils, rates, life insurance, savings, accident or benefit societies, loss of employment, union pay, books and newspapers, tram and train fares, sewing machine, mangle, school requisites, amusements and holidays, intoxicating liquors, tobacco, sickness and death, domestic help [and] expenditure for unusual contingencies, religion or charity."[13] After extensive investigation Higgins determined that a living wage (for unskilled workers) meant a weekly wage of two pounds, two shillings or seven shillings a day for a six day week, which was above the wage paid by H. V. McKay. Skilled workers were awarded higher wages in recognition of their training and experience. In a detailed study, historians Charles Fahey and John Lack have estimated that the average wage increase awarded by Higgins in the Harvester case was 20 percent per worker, while one-fifth had their wages increased by 25 percent.[14]

Although the High Court shortly declared the Excise Tariff Act unconstitutional (as usurping the industrial powers of states) the idea of a "living wage" was institutionalized through subsequent Arbitration Court awards (covering disputes that crossed state boundaries) and State Wages Board decisions, as M. B. Hammond observed in the *American Labor Legislation Review*. The standard set by Higgins had "exercised a profound influence upon public opinion and upon the determinations of other arbitration courts and wages boards."[15] It became Higgins's greatest legacy, as Frankfurter noted in a letter expressing regret at Higgins's resignation from the Court in 1920: "the great work that you have done establishes traditions and a body of experience which will survive."[16]

The impact of Higgins's work was also felt across the Pacific, in part because of the advocacy of Hammond and other reformers such as the members of the National Consumers' League and the commendation of Progressive judges such as Frankfurter, Oliver Wendell Holmes, Louis Brandeis, and Learned Hand, the latter summarizing Higgins's *Harvard Law Review* article in an article on "The Hope of the Minimum Wage" in *The New Republic* in November 1915.[17] As Jerold Waltman noted of early twentieth-century American reformers: "They often quoted with approval the Australian standard: a minimum wage is one supporting the "normal needs of the average employee regarded as a human being living in a civilized community."[18] Why was the first legal minimum wage introduced in Victoria in 1896?

Protection against Underpaid Labor of Other Lands

In the years following the inauguration of the Commonwealth of Australia in 1901, many Americans, animated by what Theodore Roosevelt liked to call "fellow feeling," identified with Australia as an advanced "white man's country" that enshrined a "white man's standard of living."[19] The Australian project of securing high living standards through minimum wages and maximum hours was framed by the White Australia policy, which introduced race-based immigration restriction and legislation to deport Pacific Islanders, imported in the late nineteenth century to labor in the sugar plantations of north Queensland. The humanitarian idea of a "living wage" based on the "human needs" of a man living in a "civilized society" was initially formulated as a response to the perceived threat posed by Chinese immigrants to Australian working conditions—especially in the furniture industry in Melbourne—and the rapacious and deadly labor trade in Pacific Islanders.

Thus the eminent Liberal leader, Alfred Deakin, a member of the Victorian Legislative Assembly in 1896 and Attorney General and then Prime Minister in the first federal government, who would welcome the US Naval Fleet in 1908 as "white man greeting white men," theorized the White Australia policy as an exercise in social justice: "it means maintenance of conditions of life fit for white men and white women; it means equal laws and opportunities for all; it means protection against the underpaid labour of other lands; it means social justice so far as we can establish it, including just trading and the payment of fair wages."[20] Just as the United States emulated Australian labor standards—such as the eight-hour day introduced in Victoria in 1856—so the republic also looked to learn from Australia's restrictive immigration policies, with the Boston-based Immigration Restriction League obtaining a copy of Australian's Immigration Restriction Act as soon as it was passed in 1901.[21]

American reformers were especially keen to learn about Australia's pioneering legislation for a compulsory minimum wage, enacted in the Victorian Factories Act of 1896, which also established wages boards for particular trades, several years before Britain followed suit in 1910. At the annual meeting of the Council of the National Consumers League in Providence, Rhode Island, in 1909, the general secretary reported on the first international meeting of Consumers' Leagues, held the year before in Geneva, at which an English delegate reported on the Victorian legislation. The National Consumers' League resolved immediately to prioritize the goal of legislation over their traditional tactic of consumer boycotts. They established a special committee to investigate the Victorian legislation and circulated a list of references to its state branches in which studies of Australian experiments (including works by Clark, Henry Macrosty, A. F. Weber, W. P. Reeves, Helen Bosanquet, George W. Gough, J. Ramsay McDonald and Ernest Aves) were prominent.[22]

I have argued elsewhere for the need to locate the pioneering Victorian legislation in a world history context that includes the encounter between Chinese imperial subjects and British imperial subjects in the Australian colonies in the nineteenth century and the *longue durée* of labor relations that saw the abolition of slavery in the British empire followed by the widespread use of contract coolie labor across the Caribbean, South America, Mauritius, Fiji, and Australia.[23] Perceptions of Chinese labor as "coolie labour" shaped the determination of the coalition of liberal and labor members of the Victorian parliament to introduce a compulsory minimum wage that would apply to all workers, Chinese and European. H. B. Higgins, then a member like Deakin of the Victorian Legislative Assembly, was a leading supporter. "It was by no means extraordinary or extravagant for us in this colony," he told the Victorian parliament, "to pass exceptional legislation for the protection of our workmen."

Our people were European in origins and we did not want to have our workers degraded to the position of the people who lived in China. In China the people worked more hours and got less pay than the people here, and it was our policy to try to raise the standard of living and not to lower it.[24]

All workers were subject to the provisions of the Act, but it is clear that Australia's pioneering introduction of a minimum wage was primarily intended to secure the status of white male workers.

Higgins carried this determination into the new federal parliament to which he was elected in 1901. There he joined the majority of members in offering strong support for the Immigration Restriction Act and the Pacific Islander Labourers Act. He felt a personal connection to the issue of Pacific Island labor because his brother-in-law, G. E. Morrison (later "Chinese Morrison," the London *Times* journalist in Peking) had worked as an investigative journalist researching the labor trade. "I feel convinced," Higgins told parliament, "that people who are used to a high standard of life—to good wages and good conditions—will not consent to labor alongside men who receive a miserable pittance and who are dealt with very much in the same way as slaves."[25] Accordingly, Higgins would also later insist that Aboriginal pastoral workers be paid the same rates as white men: "I do not put in my award, black, white, or anything," Higgins told the trade union representatives. "If he is a member of your organisation and an employee it is quite enough."[26] Awards would cover all trade union members and unionization was considered vital to securing wage justice.

In this essay, I focus on the influence of Higgins's advocacy on American reformers and the importance of his trip to the United States in June 1914 in building momentum for the US minimum wage campaign. As a special issue of the *Survey* put it: "In 1910 a legal minimum wage was considered in America a fantastic proposal. But by 1915 nine states had enacted laws." There had been a "change from scepticism to championship."[27] Arguably Higgins's championship, through personal networks, interviews and professional writing, was central to this change. In the context of political struggle over "how society should value labor" (as Glickman put it), Higgins had an impact, because it was he, in Hammond's words, who set "forth so clearly the principles which he [had] followed in establishing a minimum wage."[28] Most influential in this regard was his article, "A New Province of Law and Order: Industrial Peace through Minimum Wage and Arbitration" commissioned by the *Harvard Law Review* in 1914.[29] In thanking Higgins for his contribution, editor Gerard Henderson noted that "many lawyers here will say that it doesn't deal with a legal topic." "To me," he added, "the principles and precedents that you have worked out seem to be of the essence of law—a new branch of jurisprudence that must be scientifically studied and developed."[30]

Three years later the *Harvard Law Review* solicited a second article from Higgins, explaining:

> Your first article we have always considered to be one of the best
> that ever appeared in our Review. . . . The work now being done by
> Professor Frankfurter in the matter of settling labor disputes makes
> it particularly timely.[31]

Following the entry of the United States into the war, Frankfurter had taken up a position with Woodrow Wilson's Democratic administration as Chair of the War Labor Policies Board. In that capacity he urged Americans to follow "the experiments and legislations of the more progressive countries" such as Australia[32] In the 1930s, as an adviser to FDR, with whom he had worked during World War I, Frankfurter became a key architect of the Fair Labor Standards Act.

Looking to Australia

Australasia's reputation in pioneering "state experiments" to secure minimum wages, maximum hours, and industrial peace was already well established before Higgins's trip to the United States in 1914 excited fresh interest.[33] Initially it was New Zealand, "the country without strikes," which had introduced compulsory arbitration in 1894, that had attracted attention, but with the introduction of the legal minimum wage and establishment of Wages Boards in Victoria in 1896, the founding of the Commonwealth of Australia in 1901 and the establishment of the Commonwealth Conciliation and Arbitration Court in 1904, investigators began to look more closely at Australian developments. Victor S. Clark visited in 1904 to conduct an investigation into industrial conditions for the US Bureau of Labor; Harris Weinstock visited in 1907 on behalf of the state of California.[34] Clark attributed the good labor conditions found in Australasia to the countries' democratic political systems:

> New Zealand and Australia are the most interesting legislative
> stations in the world, and they experiment so actively because their
> political institutions are so democratic. They are doing what people
> in the United States might do were they able to enforce their will
> with equal directness through the ballot.[35]

Increasingly American reformers were intent on following the Australasian example in pursuing legislative reform. Legislation was the focus of the American Association for Labor Legislation (AALL) founded as a branch of the International Association for Labor Legislation in 1906. And in 1908, as we have seen, members of the National Consumers' League, having learned about Victoria's minimum wage and wages boards when attending an international conference of Consumers Leagues in Geneva, determined to pursue legislative reform.

In 1911, M. B. Hammond, professor in the Economics and Sociology Department at Ohio State University, embarked on a year's study leave to investigate labor law reform in Australia and New Zealand and in particular the state implementation of a minimum wage. As he explained to John Andrews of the AALL:

I have a year's leave of absence from the University and am planning to spend most of it in New Zealand and Australia in studying the experimental legislation of those lands rather than go to the old world countries.... I shall be very glad if later my observations can assist in any way the Association for Labor Legislation. Since the subject of Minimum Wage laws is in the air in this country, perhaps I can get material of interest.[36]

It was a timely offer as the AALL had been asking the British branch of the International Association, which still spoke for the "colonies," for "special information and publications on the subject of the minimum wage." "I hope you may be able to send us something in the near future," Andrews reminded British Secretary Sophy Singer in August 1911, "as this question is becoming more important week by week."[37]

The AALL was grateful to Hammond for his offer of help. "We are receiving many inquiries for information on the subject of minimum wage boards from members of state commissions and our members, and we wish you would consider yourself specially delegated to represent our Association on your trip ... and collect and mail to us from time to time, such documents and news on this subject as you think we ought to have in our little office library."[38] In subsequent articles Hammond emphasized the importance of investigating Australian developments, rather than English ones:

English experience with the minimum wage has been too brief and too limited in its industrial range to afford much information for constructive purposes or to enable us to judge as to the general acceptability of the principle. Throughout Australasia, on the other hand, the principle of the minimum wage has now found general acceptance. [39]

Indeed Britain had not introduced Boards of Trade until 1910, following an investigative trip to Australia and New Zealand by Ernest Aves on behalf of the Secretary of State for the Home Department. As it happened Aves recommended against Britain following the Australian example because its geopolitical conditions were so different. He was alert to Australia's different and distinctive location in the world. "Australia," he wrote in his report, was located in the Asia-Pacific region, and

> though far from Europe is comparatively near to India, China, Java and Japan, and in this lies another fact greatly affecting the outlook—political, economic and social. Within some three to five thousand miles of its small British population there dwell some 750 millions of the human race, spread over an area hardly greater than its own. [40]

Australians intended to adhere to "the principle of the legal minimum wage," he explained, because the "standard of the race is felt to be at stake." Despite his view that Britain did not need such legislation, the British parliament proceeded nevertheless to enact such a law in 1909.

Hammond thought his time would be better spent in Australia than Britain. His research was extensive. He reported at length on his interviews with, and the writings of, a wide range of Australian judges and trade union and employer representatives. They told him about the different methods of regulating minimum wages—arbitration courts and wages boards—and their results. Hammond quoted Higgins's statement on what might constitute "a fair and reasonable wage" in the *Harvester* case and later elaborations in the *Marine Cooks'* and the *Engine Drivers'* cases and perhaps most important provided an analysis of the principles and values underlying Higgins's judicial arbitration.[41]

In his article in *American Economic Review*, in 1913, Hammond emphasized the humanism that underpinned Higgins's judgments ("a growing sense of the value of human life") and concluded with a glowing tribute to his seminal role as a theorist of Australia's world-historic experiment in social democracy:

> He has certainly expressed, at greater length and with greater clearness than has any one else, the ideals which have animated the Australian people and the Australian lawmakers in placing on the stature books the body of social legislation which has drawn the eyes

of all the world to Australasia, and which marks the most notable experiment yet made in social democracy.[42]

According to Glickman, "the growing sense of the value of human life" and the "replacement of market value with human value became a key element of the minimum wage argument" in the United States.[43]

In Australia, Higgins had been to the fore in emphasizing the "human factor" and he played multiple roles in establishing Australia's pioneering social democracy: as a member of the Victorian parliament that introduced the first minimum wage; as delegate to the constitutional conventions that established the new nation-state; as a member of the House of Representatives in the first federal parliament; as Attorney General in the short-lived Labor government of 1904; as judge on the High Court and President of the Commonwealth Court of Conciliation and Arbitration, when he presided over the historic *Harvester* judgment.

A radical liberal lawyer, Higgins was, as biographer John Rickard noted, "a friend of labour," but not a member of the Australian Labor Party.[44] When invited to serve as Attorney General in the government formed by Labor leader, J. C. Watson, in 1904, Higgins consulted his colleague and future Liberal leader, Alfred Deakin, and decided to support the Labor government. "I saw that the party was waxing," he later told Frankfurter, "and I wanted that the leaders should face the responsibilities of office."[45] That government lasted only a few months, but when in the 1910 elections, the Labor Party, led by Andrew Fisher, won a majority of seats in both the House of Representatives and the Senate, the first national Labor government in the world held office until 1913. Australia's version of "state socialism" and the role of Higgins's "new branch of jurisprudence" in securing living standards were well known to American labor reformers, when the Progressive apostle of industrial efficiency, Robert Valentine, invited him to visit Boston.

Closely Questioned

Formerly a teacher, civil servant, and Commissioner for Indian Affairs, Valentine had recently become interested in the potential of "scientific management" for improving working conditions. Well connected in academic, business, and legal circles, Valentine proved to be an excellent contact. Living in Boston and Washington, he was at the center of a network that included enlightened Massachusetts shoe manufacturer Stanley King, Walter Lippmann, Frankfurter, and Justice Oliver Wendell Holmes, who had dubbed Valentine's home in Washington the "House of Truth."[46]

Described by Joseph McCartin as "a renegade member of the Taylor society," Valentine critiqued the Taylorists for their opposition to dealing with trade unions. [47] Workplace efficiency, he believed, could not be improved without the consent and empowerment of workers, preferably secured though unions. The Australian Conciliation and Arbitration Court required workers to be represented collectively by trade unions, whose numbers and membership had increased dramatically as a result. The role and legitimacy of trade unions were subjects Higgins discussed in "A New Province of Law and Order" and promoted in the same year in writings by Herbert Croly and Walter Lippmann and other Progressive luminaries in the *New Republic*.

Among those persuaded by Valentine's approach was Assistant Secretary of the Navy Franklin D. Roosevelt, who hired him in 1916 to introduce "the principles of true democracy" to the Charleston Navy Yard. In his draft autobiography, Higgins recalled that "Valentine, who called himself "industrial counsellor" had written to me in Melbourne about my work in labour matters and I had arranged to call on him on my way to London."[48] His resulting visit to the United States proved to be rather more significant than the brief stopover anticipated. "I wish (except for the expense) that I had left more time for this great America," he wrote to Frankfurter as he boarded ship for England in July.[49] Higgins and Frankfurter became close friends and confidantes, sharing their hopes and tribulations in a long correspondence that lasted more than fifteen years and is preserved in Frankfurter's papers in the Library of Congress.

Higgins was deeply moved by the interest shown in his work in the United States and the recognition of the significance of his innovative jurisprudence. In "A New Province for Law and Order," he paid a tribute to his American interlocutors. He had "had the good fortune to meet many men and women of broad and generous outlook and of admirable public spirit," who were anxious to learn what he could tell them of Australian methods of dealing with labor questions.[50] He wrote to Frankfurter: "They may differ in details of policy; but what I look at is the general effort for the public good. . . . The young century is yours—what will you do with it?"[51]

Through Valentine and Frankfurter, Higgins met Louis Brandeis, who had represented the state of Oregon in 1907 in *Muller v. Oregon* at the US Supreme Court. At issue was whether it was constitutional for a state law to limit the working hours of female workers or whether such regulation represented an "unreasonable infringement of freedom of contract." Brandeis had been asked to take on the case by Josephine Goldmark, of the National Consumers' League, who did most of the research for the "Brandeis brief," a legal argument that relied more heavily on sociological evidence than abstract law, that included more than a hundred pages of documentation, including social worker reports, medical investigations, factory inspector observations and other expert testimonials. "We would contrast evil and good," Goldmark later wrote of their "scientific" approach, "the dangers to health, safety, morals, and the general welfare from excessive hours; the corresponding benefits from shortened hours."[52] Higgins had taken the same sociological approach—though less "scientifically based"—to his task of determining a living wage in the *Harvester* case in 1907, when he had investigated household budgets and sought "expert" evidence from Melbourne housewives.

On June 23, 1914, Higgins lunched with Frankfurter and Professor Roscoe Pound, the leading proponent of legal realism, who was also a member of the Council of the AALL and soon to be appointed Dean of the Harvard Law School. It was Pound's view that there was "much more juristic kinship between Australian and American writers than ... between Americans and Englishmen"[53] The next day, Frankfurter introduced Higgins to social reformer Elizabeth Glendower Evans, a graduate of Radcliffe College and close friend of Brandeis and Florence Kelley.

Evans was a proud founding member of the Massachusetts Minimum Wage Commission, the first in the United States, established in 1912. She was an admirer of Victorian wages boards, as she made clear in a luncheon address at the City Club of Philadelphia. Wages boards were not a panacea she told her audience: "They will not bring in the kingdom of heaven." But where they had been tried, as in Australia, "It has been found that they do tend to correct certain flagrant abuses. They tend to bring the standard of the worst employer up to the standard of the best."[54] After lunch with Evans, Higgins attended a sitting of the Massachusetts candy-workers' wages board and, as he reported, was once again "closely questioned."[55]

Higgins and his wife Mary Alice then traveled to New York where he met Florence Kelley, Josephine Goldmark and Mary Chamberlain, to whom he granted an interview on the subject of the minimum wage, which was the basis of an article published in the August issue of *Survey*.[56] He also met Dr. John Andrews and his wife Irene Osgood Andrews of the AALL to whom Hammond had reported in 1911. Its Council members included, as well as Roscoe Pound, Professor John Commons of the University of Wisconsin, Margaret Dreier Robins of the National Women's Trade Union League (who became a good friend of Australians Alice Henry and Miles Franklin in Chicago), Goldmark of the National Consumers League and Alice Hamilton of Hull House.

On June 30, Higgins and his wife went south to Washington where they met Secretary of Labor W. B. Wilson and Assistant Secretary Louis Post, who took them to the East Room of the White House to see President Wilson receiving "the suffrage ladies" as he told Frankfurter.[57] That evening Higgins and Mary Alice were visited in their hotel by Theodore Roosevelt ("He had been urged by his 'progressive' friends in Boston and New York to meet me") and again by Brandeis:

> he came in Wednesday evening . . . for a chat at our hotel. He also brought me to what (I think) they call the "Common Council" luncheon—a body of men who are connected with the present "democratic" administration. Their talk was most interesting. Surely it is a good augury for the United States—& for the world—that so many well-trained men throw themselves so unselfishly into the movement for a better social order.[58]

The meeting of the Common Council made a lasting impression on Higgins and he often referred to it. That evening he dined with Judge Learned Hand, at his club, where he "had a most profitable time."[59] Another graduate of the Harvard Law School, Hand was a federal judge, legal scholar, and a supporter of Theodore Roosevelt's campaign for the presidency. The following year Hand wrote a summary and commendation of Higgins's "A New Province of Law and Order" for *The New Republic*.

A New Province for Law and Order

Higgins's article "A New Province for Law and Order" was widely circulated and discussed. It was printed as a separate publication by Josephine Goldmark as No. 4 in the National Consumers' League Minimum Wage Series and summarized in other publications, including John Commons and John Andrews's volume *Principles of Labor Legislation* in which they noted the effective operation of the minimum wage in Australia; and in Robert Bruere's "The Meaning of the Minimum Wage" in *Harper's Monthly Magazine*.[60] Florence Kelley edited a special issue of *Survey*, in 1915, called *The Case for the Minimum Wage*, to which Hammond contributed a long article on "The Australian Experience with Wages Boards" in which he discussed Higgins's work on the minimum wage and the operation of the Arbitration Court.[61] Walter Lippmann wrote on the campaign for a minimum wage in the *New Republic* in March 1915: "What we are struggling for is a minimum that shall be a living wage. . . . We are against sweating. That means we are against cheap labor and for the economy of high wages."[62]

Higgins was also a champion of the eight-hour day and his evidence about Australian working hours was cited in *Bunting v. Oregon*, in 1915, when the Oregon Supreme Court upheld a ten-hour workday for men and women. Frankfurter had taken over the case from Brandeis, who had been appointed to the Supreme Court. Goldmark again compiled a vast body of material about the benefits of a shorter working day, in which Australasian experience featured prominently:

> The best examples of the benefit to society and to workers arising from the short workday are found in Australasia. The movement for the 8 hour day began in Victoria over fifty years ago. . . . the wages boards or arbitration courts are empowered by law to fix maximum hours of labor. According to Mr Justice Higgins, President of the High Court of Australia [sic], the "general Australian standard" is the 48 hours week. [63]

Goldmark sent a copy of their brief to Higgins in Melbourne. "It was a noble argument by Mr Frankfurter," she wrote, "who I trust may be able to take part in the defence of another minimum wage case in the state of Minnesota." She passed on the good wishes of Brandeis and his wife adding hopefully: "We have moved fast in these last few months."[64]

Learned Hand summarized and endorsed the arguments of "A New Province for Law and Order" in an article on "The Hope of the Minimum Wage" in *The New Republic*, in which he emphasized its importance for thinking about the meaning of "full citizenship" and offered his own significant endorsement: "We must insist upon the reasonable expectation of those who view it hopefully, and we must seek to advance it, at least until it has been demonstrated to be false."[65] Full citizenship demanded that all citizens be guaranteed a living wage that would support their equal and full participation in society and government.

In its origins, conception, arguments, circulation, and impact, "A New Province for Law and Order" was a transnational text written by an Australian judge about Australian experience to educate and persuade an American audience of the merits of the minimum wage as a living wage. More generally, Higgins's account of his jurisprudence encouraged the work of Brandeis, Frankfurter, Holmes, Pound, and others in developing a "new body of law" to meet the "industrial and social needs of the time" and put "the human factor in the central place."[66] Frankfurter commended Higgins's essay in a letter to Oliver Wendell Holmes: "I wonder if you thought as well as I did of Justice Higgins' article in this month's *Harvard Law Review*?" he wrote. "It seemed to me to have all the romance of bending theories to the test of life—of trying to adjust conflicting demands to larger common interests, or at least making men know their demands through disinterested expert guidance."[67] As noted, Holmes would draw on Higgins's arguments for his important dissent in *Adkins* in 1923 at a time when the US courts were regularly striking down legislation establishing shorter hours and minimum wages.

World War I and After

In 1917, when the United States entered the war, Frankfurter was appointed head of the War Labor Policies Board in Washington, where he was able to extend regulation of working hours and minimum wages in certain industries as a means of securing industrial peace, the strategy and rationale of the Australian Arbitration Court. As Crowther's fulminations in *Collier's* suggested, an example was set that might influence a new postwar order and indeed substantial gains were made. Between 1910 and 1923 almost half the states in the union adopted minimum wage laws for women workers, responding to vigorous lobbying on the part of female reformers in the National Consumers League and social workers.[68]

But then a backlash, presaged by Crowther's article in *Collier's*, set in. The majority in *Adkins v. Children's Hospital*, a case that challenged the constitutionality of the Washington, DC, minimum wage law, for which Frankfurter had written the brief, voiced concerted opposition to the cause of the minimum wage, declaring it unconstitutional and in violation of "economic law." In his dissenting judgment Holmes referred to Australian experience and quoted Higgins:

> In Australia the power to fix a minimum for wages in the case of
> industrial disputes extending beyond the limits of any one State
> was given to a Court, and its President wrote a most interesting
> account of its operation. If a legislature should adopt what he thinks
> the doctrine of modern economists of all schools, that "freedom of
> contract is a misnomer as applied to a contract between an employer
> and an ordinary individual employee" I could not pronounce
> an opinion with which I agree impossible to be entertained by
> reasonable men. If the same legislature should accept his further
> opinion that industrial peace was best attained by the device of a
> Court having the above powers, I should not feel myself able to
> contradict it.[69]

By then Higgins had encountered a conservative backlash in his own country, that had been overtaken by imperial and conservative political forces unleashed by World War I. The Labor government had lost office, not to regain it at a federal level until 1929. Resigning his position as president of the Conciliation and Arbitration Court, following relentless political attacks from ex-Labor Prime Minister W. M. Hughes, his position, he told Frankfurter, had become impossible.[70] The Prime Minister, he lamented, was "ruining our social experiments" adding ruefully: "You say that progress is not in a straight line, but what ground have we for assuming that there is progress, in the highest sense, at all?"[71] But in a last reforming act, he used a judgment in the *Timber Workers'* case to reduce the standard working week from 48 to 44 hours, invoking the authority of Josephine Goldmark, whose research on the impact of longer working hours, reported in *Fatigue and Efficiency,* he was again pleased to quote.[72]

In the United States, the advent of the Depression saw new demands for federal intervention to ameliorate the dire effects of unemployment and reduced wages. When finally as a result of the revival of a campaign for a minimum wage on the part of an alliance of forces that included the National Consumers' League and Secretary of State, Frances Perkins, who had earlier worked with the League, trade unionist Sidney Hillman, leader of the Amalgamated Clothing Workers of America and a legal group that included Thomas Corcoran and Benjamin Cohen, Frankfurter helped draft the bill to regulate labor standards in a way that would avoid further constitutional obstruction. They decided to invoke the federal government's authority to regulate "interstate commerce."[73]

Interestingly, Higgins had suggested this strategy in an article he had written critiquing America's "Rigid Constitution" in the US *Political Science Quarterly* in 1905. There he lamented the extent to which current generations were shackled by the thinking of earlier ones and pointed to the possibilities of reform through "judicial decision":

> From the short clause enabling Congress "to regulate commerce
> with foreign nations and among the several states" the court has
> deduced an implied power to legislate for the control of all navigable
> waters ... for the construction of wharves and other works, for the
> prohibition of immigration, for laying an embargo on shipping,
> for the establishment of an interstate commission with power to
> interfere with railway companies and with transportation rates.[74]

In their decision to base the constitutionality of the new minimum wage in the US Constitution's "interstate commerce power," the authors of the Fair Labor Standards Acts 1938 (FLSA), adopted this very strategy. In doing so they also emulated the Australian example of the Commonwealth Arbitration Court, outlined by Higgins in "A New Province for Law and Order" of securing nationwide labor reform by invoking federal jurisdiction over industrial matters "extending beyond the limits of any one State."

Conclusion

The benefits of the US minimum wage were thus limited to employees working in interstate commerce. Only a relatively small number of workers were directly advantaged by the law, whose interstate provisions also favored masculine occupations, but it nevertheless marked "a turning point in American social policy" embodying the principle of "social responsibility [on the part of] the Federal Government towards American wage earners."[75] The idea of the minimum wage as a humanist principle was accepted even as the actual amount specified in legislation fell far below what could be called a living wage. Australian argument and precedent were important to the campaign, which was conducted in a transnational discursive space, but the American reform also saw a significant departure from the Australian example. In response to pressure from the women activists in the National Consumer's League, who played such an important role in the American campaign and Frances Perkins's leading role, the new minimum wage prescribed by the Fair Labor Standards Act applied equal rates to female and male workers.

In Australia, where Higgins had placed such store on the "human factor" and theorized "human needs" as the basis for a minimum wage, women workers were awarded around half the male rate, because the "human being" Higgins had imagined was a white male worker, whose status he was determined to secure and whose normal obligations included the support of a wife and children. "Fellow feeling" was a racialized and gendered condition.[76] When challenged by feminist and labor activist Mary Gilmore, who suggested that the living wage should have been based on the needs of the individual, not the family, Higgins responded that he was simply carrying out the will of parliament expressed in legislation. "Among normal wants," he wrote, "I include food, shelter, clothing—and family life. This family life cannot be had under existing conditions without money wherewith to maintain a wife and children."[77] Gilmore agreed that the *Harvester* judgment was an "amazing thing" that marked a high stage of "national civilization," but she and other feminists saw its gendered consequences. In 1913 a large industrial meeting in Melbourne called for the Arbitration Court to implement the principle of "the rate for the job" and not the sex. Campaigns for the "rate for the job"—equal pay—continued until 1938, the same year in which the Fair Labor Standards Law introduced an equal minimum wage for female and male workers in the

United States, when Australian women activists, led by veteran Labor Party member Muriel Heagney, established the Campaign of Action for Equal Pay.

The campaign for a legislated minimum wage in the United States drew inspiration and momentum from Australian precedent and the publicity accorded the work of President of the Commonwealth Court of Conciliation and Arbitration, H. B. Higgins, who theorized the minimum wage as a living wage that put human needs before productivity and the human factor before profit to ensure that white men would not be treated like "slaves" or "coolies." State Wages Boards and the Commonwealth Conciliation and Arbitration Commission worked to secure the standard of living and status of the white male worker, but whose compulsory benefits extended to all unionized male workers including Chinese and Aboriginal workers. In the United States early campaigns for minimum wages and maximum hours focused on the protection of women and children. Leading trade unionists such as Sam Gompers argued that the extension of state protection for men would emasculate them. When finally the political circumstances were right for the second Roosevelt administration to legislate for a federal minimum wage with the Fair Labor Standards Act in 1938, the long-time activism of women reformers ensured that it was an equal wage for men and women, if not, perhaps, an actual living wage for either sex.

NOTES

1. Vivien Hart, "Minimum-Wage Policy and Constitutional Inequality: The Paradox of the Fair Labor Standards Act of 1938," *Journal of Policy History* 1, no. 3 (1989): 0319–43.

2. Alice Kessler-Harris, *In Pursuit of Equity: Women, Men, and the Quest for Economic Citizenship in 20th-Century America* (New York: Oxford University Press, 2001), 106.

3. Jonathan Grossman, "Fair Labor Standards Act of 1938: Maximum Struggle for a Minimum Wage," *Monthly Labor Review*, June 1978; Lawrence B. Glickman, *A Living Wage: American Workers and the Making of Consumer Society* (Ithaca, NY: Cornell University Press, 1997); Lizabeth Cohen, *Making a New Deal: Industrial Workers in Chicago, 1919–41* (Cambridge: Cambridge University Press, 1990); Jerold L. Waltman, *The Politics of the Minimum Wage* (Urbana: University of Illinois, 2000); and Kessler-Harris, *In Pursuit of Equity*.

4. M. B. Hammond, "Judicial Interpretation of the Minimum Wage in Australia," *American Economic Review* 3, no. 2 (June 1913): 262, 285.

5. Alice Henry, "The Living Wage," *Life and Labor* 111, no. 7 (July 1913): 195. For a biography of Alice Henry, see Diane Kirkby, *Alice Henry: The Power of Pen and Voice. The Life of an Australian-American Reformer* (Melbourne: Cambridge University Press, 1991).

6. Frankfurter to Higgins, July 10, 1918, p. 2, Frankfurter papers, Library of Congress.

7. Samuel Crowther, "Who Wants a Living Wage?" *Collier's*, 1922, 8.

8. Ibid.

9. H. B. Higgins, "A New Province for Law and Order: Industrial Peace through the Minimum Wage and Arbitration," National Consumers' League Minimum Wage Series no. 14 (New York, 1915); Josephine Goldmark, *Fatigue and Efficiency* (Russell Sage/Survey Associates, 1913; reprint, Boulder: University of Colorado, 2013, bibliolife network).

10. *Harvester* Judgment [1907] (ex parte HV McKay), *Commonwealth Arbitration Reports*, vol. 2, pp. 2–18; John Rickard, *H. B. Higgins: The Rebel as Judge* (Sydney: Allen and Unwin, 1984), 171–6.

11. Charles Fahey and John Lack, "Harvester Men and Women: The Making of the Harvester Decision," in Julie Kimber and Peter Love, eds., *The Time of their Lives: The Eight Hour Day and Working Life* (Melbourne: Australian Society for the Study of Labour History, 2007), 65–85.

12. *Harvester* Judgment (ex parte HV McKay), *Commonwealth Arbitration Reports*, vol. 2, pp. 2–18.

13. Ibid., 172–3.

14. Fahey and Lack, "Harvester Men and Women," 79.

15. M. B. Hammond, "General Discussion," *American Labor Legislation Review* 92 (1913): 110.

16. Frankfurter to Higgins, December 23, 1920, Frankfurter papers, Library of Congress.

17. Learned Hand, "The Hope of the Minimum Wage," *New Republic*, November 19, 1915.

18. *American Labor Legislation Review* 3 (1913), cited in Jerold Waltman, *The Politics of the Minimum Wage* (Urbana: University of Illinois Press, 2000), 14.

19. Marilyn Lake, "Fellow Feeling: A Transnational Perspective on Conceptions of Civil Society and Citizenship in 'White Men's Countries', 1890–1910," in *Civil Society, Public Sphere and Gender Justice: Historical and Comparative Perspectives*, ed. Karen Hagemann, Sonya Michel, and Gunilla Budde (Oxford and New York: Berghahn Publishers, 2008; paperback edition, 2011); Marilyn Lake and Henry Reynolds, *Drawing the Global Colour Line: White Men's Countries and the International Challenge of Racial Equality* (Cambridge: Cambridge University Press, 2008), 199.

20. Ibid., 55.

21. Ibid., 138.

22. Victor S. Clark, "Labour Conditions in Australia," US Bureau of Labor, Bulletin 56; Victor S. Clark, *Labor Movement in Australasia: A Study in Social Democracy* (New York: Henry Holt, 1906); Henry McCrosty, "State Arbitration and the Minimum Wage in Australasia," in *Trade Unionism and Labor Problems*, ed. John Commons (Boston: Ginn, 1905); A. F. Weber, "The Report of the Victorian Industrial Commission," *Quarterly Journal of Economics* 17 (August 1903): 614–42; W. P. Reeves, *State Experiments in Australia and New Zealand*, vol. 2 (London: Grant

Richards, 1902); Helen Bosanquet, *Strength of the People: A Study in Social Economics* (London: Macmillan, 1902); George W. Gough, "The Wages Boards of Victoria," *Economic Journal* (London) 15 (1905): 361–73.

23. Marilyn Lake, "Challenging the 'Slave-Driving Employers': Understanding Victoria's 1896 Minimum Wage through a World-History Approach," *Australian Historical Studies* 45, no. 1 (2014): 87–102.

24. H. B. Higgins, *Victorian Parliamentary Debates*, Legislative Assembly, November 12, 1895, 3129.

25. Lake and Reynolds, *Drawing the Global Color Line*, 151.

26. Jude Elton, "Comrades or Competition? Union Relations with Aboriginal Workers in the South Australian and Northern Territory Pastoral Industries 1878–1957," PhD thesis, University of South Australia.

27. *The Survey*, February 6, 1915, Higgins papers, National Library of Australia (NLA), ms 1057, series 7, folio 1.

28. Glickman, *A Living Wage*; M. B. Hammond, "The Wages Boards in Australia," Quarterly Journal of Economics 29, no. 1 (November 1914): 576.

29. H. B. Higgins, "A New Province for Law and Order: Industrial Peace through Minimum Wage and Arbitration," *Harvard Law Review* 29, no. 1 (November 1915): 13–39; Editor, *Harvard Law Review*, to Higgins, September 30, 1914, Higgins papers, NLA, ms 1057/223.

30. Editor, *Harvard Law Review*, to Higgins, August 26, 1915, Higgins papers, NLA, ms 1057/238.

31. *Harvard Law Review* to Higgins, September 30, 1918, Higgins papers, NLA, ms 1057/336.

32. Felix Frankfurter, "New Labor Ideas Taught by War: Felix Frankfurter, Secretary of War Labor Board, Calls on Employer and Employee to Take Lessons to Heart," *New Republic*, December 15, 1918, 8.

33. Henry Demarest Lloyd, *A Country without Strikes: A Visit to the Compulsory Arbitration Court of New Zealand* (New York: Doubleday, Page, 1900); Henry Demarest Lloyd, *Newest England: Notes of a Democratic Traveller in New Zealand, with some Australian Comparisons* (New York: Doubleday, Page, 1900); Clark, *The Labour Movement in Australasia*; Victor S. Clark, "Present State of Labor Legislation in Australia and New Zealand," *Annals of the American Academy of Political and Social Science* 33, no. 2 (March 1909): 216–23; Philip S. Eldershaw and Percy P. Olden, "Industrial Arbitration in Australia," *Annals of the American Academy of Political and Social Science* 37, no. 1 (1911): 203–21. See Peter Coleman, *Progressivism and the World of Reform: New Zealand the Origins of Welfare States* (Lawrence: University of Kansas press, 1987).

34. Victor S. Clark, "Labor Conditions in Australia," *Bulletin of the United States Bureau of Labor* 56 (January 1905): 71–2; Harris Weinstock, *Special Labor Report on Remedies for Strikes and Lockouts*, Sacramento, 1910.

35. Clark, "Present State of Labor Legislation in Australia and New Zealand," 223.

36. Hammond to Andrews, August 14, 1911, correspondence files, series 5001, box 4, AALL papers, Kheel Center, Cornell University.

37. Andrews to Sanger, August 17, 1911, AALL papers.

38. Andrews to Hammond, August 23, 1911, AALL papers.

39. Hammond, "Judicial Interpretation," 259; M. B. Hammond, "The Minimum Wage in Great Britain and Australia," *Annals of the American Academy of Political and Social Science* 48 (1913): 22, 24.

40. Ernest Aves, *Report to the Secretary of State for the Home Department on the Wages Boards and Industrial Conciliation and Arbitration Acts of Australia and New Zealand* (London: Darling, 1908), 7, 10.

41. Hammond, "Judicial Interpretation," 285.

42. Ibid.

43. Glickman, *A Living Wage*, 153.

44. Rickard, *H. B. Higgins*, 123–52.

45. Higgins to Frankfurter, October 15, 1916. Frankfurter papers, Library of Congress, ms 18,868, reel 40.

46. Joseph A. McCartin, *Labor's Great War: The Struggle for Industrial Democracy and the Origins of Modern American Labor Relations, 1912–1921* (Chapel Hill: University of North Carolina Press, 1997), 52.

47. Ibid.

48. Higgins draft autobiography, NLA.

49. Higgins to Frankfurter, July 3, 1914.

50. Higgins, "A New Province for Law and Order," 13.

51. Higgins to Frankfurter, July 3, 1914.

52. Josephine Goldmark, *Impatient Crusader: Florence Kelley's Life Story* (Urbana: University of Illinois Press, 1953), 157.

53. Quoted in Michael Roe, *Nine Australian Progressives: Vitalism in Bourgeois Thought, 1890–1960* (Brisbane: University of Queensland Press, 1984), 53.

54. *Philadelphia Inquirer*, January 5, 1913, 9.

55. Higgins diary, June 24, 1914, Higgins papers, NLA, ms 1047/3.

56. Mary Chamberlain, "Settling Labor Disputes in Australia," *Survey*, August 1, 1914.

57. Higgins to Frankfurter, December 16, 1916.

58. Higgins to Frankfurter, July 3, 1914.

59. Ibid.

60. John R. Commons and John B. Andrews, *Principles of Labor Legislation* (New York: Harper, 1916); Robert Bruere, "The Meaning of the Minimum Wage," *Harpers Monthly Magazine*, December 1915–May 1916.

61. M. B. Hammond, "Where Life Is More than Meat: The Australian Experience with Wages Boards," *The Case of the Minimum Wage, Survey* 33, no. 19 (February 6 1915): 495–502.

62. Walter Lippmann, "The Campaign against Sweating," *New Republic*, March 27, 1915, 22–25.

63. *Bunting v. Oregon*, Felix Frankfurter, "Brief for the Defendant," "The Case for the Shorter Working Day," Supreme Court, 1915, vol. 2, p. 523.

64. Goldmark to Higgins, October 28, 1917, Higgins papers, NLA, ms 1057/293/293a.

65. Learned Hand, "The Hope of the Minimum Wage," *New Republic*, November 20, 1915, 66–8, 66, 67.

66. Roscoe Pound, Dean of the Law School, *Report of the President of Harvard University 1915–16*; Felix Frankfurter, "The Law and Law Schools," reprinted from *Reports of the American Bar Association* 40 (1915), Higgins papers, NLA, ms 1057, box 12.

67. Frankfurter to Holmes, November 11, 1915. Robert Mennel and Christine Thompson, eds., *Holmes and Frankfurter: Their Correspondence 1912–34* (Hanover, NH: University Press of New England, 1996), 39.

68. Glickman, *A Living Wage*, 135.

69. *Adkins v. Children's Hospital of the District of Columbia*, Supreme Court of the US, April 9, 1923, no. 795, LexisNexis 20.

70. Higgins to Frankfurter, February 6, 1921.

71. Higgins to Frankfurter, May 1, 1921.

72. Chris Nyland, "Scientific Management and the 44-Hour Week," *Labour History* 53 (1987): 23.

73. Kessler-Harris, *In Pursuit of Equity*, 101–16.

74. H. B. Higgins, "The Rigid Constitution," *Political Science Quarterly*, June 1905, 211–12.

75. Grossman, "Fair Labor Standards Act," 29.

76. Lake, "Fellow Feeling," in Hagemann et al., eds., *Civil Society, Public Sphere and Gender Justice*.

77. Mary Gilmore to Higgins, July 17, 1909, and draft response, Higgins papers, NLA, ms 1057/156–158.

5

American Protestant Missionaries, Moral Reformers, and the Reinterpretation of American "Expansion" in the Late Nineteenth Century

Ian Tyrrell

William Henry Seward was ailing in the spring of 1870. He had just two years to live. One of the most powerful men in Washington during his term as US Secretary of State, he was now a private citizen. Hoping that travel might reinvigorate him, he resolved to see the world. In August of that year, Seward left New York with several family members, bound for San Francisco and then Yokohama on an around the world tour. The sixty cabin passengers crossing the Pacific included British, American, and Russian officials, and five hundred Chinese laborers returning to their homeland were in steerage. Among the throng on board one group stood out for commendation. "Great," it must be confessed, "is the company of the preachers: Fifteen American missionaries with their wives and children!—the elder families returning, and the younger going for the first time to fields of labor in Japan, China, Siam, and India."[1] Wherever he went in Japan, China, India, the Middle East, and even Europe on his way home, Seward encountered missionaries and commented upon them. Among them were men and women; Catholics and Protestants; English, Germans, and Americans; and Methodists, Moravians, Congregationalists, Reformed Church, Baptists, and Presbyterians.[2] His adopted daughter recorded that: "The American and British missionaries, residing at Peking, passed the afternoon with Mr. Seward. They leave on the minds of our whole party an impression that they are earnest, true, and good men and women. The labor which they are performing in this benighted land fully justifies the Christian charity which has sent them hither."[3] Although he was not a staunch evangelical, for the Episcopalian Seward the missionaries were pathfinders for humanitarian and spiritual improvement.[4] At the Arcot mission in the Madras presidency of British India, he toured schools and hospitals administered by the Scudder family of New Jersey. Upon visiting the Zenana Mission of the Woman's Union Missionary Society of America for Heathen Lands in Calcutta, Seward's party was overcome with the achievements of these moral ambassadors for the United States: "It is the proud distinction of the United States that our countrywomen have designed and brought into execution a practical plan for the amelioration of society in India."[5]

American Protestant missionaries had been preaching abroad since the arrival of Adironam Judson and his wife Ann Hesseltine Judson in British India and, soon after, Burma in 1812.[6] Early nineteenth-century concentrations on the Middle East and the Pacific Islands had notable impacts on the target societies, though often in unintended ways.[7] Despite such evidence of ubiquitous activity, as well as the presence of voluminous records, and a formidable amount of scholarship, missionary history made little impact within mainstream US historiography for several decades from the 1960s.[8] Within scholarship on colonial and non-Western history, missionary activity was often taken for granted from the 1960s to the 1990s, but the missionaries' role was also marginalized in secular accounts and even reduced to an aid to or apology for Western rule.[9] Only in women's history were significant advances made. Thanks to the flowering of women's history in the United States, American missionary women began to be integrated into a wider social and cultural history. Historians Barbara Welter, Patricia Grimshaw, Patricia Hill, and Jane Hunter, among others, dealt with missions as a field for exploring gender roles and women's culture.[10] Some of this work explored transcultural contacts, but its potential as a model for transforming mainstream historiography on US contacts with the wider world history was not immediately realized.

In the last ten years there has occurred a resurgence of missionary history tied to the growing interest in imperial, global, and transnational history. This essay maps transnational networks for American Protestant missionaries in the late nineteenth century and explains their power, contexts, and limitations.

Much of the existing work has been done within British historiography rather than American and has reasserted both the importance of missionaries to the non-Western world, and defended the missionaries as a whole from charges of being servants of imperial power as cultural imperialists.[11] The importance of Christianity as belief and theology rather than as functional support of secular power within colonial structures has also been stressed.[12] Historians have portrayed the heterogeneous and often contradictory attitudes of (British) missionaries toward formal empire,[13] but the historiography has gone further than that. Rather than seeing missionary impacts as self-evident, recent scholarship has focused on the complexity of local reception.[14] Where the missionary's Christianity "succeeded," it did so through the critical roles of the indigenous in spreading conversion, and in adapting Christian faiths to local circumstances.[15] These more nuanced interpretations note the significance of the go-betweens or "cultural brokers"—people such as the indigenous "Bible women" of South Asia—and the traditions of religious and cultural adaptation that occurred through new sects and even new religions.[16] As part of the uneven take-up of Christianity in the non-Western world, more emphasis is also being placed on Christianity as a "world" or "global" phenomenon that is multicultural rather than purely a European imposition.[17]

While this work often stresses the role of the indigenous as carriers of adapted Christian values and culture, Ryan Dunch has shown why Western missionaries remain important in this transnational process. Indeed, they have a new importance hardly realized yet. Dunch indicates the possibilities for transnational and intercultural communications that the missionary enterprise facilitated. Missions "were uniquely placed" for cultural exchanges. Missionaries not only interacted with host societies and with other missionary groups. Through mission boards, they also "remained connected to their home countries and churches, and to missionaries of their own denomination or order working all over the world." The influences upon them, he concludes, were "highly diverse and international."[18] However, few historical accounts have applied this insight to US historiography.[19]

Although missionary historiography has embraced in recent years the study of empire, most works have operated along national lines. Despite what William Henry Seward stated about British and American missionary groups working together in the 1870s, the study of their interaction is still at a stage almost of terra incognita for transnational history. Of the advances in scholarship in British Empire history, little of that has been connected to the American missionary effort. The *Oxford History of the British Empire* Companion Series volume, *Missions and Empire*, edited by Norman Etherington (2005) remains within the formal bounds of its subject: it contains virtually nothing on this

American connection apart from the obvious inclusion of the colonial period when the thirteen colonies were part of the British Empire.[20]

While missions are now recognized as important sites for transnational interactions, the focus has typically been on the links between home and metropole. Where done, this approach tends to be bilateral rather than multilateral, as in studies of British missions' domestic impacts.[21] There has been a failure to treat the transnational space between empire and colony, and the transnational connections of different national missionary groups. What is missing is the study of people who circulated between colonies and between imperial centers. Such study of the transnational public and private spaces within which missionaries operated is in its infancy. These spaces, too, seem to have developed noticeably in the late nineteenth century.[22]

Of course, historians have not ignored the important surge of US missionary involvement in the late nineteenth century, but they have treated it as the product of an internal impulse deriving from and supporting an outward thrust of American power. Thus, Paul Varg found a national spirit of progressivism, humanitarianism, and nationalism behind the surge of American missionary activity in that era. Michael Parker's *Kingdom of Character* (1997) credits the YMCA, revivalism, and premier nineteenth-century American evangelist Dwight Moody's work as being at the root of the huge outpouring of US missionary effort in the 1890s and beyond.[23]

This parallels the larger US historiography of the post–Civil War years: in that view, the United States consolidates, pressure builds to bursting point like a soft drink can that has been shaken—then spurts out in a process of expansion in the late 1890s. A confident and aggressive nation begins to exert its muscle. As Stephen Ambrose put it for the Spanish-American War, "With the frontier gone, there was something akin to a panic among people. . . . We had to find some new outlet for our energy, for our dynamic nature, for this coiled spring that was the United States."[24] Such interpretations have rarely engaged the international context. To be sure, some historians have acknowledged missionary impacts on American culture and politics, but always conceived as a product of internal pressures. Following in the tracks of Julius Pratt's documentation of extensive missionary lobbying for the Spanish-American War and for retention of the Philippines in 1898, Richard Hofstadter argued that Americans were experiencing an internal psychic crisis in the 1890s over status shifts, a circumstance demanding a cathartic external crusade.[25] Paul T. McCartney's *Power and Progress: American National Identity, the War of 1898, and the Rise of American Imperialism* reinforces the argument for a missionary investiture of empire, but nowhere considers the external influences shaping an American national identity and sense of mission.[26]

None of this fits the world that Seward described. In the 1870s the US missionary presence was already noticeable; it would become more so in the 1880s. By 1890 some 900 US missionaries served abroad (all of them representing Protestant churches); by 1900 this number had more than trebled. The organization of this unprecedented missionary force came before the United States took its formal territorial acquisitions abroad from 1898 to 1903.[27] An alternative explanation for missionary expansion can be found that moves beyond the simple evocation of events and processes endogenous to US society. This lies in profound globalization that presented both challenges and opportunities. These changes had their roots in the 1870s, at the time Seward was traveling. First, there was the circulation of the globe by cable starting from the 1866 Atlantic crossing through to the Singapore cable laid by 1870, and eventually to the cross-Pacific cables of the British all-red route in 1902, and the American equivalent from Manila to San Francisco (1903). This was a process linking the world. It produced a rapid spread of information concerning shipping, travel timetables, the price of gold on which the world economy depended, and information on war and peace. Second, the building from the 1870s to 1914 of railroad networks in places such as India, Central Europe, and Russia, including the trans-Siberian railway, complemented the cable and the iron rails that bonded the eastern and western United States from 1869. Third, steamship travel became common. Facilitated especially by the opening of the Suez Canal in 1869, regular and reliable steamship services operated well beyond the transatlantic circuit, and became global in scope. From 1869 also, services included the San Francisco to Yokohama route of the Pacific Mail Steamship Company, on which Seward traveled, and the San Francisco, Hawaii, Auckland, and Sydney route that became a regular steamship service from 1885.[28]

Historians have not adequately explored nineteenth-century globalization's meanings for the United States. Arguably, the impact of "imperial" or "Victorian" globalization in the late nineteenth century was greater than that of the worldwide web today, because the rate and scope of change reducing time constraints was so dramatic. Due to the telegraph to Singapore, a six-week gap in news received in China (beyond the reach of cable in 1870) became twenty-four hours in Singapore as Seward's party moved south.[29] On arriving in Singapore, the Sewards' "first inquiry" concerned "whether the telegraph-cable [had] been laid from Point de Galles [sic] to this place." The answer was affirmative. The completion of the cable from Ceylon (now Sri Lanka), and hence the link with London and New York, was part of a profound if uneven communications revolution changing the world, and one that would intensify over the next two to three decades. Yet the impacts were not technologically determined.[30] They were mediated by cultural perception, with the shrinking of time and space experienced as emotional change in distance and social immediacy. "It is reassuring to come again into instantaneous communication with home and 'the rest of mankind,'" commented Seward.[31] The change was not lost upon missionaries either. The accounts of American missionaries and their supporters indicate that they saw global communications as central to their endeavor. The American Young Men's Christian Association (YMCA) missionary to India, Sherwood Eddy, rejoiced in 1896 at the "students of Christendom awaking, with steam and electricity to carry us to the ends of the earth in a month, with typewriter and telegraph for our epistles, [and] bicycle and railways to speed the gospel."[32] Long before this, Protestant evangelicalism had global ambitions based on biblical injunctions, and these Christian impulses, not new technology, continued to provide the key motivations of the missionaries. Changing communications allowed these ambitions to be realized more fully in the 1880s and beyond, but missionaries and moral reformers networked to take advantage of technological shifts. They created the circuits of transnational evangelical action through personal contacts and international reform and missionary organizational activity that gave substance to such an impersonal process as "globalization."[33]

This globalizing of American missionary and moral reform poses a question for American history. The post–Civil War years are thought among the most isolated, the era in which the United States retreated into itself, consolidated the nation's new continental frame, and healed the wounds of bitter internal division. There are paradoxes here—of a consolidating nationhood, yet at the same time strengthening cross-national connections. The post–Civil War "inside" of the United States needs to be related to the "outside" to illuminate this period, especially for the years from 1880 to 1900 when the effects of "Victorian" or "imperial globalization" began to be felt strongly.[34] This is particularly true for missionaries.

Perhaps the end of Reconstruction stimulated the missionary expansion that followed in the 1880s and beyond by releasing for new directions old antislavery and antiracist enthusiasm. The case of Vermonters Mary Ann Leitch and Margaret Winning Leitch could be invoked. Devout evangelicals with antislavery sympathies, the two young sisters (born in 1849 and 1857, respectively) served as teachers in the Reconstruction South in Virginia from 1873 to 1879, then resolved to go as missionaries for the American Board of Commissioners for Foreign Missions (ABCFM) in British Ceylon. They preached from their base in Jaffna the equality of the Tamil people with their European overlords and explicitly invoked the example of slavery's racialized structures to make their point.[35]

Yet these humanitarian sensibilities were themselves the product of changing personal and transnational influences. The sisters had long seen foreign, not domestic, missionary work as their ultimate objective, but Margaret Leitch was too young to go as an independent missionary until the late 1870s, and an opening did not come until 1879.[36] Among transnational influences, transatlantic Quaker and evangelical linkages of antislavery groups stretching back into the antebellum years had not been lost, but reformers tapped these connections anew in the 1870s and beyond as improved communications allowed. The first thing that the Leitch sisters did on their overseas adventure was to confer in London with British missionary leaders on strategies to pursue before they headed for Jaffna in late 1879 via Suez; and on their return in 1886–1887, they first stopped in Britain to raise money for missions.[37] Stimulated by the technological changes that accelerated the flow of information and people, the late Victorian phase of globalization also witnessed the first surge in what today are called today transnational NGOs.[38] Americans began to participate in a range of international organizations founded in that decade, such as the International Prison Congresses from 1872, and the movement against the state licensing of prostitution organized by England's Josephine Butler in 1877.

The emergence of both governmental and nongovernmental organizations on an international level in the 1870s coincided with a rise in transatlantic religious revivals. Dwight Moody's highly publicized and successful visits to Britain in 1873–1875 drew upon and in turn changed the nature of this revivalism.[39] It now focused more on systematic organization and follow-up for conversions and introduced the hymns and singing of Ira Sankey, Moody's collaborator. The improvement in transportation facilitated these revivals and adoption of their techniques through ease of movement and exchanges of information, allowing Moody to make many more trips to Britain before his death in 1899. Although Charles Finney and others had shaped the transatlantic revival tradition in the antebellum period,[40] these revival currents of the postbellum years were wider in geographic scope. Itinerant evangelists operated increasingly on a global level, but particularly within the British Empire and the United States. Thus, in 1877 the Glasgow-based Revd Alexander Somerville "set out for our Australian colonies" and spent eighteen months on a journey of 34,000 miles during which he spoke to "610 audiences."[41] In the 1880s Somerville continued to tour, taking in South Africa, Europe, and the Middle East. The German-born premillennialist George Müller developed after 1875 a seventeen-year evangelizing ministry, including stints in Australia, India, and the West Coast of the United States.[42] Such revivalism provided a transnational cultural context and stimulus to the development of a new missionary outpouring from a number of countries.

The growth of missions was not limited to the United States. A quickening of Scandinavian missionary activity coincided with the founding of the Svenska Missionsförbundet in 1878, and student support groups were established in universities and colleges in Norway, Denmark, Britain, Canada, and the United States in the early 1880s. Influential for the United States was the example of the China Inland Mission. Although founded in 1865 in Britain, the growth of this organization and its fame proceeded apace from 1875 when the Revd J. Hudson Taylor made a public appeal for more missionaries for China to go into nine provinces where Protestant clergy had never been based. Hudson Taylor indirectly influenced the American missionary movement through the Cambridge Seven, a group of young, well-educated British men, including Cambridge University graduates, who committed to serve in China for Taylor in 1885.[43] From the Cambridge group came the inspiration and the model for the beginnings of the Student Volunteer Movement for Foreign Missions (SVM) in 1886 at Northfield, Massachusetts.[44] Dwight Moody's Bible Institute at Northfield (itself partly modeled on the Keswick and Mildmay precedents in Britain) was the site. A type of evangelical summer camp, the meeting organized by Moody in 1886 was devoted to stimulating the interest of young college students in Christian service overseas. These summer meetings continued in 1887 and 1888, leading to formation of the SVM to stimulate and coordinate the recruitment of young missionaries. Taylor himself attended the 1888 meeting of the Northfield group and reportedly "exerted a deep spiritual influence on the entire conference."[45] His accounts of mission work in China provided feedback to supplement the calls from American missionaries for new recruits, and further evidence of a complicated triangular interaction across national boundaries concerning Britain, China, and the United States.[46]

Another influence on American missionary expansionism in the 1880s was this feedback from the mission fields provided by experienced missionaries. As with Britain's Hudson Taylor and the American William Ashmore, this period saw furloughs in the home country becoming easier to obtain, with cheaper, more predictable and speedier transport. Having served the American Baptist Missionary Union since the 1850s, Ashmore was forced to return to the United States several times on account of family illnesses. During his 1886 stay, he proclaimed at the Northfield conference a "summons to Christian duty" on behalf of East Asia.[47] The 1870s to 1880s also saw key individuals within the earlier, much smaller generation of American missionaries to China and India who had gone out mostly in the 1840s to 1860s returning home permanently where they could staff missionary magazines or run support societies. Thus Esther Jerman Baldwin, who had first gone to China with her Methodist missionary husband in 1862, served two decades, then spent a further twenty years as the president of the New York Woman's Missionary Society; her book *The Chinese Question* (1882) was a vigorous rebuttal of the anti-Chinese agitation in the United States based on first-hand experience of the Chinese people in the mission field. Her husband, Stephen Livingstone Baldwin, was an organizer of the 1900 Ecumenical Missionary Conference in New York and produced the report on mission work for the conference.[48] Another from China was John Nest Talmage, returning after forty-two years in 1889. His clergyman brother Thomas DeWitt Talmage was a prominent supporter of humanitarian and missionary work in the 1890s.[49] From India, Royal Wilder, whose son would later be a leader of the SVM, returned in 1875 to Princeton and founded the *Missionary Review of the World*, which was influential in the United States in advocating a foreign missionary re-engagement and expansion.[50]

Arguments made on return focused on the need for more volunteers and money. It became commonplace for missionaries to attack the home base as irresponsible or lukewarm toward missions. Underlying the increasingly urgent calls was the role of syncretic and millenarian indigenous movements forged out of the turmoil on the periphery of the European colonial world. The syncretic religion of China's Taiping Rebellion (1851–1864) was partly Christian inspired and reflected the impact of European commerce, culture, and religion. So too the Indian Mutiny of 1857, a nativist uprising that shook the foundations of the old British East India Company rule and led to the assumption of direct British imperial control. Mission workers of the 1860s and 1870s were exposed to the eddying effects of this earlier colonialism and the indigenous reactions against it.[51] In India and Ceylon, Hindu revivalism had strengthened as a consequence of the missionaries' vigorous attempts at Christian conversion. From 1877 to 1888, Hindu mobs in Madras Presidency picketed missionary meetings, stoned houses, and tried to drown missionaries out with noisy counterdemonstrations. In Ceylon, the Wesleyan-educated Arumuga Navalar incorporated Western teachings into his scholarship critiquing Christianity, established his own Hindu schools in competition with Christian ones, and became a prominent Shivite revivalist before his death in 1879.[52] Returning missionaries also added to the alarm. Samuel Kellogg came back from India and wrote *The Light of Asia and the Light of the World* (1885), to show the appeal of Buddhism to secularists (he was thinking of the English poet Sir Edwin Arnold who had extolled the virtues of the Buddha in *The Light of the World* in 1879) and yet also Buddhism's "moral weakness" from the evangelical premillenarian Christian viewpoint to which Kellogg adhered.[53] There was, too, the direct impact of Hindu proselytizers who visited the United States. Thus, Gopalrao Joshee, a Hindu Brahmin, who toured the United States from

1884 to 1886, attracted notoriety when he proclaimed the superiority of Indian culture.[54] Later, in 1893, Swami Vivekananda, a prominent Hindi revivalist, attended the meetings of the Parliament of Religions in Chicago during the World's Columbian Exposition, whereupon missionary groups attacked him for launching "an aggressive movement" to promote "heathen propaganda."[55] The missionary expansion of the 1880s and 1890s was conditioned by news coming back from the mission fields (and from foreign visitors) concerning such "infidel" competition.

A complicated transnational process intensified this competition. Evangelicals believed that Asian resistance to their messages was encouraged by the work of European and American theosophists advocating the syncretic mixture of religions.[56] Former *New York Tribune* journalist Henry S. Olcott and the Russian "Madame" Helena Blavatsky established the headquarters of the theosophy movement in Madras in the early 1880s, where they proceeded to play "an active role" in the revival of Buddhism.[57] When the premillennialist Arthur Tappan Pierson proclaimed the "crisis in missions" in 1886 at the Northfield meetings of the Moody Institute and called for renewed missionary efforts against the rising tide of unbelief, he did so amid growing concern about the complementary resurgence of competitor faiths and European "irreligion" being exported to Europe's colonies.[58] The missionary impulse was a reciprocal one with complicated roots in the interaction of Europeans, Americans, and indigenous groups in the colonial world. It was not simply a unidirectional thrust inspired by developments solely within the United States.

The answer to the missionaries' pleas was, first, to send more missionaries. The Student Volunteer Movement was organized out of the evangelical energy of the Northfield revivals, with a program to canvass college students to pledge future service, upon graduation, in a foreign missionary field.[59] A second and supplementary response to the call for help from the "field" was to provide more ancillary groups that would support missions. One of the most important of these was the World's Woman's Christian Temperance Union, founded in 1884, which sent out its own round-the-world missionaries from that date to encourage abstinence from alcohol and established a special Department of Temperance and Missions.[60] The other key group was the YMCA. A British society in origin, it mutated into a more aggressive and college-centered evangelical organization in the 1870s in the United States and, in 1887, began evangelizing abroad as a backup for the missionaries' work. Traveling secretaries went out under the auspices of the International Committee of the YMCA of North America. The World's YWCA followed suit in the 1890s.[61]

Again, the stimulus came from abroad—from missionaries in Asia. An American medical missionary, the Revd Jacob Chamberlain, working at the

Reformed Church mission at Arcot in Madras Presidency, pushed this issue. He believed the American YMCA would systematically organize the educated youth of India, introduce effective nondenominational methods, and heighten the evangelical temper of youth work. Chamberlain raised alarm at lost opportunities for conversions because "India's educated young men" were "running off into infidelity, Rationalism & Agnosticism and poisoning the minds of their uneducated friends," while the missionaries were "failing to reach them and apprehend them for Christ."[62]

Why Asia and not Africa, or the Middle East, where Americans had another strong missionary presence, and why India in particular? It was in India that higher and secondary education was expanding most, with increasing numbers going to colleges and universities. Some of these institutions were secular, while others were religious schools. This expansion underwrote nationalism and competing religions, since Hindus sponsored their own schools to combat Western influences. Small wonder that the YMCA was reshaped into a proselytizing missionary force to work for the conversion of college-educated young men. These students were the targets and it was in India where the YMCA expansion of the 1880s first began, not China. Similar processes with higher education drew the YMCA at the same time into Japan.[63] By around 1900, the emphasis had begun to change. China was now the most important YMCA target in Asia. With the old regime decaying irrevocably after the Boxer Rebellion of 1900 and the evidence in that rebellion of disaffected youths embracing a millenarian and syncretic religion, the YMCA gave great attention to the disintegrating Qing Empire. The American input was designed to take advantage of that decay, and to work in partnership with indigenous groups that also wanted to transform their society morally and materially.[64]

There was a thinly veiled geopolitics to these Asian-centered targets that reflected the patterns of globalization and communications changes. Arthur Tappan Pierson was one of the most influential strategists for the organization of the Student Volunteers. In the bestselling *The Crisis of Missions* (1886), and at the Northfield meeting of the same year, he argued that South and East Asia had advantages for missionaries: Japan was enterprising and modernizing, and China, once converted, would provide a self-made Christian diaspora across Southeast Asia and the Pacific, because Chinese "swarm[ed] everywhere like bees."[65] Yet South Asia was of particular importance because of the prevalence of English-speaking and non-"Papal" missionaries. The use of English was widespread, colonial rule was consolidated, and economic and commercial changes associated with Victorian-era globalization were taking effect.[66] India, in particular, would provide the lynchpin for the conversion of colonial peoples across Asia, and then the world. In Pierson's words of 1886,

India was "a controlling fortress guarding the very highway to other Oriental empires."[67]

Africa and Latin America were not major targets.[68] Small Latin American missions existed (e.g., in Mexico) from the 1870s, established by the ABCFM and Methodists,[69] but, in general, American missionary boards thought it preferable to carry the message of salvation to those countries that could provide leadership for indigenous reform in the non-Christian world. The United States did have missionary involvement in Africa, at first with the ABCFM in Liberia in the 1830s, but mostly associated with African American churches: in Liberia with a "permanent" but marginal African Methodist Episcopal Church mission from 1878,[70] and in South Africa from 1901 grafted onto an expanding indigenous Christian movement.[71] After 1900, white Americans led by Charles Hurlburt of Pennsylvania contributed to the faith mission established by the British in East Africa, the Africa Inland Mission.[72]

The most notable case in late nineteenth-century Africa suggests one reason why that continent was not the central focus on this American-led (white) missionary revival of that time. The Presbyterian Church mission in the Belgian Congo under the African American William Sheppard was a small Protestant enclave in a Catholic missionary country. As James T. Campbell shows, the Presbyterians were reluctant to send out African Americans on their own, and these were the ones most desirous of going to Africa, a continent reputed to be disease affected and unsuitable for whites. African mission work remained more "pronounced in black [American] churches."[73]

Yet underlying the choice was the fact that the educational level of Europe's African colonial targets was low in comparison with Japan and India. YMCA leaders in the formative years from 1889 to 1900, such as Luther Wishard, went only (briefly) to Egypt and South Africa, where the target student population was more developed and numerous, though small in comparison with India. African circumstances in the 1880s and 1890s did not allow the YMCA to quickly target a cadre of educated students to overcome the sheer numerical inadequacy of all European missions and make the indigenous themselves the directors of their own path to salvation.[74]

Missionary support organizations in turn required the assistance of laypeople and extra money. The need to support the increased level of foreign missionary engagement led to funding drives, and new organizations such as the Forward Movement of the Congregational Church in the 1890s, and the Laymen's Missionary Movement of 1905 to bankroll evangelism. By that time, a powerful American missionary and mission support force was at work with distinctive features: lay, interdenominational, and based on business methods, especially the targeting of markets for conversion with the aid of statistics and maps; and the systematic canvassing of funds, often aimed at specific audiences such as groups of wealthy businessmen and community leaders. This work was also aggressively evangelical. It shared with American society a profoundly Protestant temper and was indifferent to or hostile toward Catholicism. Some of the most prominent churches, especially Methodists, were happy to campaign in Catholic lands,[75] though Episcopalians wished to avoid such conflict.

There were great tensions between this newer approach and the existing missionary force, especially British missionaries. YMCA officials such as Sherwood Eddy and David McConaughy regarded their British counterparts as ineffectual, though individual workers were judged according to evangelical—not national—standards. They also viewed British authorities as class-bound people who supported the racial hierarchies of the colonies. American YMCA officials were more prepared to adapt to nationalist pressures and to emphasize modernization of non-Western cultures through education.[76]

A paradox remained in the objectives of this disruptive new missionary style because its leaders were at the same time anxious to foster cooperation within the Christian missionary forces. The paradox stemmed from the fact that efforts to enhance cooperation flowed from the experience of the missionary movement, where the disruptive impacts of new missionary styles were being felt.[77] In 1900 the Ecumenical Missionary Conference in New York saw the issue debated extensively. So long as the mission boards had the power and the money, no agreement on fusion could be easily achieved, but the principle of "comity" gradually spread, with cooperation on hospitals foreshadowed.[78] Some missions, for example the German Moravians in Labrador, signaled a willingness to withdraw from the field because there was only room for the better-established Lutherans.[79] This principle was taken further at the 1910 World Missionary Conference in Edinburgh, which "broke new ground" in embodying "missionary co-operation in a structured form."[80]

There the American delegation included Episcopal Bishop Charles Brent and YMCA and SVM leader John Mott. Both of these men had wide experience of practical conditions in the mission field. Brent's Christian ecumenicalism reflected the impact of his time in the Philippines. He found it "little short of absurd to try to bring into the Church of Christ the great nations of the Far East unless we can represent an undivided front."[81] John Mott had cultivated many colleagues from different denominations in the Euro-American world in the course of his travels for the Student Volunteers and the World Student Christian Federation (1895), and was acutely aware of the need for cooperation. Selected as chair of the 1910 conference, he was instrumental in arguing for a Continuation Committee of that meeting. Though interrupted in its work by the onset of World War I, the Continuation Committee became a de facto secretariat for the international mission movement. Together with his friend, Joseph H. Oldham, the Indian-born Scot, Mott used the Continuation Committee to steer the missionary movement toward greater cooperation, culminating in the founding of the International Missionary Council in 1921.[82]

The Edinburgh conference and its aftermath marked an important step in the development of Christian ecumenicalism and showed a strong American influence. As Brian Stanley notes, "There is little doubt that it was the American members of the Commission who were setting the pace, and the British who were at best cautious and at worst sceptical about the possibilities for a viable organ of missionary co-operation."[83] To be sure, the ecumenical endeavor still had a long way to travel. The conference bypassed questions of faith and order and, to satisfy objections from High Church Anglicanism, Mott had to excise discussion of proselytizing in Catholic countries. The conference could only deal with missions to the non-Christian world, and its surveys and deliberations therefore excluded Latin America.[84] Although Mott's conviction on the indissolubility of global missionary objectives faced resistance, US hegemony over the international Protestant missionary apparatus was growing. The focus on formal reporting, specialized studies by committees, and compilation of data adopted by the 1910 conference flowed from methods already pioneered by the Student Volunteers and their American allies in the mission societies. The Continuation Committee conformed to this practice, stressing "business efficiency" and standardized formats for the subsidiary conferences that Mott convened in cities across Asia after 1910 as he promoted Christian ecumenical cooperation.[85]

Brent also worked to advance the ecumenical agenda. In 1925 he attended the Protestant churches' Life and Work Conference at Stockholm, which sought "mutual cooperation . . . in the area of social and political life." But he was more interested in "questions of doctrine and church structures" concerning "baptism, Eucharist, ordained ministry, the church and concepts of its unity."[86] As president of the first World Conference on Faith and Order in Lausanne (1927), Brent reminded delegates that the cacophony of competing Christian beliefs had hurt the progress of missions. The persistence of so many different missionary societies in China, for example, was, in Brent's view, "suicidal for Christianity."[87]

The American urge to reorganize the global Protestant missionary forces and infrastructure had flow-on effects in these patterns of cooperation between national groups at the level of the metropoles as well as in colonial situations. Although the urge was, indeed, toward international cooperation, it was under an American-influenced model. In the 1920s, ecumenism paralleled the wider move in American relations with other nation-states toward a cooperative yet non-binding form of internationalism. Such "internationalism" would ideally involve the interaction of nongovernmental organizations in free association, and the free exchange of goods and services across national boundaries, based on market principles.[88]

It is possible to generalize from this process of missionary expansion and to posit a model for further elaboration and testing: to argue that the European empires and the entire process of imperial globalization had antagonized the indigenous peoples of South and East Asia, and to conclude that Americans fashioned new responses designed to "rescue," as it were, this situation by providing an innovative and vigorous form of evangelical competition for the rising force of nationalism, revitalization of traditional religions, and secularism. Focusing on modernization and rationalization of the missionary force, this approach drew upon the fund-raising experiences of particular church groups and mission boards, both British and American. The reaction at home synthesized this transnational experience into an increasingly American-led agenda on missions implemented by the Student Volunteers, the YMCA, and ancillary groups.

While these modernizing characteristics came to be thought of as "American," they were shaped from encounters between colonial peoples and missionaries on the ground; it was colonial experience that drew the attention of missionaries to the possibilities for modernization. As Mary Leitch wrote of Jaffna, "I begin to think that he who could make two spears of paddy [rice] grow where only one grows now would be a benefactor indeed. There is not a plough in this province." Leitch immediately corrected herself, but only to re-emphasize the point: "They still use a crooked stick, which only scratches the surface of the ground and when a drought comes everything is burnt up, and we have a famine. I am mistaken; there is one plough here, but it is too heavy for use."[89] The American missionary exercise's modernizing impulse was in such ways transnationally produced and not exceptional.

The external expansion of the American missionary effort of the late nineteenth century was self-consciously projected as evangelical Christianity, involving for this reason international cooperation with like-minded foreign evangelicals. Evangelical Christian missionaries learned from one another. The Leitch sisters learned much about methods of fund-raising used in the Scottish Presbyterian churches in the early 1890s and developed the New England Congregational Church's Forward Movement campaign from this example of systematic canvassing. For its part, the SVM was inspired by the energy of Hudson Taylor's China Inland Mission and frequently addressed by English and Scottish evangelical preachers, such as the Revd Frederick B. Meyer. All this is evidence for transnational interchanges of ideas and tactics.[90]

Yet the American missionary force's enhanced reliance on well-organized bureaucracies and fundraising differed from the China Inland Mission in that the latter was a faith mission, and Taylor did not make organized appeals for funds.[91] Moreover, American missionary groups and their lay ancillary supporters became embroiled in competition with other national missionary groups, as Americans, spurred by the infusion of Student Volunteer support, pushed toward the position of number one Protestant missionary force in the world.[92]

So what has this to tell about larger themes of US history? Clearly the outside and the inside of American history are closely related. Americans honed their sense of national difference from international action, cooperation, and conflict, even as they conceded that what passed for American exceptionalism was a variant on an Anglo-American pattern, and, in the case of missionary "expansion," a Christian evangelical pattern.

As far as the direction of US history is concerned, the missionary movement created networks that brought a greater American entanglement with the wider world. Moreover, the impact of missionaries lends weight to the argument that missions became a major source of knowledge of the non-Western world for Christian evangelicals. This extends, perhaps providing a special case for, the arguments of historians impressed by the rising interest among American middle-class people in travel and stories about foreign places. Arguably the United States developed out of these transnational experiences a more cosmopolitan orientation in the 1880s and 1890s than before 1880. Narrow as the view of missionaries could be at times, encounters often led to partial identification with the Other, as the example of Ester Baldwin suggests, and also provided opportunities to convey to home churches the diversity of cultures abroad. Far from dismissing the "heathen" as just that, early twentieth-century American study texts drawn from the mission enterprise were heterogeneous and complex. Americans possibly knew more about the geography of foreign places at that time, than in the 1930s after immigration and missionary expansion had, temporarily, ceased.[93]

Those same missionaries grew in key cases to identify with foreigners, critique racism at home, and oppose xenophobic anti-immigration restrictions that would antagonize their potential converts in Asia. Ester Baldwin announced of the Chinese: "knowing them as I do, not from newspaper items ... but from a personal knowledge of all classes of the people in their own country[,] ... I no longer wonder that the Creator has made one-third of the human race after the Chinese pattern, and only, nay, less than 50,000,000 Americans."[94] In a similar fashion, missionary Sidney Gulick, who returned to the United States in 1913 from Japan, became a leading figure in the agitation against Japanese exclusion, and for Japanese–US friendship.[95]

Given the extent of the missionary organization, it is not surprising to find historians emphasizing the missionary ethos and humanitarian rhetoric of American foreign policy in the late nineteenth and early twentieth centuries.[96] This is not to say that the mission lobby developed a substantial influence over the direction of US foreign relations. To be sure, missionary expansion took Americans to places where they could come into harm's way. On these occasions, missionaries called on their government for aid, as in the case of the Congregationalist Ellen Stone, when irredentist bandits in Bulgaria held her to ransom in 1901–1902. But President Theodore Roosevelt refused to pay the money (which then had to be raised privately) principally because he did not wish to upset Russia with a Mediterranean military intervention. To do so might disturb the balance of power in Europe, in a place that lay outside critical US strategic interests.[97]

While Protestant missionary work came to overlap with the exercise of state power, foreign policymakers preferred missionaries to stick to the arena of spiritual life rather than political lobbying that might interfere with *Realpolitik*.[98] But the very presence abroad of missionaries complicated the equation for diplomacy. Evangelical pressure did not decide US entry into the war of 1898 with Spain, for example; indeed, the clergy was divided over the efficacy of intervention,[99] but missionary activities in aiding victims of famine, war, and civil unrest in that decade created a context in which such a decision could be encouraged. That is, the humanitarian interventions of the 1890s, whipped up by the missionaries especially in regard to the Armenian massacres of 1894–1896 in the Ottoman Empire and the Indian famine of 1897–1900, provided a template within which the humanitarian crisis over the Spanish action in Cuba was acted out. Thus, the WCTU's organ, the *Union Signal*, editorialized that "we must not consent to have another Armenia at our very doors."[100] When the Red Cross leader Clara Barton saw the extent and nature of Cuban casualties at the hands of General Valeriano Weyler's *Reconcentrado* policy, she proclaimed that the Armenian massacres paled in comparison.[101]

The missionaries did contribute to humanitarian and missionary rationalizations of American empire, and policymakers frequently extolled, though not by name, the virtues of "soft" diplomacy in the form of missionaries. Seward's evocation of US missionaries aiding the spread of a peaceful world of commercial exchange and social progress through their contribution to modernization of non-Western countries was but an early example. If a humanitarian missionary ethos developed in a more secular way, especially after the 1914–1918 war, its roots lay in the nineteenth-century missionary experience. Seward would probably have been pleased with this outcome.

NOTES

1. *William H. Seward's Travels around the World*, ed. Olive Risley Seward . . . with two hundred illustrations (New York: D. Appleton, 1873), 29–30.

2. Seward went with his adopted daughter, Olive Risley Seward, nephew George Seward (US Consul-General in Shanghai), and Kate Sherman Seward (wife of the consul). To cite just one observation: In Syria the Armenians and Coptic churches were not evangelical, but "On the other hand, the Protestant missionaries from Germany, Great Britain, and the United States, are the living, active preachers and teachers of the Gospel" (ibid., 604).

3. Ibid., 204.

4. Seward claimed that "most of the Americans residing in China are missionaries" (ibid., 215).

5. Ibid., 370–1.

6. All American missions in the nineteenth century were Protestant. Indeed, until 1908, the Roman Catholic Church treated the continental United States itself as a missionary field, principally due to the presence of Indian tribes; and American Catholic missions abroad were not established for another decade.

7. Joan Jacobs Brumberg, *Mission for Life: The Story of the Family of Adoniram Judson, the Dramatic Events of the First American Foreign Mission, and the Course of Evangelical Religion in the Nineteenth Century* (New York: Free Press, 1980); Patricia Grimshaw, *Paths of Duty: American Missionary Wives in Nineteenth-Century Hawaii* (Honolulu: University of Hawaii Press, 1989); Ussama Makdisi, *Artillery of Heaven: American Missionaries and the Failed Conversion of the Middle East* (Princeton: Princeton University Press, 2008); Heather J. Sharkey, *American Evangelicals in Egypt: Missionary Encounters in an Age of Empire* (Princeton: Princeton University Press, 2008); James A. Field, *America and the Mediterranean World, 1776–1882* (Princeton: Princeton University Press, 1969). Americans also maintained missionaries to indigenous Americans that performed kindred functions, and the American Missionary Association performed a similar duty in American territory for African Americans after the Civil War and, after 1898, in Puerto Rico. The nineteenth-century missionary force outside the United States was exclusively Protestant.

8. Among the more important studies have been James C. Thomson Jr., Peter Stanley, and John Curtis Perry, *Sentimental Imperialists: The American Experience in East Asia* (New York: Harper and Row, 1981); James Reed, *The Missionary Mind and American East Asia Policy, 1911–1915* (Cambridge, MA: Harvard University Press, 1983); John K. Fairbank, ed., *The Missionary Enterprise in China and America* (Cambridge, MA: Harvard University Press, 1974); Paul Varg, *Missionaries, Chinese,*

and Diplomats: The American Protestant Missionary Movement in China, 1890–1952 (Princeton: Princeton University Press, 1958); William R. Hutchinson, *Errand to the World: American Protestant Thought and Foreign Missions* (Chicago: University of Chicago Press, 1987).

9. Hutchinson, *Errand to the World*, ch. 4; Arthur Schlesinger Jr., "The Missionary Enterprise and Theories of Imperialism," in Fairbank, *Missionary Enterprise*, 336–73. Andrew Porter, "Church History, History of Christianity, Religious History: Some Reflections on British Missionary Enterprise since the Late Eighteenth Century," *Church History* 71 (September 2002): 555–84, esp. 556–7.

10. Patricia R. Hill, *The World Their Household: The American Woman's Foreign Mission Movement and Cultural Transformation, 1870–1920* (Ann Arbor: University of Michigan Press, 1985); Jane Hunter, *The Gospel of Gentility: American Women Missionaries in Turn-of-the-Century China* (New Haven: Yale University Press, 1984); Ann White, "Counting the Cost of Faith: America's Early Female Missionaries," *Church History* 57 (March 1988): 19–30; Dana L. Robert, ed., *Converting Colonialism: Visions and Realities in Mission History, 1706–1914* (Grand Rapids, MI: William B. Eerdmans, 2007); Grimshaw, *Paths of Duty*; Barbara Welter, "'She Hath Done What She Could': Protestant Women's Missionary Careers in Nineteenth-Century America," *American Quarterly*, special issue: Women and Religion, 30 (Winter 1978): 624–38; Gael Graham, *Gender, Culture, and Christianity: American Protestant Mission Schools in China, 1880–1930* (New York: Peter Lang, 1995); Carol C. Chin, "Beneficent Imperialists: American Women Missionaries in China at the Turn of the Twentieth Century," *Diplomatic History* 27 (June 2003): 327–52; Kathryn Sklar, Barbara Reeves-Ellington, and Connie Shemo, eds., *Competing Kingdoms: Women, Mission, Nation, and Empire* (Durham, NC: Duke University Press, 2010); Maina Chawaal Singh, *Gender, Religion, and "Heathen Lands": American Missionary Women in South Asia (1860s–1940s)* (New York: Garland Publishing, 2000). For Britain, see the recent work of Elizabeth Prevost, *The Communion of Women: Missions and Gender in Colonial Africa and the British Metropole* (New York: Oxford University Press, 2010); Elizabeth Prevost, "Assessing Women, Gender, and Empire in Britain's Nineteenth-Century Protestant Missionary Movement," *History Compass* 7, no. 3 (2009): 765–99. See also Gülen Cevik, "American Missionaries and the Harem: Cultural Exchanges behind the Scenes," *Journal of American Studies* 3 (2011): 1–19.

11. Porter, "Church History, History of Christianity, Religious History"; Andrew Porter, *Religion versus Empire?: British Protestant Missionaries and Overseas Expansion, 1700–1914* (Manchester: Manchester University Press, 2004); Ryan Dunch, "Beyond Cultural Imperialism: Cultural Theory, Christian Missions, and Global Modernity," *History and Theory* 41 (October 2002): 301–25; Hutchinson, *Errand to the World*.

12. Porter, "Church History, History of Christianity, Religious History," 583.

13. Ibid.

14. Makdisi, *Artillery of Heaven*.

15. Andrew Porter, "Evangelical Visions and Colonial Realities," *Journal of Imperial and Commonwealth History* 38, no. 1 (2010): 145–55; Robert Frykenberg, "Christian Missions and the Raj," in Norman Etherington, ed., *Missions and Empire*,

The Oxford History of the British Empire Companion Series (Oxford: Oxford University Press, 2005), 107–31; Ryan Dunch, *Fuzhou Protestants and the Making of a Modern China, 1857–1927* (New Haven: Yale University Press, 2001); Maina Chawal Singh, "Gender, Thrift and Indigenous Adaptations: Money and Missionary Medicine in Colonial India," *Women's History Review* 15 (November 2006): 701–17. See also the contributors to Sklar, Reeves-Ellington, and Nemo, *Competing Kingdoms*, passim.

16. Frykenberg, "Christian Missions and the Raj," 107–31; Eliza F. Kent, "Tamil Bible Women and the Zenana Missions of Colonial South India," *History of Religions* 39 (November 1989): 117–49; Singh, "Gender, Thrift and Indigenous Adaptations." For the idea of cultural brokers, Brian C. Hosmer, "Reflections on Indian Cultural 'Brokers': Reginald Oshkosh, Mitchell Oshkenaniew, and the Politics of Menominee Lumbering," *Ethnohistory* 44 (Summer 1997): 493–509; Ilana Gershon, "When Culture Is Not a System: Why Samoan Cultural Brokers Can Not Do Their Job," *Ethnos* 71 (December 2006): 533–55.

17. Andrew F. Walls, *The Cross-Cultural Process in Christian History: Studies in the Transmission and Appropriation of Faith* (Maryknoll, NY: Orbis Books, 2002); *Cambridge History of Christianity*, vol. 8: *World Christianities c.1815–c.1914*, ed. Sheridan Gilley and Brian Stanley (Cambridge: Cambridge University Press, 2006); Jay Riley Case, *An Unpredictable Gospel: American Evangelicals and World Christianity, 1812–1920* (Oxford: Oxford University Press, 2012).

18. Dunch, "Beyond Cultural Imperialism," 320 (quotes); Dunch, *Fuzhou Protestants*.

19. Sharkey, *American Evangelicals in Egypt*, treats the Protestant missionary encounter as transnational, with two-way flows.

20. Etherington, *Missions and Empire*. Jeffrey Cox, *Imperial Fault Lines: Christianity and Colonial Power in India, 1818–1940* (Stanford, CA: Stanford University Press, 2002), however, contains material on American as well as British missionaries in the Punjab. The careers of the earliest US missionaries such as Adoniram and Ann Hasseltine Judson in Burma from 1812 are well known. See Brumberg, *Mission for Life*.

21. Catherine Hall, *Civilising Subjects: Colony and Metropole in the English Imagination, 1830–1867* (Chicago: University of Chicago Press, 2002); Susan Thorne, "Religion and Empire at Home," in *At Home with the Empire: Metropolitan Culture and the Imperial World*, ed. Catherine Hall and Sonya O. Rose (Cambridge: Cambridge University Press, 2006), 143–65; Susan Thorne, *Congregational Missions and the Making of an Imperial Culture in Nineteenth-Century England* (Stanford, CA: Stanford University Press, 1999).

22. Thomas Faist, *The Volume and Dynamics of International Migration and Transnational Social Spaces* (Oxford: Oxford University Press, 2000).

23. Paul Varg, "Motives in Protestant Missions, 1890–1917," *Church History* 23 (March 1954): 77, 81. Hutchinson, *Errand to the World*, 92, stresses civilizing and westernizing impulses within the American churches and the outward projection of a "spiritual imperialism." Michael Parker, *The Kingdom of Character: The Student Volunteer Movement for Foreign Missions, 1886–1926* (Lanham, MD: University Press

of America and American Society of Missiology, 1998), unpaginated introduction.
More generally on American "expansion," see Emily S. Rosenberg, *Spreading the
American Dream: American Economic and Cultural Expansion, 1890–1945* (New York:
Hill and Wang, 1982).

24. Cited in *Crucible of Empire: The Spanish-American War*, http://www.pbs.org/
crucible/frames/_film.html.

25. Julius Pratt, *Expansionists of 1898: The Acquisition of Hawaii and the Spanish
Islands* (Baltimore: Johns Hopkins University Press, 1936), 316; Richard Hofstadter,
"Cuba, the Philippines, and Manifest Destiny," in *The Paranoid Style in American
Politics and Other Essays*, by Richard Hofstadter (New York: Knopf, 1965), 145–87.

26. Paul T. McCartney, *Power and Progress: American National Identity, the
War of 1898, and the Rise of American Imperialism* (Baton Rouge: Louisiana State
University Press, 2006), 201–5.

27. Stephen L. Baldwin, *Foreign Missions of the Protestant Churches*
(New York: Eaton & Mains, 1900), 254–60; *Almanac of Missions for 1889* (Boston: n.p.,
n.d.), 38.

28. For the early history of this latter route, Sylvia Masterman, *The Origins
of International Rivalry in Samoa: 1845–1884* (London: George Allen and Unwin,
1934), 112–14; E. Mowbray Tate, *Transpacific Steam: The Story of Steam Navigation
from the Pacific Coast of North America to the Far East and the Antipodes, 1867–1941*
(New York: Cornwall Books, 1986), chs. 1–3.

29. Stephen Kern, *The Culture of Time and Space, 1880–1918* (Cambridge,
MA: Harvard University Press, 1983), 2; Daniel C. Headrick, *The Tools of
Empire: Technology and European Imperialism in the Nineteenth Century*
(New York: Oxford University Press, 1981).

30. Emily S. Rosenberg, ed., *A World Connecting, 1870–1945* (Cambridge,
MA: Harvard University Press, 2012), 351.

31. *William H. Seward's Travels*, 271–2.

32. Letter No. 1, November 15, 1896, in India, Eddy, G. Sherwood, Report Letters,
1896–1903, National Committee, 1891–1926, Y-57-1, Kautz Family YMCA Archives,
University of Minnesota (hereinafter KFYMCAA).

33. For an example, see Revd David James Burrell, "Introductory letter," in
Francis E. Clark, *World Wide Endeavor: The Story of the Young People's Society of
Christian Endeavor from the Beginning and in All Lands* (Boston: United Society of
Christian Endeavor, 1895), 11: "The coming historian will characterize the nineteenth
century as The Age of New Forces. He will make mention of steam and electricity,
and of their wonderful application and adjustments in the industrial world. . . . But he
will dwell with vastly greater emphasis on certain new forces and new adjustments
of religious things; such as the Sunday-School, the Missionary Propaganda, the
Temperance Reform, Women's Work, and the Endeavor Movement."

34. For this concept though not the application, see Robert Gregg, *Inside Out,
Outside In: Essays in Comparative History* (New York: St. Martin's Press, 2000).

35. Ian Tyrrell, *Reforming the World: The Creation of America's Moral Empire*
(Princeton: Princeton University Press, 2010), ch. 2; Mary Leitch and Margaret

Leitch, *Seven Years in Ceylon: Stories of Mission Life* (New York: American Tract Society, 1890). When mission boards began "interfering on the rights of the natives," the sisters recalled the practice of antebellum "Southerners" and others who "contended that the *black man had no rights which a white man was bound to respect*." Mary and Margaret Leitch to N. G. Clark, May 17, 1890, reel 459, ABCFM Papers (emphasis in original). In contrast, the Leitches stood for human rights, which they saw as a direct outgrowth of their missionary work and evangelical faith. Mary and Margaret W. Leitch to G. Henry Whitcomb, January 2, 1899, in "Our Experience in Collecting Funds: Some Lessons Learned," 15, in Biographical File, box 43, Women's Board of Missions: Supplementary Papers and Correspondence, 1873–1947, ABC 9.5.1, Houghton Library, Harvard University.

36. The sisters' mother, who died in 1872, had long wanted them to go overseas as missionaries. Ellen Wheeler, "New York State Christian Endeavor Convention," *New York Evangelist*, October 29, 1891, 2; Edward Miller and Frederic P. Wells, *History of Ryegate, Vermont, from its Settlement by the Scotch-American Company of Farmers to Present Time. With Genealogical Records of Many Families* (St. Johnsbury, VT: Caledonian Company, 1913), 406.

37. For transatlantic Quaker and evangelical networks of the 1870s and 1880s, see the examples in the Hannah Whitall Smith Papers, boxes 1–2, Lilly Library, Indiana University; for antislavery transnational connections, Bonnie Anderson, *Joyous Greetings: The First International Women's Movement, 1830–1860* (New York: Oxford University Press, 2000).

38. Martin H. Geyer and Johannes Paulmann, eds., *The Mechanics of Internationalism: Culture, Society, and Politics from the 1840s to the First World War* (London and Oxford: Oxford University Press, 2001); Leila Rupp, "The Making of Women's International Organizations," in Geyer and Paulmann, *The Mechanics of Internationalism*, 208; F. S. L. Lyons, *Internationalism in Europe, 1815–1914* (Leyden: A. W. Sythoff, 1963), 215–22.

39. James F. Findlay, *Dwight L. Moody: American Evangelist, 1837–1899* (Chicago: University of Chicago Press, 1969), 145–6, 342–3. Moody had first visited Britain briefly in 1867.

40. Richard Carwardine, *Trans-Atlantic Revivalism: Popular Evangelicalism in Britain and America, 1790–1865* (Westport, CT: Greenwood Press, 1978).

41. On Somerville, see Andrew Aird, *Glimpses of Old Glasgow* (Glasgow: Aird & Coghill, 1894), 361–2.

42. Dana L. Robert, *Occupy Until I Come: A. T. Pierson and the Evangelization of the World* (Grand Rapids, MI: William B. Eerdmans, 2003), 103–9; Arthur T. Pierson, *George Müller of Bristol and his Witness to a Prayer-Hearing God* (New York: Baker and Taylor, 1899), 246–56.

43. Alvyn Austin, *China's Millions: The China Inland Mission and Late Qing Society, 1832–1905* (Grand Rapids, MI: William B. Eerdmans, 2007), 180–7, 206–9. Of the Cambridge Seven, five were Cambridge students, and two were soldiers, but these were also members of the elite of British society, and one soldier was the brother of a Cambridge student.

44. John Mott, *The American Student Missionary Uprising: or, The History and Organization of the Student Volunteer Movement for Foreign Missions* (n.p., 1892), 11–12.

45. T. J. Shanks, ed., *College Students at Northfield; or A College of Colleges, No. 2* . . . (New York: Fleming H. Revell, 1888), 12.

46. Parker, *Kingdom of Character*; Clifton J. Phillips, "The Student Volunteer Movement and Its Role in China Missions, 1886–1920," in John King Fairbank, ed., *The Missionary Enterprise in China and America* (Cambridge, MA: Harvard University Press, 1974), 91–109; William H. Beahm, "Factors in the Development of the Student Volunteer Movement for Foreign Missions" (PhD diss., University of Chicago, 1941).

47. *Springfield Republican*, August 2, 1886, p. 1, folder 5234, box 449, Archives of the Student Volunteer Movement for Foreign Missions, Record Group 42, Yale Divinity School Library; "William Ashmore, D.D.," in *The Baptist Encyclopedia*, ed. William Cathcart (Philadelphia: Louis H. Everts, 1881), 45.

48. *New York Times*, July 29, 1902, 9; Baldwin, *Foreign Missions of the Protestant Churches*; Esther Jerman Baldwin, *The Chinese Question by One Who has Found a Home in China for Nearly 20 Years, and Claims to Know the People* ([New York?]: n.d. [1882]), 13.

49. Philip Wilson Pitcher, *Fifty Years in Amoy: Or, A History of the Amoy Mission, China, Founded February 24, 1842* . . . (New York: Board of Publication of the Reformed Church in America, 1893), 74–9.

50. Robert A. Schneider, "Royal G. Wilder, New School Missionary in the ABCFM, 1846–1871," *American Presbyterian* 64 (Summer 1986): 73–82.

51. C. A. Bayly, *The Birth of the Modern World, 1780–1914: Global Connections and Comparisons* (Oxford: Blackwell Publishers, 2004), 148–50; Jonathan D. Spence, *The Search for Modern China* (New York: Norton, 1999), 170–8; Jonathan D. Spence, *God's Chinese Son: The Taiping Heavenly Kingdom of Hong Xiuquan* (New York: W. W. Norton, 1996). Cf. Thomas H. Reilly, *The Taiping Heavenly Kingdom: Rebellion and the Blasphemy of Empire* (Seattle: University of Washington Press, 2004); Eugene P. Boardman, "Christian Influence upon the Ideology of the Taiping Rebellion," *Far Eastern Quarterly* 10 (February 1951): 115–24; Matthias Middell and Katja Naumann, "Global History and the Spatial Turn: From the Impact of Area Studies to the Study of Critical Junctures of Globalization," *Journal of Global History* 5, no. 1 (2010): 149–70.

52. D. Denis Hudson, "Tamil Hindu Responses to Protestants: Nineteenth-Century Literati in Jaffna and Tinnevelly," in *Indigenous Responses to Western Christianity*, ed. Steven Kaplan (New York: New York University Press, 1995), 95–123; Geoffrey A. Oddie, *Hindu and Christian in South Asia* (London: Curzon Press, 1991), 189, 191, 192.

53. Samuel H. Kellogg, *The Light of Asia and the Light of the World* (London: Macmillan, 1885), 21 (quote), 371 ("moral weakness"); Thomas A. Tweed, *The American Encounter with Buddhism, 1844–1912* (Chapel Hill: University of North Carolina Press, 1992); Edwin Arnold, *The Light of Asia: Or the Great Renunciation (Mahabhinishkramana) Being the Life and Teaching of Gautama, Prince of Indian and Founder of Buddhism* . . . (New York: Home Book Company, [1879]). Theosophists approved. See "The Light of Asia, as Told in Verse by an Indian Buddhist," *The*

Theosophist 1 (October 1879), at http://www.theosociety.org/pasadena/theosoph/theos1b.htm#light.

54. Meera Kosambi, "Anandibai Joshee: Retrieving a Fragmented Feminist Image," *Economic and Political Weekly* 31, no. 49 (December 7, 1996): 3191; Meera Kosambi, "Introduction: Returning the American Gaze: Situating Pandita Ramabai's American Encounter," in *Pandita Ramabai's American Encounter: The Peoples of the United States (1889),* ed. Meera Kosambi (Bloomington: Indiana University Press, 2003), 15–16; "Row Sattay's Folly," *New York Times,* August 30, 1886, 4; Caroline Healey Dall, *The Life of Dr. Anandabai Joshee, a Kinswoman of the Pundita Ramabai* (Boston: Roberts Brothers, 1888), 139–40; Edith Blumhofer, "'From India's Coral Strand': Pandita Ramabai and U.S. Support for Foreign Missions," in *The Foreign Missionary Enterprise at Home: Explorations in North American Cultural History,* ed. Daniel H. Bays and Grant Wacker (Tuscaloosa: University of Alabama Press, 2003), 152–70.

55. Carl T. Jackson, *Vedanta for the West: The Ramakrishna Movement in the United States* (Bloomington: Indiana University Press, 1994), 27.

56. Jacob Chamberlain to Cephas Brainard, October 6, 1887; extract from the minutes of the Madras [Missionary] Conference of date 12th of March 1888, with Richard Morse minute, April 6, [1888]; Jacob Chamberlain to Morse, March 20, 1888; Chamberlain to Luther Wishard, May 19, 1888, folder Correspondence and Papers 1888, India Correspondence and Papers 1887–90, box 356, Y.63-4, KFYMCAA; Kellogg, *Light of Asia and the Light of the World,* 21.

57. Jackson, *Vedanta,* 5; David L. McMahan. *The Making of Buddhist Modernism* (New York: Oxford University Press, 2008); Stephen R. Prothero, *The White Buddhist: The Asian Odyssey of Henry Steel Olcott* (Bloomington: Indiana University Press, 1996).

58. Arthur Tappan Pierson, *The Crisis of Missions: Or, the Voice Out of the Cloud* (New York: Robert Carter and Brothers, 1886), 92–3, 297–8.

59. See esp. Phillips, "The Student Volunteer Movement and Its Role in China Missions," 110–34; Beahm, "Factors in the Development of the Student Volunteer Movement for Foreign Missions"; Mott, *The American Student Missionary Uprising.* See also Ruth Franzen, *Ruth Rouse among Students: Global, Missiological, and Ecumenical Perspectives* (Uppsala: Swedish Institute of Mission Research, 2008).

60. Ian Tyrrell, *Woman's World/Woman's Empire: The Woman's Christian Temperance Union in International Perspective, 1880–1930* (Chapel Hill: University of North Carolina Press, 1991).

61. On the YWCA abroad, see Karen Phoenix, "Not by Might, Nor by Power, But by Spirit: The Global Reform Efforts of the Young Women's Christian Association of the United States, 1895–1939" (PhD diss., University of Illinois, 2010); on the YMCA abroad, see Tyrrell, *Reforming the World,* ch. 4; and C. Howard Hopkins, *History of the Y.M.C.A. in North America* (New York: Association Press, 1951).

62. Jacob Chamberlain to R. C. Morse, March 20, 1888, folder Correspondence and Papers 1888, India Correspondence and Papers 1887–90, box 356, Y.63-4, KFYMCAA.

63. "Main Facts Connected with the Beginning of the Foreign Work" and "Main Points by Elbert Munrow [Monroe] of New York and John Trumbull Swift," folder Correspondence and Papers 1888, India Correspondence and Papers 1887–90, box 356, Y.63-4, KFYMCAA; Jon Thares Davidann, *A World of Crisis and Progress: The American YMCA in Japan, 1890–1930* (Bethlehem, PA: Lehigh University Press, 1998).

64. Shirley S. Garrett, *Social Reformers in Urban China: The Chinese Y.M.C.A., 1895–1926* (Cambridge, MA: Harvard University Press, 1970), 49, 77–81, and passim.

65. Pierson, *Crisis of Missions*, 94 (quote); *Springfield Republican*, August 2, 1886. Racially based though this assessment was, it was a far cry from the usual Western categorization of Chinese as systematically inferior.

66. Pierson, *Crisis of Missions*, 50–1.

67. Ibid., 52.

68. In Japan, 1873 marked the real beginnings of the Protestant missions. Korea was not a possible target until the next phase of missionary expansion, the 1880s.

69. Deborah J. Baldwin, *Protestants and the Mexican Revolution: Missionaries, Ministers, and Social Change* (Urbana: University of Illinois Press, 1990), 21–23.

70. James T. Campbell, *Songs of Zion: The African Methodist Episcopal Church in the United States and South Africa* (New York: Oxford University Press, 1995), 88–89.

71. Ibid., 215.

72. Evanson N. Wamagatta, "The Presbyterian Church of East Africa: An Account of Its Gospel Missionary Society Origins, 1895–1946" (PhD diss., University of West Virginia, 2001), 62, 80; Theodore Roosevelt, *African Game Trails* (1927 repr.; New York: Charles Scribner's Sons, 1909, 1910), 146. On faith missions in West and South Africa, see Case, *An Unpredictable Gospel*, chs. 4, 7, 9.

73. James T. Campbell, *Middle Passages: African-American Journeys to Africa, 1787–2005* (New York: Penguin, 2006), 142 (quote), 149, 164–5, 181–3.

74. Charles K. Ober, *Luther D. Wishard: Projector of World Movements* (New York: Association Press, 1927), 164, 167.

75. Kenton J. Clymer, "Religion and American Imperialism: Methodist Missionaries in the Philippine Islands, 1899–1913," *Pacific Historical Review* 49 (February 1980): 29–50; Clymer, *American Protestant Missionaries in the Philippines, 1898–1916: An Inquiry into the American Colonial Mentality* (Urbana: University of Illinois Press, 1986); Clymer, "The Methodist Response to Philippine Nationalism, 1899–1916," *Church History* 47 (December 1978): 421–33.

76. Robert Wilder to unidentified correspondent, February 9, 1890, folder February 1890, India Correspondence and Papers 1887–90, box 356, Y.63-4, KFYMCAA; David McConaughy to My Dear Friend [Richard C. Morse], June 3, 1890, folder March 1890, India Correspondence and Papers 1887–90, box 356, Y.63-4, KFYMCAA.

77. *New York Times*, August 4, 1927, 20; Eugene C. Bianchi, "The Ecumenical Thought of Bishop Charles Henry Brent," *Church History* 33 (December 1964): 448.

78. "Fruits Expected from the Conference; Three Important Results from Its Deliberations Anticipated. Comity in Mission Work; Fields to be Divided for More Efficient Efforts," *New York Times*, May 3, 1900, 6.

79. Ibid.

80. Brian Stanley, *The World Missionary Conference, Edinburgh 1910* (Grand Rapids, MI: William B. Eerdmans, 2009), 278, 280–1.

81. Quoted Bianchi, "The Ecumenical Thought of Bishop Charles Henry Brent," 448.

82. Stanley, *World Missionary Conference*, 301–2.

83. Ibid., 287.

84. Ibid., 66–72.

85. Harlan Beach, *Findings of the Continuation Committee Conferences, Held in Asia, 1912–13* (New York: Student Volunteer Movement, 1915), 407.

86. Jürgen Schuster, "Edinburgh 1910 and Beyond: Mission in Unity: Historical, Theological and Practical Reflections," 5, ms in author's possession.

87. H. N. Bate, ed., *Faith and Order: Proceedings of the World Conference, Lausanne, August 3–21, 1927* (London: Doran, 1927), quote at 7. That this ecumenical feeling was rooted in Brent's experience in the Philippines is shown by, for example, Charles Brent to Revd E. A. Silbey, October 20, 1916, fl Oct 1916, box 12, Charles Henry Brent Papers, Library of Congress.

88. On American "internationalism" in the 1920s, see William Appleman Williams, "The Legend of Isolationism in the 1920s," *Science and Society* 18 (Winter 1954): 1–20; Robert H. Ferrell, *Peace in Their Time: The Origins of the Kellogg-Briand Pact* (New Haven: Yale University Press, 1952); Joan Hoff Wilson, *American Business and Foreign Policy: 1920–1933* (Lexington: University Press of Kentucky, 1971), x.

89. Leitch and Leitch, *Seven Years in Ceylon*, 24–5.

90. Wilder, *Student Missionary Uprising*, 11–12; Benjamin Broomhill, *The Evangelisation of the World: A Missionary Band*, 2d ed. (London: Morgan and Scott, 1887).

91. Austin, *China's Millions*, 95–6.

92. Baldwin, *Foreign Missions of the Protestant Churches*, 254–60.

93. Frank O. Erb, "The Development of the Young People's Movement," *Biblical World* 48 (September 1916): 173; James Mills Thoburn, *The Christian Conquest of India* (New York: Young People's Missionary Movement, 1906). For a model study of wider travel impacts, see Kristin Hoganson, *Consumers' Imperium: The Global Production of American Domesticity, 1865–1920* (Chapel Hill: University of North Carolina Press, 2007).

94. Baldwin, *The Chinese Question*, 13.

95. Sandra C. Taylor, *Advocate of Understanding: Sidney Gulick and the Search for Peace with Japan* (Kent, OH: Kent State University Press, 1984); Jennifer C. Snow, "A Border Made of Righteousness: Protestant Missionaries, Asian Immigration, and Ideologies of Race, 1850–1924" (PhD diss., Columbia University, 2003).

96. Pratt, *Expansionists of 1898*; McCartney, *Power and Progress*. See also Joseph L. Grabill, *Protestant Diplomacy and the Near East: Missionary Influence on American Policy, 1810–1927* (Minneapolis: University of Minnesota Press, 1971).

97. Randall B. Woods, "Terrorism in the Age of Roosevelt: The Miss Stone Affair, 1901–1902," *American Quarterly* 31 (Autumn 1979): 478–95.

98. Tyrrell, *Reforming the World*, ch. 9.

99. Winthrop Hudson, "Protestant Clergy Debate the Nation's Vocation, 1898–1899," *Church History* 42 (March 1973): 110–18.

100. *Union Signal*, March 19, 1896, 8.

101. Clara Barton, *The Red Cross: A History of This Remarkable International Movement in the Interest of Humanity* (Washington, DC: American Historical Press, 1898), 520–2; Merle Curti, *American Philanthropy Abroad* (New Brunswick, NJ: Rutgers University Press, 1963), 204; Elizabeth Brown Pryor, *Clara Barton: Professional Angel* (Philadelphia: University of Pennsylvania Press, 1987), 303. For the newest and best history of the Red Cross's international work, see Julia Irwin, *Making the World Safe: The American Red Cross and a Nation's Humanitarian Awakening* (New York: Oxford University Press, 2013).

6

The Body in Crisis

Congo and the Transformations of Evangelical Internationalism, 1960–1965

Melani McAlister

On November 24, 1964, the white American missionary Dr. Paul Carlson was gunned down in the streets of Stanleyville, Congo, by antigovernment guerillas. Carlson had been held hostage for several weeks by the Conseil National de Lebération (CNL), the so-called Simba rebels, who were fighting a Congolese government they saw as being merely an extension of Belgian colonialism. The rebels had sentenced Carlson to death several times, then reprieved him, then sentenced him again—all part of the group's strategy for negotiating with the US- and Belgian-backed government.

Carlson was taken prisoner while serving as a doctor in a remote region of Congo. By 1964, most missionaries, whether Belgian, American, or other European, had already been evacuated; often seen by Congolese as remnants of colonialism, they were targets of violence in a country torn by civil war. Because the rebels had singled him out, Carlson was already a figure of some notoriety when he was killed, along with fifty-nine other people (mostly Belgian priests, nuns, or business people) in a spasm of violence as the rebels were being attacked by Belgian paratroopers.[1] Carlson was one of only two Americans to die that day, and he immediately became a national martyr.

Carlson was featured on the cover of *Time*, as well as in *Life*, which did an emotional story about his family that also featured shocking photos of the deaths in Stanleyville. A large close up of Carlson's dead body was part of a sixteen-page spread that melodramatically recounted the hectic, fearful final moments of the hostages.

"The Radio Shrilled: Kill Them All," one headline read, next to a photo of a white man standing on the street, his shirt covered in blood. The photographs, massed in a constellation of death images, invited fear, anger, a sense of confusion. *Time* and *Newsweek* also featured Carlson on their covers, presenting him as a symbol of how "good whites" were being treated by what *Time* called the "dazed, ignorant savages" who failed to appreciate the help they were being offered by Americans like Carlson.[2]

White American evangelicals were particularly riveted by this story of one of their own. In the dozens of denominational journals and missionary magazines that circulated in the 1960s, Carlson's death, and that of other missionaries in Congo during the civil war, was a prominent topic. Just after Carlson's death, Billy Graham devoted two episodes of his weekly radio program, *The Hour of Decision*, to events in Congo. Graham, who at this point in his career understood nearly every international event as an example of communist subversion, also saw the attacks in Congo as proof of the inherently problematic nature of African decolonization. What happened to Carlson, Graham said, "should arouse the people of the Western world"; it "is a warning and a foretaste of things to come." The world was changing rapidly, Graham pointed out, and the nations of Africa "have a lust for freedom."

> Right or wrong, wise or unwise, they long to be free: to chart their
> own course! To protect their own interests. And to plan their own
> future. Many of them however are failing miserably. Because they
> are not prepared to be free. Freedom imposes responsibility. And an
> irresponsible nation is not eligible to be free.[3]

With clear parallels to a parent talking to a teenager, Graham's comments suggested that the irresponsible Africans had not yet proven their maturity to those who held the keys to eligibility for self-determination.

A few weeks later at the end of December 1964, college students who attended Urbana 64, the biannual conference of Intervarsity Christian Fellowship, gathered at a special memorial service for Carlson. Revd Wilbert Norton read from Matthew 16, in which Jesus tells his disciples that they must take up their cross and follow him. The pastor then described the impact of Carlson's death:

> Not since the brutal murders of John and Betty Stam by the
> Communists in North China thirty years ago has the Christian
> world been so stunned as in recent weeks by the slaughter of men
> and women and children of peace and good will, who died from the
> gunfire of men of hate, ignorant of God's love and peace.

Revd Norton introduced a tape recording made by Carlson a few months before he died. Carlson's recording expressed the hope that the Congolese church would be steadfast in the face of coming difficulties. The Intervarsity service included a prayer asking that those in attendance should also prove themselves worthy, should their time come to be loyal to Jesus unto death. As Norton described the experience of listening to Carlson's recorded comments: "Dr. Carlson's voice carries across the jungles of Congo as it speaks to us tonight on behalf of all the missionaries slain in recent times, of the charge unparalleled, the witness unashamed, and the triumph unquestioned."[4] In fact, the triumph was questioned, and the witness was not without its shame. That was precisely the problem.

By the time of Carlson's death, Congolese Protestants had begun to raise very serious questions about missionary behavior. Congolese often identified all Christian missionaries with Western power and Belgian colonialism. In the wake of independence, missionaries (mostly Catholic but including scores of US Protestants) had been attacked in the successive waves of violence and various anticolonial and antigovernment rebellions that convulsed Congo in the early 1960s. US Protestants evacuated their missionaries from Congo four times from 1960 to 1965, twice under the orders of the US State Department. The first two times, in 1960 and 1961, turned out to be mostly false alarms: the missionaries who stayed behind did not face significant danger. Those who evacuated and then returned, however, found not infrequently that they were met with some tough questions from the Congolese Christians they had left behind to tend to the churches, missionary schools, and hospitals. In 1964, as the CNL rebellion swept across eastern Congo and into the important city of Stanleyville, it was a rather different story, as the danger to Europeans and Americans was imminent and obvious.[5] Relationships on the ground between Congolese and US missionaries had also changed a great deal, and tensions between the two groups were profound. In a postcolonial state, albeit one still struggling to establish a secure central government, the old ways of imperialist missions could no longer be taken for granted.

Although the mainstream media embraced the story of benevolent white missionaries slain by a group of African "savages," African American observers in the United States tended toward a rather different assessment of the Carlson story. In general, African Americans, including theologically conservative African American Protestants, were more supportive of nationalist movements in Africa and more critical of US policies than white Protestants. At least some black churches saw links between Congo and the domestic politics of civil rights. African American church leaders saw Congo as a political and a religious issue, but found that their support for global black liberation was sometimes in tension with their enthusiasm for missions and their sober recognition of the reality of anti-Christian violence, in Congo and elsewhere.

Thus, violence against Christian missionaries in Congo became a symbolic site for the figuration of race, faith, and domestic and international politics in the early 1960s. African American believers struggled to position themselves between what seemed like competing loyalties. For white evangelicals, Carlson's death was also part of a much larger story: it was the image, the concentrated essence, of how white American evangelicals had begun to see themselves. They were well aware that Christians had faced hostility before, but now it appeared that missionaries were everywhere being attacked by the people they had served, citizens of assertive young nations who no longer, it seemed, wanted to be saved.

Historicizing US Evangelicalism in a Global Frame

This essay analyzes the crisis in Congo in the early 1960s in relation to a set of important transformations in US evangelical Christianity. In tracing this history, I make three interrelated arguments, joined by one proposition.

My first argument is that decolonization was of central importance to US evangelicals. This is not only because it transformed missionary work, although it did, as this essay shows and as other scholars have aptly traced.[6] Decolonization also mattered because the post–World War II challenges to European colonialism fundamentally threatened the presumptions of European and American cultural supremacy that had been at the heart of imperialist missions. Missionaries were still very much at work in the 1960s (as they are today), but in the vacuum left by the disintegration of the logic of missionary benevolence, new relationships were forged. This led to a struggle by at least some theologically conservative Protestants to fashion new, post-imperial self-conceptions. This undertaking was strikingly uneven, and decolonization certainly did not put an end to the condescension, self-aggrandizement, and sometimes even hostility with which some Americans viewed Christians outside the United States. But it altered the terms of the debate.

My second argument is related to the first: during and after decolonization, the moral geographies of global evangelicalism began to slowly change in order to more fully account for the dramatic rise in the number of Christians beyond the West.[7] In the 1960s, evangelicals were on the cusp of this transformation, just beginning to recognize that, in the postcolonial era, the success of missions might mean that black and brown Christians outside the United States might not welcome the continued presumption of American leadership in the faith. By the early 1970s, as millions of people in Latin America, Africa, and Asia converted to some form of Protestantism, evangelicals around the world became acutely aware that Christian demographics were changing. At the historic meeting of the 1974 Congress on World Evangelization in Lausanne, Switzerland, for example, Billy Graham, the reigning dean of evangelicalism, cheered the visibility and energy of "younger churches," as he stood before a multinational and racially diverse crowd of 4,000 delegates who themselves spoke forcefully at the meeting as equals, not as missionary objects.[8] Over the next few decades, Christians from Africa, Asia, and Latin America would play ever more prominent roles in the institutions of global evangelicalism. By 2010, more than 50 percent of the world's evangelicals would live outside the United States and Europe.[9] As an awareness of imminent changes began to take hold in the 1970s and 1980s, and as evangelicals around the world became more self-consciously assertive, an important segment of the US evangelical community began to embrace an understanding of Christian identity as fundamentally multiracial and transnational.

This expansive sense of identity was not only geographical but also spiritual and affective. As American evangelicals turned toward the Global South in the later part of the twentieth century, they constructed a particular narrative about Christians outside Europe and the United States that saw in those believers an admirable authenticity and zeal, which was also viewed as linked, paradoxically, to their great susceptibility to danger and persecution. Passion and martyrdom would soon become the twin pillars for Americans' narration of Christian faith in the Global South. In the charismatic worship styles of much of the evangelical community in Africa and Latin America, their stories of miracles and faith healings, and their supposed freedom from the shackles of excessive wealth that bound Americans, US evangelicals saw in their fellow believers an exemplary faith: an embrace of sensuous, emotive intensities that seemed to make them more passionate, more ideally Christian than most Europeans and Americans. In the 1960s, this embrace—with its mix of exoticism, primitivism, and genuine respect—was still incipient among evangelicals, although not uncommon among mainline Protestants.[10]

At the same time, US Protestants were becoming increasingly likely to focus on persecution and martyrdom as hallmarks of their faith. This attention was not new, of course. From its early days, martyr veneration had been part of the DNA of Christian culture-making. Protestants had laid claim to that heritage, and narrations of persecution of Protestants, particularly by Catholics, had long been part of Protestant print culture in Europe: the first edition of *Foxe's Book of Martyrs* was in 1563. That was followed by scores of other editions, including several in the United States in the nineteenth century. The iconography of martyrdom was evoked, too, in the spectacles of suffering that were such an important part of anti-slavery politics in the eighteenth- and nineteenth-century United States and Britain, where the bodies of slaves were displayed as anti-abolitionist rhetoric.[11] American Protestants also found a source of martyr stories in the lives and deaths of missionaries, although the glorious faithfulness of a local convert was also occasionally part of pious literature. [12] By the early twentieth century, most accounts of missionary deaths were moving toward more circumspect formulations. As Catholic immigration to the United States increased in the later part of the nineteenth century, Protestants begin to separate themselves more fully from what they saw as Catholic practices of saint worship, tainted by excesses of emotion and even idolatry.[13] Still, the emotionally vivid accounts of physical suffering never entirely disappeared. In 1956, five American missionaries in Ecuador were hacked to death by a local tribe. The story of the "Acua martyrs" made national news, chronicled multiple times in *Life* and in a best-selling book that was excerpted in *Reader's Digest.*[14]

As I will show, the Carlson story indicates how much evangelicals in the early 1960s were still invested in the narrative of missionary benevolence and sacrifice. And yet, the guilt and frustration that missionaries and their supporters experienced in Congo was tied to their own ambivalence, to the recognition that they were being judged, and sometimes found wanting, by people who considered themselves to be spiritual brothers, not pupils. Within fifteen years of Carlson's death, those brothers would become the exemplars of Christians who suffered and died for their faith (now usually at the hands of Muslims). They would also begin to become teachers, their "spiritual power" authenticated by both their faithful passion and their suffering, acknowledged and to some degree emulated by American evangelicals. This essay traces the fitful early stages of a set of linked transformations regarding race, decolonization, and a globalizing church.

My third argument is that fully understanding this history requires studying theologically conservative Protestants across the lines of race. In particular, both African American and white Protestants were deeply engaged with Africa, in ways that put them in conversation with each other. In making this argument, I share the approach of recent scholarship that defines as "evangelical" any theologically conservative Protestant with a relatively literal approach to the Bible, who believes in the necessity of personal salvation and the importance of evangelizing others. This model allows us to bring together black, white, and other believers who share a range of faith statements and practices. Interracial religious histories have become more common in recent years, as historians like Randall Stephens and Paul Harvey have examined the cross-racial interactions of religious people in regional contexts.[15] These models are crucial, because they challenge the presumptions that are built into the separate historiographies.

In many ways, of course, black and white evangelicals in particular have remained "divided by faith," both in terms of where they worship and how they stand on domestic social justice issues.[16] But studying both black and white evangelicals does not mean denying their differences—far from it. As I show here, historically black churches such as the African Methodist Episcopal (AME) church embraced African decolonization far earlier and more fully than white evangelicals did.[17] Yet, as I also demonstrate, debates about racism in the domestic context were not uncommon among white evangelicals, and postcolonial attitudes toward Africans were not universal among African Americans.[18] To understand the ways in which US evangelicals have engaged the world, we need to analyze—not assume—the ways that race, globalization, and religion interact.[19]

Finally, my proposition is this: it is time for scholars to rethink the history of the evangelical Christians in the United States by reframing that history on international terrain.

Doing so will necessarily challenge the logic that equates theological conservatism with right-wing politics. Political conservatism was and is a dominant part of the evangelical posture, globally as well as domestically.[20] But it is far from the whole story, especially on international issues. Yet presumptions about theologically conservative and presumably white Protestantism remain entrenched—so much so that the very idea of a "post-imperial" US evangelicalism can strike many people as rather absurd.[21] It is time we move beyond the presumptions that underlie this incomprehension.

The Congo Crisis

The move to independence was a tumultuous affair in Congo. In early 1960, Belgium announced that it would grant independence to its colony in just six months, a remarkably rapid transition, despite the fact that Belgium's rule had explicitly inhibited the development of national-level political institutions and had all but prohibited higher education among the Congolese. The one political organization with some kind of national base, the Congolese Liberation Movement (in French: Mouvement de Libération du Congo, or MLC), was led by an outspoken young nationalist, Patrice Lumumba, who was elected as prime minister. The venerable and relatively conservative leader Joseph Kasavubu became president in what was an uneasy power-sharing arrangement.

The idea of a postcolonial Africa had captured the imagination of liberals, leftists, and black nationalists around the world, and Lumumba, like Ghana's Nkrumah, embodied that dream for many people. The young nationalist soon earned the enmity of the Belgians, however, who had expected to maintain a leading hand in their former colony.[22] Lumumba also ran quickly afoul of the Eisenhower administration.[23] Although by 1960 US policymakers had adopted the perspective that Africans were no longer to be treated as children, unready for freedom, their new and barely improved view was that Africans were more like adolescents, whose moves toward freedom were dangerous precisely because they might be seduced by an unwelcome suitor—the Soviet Union. Lumumba was an unknown; he seemed erratic and inexperienced, a nationalist with pan-Africanist leanings and a populist appeal. Congo itself was rich in minerals, particularly in the province of Katanga; its wealth had been a lure for the Belgian colonizers and remained a prize for the European mining companies that dominated the Congo's economy. President Joseph Kasavubu, Lumumba's rival for power, was considered friendlier to the West, and more stable.

When Congo became officially independent on June 30, 1960, the immediate response among the general Congolese population was delirious joy. Within two weeks, however, the army had mutinied; the province of Katanga under the leadership of Moise Tshombe had seceded; and the United Nations had dispatched troops to stabilize the country and limit Belgian interference. Shortly after began what would become a deadly struggle for power in the new government. Starting in early September 1960, a complex series of political moves and countermoves began when Kasavubu dismissed Lumumba as prime minister. Lumumba refused to accept this dismissal and continued to vie for power. A few weeks later, a coup led by the young colonel Joseph Mobutu, the head of the army, pushed both Kasavubu and Lumumba aside. (In 1965 Mobutu would become president of Congo in another coup and go on to rule as a dictator until 1997.) In late September, Mobutu arrested Lumumba, then released him. Lumumba was then held in a form of house arrest, "guarded" simultaneously by the UN and the Congolese army.

Lumumba still maintained his right to govern as the democratically elected prime minister, and he still had a good bit of popular support in Congo. However, after weeks of wrangling, Kasavubu was accepted by the United Nations as the legitimate head of government, although only after a great deal of negotiation with the United Nations, United States, and Belgium. On November 27, shortly after this political defeat at the United Nations, Lumumba escaped his house arrest. A week later, he was arrested again by Mobutu and held for several weeks (and treated brutally) as the world looked on. Then, in January 1961, Lumumba was secretly transferred to his arch enemies in Katanga, where he was murdered while Belgian military "advisors" looked on. Lumumba's death was not announced until February, when Mobutu claimed, with absolutely no credibility, that the former prime minister had been murdered by angry villagers.[24] The obvious charade made clear that high-level Congolese leaders were making the barest attempt to cover up the brutal murder. Lumumba's supporters, both in Congo and abroad, were outraged. Immediately, there were demonstrations in a dozen or more cities, from Accra to Amsterdam.[25]

After President John F. Kennedy came to office in January 1961, he adopted a policy of "restraint" in Congo, paired with a generalized commitment to support decolonization. But JFK's foreign policy team also saw Congo as dangerous, a place where conflict over resources and the realities of civil war threatened to give the Soviets a significant opportunity. In the early days, before Lumumba's death was announced, Secretary of State Dean Rusk and his team believed it was possible to "find some consensus which would provide a basis upon which some sense can be made out of the Congo picture."[26] But by 1962, it was in Congo, according to Odd Arne Westad, where "the stakes were by far the highest for both the United States and its rivals."[27] The five-year conflict that emerged after independence would become a key site for the African Cold War and the most intensive US intervention in Africa in the 1960s, as Kennedy and then Johnson backed chosen allies with military aid and intelligence.

African American Christians Respond

As the crisis in Congo initially unfolded in the fall of 1960, African American Christians were already responding—forestalling any lingering sense that African Americans were interested only in domestic issues, or that churches were generally quiescent on political matters beyond civil rights. Already, nearly a year before Lumumba's murder, in March 1960, the massacre of sixty-nine people in Sharpeville had led leaders of the AME church to petition the United Nations to expel South Africa from its ranks. A group of ministers silently protested at the South African consulate in New York wearing signs that asked "What Color is Christ? Would Jesus Need a Pass in South Africa?"[28] At their national meeting in Memphis a few months after Sharpeville, the AME Council of Bishops expressed shock and outrage in specifically religious terms: "the fact that these crimes are perpetrated by a so-called Christian nation fills us with a sense of shame and horror."[29]

Then, just a few months later, as events in Congo escalated, the missions magazine of the AME, *Voice of Missions* (*VOM*), carried several stories about Lumumba. Many African Americans believed that the attacks on Lumumba were part of a larger colonial plot that favored Belgian interests and the pro-Belgian leader of Katanga, Moise Tshombe. (In fact, as Thomas Borstelmann has argued, whites in the United States and Europe understood the struggle in similarly racialized terms, and Tshombe had a number of American segregationists as his allies.[30]) In the winter of 1960–1961, as Lumumba struggled to get back into power, *VOM* enthusiastically recounted that his following was increasing.[31] Then, once his death had been reported, the magazine angrily followed the international response. The magazine reported on a speech by Ghana's Nkrumah that denounced UN and Belgian actions in Congo. "Dr. Nkrumah," the magazine commented, "said that the murder of Patrice Lumumba was not merely the murder of an individual, but the murder of that principle of legality which the United Nations has been advocating in the Congo."[32] Other African American church leaders were also outspoken. These included not only Protestants associated with mainline Protestant denominations, like Revd Fred Shuttlesworth of the American Baptists (Martin Luther King's denomination), but also people like Revd Smallwood Williams, the head of the Bible Way Church, an assembly of African American Pentecostal churches with a characteristically conservative theology. Writing to the *Pittsburgh Courier* several weeks after the UN protests, Revd Williams noted that the US administration had seemed unable to distinguish nationalism from communism, and that anti-communist rhetoric used against Lumumba was the same kind of smear used against civil rights activists at home.[33]

In addition, in the summer and fall of 1960, both the National Baptist Convention (the largest African American denomination) and the AME General Board voted to step into the breach after white missions groups evacuated in the face of instability and violence. At the time, there were relatively few African American missionaries to Congo. An African American Presbyterian, William Sheppard, had been on the first two-person team to go to Congo, in 1882.[34] But when the government of Belgium took over the colony from King Leopold in the early twentieth century, it had discouraged African American missionaries. By the time of Congolese independence, there were probably fewer than twenty African Americans on the missions field there, generally serving with one of the mainline churches, Methodist or Presbyterian.[35] African American churches like AME or Church of God in Christ, with missions programs in other parts of Africa, had small churches in Congo, built by migrants who had previously lived in areas where those denominations had missions and/or strong churches, such as South Africa. But there were no missions programs per se.[36] Nonetheless, AME Bishop John Bright announced that he was leaving to visit Congo, while George Baber, the Bishop who put forth the resolution for the AME church, declared the "present situation in Africa" to be "the greatest challenge" the denomination had ever faced.[37]

African American Christians were not the only ones concerned. Secular papers like the *Chicago Defender* and the *Pittsburgh Courier* also followed Lumumba's rise and fall. And on February 16, 1961, as riots wracked other cities around the world, a group of two hundred or more demonstrators, mostly African American, gathered outside the UN building, wearing black armbands to protest Lumumba's death and their presumption that the United States had supported his murder. (Many years later, their suspicions were confirmed. Eisenhower had ordered the CIA to assassinate Lumumba in the fall of 1960, although the plot was never carried out.[38]) The demonstrators included writers Maya Angelou and LeRoi Jones, as well as jazz singer Abbey Lincoln. A dozen or more made their way into the Security Council chambers, where they shouted down the speaker, US Ambassador to the United Nations Adlai Stevenson, as he defended US support for the Belgian-backed government. The protest ended in a melee, with approximately twenty people injured. Demonstrations continued outside the building throughout the day, and, for the first time in its history, the UN building was closed to the public for two days.[39]

Missionary Views and the Politics of Race

The United Nations had declared 1960 the Year of Africa. By then, it was virtually impossible for most American Christians, evangelical or not, to avoid a sense that the world was moving under their feet, and that Western Christianity's global reach was changing rapidly. The very basis of imperialist missions was being undermined by decolonization and postcolonial arguments about cultural imperialism.

Race was also an issue, as believers in the Global South raised questions about US racial practices at home—and missionary racism abroad. In 1959, an American missionary to South Africa had taken his fellow missionaries to task in *HIS*, the magazine of Intervarsity Christian Fellowship: "[I]f I were an African, and some missionary came around fishing for my soul, but obviously didn't want to have anything to do with *me*, I'd soon tell him to go back where he came from." "It must seem like hypocrisy to the Africans," he continued, "that you invited the believers to the Lord's table, but they can never expect to sit down to yours."[40]

US policymakers in this period worked from a similar logic: they began to support civil rights because it was good for the US position globally. Racism at home was a Cold War liability.[41] The evangelical story followed a similar path, but the stakes were different. US evangelicals believed they needed to take racism seriously because it was affecting a global Christian witness.[42] While these believers were generally also Cold Warriors, they also expressed concerns about creating a truly global community of believers, not just a well-positioned nation-state. In other words, they were worried less about the image of America than about the image of Jesus.

Racism was a problem in two ways. First was the sense that many missionaries continued to evince a sense of white superiority when they were on the field. Second was the problem of domestic evangelical opposition to civil rights. Despite the visibility of outspoken leaders like Jerry Falwell, whose hostile stance positioned him as the voice of a large segment of conservative Christians in the South, many of the major evangelical institutions were deeply concerned about racism. Historian Mark Newman has described the slow, incremental, and internally controversial process by which the Southern Baptist Convention (SBC) moved toward accepting desegregation.[43] In the 1950s and 1960s, the Christian Life Commission of the SBC was at the heart of the denomination's progressive wing. The Commission's 1954 report on *Brown v. Board* laid out the three primary reasons that Southern Baptists should accept school desegregation: it was now the law, and Christians had an obligation to "render unto Caesar"; segregation was hurting missionary enterprises; and it was against "the scriptural teaching that every man is embraced in the love of God." The General Convention passed a resolution endorsing *Brown*.[44] But while the national leadership of the SBC, along with Baptist press editors, and several state Baptist conventions took stances in favor of school desegregation and, in the 1960s, the Civil Rights Act, the local churches largely remained either quiescent or actively resistant, particularly when it came to desegregating their own churches. The activists who supported segregation were quite as vocal in the SBC as those who opposed it. And local ministers who might push a desegregationist position could find themselves quickly out of a job.[45]

Some scholars have argued that the seeming incongruity of the divergent views about race among theologically conservative white Protestants can be explained by the evangelical/fundamentalist divide. The more "respectable" and outward-looking neo-evangelicals at the National Association of Evangelicals and *Christianity Today* tended to have more liberal race politics, while those who still embraced the title "fundamentalist" were also more politically conservative—at least until the rightward swing of the 1980s that narrowed the divide. This argument has some truth: certainly it was the case that self-declared fundamentalists like Falwell, Pat Robertson, Bob Jones, and Carl McIntire had been outspoken against integration.[46] But as the divisions in the SBC make clear, there were racial liberals in a range of locations in the evangelical/fundamentalist spectrum. And it was international issues, particularly the impetus toward missionary work, that pushed some believers toward more liberal views on race.

For many, the single most powerful argument was that racism was devastating the missionary movement. "Nothing reached my heart more than the pleas of our missionaries around the world," wrote one Florida minister in *Christianity Today* in 1962, discussing his own struggle with racism. "The eyes of the world were focused on our treatment of minority groups. Missionary after missionary warned that our attitudes were making their work less effective."[47] African American ministers also criticized racism from the standpoint of missions. Howard Jones, who worked with Billy Graham in Liberia, told *HIS* that on his recent trip to Africa, he was "plagued" by detailed questions: "They quizzed us about the Emmett Till lynching in Mississippi and other racial disturbances," which, Jones said, they had heard about through Radio Moscow and other communist outlets. "We knew that the broadcasting of such tragic news by the Communists spoils America's image abroad, and impedes the progress of Christian missions in Africa, Asia and other parts of the world."[48]

This multiplicity of visions about race was related to what can only be described as the near schizophrenia of white US evangelical attitudes toward decolonization. By the time of independence, the European and American communities in Congo had been swirling with anxiety for months, ever since Belgium had announced its intention to withdraw. In early 1960 US missionaries serving with African Inland Mission warned that the Congolese were being influenced by "extremist propaganda" and potentially susceptible to communism.[49]

Evangelicals in the United States had for several years been discussing the rise of nationalism in Africa, Asia, and Latin America. The more socially aware wing of the evangelical movement, epitomized by Intervarsity Christian Fellowship and, to a lesser degree, by *Christianity Today*, was clear that, while Christians still needed to be concerned about communism, their fellow believers and/or potential converts were more likely to be committed to Third World nationalism. As the widely circulated book *Missions in Crisis* put it in 1961:

> The growing tide of nationalism and anti-white feeling throughout much of the world make a critical reappraisal of missionary strategy essential . . . we must be willing to adapt ourselves, in the best biblical manner, to the situation as it exists. . . . We shall need a spirit

of divine humility if we are to learn from recent missionary history. And learn we must.[50]

That said, many missionaries were quite dubious about nationalist sentiment in the populations where they worked, and their views of Congo were distinctly mixed. White evangelical missionaries generally believed, and told whoever would listen back in the States, that the Congolese had not been "ready" for independence. "They had no real conception of freedom," said the wife in one Baptist missionary couple. "They thought it meant money and all the things they wanted."[51] Another anonymous missionary wrote a caustic mimeographed report in which he vented about the dangerous, materialistic trends he saw around him. "Those [Congolese] who desire spiritual values ... are in the minority." Rather, he said, a "malignant and violent'" nationalism—a force both "sadistic and self-destructive"—had swept the naïve Congolese off their feet "with bottomless promises of quick material riches and a future communist utopia." God might yet work miracles in Congo, the missionary said, though he had doubts that a just God would be willing to redeem such people, who had "rejected so much grace and light." Still, one should pray.[52] Although such vitriol was hardly typical—Congo missionaries were often condescending but rarely so hostile—the broad sentiment was not uncommon: nationalism and independence were naively embraced by a people who had little understanding of what they meant, but who longed for them out of a kind of selfishness.

African American missionaries in Congo were few and far between, but they were not necessarily of a different mind than white evangelicals. Deighton Douglin served with the staunchly fundamentalist and largely white Conservative Baptist Foreign Missions Society (CBFMS)—a group that would soon find itself in a grave and contentious struggle over mission politics. Douglin told the black newspaper *Chicago Defender* that, in his view, the Belgians had ruled the Congo well, but they had failed to respond to uprisings with the firm hand that was necessary. Things had moved too quickly toward independence. Now, he said, the chaos made Congo ripe for the Communists.[53]

The back and forth logic of much evangelical commentary on race and decolonization was not simply a matter of one's position on the evangelical political spectrum, or the differences in editorial visions at particular magazines. Instead, it bespoke of a particular kind of aporia about Christianity's claims to universalism in a rapidly transforming world. American evangelicals believed that everyone had a soul and that God longed for the salvation of each person, without distinction. But they had lived in a national environment deeply saturated with colonialist views of Africa, and in a religious culture in which most mission organizations depended on selling an image of benighted continent in order to raise support for their work.[54] Even though missionaries had been and remained an important source of often nuanced and thoughtful accounts of life in their areas of service—for that reason, they were sometimes sought out by US diplomats for insider knowledge—they also built lives and careers around assumptions of superiority. Missionaries and their supporters were, then, often deeply ambivalent.

Such ambivalence was apparent, for example, in Africa Inland Mission's (AIM) official magazine *Inland Africa*. In the fall of 1960, AIM's General Director surveyed the situation in Congo just after independence. Congolese church leaders, he announced smugly, had told him that they themselves had doubts about independence: "Bwana, (Sir), we are far from ready for our freedom. We have already found what we want in our belief in Christ and what we need is advancement in the things of Christ."[55] In the next issue, however— the "Congo Crisis Issue"—the magazine carried an article highlighting the importance of Westerners accepting the leadership of the indigenous church.[56] It was an early example of Americans moving toward an embrace of the spiritual legitimacy (if not yet idealization) of Congolese Christianity. And, in the coded debates of this period, such acceptance of African leadership in religious matters was also a quiet statement of willingness to fully accept Congolese independence, both religious and political.

Congolese Christians

With the coming of political independence in 1960, Christian Congolese, specifically evangelicals, had become increasingly vocal about the issues of independence within the churches, and it was in the urgent and concrete struggles over resources that many of the most emotionally powerful performances of race, nation, and religious identity played out. Officially, local Congolese churches were separate from the missions structures. And, in theory, most evangelical missionary organizations saw their role as converting an initial set of believers, then training pastors, and then ideally stepping back to allow complete control by the indigenous church.[57] In Congo, this by and large had not happened, and missionaries remained powerful as pastors, directors of medical clinics, and administrators for church-based schools. Those Congolese who had been converted by evangelical missionaries (either from Catholicism or from indigenous African forms of worship) frequently expressed their fealty to their churches, even as they often complained about their treatment at the hands of arrogant and/or incompetent missionaries, and demanded more control. The issues were not just internal to the churches; the United States may not have had colonies in Africa, but it had missionaries, whose roles and status were virtually inseparable from the national and international situation around them. In this context, conflicts over school fees or pastoral ordination were also sites of decolonization.

In July 1960, as chaos swept across the country shortly after independence, the US consulate in Kampala, Uganda, recommended that all missionaries in Eastern Congo evacuate. Most did, heading out to nearby countries, or in some cases back to the United States. In at least one situation, a group of Congolese initially tried to prevent the missionaries from leaving by impeding an evacuation plane as it tried to land; the crowds were not hostile, the *Chicago Tribune* reported, they "simply wanted to head off the departure of men who served as doctors and teachers."[58]

These evacuations were the source of a great deal of confusion, anxiety, and even anger for at least some Congolese, and those missionaries who left sometimes felt the need to justify their decision. In one private letter back to AIM's New York office, a missionary evacuated to Kenya explained the reasons for his departure, including the disturbing presence of soldiers in the streets and the breakdown of law and order. Every day was more fearful than the last, he reported, in a letter as notable for its defensiveness as its presumption:

> I cannot see how we would have hoped to continue [to stay] very
> long when every time we heard a truck, we wondered if they were
> soldiers, and every time we had a knock on the door, the knocker
> would walk straight into the house without asking, and all our goods
> needed to be tied down under lock and key ... and every time people
> came to the yard, they peered into the house windows or into the
> garage or onto the porch ... times just are not what they used to be,
> Sid, believe me.

This missionary was also not above raising the familiar specter of black men as rapists: "Those with families and especially those with growing girls in the family, were especially warry [sic] about these matters."[59]

Conflict in Kivu

While missionary behavior in general was a site of tension, control over mission schools in particular was deeply fraught. It is hard to overstate the political and affective centrality of education for Congolese Protestants who were being trained—inadequately—in the mission schools. In fact, the issue of education, or rather the limits of it, angered Congolese Christians so deeply that it became a kind of proxy for claims to autonomy and independence for churches overall. By 1960, according to one estimate, Protestant missions overall had provided at least some primary school education to approximately one million Congolese.[60] But this education was a mixed bag. Many of the mainline Protestant missions followed the government-approved curriculum, and so provided a standard, if minimal, education. But organizations like AIM and the Conservative Baptist Foreign Missions Society (CBFMS) in Kivu (eastern Congo) had refused to accept state subsidies, or to teach the regular curriculum.[61] The missions were determined to keep their religious independence, and to avoid what they saw as a Catholic-tinged, state-sponsored program of study. This meant, however, that when Congolese left these mission schools, they did not have certifications that would allow them to attend public high school. Moreover, as independence neared, it became clear that the good jobs opening up would be filled almost entirely by graduates of the Catholic schools; a mission education from the Conservative Baptists or most AIM schools was almost useless outside the church and mission itself.[62]

It was in this context that, when the Conservative Baptist missionaries were evacuated in 1961 (for the second time), they returned to Kivu to find that their positions had changed. Two groups, one more closely allied with missionaries and the other more closely allied to Lumumbist sentiments, battled for control over the churches and associated schools. Both sides—the missionaries and their allies, on the one hand, and the "insurgent" church leaders, on the other—appealed to the Congolese government for recognition, and as different local and national governments came into power, the ascendency also shifted on the ground. Things got so bad that in the early 1960s that one Congolese official commented that, while political conflicts had settled down in the area, religious ones were still churning: "The Affairs of the [Kivu] area seem to be quiet except the war that is going on inside the protestant church!"[63]

At one point, when Congo's President Kasavubu had been convinced to weigh in on the side of the missionaries and their supporters, some of the insurgent (anti-missionary) faction decided to try to appeal to a higher power: they wrote a letter to President Kennedy complaining that "your compatriots at the Baptist Mission of the Kivu" had repeatedly repudiated democratic proceedings in the church. The Congolese explained that the missionaries had fled the country and abandoned their missionary service, only to return "to proceed by armed force against our pastors and our churches. ... Is it the Baptist mission of rifles and cudgels?" The letter went on: "We ask you ... to recommend to your compatriots to treat us as men and not as beasts, as men who wish to learn and to develop themselves and not as men for whom one shuts the schools."[64]

The schools were a central node in the larger nexus of political and religious power that marked the evangelical missions programs. Without this understanding—an awareness of the ways in which political debates about power and colonial mentalities were often funneled through discussions about education (or, in other cases, seemingly arcane debates over how pastors would be paid)—it is easy to miss the multiple ways that decolonization happened in Congo, and the terms under which Americans were forced to rethink their benevolence.

Perhaps the most striking argument for a transformation in Congolese-missionary relationship came in the form of a long 1961 article written by Congolese minister Philippe Decorvet on the state of the church in Congo. The seemingly innocuous piece was published in *Congo Mission News*, a magazine distributed to Protestants in Congo as well as missionary supporters in the United States. By 1961 the magazine was publishing articles not just about Congolese but also by them. Even more strikingly, Decorvet wrote his essay in French—something that happened only a few times in the early 1960s.[65]

Decorvet's article was at one level uncontroversial; it was a simple call for more theological training. Congolese Christians, he said, needed to understand the Gospel more deeply. This was entirely congruent with the evangelical focus on individual encounters with scripture, and the importance of local church leadership rather than a central hierarchy. At the same time, however, Decorvet's essay was a quiet attack on missionary attempts to control the meaning of the Bible. Writing at a time when the Bible had been translated into most of the major African languages for several decades, Decorvet argued that it was not enough to have Bibles available in the local languages. Those translations were inadequate because the Old Testament lost something crucial when translated from the French (as Belgian missionaries often did). African languages are vivid and concrete, Decorvet said, more like Hebrew than French, with its abstractions and formalisms that distorted the original text.[66] In this sense, African languages were better vehicles for key components of the Bible than European languages. Thus, Decorvet argued, Africans must be educated in Hebrew so they could do the translations themselves. While this might not seem particularly radical, it was a rather startling call in 1961, in a nation where there were no universities and as yet no functioning Protestant colleges or seminaries of any kind.[67] This was part of Decorvet's point; he wanted to make clear the links between religious education and postcolonial politics: "They render an immense service in learning Hebrew, those African pastors who have the possibility of doing so; this is the best way of 'deoccidentalizing' the Church, and that is what we must do."[68] De-occidentalizing the church: postcolonialism happened in the register of theology as well as the battle for control over resources. Of course, this project was ultimately no simpler for the church than for the state. Missions organizations still had the money; American and European dollars built church hospitals and eventually would fund those seminaries that Decorvet talked about. But the long-term transformations in the church–mission relationship would be profound.

Thus, the fundamental premise of missionary benevolence was being challenged by the battles over control—over churches and schools, and over the Bible itself. It was in this context of struggle, of multilayered debates about power within and outside the churches, that a large number of missionaries evacuated in 1960 and 1961, and then again in 1964. Many of the American missionaries faced profound criticism for having abandoned their mission stations. For their part, missionaries castigated Congolese for being too politicized, for putting nationalistic pride ahead of Christian community. Congolese denounced missionaries for the American version of the same thing: rather than stay with their fellow Christians in times of trouble, they evacuated, using the privileges of being American to depart and expecting the privileges of whiteness when they returned. Loyalties were divided, it seemed, while each side accused the other of excessive worldliness.

Missionary Martyrdom

By 1964, when Carlson was killed, the situation in Congo had deteriorated even further. The country was wracked by a complex series of rebellions launched by a number of competing groups. The most successful of these were the CNL (the Simbas), who in the spring of 1964 swept across Congo's east and north, taking over nearly half of the country in three months. As the rebels claimed a series of dramatic victories, they also increasingly faced planes and helicopters provided by the United States (and piloted by anti-Castro Cuban exiles), a fact that led their leader, Christophe Gbenye, to become more overtly anti-American.[69] In April and May 1964, there was rioting in the capital of Kivu province and an important regional city fell to the rebels. In August, Stanleyville fell in a bloody battle. In advance of the rebels' sweep, missionaries evacuated in droves, and scores of mission stations were soon in rebel-controlled territory.[70]

But Paul Carlson did not leave. He ignored an evacuation order from the US embassy, although his wife and children had left earlier in the year. In October

1964, he was captured by the rebels in Stanleyville, who initially identified the missionary doctor as a military officer. For the CNL leader Gbenye, Carlson was among those he routinely referred to the "impérialistes américains."[71]

Carlson was far from the only missionary to die in the violence of the 1964 conflict between rebels and the Congolese government. Perhaps not surprisingly, after Carlson's death made news, dozens of US church magazines began to publish their own accounts of missionary sacrifice and martyrdom. The *Pentecostal Evangel, Christian Leader, Conservative Baptist*, and others all published similar stories about their missionaries in Congo.[72] The World Evangelical Alliance published a pamphlet that harkened to Christian narratives of giving one's life for others: "Love's summit reached!" announced the cover, describing the death of six missionaries in Congo.[73] Billy Graham's *Crusade* also reported on the rebellion and the killings of missionaries in great detail. It described the executions on the streets of Stanleyville, as well as the deaths of a smaller group of missionaries in the area of Banalia [Orientale province]. One particularly detailed and emotionally powerful account told of how a group of Belgian mercenaries had launched an exhaustive search for the missing group of seven Protestant missionaries, and five of their children, only to have the trail end at a river, where they find only blood-soaked clothes and a Bible.[74] The long history of the iconography of Christian martyrdom saturated these accounts.

There is an obvious political valence to this particular story: it is the Belgian mercenaries—those who had parachuted into Stanleyville and whose invasion had set off the massacres—who are the heroes, valiantly searching for the lost. But there is another, less obvious politics: missionaries die, their children die, and they do so because of their exemplary, timeless commitment. A theme that runs through almost every account is that of "ransom"; the Christian language asserts that, just as Jesus's death on the cross is the ransom for our sins, these missionaries' lives were a ransom for the Congolese they loved.

African American observers also expressed their concern and sadness over Carlson's death. African American newspapers, which often covered church news as proudly "ours," ran ongoing and detailed stories about Carlson's capture and then his murder.[75] Churchgoers were presumed to be a significant portion of the readership of the major black papers, and despite the history of criticizing US Africa policy, they reported Carlson's death as a tragedy, one inherently interesting to their audiences.

Still, there were ironies that African American Protestants did not fail to notice. After all, by the time Carlson died, the civil rights movement had already had its share of martyrs at home. In late February 1965, when Carlson's death the previous December was still in the news, Martin Luther King announced his plan to march from Selma to Birmingham. Many people were fearful for his life. Reporting on King's announcement, the *Pittsburgh Courier* highlighted the ways that African American Christians saw the links between domestic and global issues. A group of churches were responding to King's announcement with a prayer meeting, the paper reported. On a Sunday in February, churchgoers around the country would offer concentrated prayer for missionaries and other Christians who were under threat of violence—violence both in Africa and in Alabama.

The fact remained, however, that Carlson's death happened as many missionaries were once again facing profound criticism for having deserted their mission stations. The basic facts were undeniable: most Protestant missionaries had abandoned their fellow Christians, not once but several times, rather than risk actually becoming martyrs. Carlson had not left, and so in that sense he was the ideal, the proof, of a missionary sacrifice that in reality had not always been forthcoming.

Conclusion

In the early 1960s, violence against Christian missionaries in Congo became a symbolic site for understanding how race, faith, suffering, and politics were being refigured. African American conservative Protestants also saw Congo as a political and a religious issue, but had to negotiate their support for missions and the realities of violence against Christians with their embrace of Congolese decolonization. For white evangelicals, Carlson's death also symbolized the bitter reality of modern missions. Missions were in crisis all over the world, as "young churches" insisted on their rights to dignity, self-government, and eventually to ownership of the schools and hospitals that missionaries had once controlled.[76]

Looking back at events in Congo in the early 1960s, we can see the conflict between the missionizing impulses of US evangelicals and the evolving realities of decolonization. In Africa, as elsewhere in the Global South, political changes made it appear that old-style missionary benevolence was on its way out, replaced by the power of postcolonial nations and a newly powerful local church. But missionary impulses did not disappear over the next few decades, they transformed: soon Global South Christians would play key roles as missionaries in other parts of the world. Africans grew their own churches, and after 1989 and the fall of the communist bloc, they sent missionaries all over the world—to Eastern Europe, Asia, and the United States.

American evangelicals also began to refigure, or at least expand, their ideas about Christian martyrdom. By the early 1990s, movements to protect "persecuted Christians" from attack became a staging ground for evangelical internationalism. African, Asian, or Middle Eastern Christians became the new martyrs for the Church, often understood to be facing down an expansionist, hostile Islam. Those upstart "local" Christians were now understood to be the face of the global church, and their struggles against Islam made their bodies the suffering icons of a new kind of evangelical frontier.[77]

The intertwined nature of these involvements should make one thing clear: US evangelical history is an international history, inseparable, not only from developments in US foreign policy but also from the evolution of a transnational community of believers, of which Americans form only a part. The realities of global Christianity are lived within and across the borders of the nation. This does not mean that "American-ness" did not matter, or that domestic politics, including the politics of race, were not a central part of US evangelical life. It does mean that it is difficult—more difficult than our histories have acknowledged—to distinguish between identities forged at home or those forged abroad. The modern shape of a globally conscious US evangelical culture emerged in part from seeds planted at the moment of decolonization. In other words, the raced body of evangelical internationalism has both a Cold War genealogy and a Third World birthplace.

NOTES

1. Stephen R. Weissman, *American Foreign Policy in the Congo, 1960–1964* (Ithaca, NY: Cornell University Press, 1974), 238–47.

2. "Congo Martyr: Dr. Paul Carlson," *Life*, December 4, 1964; Staff writers, "The Congo Massacre," *Time Magazine*, December 4, 1964, http://www.time.com/time/magazine/article/0,9171,830872-1,00.html.

3. Billy Graham, "Tragedy of the Congo," *Hour of Decision*, December 13, 1964, BGCA coll 191: tape 778.

4. Wilbert Norton, "Memorial Service—God's Word," Urbana.org, December 1964, http://www.urbana.org/articles/memorial-service. The *Chicago Defender* published a UPI report that quoted an unnamed speaker at the conference saying: "These modern martyrs are essential. God has once again allowed his servants to be killed. They speak now to the age of the nuclear bomb and to the atheism of existentialism." UPI, "Dr. Carlson, 31 Others, Honored at Convention," *Chicago Daily Defender*, December 31, 1964.

5. In addition to Weissman, the best overall examination of events in the Congo in the early 1960s is Lise Namikas, *Battleground Africa: Cold War in the Congo, 1960–1965* (Stanford, CA: Stanford University Press, 2013).

6. Alan Scot Willis, *All According to God's Plan: Southern Baptist Missions and Race, 1945–1970* (Lexington: University Press of Kentucky, 2004); David R. Swartz, *Moral Minority: The Evangelical Left in an Age of Conservatism* (Philadelphia: University of Pennsylvania Press, 2012); Mark Newman, *Getting Right*

with God: Southern Baptists and Desegregation, 1945–1995 (Tuscaloosa: University of Alabama Press, 2001).

7. Mark A. Noll, *The New Shape of World Christianity: How American Experience Reflects Global Faith* (Wheaton, IL: IVP Academic, 2009); Philip Jenkins, *The Next Christendom: The Coming of Global Christianity* (New York: Oxford University Press, 2002).

8. Rene Padilla, *The New Face of Evangelicalism: An International Symposium on the Lausanne Covenant* (Downers Grove, IL: InterVarsity Press, 1976). See also McAlister, "A Call to Action: The Lausanne Congress of 1974 and 'Social Concern,'" *Journal of American Studies* (forthcoming).

9. "Global Christianity: A Report on the Size and Distribution of the World's Christian Population" (Washington, DC: The Pew Forum on Religion and Public Life, December 2011), http://www.pewforum.org/christian/global-christianity-exec. aspx.

10. Melani McAlister, "What Is Your Heart For? Affect and Internationalism in the Evangelical Public Sphere," *American Literary History* (Winter 2008): 870–95. On mainline Protestants' embrace of Global South spirituality, see Gretchen Boger, "American Protestantism in the Asian Crucible, 1919–1939" (PhD diss., Princeton University, 2008); Joseph Kip Kosek, "Richard Gregg, Mohandas Gandhi, and the Strategy of Nonviolence," *Journal of American History* 91, no. 4 (March 2005): 1318–48.

11. On the iconography of abolitionism, see Jean Fagan Yellin, *Women and Sisters: The Antislavery Feminists in American Culture* (New Haven: Yale University Press, 1992).

12. Dana Lee Robert, *American Women in Mission: Social History of Their Thought and Practice* (Macon, GA: Mercer University Press, 1996), 49. On the circulation of the story of As'ad Ashidyaq, a convert to Protestantism from Catholicism in the nineteenth century, see Ussama Makdisi, *Artillery of Heaven: American Missionaries and the Failed Conversion of the Middle East* (Ithaca, NY: Cornell University Press, 2008), esp. 150–4.

13. One example of a rather dispassionate recounting is Marshall Broomhall, *Martyred Missionaries of the China Inland Mission, with a Record of the Perils & Sufferings of Some Who Escaped* (London: Morgan & Scott, 1901).

14. Elisabeth Elliot, "Through Gates of Splendor," *Reader's Digest,* August 1956; "'Go Ye and Preach the Gospel': Five Do and Die," *Life,* January 30, 1956, 599: O240; Elisabeth Elliot, "Child among Her Father's Killers: Missionaries Live with Aucas," *Life,* November 24, 1958, 349: OS1. Elisabeth Elliot, *Through Gates of Splendor* (New York: Harper, 1958). An excellent analysis of the popular response to the Auca martyrs is Kathryn Long, "In the Modern World, but Not of It: The 'Auca Martyrs,' Evangelicalism, and Postwar American Culture," in *The Foreign Missionary Enterprise at Home: Explorations in North American Cultural History,* ed. Daniel Bays and Grant Wacker (Tuscaloosa: University of Alabama Press, 2003), 223–36.

15. On the definition of evangelical, see Mark Noll, *The Scandal of the Evangelical Mind* (Grand Rapids, MI: W. B. Eerdmans, 1994). On studying African American evangelicals in conjunction with white and other evangelicals, see Randall J. Stephens, *The Fire Spreads: Holiness and Pentecostalism in the American South*

(Cambridge, MA: Harvard University Press, 2010); and Paul Harvey, *Freedom's Coming: Religious Culture and the Shaping of the South from the Civil War through the Civil Rights Era* (Chapel Hill: University of North Carolina Press, 2005).

16. Michael O. Emerson and Christian Smith, *Divided by Faith: Evangelical Religion and the Problem of Race in America* (New York: Oxford University Press, 2000).

17. I have chosen to consider the AME church as an evangelical church, despite its formal affiliation with world Methodism. In terms of their positioning on the Protestant continuum, Methodists of all races were and are a complex denomination. The AME church in particular joined the World Council of Churches in 1948, and was actively enthusiastic about the world ecumenical movement starting at least in the 1960s. By many standards, this would make the church decidedly not evangelical. And yet the AME Church espoused doctrines and held worship services almost identical to those of churches like the Southern Baptist Convention. And the WCC made clear that it welcomed evangelical churches, as long as they were willing to join an ecumenical movement. In my forthcoming book, I trace the debate over which Protestant churches were considered evangelical, and by whom, in the fifty-year period beginning in 1960.

18. James H. Meriwether, *Proudly We Can Be Africans: Black Americans and Africa, 1935–1961* (Chapel Hill: University of North Carolina Press, 2002).

19. Alan Wolfe makes a similar point about the tendencies of researchers to exclude black and Latino evangelicals in his review of Michael Lindsay's *Faith in the Halls of Power:* Alan Wolfe, "Evangelicals Everywhere: Review of *Faith in the Halls of Power,*" *New York Times,* November 25, 2007. As Christian Smith points out, about 10 percent of African Americans attend megachurches, some of which are primarily African American, many of which are racially mixed, and few of which are likely to be counted in numbers of "black Protestants." See also Christian Smith, *American Evangelicalism: Embattled and Thriving* (Chicago: University of Chicago Press, 1998).

20. The scholarship on the "religious right" is too vast to list here, but it includes: Kenneth Heineman, *God Is a Conservative: Religion, Politics, and Morality in Contemporary America* (New York: New York University Press, 1998); Joel Carpenter, *Revive Us Again: The Reawakening of American Fundamentalism* (New York: Oxford University Press, 1997); William Martin, *With God on Our Side: The Rise of the Religious Right in America* (New York: Broadway, 2005); Steven P. Miller, *Billy Graham and the Rise of the Republican South* (Philadelphia: University of Pennsylvania Press, 2009). There is emerging and very valuable scholarship on the US evangelical Left. See, e.g., Swartz, *Moral Minority.* Also Brantley W. Gasaway, *Progressive Evangelicals and the Pursuit of Social Justice* (Chapel Hill: University of North Carolina Press, 2014); Charles Marsh, *The Beloved Community: How Faith Shapes Social Justice from the Civil Rights Movement to Today,* new ed. (New York: Basic Books, 2006).

21. For work on missions that re-examines its political implications, see Willis, *All According to God's Plan;* Daniel H. Bays and Grant Wacker, *The Foreign Missionary Enterprise at Home: Explorations in North American Cultural History* (Tuscaloosa: University Alabama Press, 2003); Joel Carpenter and W. R. Shenk, *Earthen Vessels: American Evangelicals and Foreign Missions, 1880–1980* (Grand

Rapids, MI: W. B. Eerdmans, 1990); Holger Brent Hansen and Michael Twaddle, eds., *Christian Missionaries & The State in the Third World* (Athens: Ohio University Press, 2002). The work on foreign policy largely considers conservative evangelicals, but does challenge the domestic focus: Andrew Preston, "Bridging the Gap between the Sacred and the Secular in the History of American Foreign Relations," *Diplomatic History* 30, no. 5 (November 2006): 783–812; Miriam Adeney, *God's Foreign Policy* (Grand Rapids, MI: W. B. Eerdmans, 1984); William Martin, "The Christian Right and American Foreign Policy," *Foreign Policy* 114 (Spring 1999): 66–80.

22. The two most important texts on Lumumba's rise to power are Emmanuel Gerard and Bruce Kuklick, *Death in the Congo: Murdering Patrice Lumumba* (Cambridge, MA: Harvard University Press, 2015); Ludo de Witte, *Assassination of Lumumba* (London: Verso, 2003). On the Congo crisis more generally, see Namikas, *Battleground Africa*; Weissman, *Foreign Policy in the Congo*; Odd Arne Westad, *The Global Cold War: Third World Interventions and the Making of Our Times* (Cambridge: Cambridge University Press, 2005); Madeleine G. Kalb, *The Congo Cables: The Cold War in Africa—From Eisenhower to Kennedy* (New York: Macmillan, 1982). On Lumumba's rise, see also Rene Lemarchand, "How Lumumba Came to Power, August 1960," in *Footnotes to the Congo Story: An Africa Report Anthology* (New York: Walker, 1967).

23. US enmity against Lumumba was such that even a year after he was killed, a major US policymaker reported in some detail on the history of US policy in Congo without once mentioning his name. George Ball, "American Policy in the Congo (January 1962)," in *Footnotes to the Congo Story: An Africa Report Anthology* (New York: Walker, 1967). See also the report from the UN commission that investigated the death in late 1961, "Excerpts from Report by U.N. Commission on Inquiry into Lumumba's Death," *New York Times*, November 15, 1961.

24. De Witte's Assassination of Lumumba was written before a number of clarifying documents were released. More detailed accounts of his escape, arrest, and murder are in Gerard and Kuklick, *Death in the Congo*, 177–214; Namikas, *Battleground Africa*, 118–21; 124–6.

25. "Rioters Protest Lumumba Death; U.S. Is Assailed by Students— Demonstrators Shout in London and Rome," *New York Times*, February 15, 1961; "Embassies Attacked in Cairo," *New York Times*, February 16, 1961; "Protests in Several Nations," *New York Times*, February 17, 1961; "Congo Issue Stirs Rioting in London; Police Halt Mob's Attempt to Rush. Belgian Embassy," *New York Times*, February 20, 1961.

26. Harriet Dashiell Schwar, ed., *Foreign Relations of the United States, 1961–1963*, vol. 20: *Congo Crisis* (Washington, DC: Government Printing Office, 1994), Document 20.

27. Westad, *The Global Cold War*, 136.

28. "AME's Picket South African Consulate," *New York Amsterdam News*, April 9, 1960.

29. Thaddeaus Stokes, "AME Bishops Council Asks African Aid," *Atlanta Daily World*, April 15, 1960. See also the call for the United Nations to remove South Africa: "Ministers Protest African Lynchings," *New York Amsterdam News*, March 26,

1960. Meriwether cites these reports, although with little attention to the specifically Christian concerns (*Proudly We Can Be Africans*, 206, 232).

30. Thomas Borstelmann, *The Cold War and the Color Line: American Race Relations in the Global Arena* (Cambridge, MA: Harvard University Press, 2003), 148–50.

31. "Pro-Lumumba Pressures Mounting in Congo," *Voice of Missions*, February 1961.

32. "UN Assembly Back at Work: President Nkrumah Speaks," *Voice of Missions*, April 1961.

33. Meriwether, *Proudly We Can Be Africans*, 232. Quoting Williams, Letter to the Editor, Pittsburgh Courier, March 19, 1961, sec. 2, 26.

34. James T. Campbell, *Middle Passages: African American Journeys to Africa, 1787–2005* (New York: Penguin Press, 2006); Ira Dworkin, "In the Country of My Forefathers," *Atlantic Studies* 5, no. 1 (April 2008): 99–118.

35. There are very few histories of African Americans in missions after 1945, although there is a rich scholarship on earlier periods. From my research, admittedly partial, it seems that there were few, if any, African American denominations with missionaries in Congo in the early 1960s. For some sense of which mainline or evangelical largely white denominations were sponsoring African American missionaries in Congo, we can see the reports in African American newspapers in this period. "Methodist Missionaries Returning to Congo," *New Journal and Guide*, November 19, 1960; "Congo Missionary Marries Chicago Methodist Minister," *Atlanta Daily World*, July 21, 1961; "Congo Missionary Funeral Held in PA," *Afro-American*, September 22, 1962; "Southern Couple Answers Need of Church and Congo," *Chicago Daily Defender*, December 1, 1965. The scholarship on early twentieth-century African American missions in Africa includes E. A. Freeman, *The Epoch of Negro Baptists and the Foreign Mission Board* (New York: Arno Press, 1980); Sylvia Jacobs, ed., *Black Americans and the Missionary Movement in Africa* (Westport, CT: Greenwood Press, 1982); Kimpianga Mahaniah, "The Presence of Black Americans in Lower Congo from 1878 to 1921," *Global Dimensions of the African Diaspora* (1982): 268–82; Lamin Sanneh, *Abolitionists Abroad: American Blacks and the Making of Modern West Africa* (Cambridge, MA: Harvard University Press, 1999); Gayraud S. Wilmore, "Black Americans in Mission: Setting the Record Straight," *International Bulletin of Missionary Research* (July 1986): 98–102.

36. Campbell, *Middle Passages*; Marvin D. Markowitz, *Cross and Sword: The Political Role of Christian Missions in the Belgian Congo, 1908–1960* (Stanford, CA: Hoover Institution Press, 1973); David Lagergren, *Mission and State in the Congo: A Study of the Relations between Protestant Missions and the Congo Independent State Authorities with Special Reference to the Equator District, 1885–1903*, Studia Missionalia Upsaliensia 13 (Lund: Gleerup, 1970); Ira Dworkin, "American Congo," *Civilisations* 55, no. 1/2 (February 2006): 165.

37. "AME Church to Meet Challenge of Congo Crisis," *Baltimore Afro-American*, July 30, 1960; "Baptist Sending Negros to Congo," *New York Amsterdam News*, September 10, 1960. John D. Bright, the Bishop who left for Congo, was one of the

AME leaders most involved in the black liberation movement. In 1966 he signed a controversial document by the National Council of Negro Churchmen that supported black power. National Council of Negro Churchmen, "A Challenge to White Power," *Negro Digest*, December 1966.

38. This is documented in detail in Gerard and Kuklick, *Death in the Congo*, 177–193.

39. Peniel E. Joseph, *Waiting 'Til the Midnight Hour: A Narrative History of Black Power in America* (New York: Holt Paperbacks, 2007), 39–42. "Riot in Gallery Halts UN Debate: American Negroes Ejected After Invading Session," February 16, 1961.

40. Peter Letchford, "Dialog on Racial Prejudice," *HIS* 20, no. 1 (October 1959): 7–10.

41. Penny Von Eschen, *Race Against Empire: Black Americans and Anticolonialism, 1937–1957* (Ithaca, NY: Cornell University Press, 1997); Borstelmann, *The Cold War and the Color Line*; Mary L. Dudziak, *Cold War Civil Rights: Race and the Image of American Democracy* (Princeton, NJ: Princeton University Press, 2000).

42. Willis, *All According to God's Plan*; Newman, *Getting Right with God*. See also Joel L. Alvis, *Religion and Race: Southern Presbyterians, 1946 to 1983* (Tuscaloosa: University of Alabama Press, 1994).

43. Newman, *Getting Right with God*. See also Nancy Tatom Ammerman, *Baptist Battles: Social Change and Religious Conflict in the Southern Baptist Convention* (New Brunswick, NJ: Rutgers University Press, 1990).

44. Newman, *Getting Right with God*, 20–34, 80–3.

45. This happened to Thomas Holmes of Tattnall Square Baptist Church near Atlanta. On the battle over segregation in that church, which, not coincidentally, involved an African student, see Willis, *All According to God's Plan*, 180–1; Harvey, *Freedom's Coming*, 244–5; Benjamin E. Mays, *Born to Rebel: An Autobiography* (Athens: University of Georgia Press, 2003), 246–9. On the struggle to desegregate churches in the South, see Joseph Kip Kosek, "'Just a Bunch of Agitators': Kneel-Ins and the Desegregation of Southern Churches," *Religion and American Culture* 23, no. 2 (June 1, 2013): 232–61.

46. Daniel K. Williams, "Jerry Falwell's Sunbelt Politics: The Regional Origins of the Moral Majority," *Journal of Policy History* 22, no. 2 (April 2010): 125–47; Susan Friend Harding, *The Book of Jerry Falwell: Fundamentalist Language and Politics*. (Princeton: Princeton University Press, 2001), 14–29; Heineman, *God Is a Conservative*, 14–24.

47. James L. Monroe, "The White Man's Dilemma," *Christianity Today*, October 26, 1962, 16.

48. Swartz, *Moral Minority*, 131.

49. Philip Dow, "The Missionary Factor in US Relations with East and Central Africa during the Cold War" (PhD diss., University of Cambridge, Clare College, 2013), 91. Dow is quoting Minutes of Congo Field Council, AIM, January 7–12, 1960, BGCA coll 81: 10–36.

50. Eric S. Fife and Arthur Glasser, *Missions in Crisis: Rethinking Missionary Strategy* (Downers Grove, IL: InterVarsity Press, 1961), 13–14.

51. Phil Casey, "Congo Families Land in Capital," *Washington Post*, July 22, 1960, D1.

52. Anonymous, "An Evaluation of the Congo Situation as Seen through the Eyes of an Evacuated Missionary," March 1, 1961, BGCA coll 165: 101–5.

53. "Ex-Congo Missionary Teacher Wins Degree," *Chicago Daily Defender*, August 22, 1960, sec. p. 9. The interview was on the occasion of his receiving an MA from Boston University, also reported in "Back from Congo," *Baltimore Afro-American*, August 27, 1960. For more on Douglin: Deighton Douglin and Alice Douglin, Lowell Historical Society Oral History Project II, November 22, 2003, http://ecommunity.uml.edu/blackhistory/; "Your Missionaries at Work: What's Happening in Congo," *Conservative Baptist*, December 1964, coll 165: 102–2; Jack E. Nelson, *Christian Missionizing and Social Transformation: A History of Conflict and Change in Eastern Zaire* (New York: Praeger, 1992), 123.

54. Bays and Wacker, *Foreign Missionary Enterprise*; Kevin Grant, *A Civilised Savagery: Britain and the New Slaveries in Africa, 1884–1926* (New York: Routledge, 2004). See also Paul S. Landau and Deborah D. Kaspin, *Images and Empires: Visuality in Colonial and Postcolonial Africa* (Berkeley and Los Angeles: University of California Press, 2002).

55. Ralph Davis, "Africa's Present Day Challenge," *Inland Africa*, October 1960, 5.

56. Revd John Gration, "Partners in the Other Boat," *Inland Africa*, December 1960.

57. This is one version of the "three selfs" model of nineteenth-century missionary theorists like Rufus Anderson. William R. Hutchison, *Errand to the World: American Protestant Thought and Foreign Missions* (Chicago: University of Chicago Press, 1987); Charles Van Engen, "A Broadening Vision: Forty Years of Evangelical Theology of Mission, 1946–1986," in *Earthen Vessels: American Evangelicals and Foreign Missions, 1880–1980* (Grand Rapids, MI: W. B. Eerdmans, 1990), 230–4.

58. "Africans Halt Flight of Missionaries," *Chicago Tribune*, July 18, 1960. The report quoted the US embassy as saying that about one-half of approximately 2,000 Americans had been evacuated, and most others were out of danger. See also "400 Yanks Quit Congo; 100 Others Decide to Stay," *Chicago Tribune*, July 14, 1960; "D.C. Couple's Daughter Evacuated from Congo," *Washington Post and Times Herald*, July 16, 1960; Milton Viorst, "Congo Rescues Related by Missionary Here," *Washington Post and Times Herald*, July 20, 1960.

59. Eddie Schuit, "Letter to Sidney Langford," February 11, 1961, BGCA coll 81: 10–31.

60. This is Philip Dow's estimate, extrapolating from the number of missionary-run schools in 1951 (based on a report from the Council of Protestant Missions in Congo), and the expected amount of annual turnover in each school. Dow argues that this is a conservative estimate, and I believe he is right in that. Dow, "The Missionary Factor in US Relations with East and Central Africa during the Cold War."

61. William J. Petersen, *Another Hand on Mine: The Story of Dr. Carl K. Becker of the Africa Inland Mission* (New York: McGraw-Hill, 1967), 165.

62. Nelson, *Christian Missionizing*, 67–73, 76–8. On the issue of mission schools and educational policy more broadly, see Markowitz, *Cross and Sword*.

63. Nelson, *Christian Missionizing*, 113.

64. Ibid., 118. Nelson is citing a letter from Lawy Bakulu and Luc Mangolopa, May 28 1962, from the CBFMS archives, US State dept. translation.

65. Once an organization dominated by missionaries, the Congo Protestant Council had in 1960 elected Pierre Shaumba as its first Congolese president. By 1961, *Congo Mission News*, which was distributed both within Congo and to missions supporters in the United States, had become a forum for Congolese Christians as well as American missionaries.

66. Many scholars have shown that Bible translators made many, often egregious, mistakes: abstract terms like Holy Spirit were difficult to get right, so it is perhaps not surprising that missionaries in Sudan ended up speaking of "clean breath" instead. Lamin O. Sanneh, *Translating the Message: The Missionary Impact on Culture*, 2d ed. (Maryknoll, NY: Orbis Books, 2008), 230, quoting Eugene Nida, *God's Word in Man's Language* (New York: Harper, 1952, 47). Michael Kasongo also argues that the missionaries made key mistakes in translating the Bible into Otetela, using overly vague or confusing Otetela words for terms like grace, charity, spirit, covenant—even Messiah and salvation. Michael Kasongo, *History of the Methodist Church in the Central Congo* (Lanham, MD: University Press of America, 1998), 70–7.

67. In 1960, the North Congo Seminary of Banjwadi, a joint effort of AIM and UFM, began with five students. In September 1963, AIM reported that it was beginning to focus on trying to build up the seminary, but at that point, it seems as if it was not actually functioning or only barely. "Report of the IFMA Africa Committee," September 1963, 3 of 8, BGCA coll 81: 37–9.

68. Phillipe Decorvet, "Des Missionaires Nouvelles," *Congo Mission News/Nouvelles Missionaires Du Congo*, October 1961, 20. My translation.

69. Weissman, *Foreign Policy in the Congo*, 213–30.

70. On the rebels' advance, Namikas, *Battleground Africa*, 189–99. On the AIM stations, see Petersen, *Another Hand on Mine*, 189–91. Paul Carlson's wife and children were evacuated from Northwest Congo in September. A timeline of Carlson's capture and the Belgian documents associated with the events is found in: C.R.I.S.P., *Congo 1964: Political Documents of a Developing Nation* (Princeton: Princeton University Press, 1966), 383–8. The status of Carlson's family is in Telégramme 24 Octobre, 383.

71. See Gbenye's telegram of October 24 and the document published in Le Martyr, October 30, 1964, both in C.R.I.S.P, *Congo 1964*, 384–85.

72. Nettie Berg, "More Heroes in the Congo," *Christian Leader*, January 1965, 7, BGCA coll 165: 102–2. Angeline Tucker, "Crisis Days in the Congo," *Pentecostal Evangel*, February 14, 1965, BGCA coll 165: 102–2. William A. Deans, "Flight from the Congo!" *Interlit*, 1964, BGCA coll 165: 102–2.

73. Worldwide Evangelization Crusade, "Congo: Tragedy or Triumph?" *Worldwide Thrust: WEC's Monthly Communique*, February 1965.

74. D. W. Truby, "Congo: The Facts," *Crusade*, April 1965, BGCA coll 165: 102–2.

75. Editorial, "The Massacre," *Daily Defender*, November 30, 1964; "Is Congo Missionary Living?" *Chicago Daily Defender*, November 18, 1964; "Kin May Follow in Footsteps of Congo Victim," *Chicago Daily Defender*, December 8, 1964.

76. On this struggle in Congo specifically, see Robert Gilbert Nelson, *Congo Crisis and Christian Mission* (St. Louis, MO: Bethany Press, 1961); Nelson, *Christian Missionizing*; Kasongo, *Methodist Church*; Markowitz, *Cross and Sword*.

77. Melani McAlister, "The Persecuted Body: Evangelical Internationalism, Islam, and the Politics of Fear," in *Facing Fear: The History of an Emotion in Global Perspective* (Princeton: Princeton University Press, 2012); Melani McAlister, "US Evangelicals and the Politics of Slave Redemption as Religious Freedom in Sudan," *South Atlantic Quarterly* 113, no. 1 (December 21, 2014): 87–108.

7

Extracted Truths

The Politics of God and Black Gold on a Global Stage

Darren Dochuk

In recent years, Alberta has become known internationally as
the great oil-producing province of Canada. Yet every time I look
at an oil well and see the pump going up and down ... I say
to myself, "Some day that well will be pumped dry, but there
is a cruse of oil which will never run dry—one that will flow
on forever and ever." We should be anxious for people to know
about the oil which in the lamp of God's Word produces a light
that shines across the darkness of this world in order that men
may find their way to Jesus Christ, the one who alone can save
and who can solve their problems, whatever they may be.[1]

Ernest C. Manning, Premier of Alberta, Canada

On a brilliant, big-sky summer day typical for July in northern
Canada, fifty finely dressed city types, belying the ruggedness of
the muskeg and boreal forest that surrounded them, clustered on a
designated spot to inaugurate an ultra-modern enterprise. The spot
rested on cleared land butting up against the once sleepy fur-trap-
ping town of Fort McMurray, Alberta, located three hundred miles
north of Edmonton.

Sleepy gave way to bustle July 2, 1964, as government officials,
corporate executives, and members of the press enjoyed a luncheon and opening ceremony and toured the site of the Athabasca
oil sands owned by Great Canadian Oil Sands Limited (GCOS).
The activities were punctuated by bold proclamations, all in keeping with the unbridled confidence of the moment. Over lunch,

S. D. Bechtel, GCOS's lead construction contractor, and Clarence Thayer, GCOS president, announced that the project "ranks high among the great industrial breakthroughs of the century," and touted its soaring potential. The highlight moment came at the opening ceremony itself, which assumed an air of religiosity. As if to caution against an enthusiasm without higher purpose, Revd Sylvio Lasage of St. John Baptist Church led his makeshift congregation in prayer, urging the luminaries to appreciate the ultimate significance of their handiwork. Next, Alberta Premier Ernest Manning, a Baptist who spoke Lasage's language, capped the festivities off with an invocation of God's blessing then drove a commemorative stake into the ground. Soldered to the stake was a plaque that summarized the superlative nature of the GCOS venture, the roots of its conception, and declared it officially begun.[2]

The blend of human energy and spiritual resolve witnessed around Fort McMurray in the summer of 1964 grew in scope over the next three years, as lofty visions became reality. By 1966, corporate newspapers were heralding the grand prospects of GCOS. Much of the excitement revolved around the mammoth machinery that was being readied by LeTourneau Incorporated, the earthmoving equipment company started by a Texas-based Christian businessman named R. G. LeTourneau. Spread over 30,000 square miles, with deposits 150 feet thick, the Athabasca oil sands represented 600 billion barrels of oil. Assuming the monumental task of extracting this "wealth under the layer cake" were gigantic bucketwheel excavators and LeTourneau's eighty-five-ton dump trucks and twenty-ton loaders, which he identified as God-given conduits for man's dominion over the earth.[3]

Finally, in late summer of 1967, the people and machinery that comprised GCOS were ready. For three years, GCOS's press release explained, three thousand workers had labored round-the-clock, turning a 235 million dollar investment into the "world's first commercial venture" to produce synthetic crude out of bitumen. Created to change the world, the GCOS was also a world's creation: over the course of thirty-six months, a multinational multitude of scientists, engineers, and equipment operators had shaped a mass of international supplies into an enormous complex able to extract "one of the world's largest single energy resources." Drawn to the unforgiving Canadian North from "comfortable cities, modest farms, rustic villages," all of GCOS's hard-working laborers and their hard-won victories, it was stressed, stood as a "tribute to man's inventiveness and determination [to overcome] the obstacles of nature" and a signal that the "dawn of a new age" had arrived.[4]

For all of the boilerplate that executives used to promote their product, GCOS's official opening in August of 1967 also reverberated, as it had three years earlier, with a more somber religious beat. Included in the media extravaganza at the plant's opening was a forty-five-minute film produced for the occasion called *Athabasca*, which celebrated the oil sands project as a benevolent effort to harness earth's bounty and civilize an uncivilized realm. Its creators cast special light on the industrialist in charge of the civilizing: J. Howard Pew, whose presence on screen and at the project's sod-turning events in 1964 and 1967 was meant to remind employees that Protestant ethics shaped the entire affair. As the former president of Sun Oil Company (Sunoco), now chairman of its board of directors (GCOS was Sunoco's subsidiary), Pew was filmed commanding the company's posh Philadelphia headquarters. A devout Presbyterian, Pew made it known that his company's successes grew out of his steadfast commitment to Christ, which is why he chose to christen functions like GCOS's unfurling with a prayer:

> Almighty God, we ask they Divine blessing. . . . Give us grateful
> hearts for the many benefits that we have enjoyed in the past and
> help us to trust in Thee as we face the future. May we remember
> the service and sacrifice of those who have helped build our
> industry. May Thy guiding spirit continue to be with the officers and
> employees of our Company that their mutual understanding may be
> for the betterment of us all.

Amid the excitement of the GCOS venture, *Athabasca*'s producers hoped that viewers would extract a quieter, fundamental truth from Pew's life: here was a man whose entrustment of nature's bounties gave meaning to his life, here was a man whose faith in God made the search for black gold something existential, something sacred, something good.[5]

As evidenced in all the action and personalities surrounding GCOS's development, Pew was hardly alone in his worldview. Indeed, what we see illustrated in the GCOS project speaks to other extractable truths, these ones historical. First, it underscores the uniquely strong bond that evangelical Protestantism and the petroleum sector shared in the twentieth century, especially at their moments of ascendancy in the Cold War years. Like Pew, countless Bible believers in North America's oil patches saw petroleum as their special providence to be used industriously for the advancement of kingdoms of their making. Viewing their place in the oil sector as divinely appointed, never doubting the virtues of their quest, they brought their theology to bear on temporal issues of energy governance, used monies accrued through secular business to build sacred empires (churches, missionary agencies), and relied on religion to facilitate and legitimate the construction of modern petroleum's most elaborate apparatuses of extraction.

This wedding of evangelical fervor to the business of oil highlights a second truth, one that historians should ponder when chronicling modern America. Among the most exciting impetuses in recent scholarship has been renewed study of American economic, political, and religious history in global contexts. Although pursuing the same goal—to account for the United States' development in the world—these lines of inquiry have typically unfolded parallel to one another, with religion set farthest apart from the other agents of change. Yet the GCOS enterprise demonstrates the value of embedding matters of faith in matters of international affairs, and of linking religious dynamics to transnational flows of money and raw materials. One of the standard bearers of the new global history is Sven Beckert's *Empire of Cotton*, which tracks the illustrious life of a commodity over millennia and multiple terrains. The successor to white gold as earth's most bountiful commodity, black gold warrants similar treatment, though with faith factored in. Commodities like cotton and oil, after all, are valuable for their values-making weight: besides lending wealth to some, burdens of labor to others, they also elicit millennial dreams, stir notions of exceptionalism, drive religious laborers to and from distant shores, and offer reason and means for church expansion. GCOS's story demands this integrated approach.[6]

It also reveals a third truth: that the type of transnational exchange apparent in the history of GCOS has always been multilateral and multidirectional. As a more textured account of the venture will further demonstrate, this fruitful partnership of oil and evangelical Protestantism was the product of a world system, in which theologies of resource management, corporate and churchly alliances, financial incentives and political interests, and outcomes of lasting import flowed into and out of northern Alberta from multiple angles. Although American initiative loomed large in Fort McMurray, it functioned alongside and in conjunction with homegrown designs derived from a host of intercontinental influences. A closer look at the GCOS's longer gestation and three of its God-fearing architects— J. Howard Pew, R. G. LeTourneau, and especially Ernest Manning—will reaffirm this point. Each represents a distinctive way in which evangelicalism's enchantment with oil produced sweeping effects. Together they illustrate how its association with this resource has always been an all-encompassing, universal affair.[7]

Despite GCOS's declarations in 1967 that stressed the careful planning behind the Athabasca oil sands project, in fact a much longer strand of luck and circumstances allowed it to reach this apex, a strand reaching back in time to the 1920s and anxiousness by Alberta's resident engineers and politicians to generate a viable homegrown oil industry.

On the technical side, it was Karl Clark, a metallurgist at the University of Alberta, who took the lead in researching the oil sands. The thousands of acres of oleaginous muskeg that encircled Fort McMurray had long been known to contain valuable deposits. Indigenous peoples, European fur trappers, and wanderlusts who made their way to the Athabasca region to carve out independent lives had always seen the bituminous sands as odd and mysterious but useful—for waterproofing canoes, medicinal purposes, and even religious ceremony. Commercially, however, the sands lacked application, and processing them was too difficult to make it worth the while. This changed in the 1920s when Clark invented a hot water separation process that essentially boiled the oil out of the soil, and facilitated development of the tar for wider use. Still expensive to implement, Clark nevertheless knew that his system would work, and be profitable, provided major players—a large corporation and willing government—stepped up to help.[8]

Alberta premier Ernest Manning, practical and big picture in his vision, soon assumed the task of making Clark's inventiveness count for the betterment of the entire province. Manning's assignment, in this regard, resonated with his vocational aspirations as a Christian politician sensitive to the needs of his constituents but also tuned to the transnational flows of religious and political ideas. His worldview was cultivated through years of tireless work in Alberta's Social Credit Party, the continent's most successful populist movement of the twentieth century. During the early heyday of this movement in the 1920s and 1930s, Manning came under the tutelage of two men, both of whom operated in a vast orb of intellectual give-and-take.

The first of these was the guru of the Social Credit movement, Major Clifford Hugh ("C.H.") Douglas. Manning's political philosophy stemmed from the interwar teachings of this British logician, whose ideas filtered into the United States, particularly populist strongholds like southern California, but found real traction in the British Commonwealth, especially its farther reaches of Australia and western Canada. At the core of Douglas's agenda was a call to reform the monetary system, which he, like other disenchanted capitalists at the time, believed was seriously broken. Douglas sought to address capitalism's failings not as socialists proposed, by centralizing production and making it more equitable through its nationalization, but by correcting deficiencies in the distribution of income and goods through a process of democratization. Douglas, in short, believed that the problem of distribution could be solved "without any disturbance of capitalism" by "a frontal attack on the modern financial system," which, in its top-heavy, monopolistic ways, had in his estimation "immobilized consumption" at society's grassroots. His was a technical more than ideological answer to the age.[9]

It was an answer that grew naturally out of his professional purview. Besides attending Cambridge University for a short time, Douglas's primary education came through employment with Westinghouse Electric Corporation and as Chief Engineer with the British government, with posts throughout the Empire. His economic theory was, accordingly, an attempt to apply lessons of this travel and rules of his trade to modern enterprise: stricter adherence to laws of distribution would, in his mind, lead to smoother mechanics in all facets of the capitalist machine, in the West but also in developing nations across the globe. The laws that he championed both in print and during his regular speaking engagements in Canada, Australia, New Zealand, Asia, and Scandinavia centered around two fundamental certainties: that smoother distribution of money to all citizens and the subsequent rise in their purchasing power, coupled with the institution of a logical price adjustment mechanism to ensure a "Just Price," would turn the working masses into empowered individual consumers, and at the macro-level free national economies from the stagnation and scarcity created by the greedy, powerful few. Although Douglas's mandates were popular in their own right, they also overlapped with those espoused by the Technocracy Movement, which enjoyed its own transnational popularity at this time. Some of Alberta's Social Credit proponents in fact cross-fertilized Technocracy's propositions with Douglas's. Besides entertaining ideas for alternative currency and money management, Social Credit and Technocracy advocates placed their trust in applied science as the answer to social problems, though the former wished for this science to be applied with a soul.[10]

The theology of Social Credit—the "soul" to Douglas's science—was provided by William "Bible Bill" Aberhart, the preacher-politician whose teachings won him the premiership of Alberta in 1935, and the deep admiration of Manning, his most ardent devotee. A proponent of exegetical teachings that planted him on the conservative side in the fundamentalist-modernist controversy that polarized Protestantism during the 1920s, Aberhart did all he could to shore up orthodoxy by founding the Calgary Prophetic Bible Institute, speaking in local churches, and preaching on his radio program, *Back to the Bible Hour*. His labors had wide appeal in the fledgling province, particularly among its American farmers and ranchers, recently relocated US plainsmen who comprised a majority in southern Alberta. Aberhart pursued politics with the same zest through Social Credit's platform of economic redistribution and community values, initiatives that had potency during the Depression. Aberhart's agenda earned him Alberta's head office, where he served for eight years. Having been educated by Aberhart at his Bible Institute, Manning slid easily into leadership in the premier's camp. Even prior to Aberhart's election,

Manning could be seen traveling the countryside with the barnstorming politician, junkets that the press referenced when deeming them a father-son team.[11]

In 1943, following Aberhart's sudden death, Manning ascended to his mentor's political post and simultaneously became Alberta's Minister of Mines and Minerals. Manning used his new authority to advance Aberhart's dogmas, though in tempered form. Whereas Aberhart was a fundamentalist who waged war for his beliefs, Manning was an irenic evangelical who bore witness to them in a diplomatic tone. This combination made him instant allies with American clerics and laymen who in the early 1940s began constructing the "New Evangelicalism" associated with a rising generation of moderate and culturally engaged preachers, laymen, and institutions such as Billy Graham, Charles Fuller, Fuller Seminary (California), and missionary agencies like Wycliffe Bible Translators. Between 1943 and 1947, Manning in fact made it his mission to enlist in several New Evangelical undertakings. He organized branches of the International Christian Business Men's Committee, spoke on behalf of the Gideons and Billy Graham, sat on many ministerial boards, and saw to it that America's leading revivalists made their way north to Calgary and Edmonton for mass meetings. Manning's pause from the work of his office to host California preacher-businessman Charles Fuller on a three-day provincial speaking tour in 1947 typified his resolve to prioritize his faith initiatives over political ones.[12]

In truth, however, he never considered the political secondary. Manning believed that if linked to evangelism, the quest to save individual souls with the New Testament gospel, politics could serve as an essential rejoinder to society's problems. "We cannot purify polluted water in a well merely by painting the outside of the pump," he would say; purification needed to happen first through a personal relationship with God, second through a willingness to act vigorously for social reform. His message that statecraft and faith should mix, and that Christian citizens needed to take ownership of their communities, did indeed stir the masses, at home as well as throughout the United States and British Commonwealth. "As I travel," he offered in 1950, "I frequently meet those who think it strange that a man in public life should be interested in the Bible. ... I wonder why." "If you are a realist you cannot deny the fact that beneath and behind all of our human and material problems there lies the one basic problem of man's broken relationship to his God." Under Manning, Social Credit continued to rally for plain people who sought escape from the clutches of eastern banks and corporate elites. Manning did not follow Douglas's doctrines to the fullest by constructing alternative credit-creating agencies and script. In his politics, as in his religion, he was more centrist

than hard-core ideological. But he did make government responsible for leveling capitalism's playing field, providing citizens with freer access to a fairer
market, and sustaining a "share-the-wealth" spirit.[13]

Manning's administration of oil reflected this pragmatism. Although the
Minister of Minerals was aware of the tar sands in Fort McMurray, his early
concerns were in developing conventional oil supplies: this, he believed, was
the easier ticket to collective wealth. His schema received a momentous boost
in 1947 when the Imperial Oil Company tapped crude on farmland in the
Leduc field, just south of Edmonton. Under the guidance of Vern "Dry Hole"
Hunter (colleagues mocked his numerous failures), and before five hundred
witnesses, an Imperial team of roughnecks opened the valves and flared the
well of their discovery rig. The flames shot fifty feet into the air and could
be seen in Edmonton, where Imperial executives partied. Within days of the
discovery other petroleum companies were investing heavily in Alberta; by
the end of the year thirty-one wells were pumping 3,500 barrels per day from
the field. Though modest, the numbers proved that Alberta was now a player
in international petroleum.[14]

As head of a new oil-rich constituency Manning gained instant sway across
national lines. The Leduc find was particularly important to an embattled
sector of North American oil: independent oilmen, small producers whose
post–World War II status had declined amid global petroleum's shift from the
American Southwest to Saudi Arabia. As American major companies turned
their attention to the voluminous subterranean pools of the Middle East, and
transformed the United States into an oil importer, the wildcatters of Texas and
Oklahoma lost leverage. As their political clout diminished, their outcries for a
revitalized domestic oil industry increased. Proximate and overseen by a politician who shared their values, Alberta's oil breakthrough struck these oilers as a
spectacular opportunity for their business, their politics, and for many of them,
their faith: here was a new frontier on which they could reap profits and sell
the virtues of local crude to a North American citizenry pressed by Cold War
anxieties, and paranoid about controlling foreign influences, be they Saudis
or Soviets. Recognizing this, Manning spent the years after the Leduc strike
shoring up already robust north–south ties between Alberta and the American
West, and making his dominion a wildcatter's paradise.

Manning's speaking itinerary grew accordingly during this time,
both in size and diversity. Even as he continued to crisscross the continent
preaching on the radio and in pulpits about the essence of fundamentalist
Christianity, he assumed a more pressing schedule of business engagements,
especially with executives, engineers, and politicians in the Southwest's oil
sector. Preaching in the region's churches on Sunday, he sermonized in its

oil associations Monday through Saturday. He completed the latter task with equal enthusiasm because in his mind Alberta had a God-given gift to offer all North Americans: a cheaper, safer supply of oil mined in accordance with Christian principles. Indeed, little separated Manning's evangelical and petroleum gospels. His was a totalizing conviction that the purest faith and fuel values were those that allowed individuals to draw freely the fortunes of God's word and God's earth.

By the early 1950s, evangelical and oil leaders in the United States were embracing Manning as a shining symbol of applied Christianity and home-grown resolve in the global fight for oil independence. One South Carolina Baptist expressed a common sentiment in American church circles when composing a letter to Manning. "We appreciate your testimony and your Christian influence. We believe the Lord has great plans for you. We shall look forward to fellowship with you in days that are ahead." This sentiment flowed upward from the grassroots as well. As Manning's reputation grew in size so too did the volume of his daily mail, which became inundated with requests from US citizens for his autograph, photo, or latest speech. American oilmen were equally welcoming of Manning and his message. They were drawn to a number of his proclamations on behalf of independent oil, and though not uniformly, heralded his blend of theology and politics in defense of the domestic producer.[15]

Three aspects of Manning's outlook particularly appealed to them, with the first impinging on policy. As his province's oil business grew, Manning framed a petroleum plan that maintained Social Credit's share-the-wealth imperatives. Manning, like C. H. Douglas, had no desire to restructure capitalism; he just wanted to make it less prone to excess and undemocratic tendencies. His mineral policy was thus simple but tough: to "ensure that the natural resources of the Province [were] developed in the interests of the people as a whole, under the most equitable conditions and with the greatest measure of freedom from regimentation." What did this mean? Although welcoming of corporate investment in Alberta's fields, Manning set firm limits. Oil companies were allowed to lease no more than 200,000 acres of Crown land for exploration and required to pay hefty deposits in advance of their work, which was reviewed yearly. Once oil was discovered, companies were allowed to continue leasing half of the allotted land but forced to set aside the other half as a Crown Reserve to be developed by the provincial government. "By this procedure," Manning proclaimed, "the Government precludes all possibility of any monopoly getting control of the natural resources of the province." There was another way that the producer's loss became the purchaser's gain. Once a company developed a field it had to pay royalties (up to 15 percent) back to the people of Alberta. In this manner, Manning added, citizens were guaranteed that private enterprise would be "properly directed" toward the public good. And it guaranteed that citizens would get their piece of petroleum's lucrative pie. For some American oilmen, Southwestern independents included, Manning's policies seemed heavy-handed, and their wishes for less government handling would eventually force him to soften his stand. But even in their caution, independent producers openly celebrated Alberta's stand against big oil. In this Canadian outpost, they saw a politician who was leveling the playing field for corporations of any size and staring down the "tyranny of monopoly."[16]

If Manning was a free enterpriser with a plain-folk edge, he was also a technocrat who privileged the engineer over Wall Street executives, Ivy League intellectuals, and government bureaucrats. This trait too—one grafted from Douglas—struck a chord with American allies. In his handling of oil, Manning relied on technological experts to draft reports and policies, design the mechanisms to extract and protect the province's resources, converse and compare notes with tacticians in other parts of the world, and generally manage everything. There was nothing surprising about this approach, since the superstructure of post–World War II petroleum demanded special knowledge. Still, Manning's reliance on technical thinkers was also testament to the Social Credit experience, which privileged those who thought in utilitarian terms and sought to make society better through applications (not abstractions) of truth. In this sense, Manning agreed with J. R. White, president of Imperial Oil, who told his audience of engineers at a national gathering in Calgary in 1954 that their status in the West was singular, for they were the ones who had imagined their region and its natural resources into being and who were now constructing a civilization out of chaos. As Manning would add at one of his own addresses to engineers, theirs was the great privilege and responsibility to mold physical material into a shape that God had intended for it. The importance Manning placed on engineers allowed him a special hearing with the petroleum guilds that he frequented throughout North America. Able to speak to them as someone who shared their deep distrust of knowledge-makers on Wall Street and in the Ivory Tower, those operating far from the dirt, grease, and splendor of their immediate environments, Manning struck a chord that rang deeper than politics. It was existential.[17]

There was yet a third aspect of Manning's oil ideology that resonated with many Southwestern independents, and that was its connection to cosmic purpose. Manning, like Aberhart before him, held to a premillennial dispensationalist view, which relied on a literalist reading of Scripture to interpret world events. As a premillennialist with technocratic sympathies, Manning continually looked to decode signs of societal strain as evidence that Christ's return was nigh. Most of his colleagues in the New Evangelicalism practiced the same approach. They believed that it was up to individual Christians to prepare society for the end of time, which in light of nuclear armament and Soviet communism appeared to be imminent. But Manning's premillennialism also ratified his popularity in broader spheres of Southwestern crude. Manning in fact consciously connected his eschatology to prevailing intellectual strands in independent oil that stressed crisis. It was at this moment that M. King Hubbert, a founder of Technocracy, crafted his theory of "peak oil," which held that US domestic production would crest by 1971 then steadily decline. The apocalyptic feel of this prediction confirmed Manning's belief that the world was entering its last phase. Not only did time seem to be running out on America—God's City on a Hill—but it was now favoring non-Christians located in the very place to which Christ would return for his followers: the Middle East. His response was twofold: first, to keep his people's eyes glued on events in the Middle East, where rising oil production and attending political power seemed to portent Christ's return, and second, to extract expeditiously whatever oil supplies were left under their soil before their dispensation expired. In Manning's scheme it was wildcatters who offered North Americans a last glimmer of hope: they alone had the courage to find new reserves and inspire patriots with pure capitalist drive.[18]

With remarkable ease Manning thus filtered eschatology and economics into a political creed that could unite oil patch citizens in the United States and Canada. In his speeches, writings, and legislation he shaped the way millions of Christians in both country's thought about energy and their place in the world, and synchronized theologies of salvation and stewardship with the politics of entrepreneurialism and access to nature's resources.

His networking on behalf of this dogma was indeed invaluable to the construction of independent oil's political front. Even as he spent the early 1950s traveling on a north–south axis to the United States, networking with like-minded evangelicals, he also approached oil producers as partners in Alberta's cause. At a summer meeting of the Interstate Oil Compact Commission, held in Banff in September 1952, Manning thanked his guests for taking their conference north of the border: "May I pay tribute to the good judgment of those responsible for arranging to hold this year's meeting in the province now recognized as the Texas of Canada." A short time later, he paid tribute to Texas in person by speaking at the Mid-Continent Oil & Gas Association in San Antonio. Texas oilmen publicized his plain-folk qualities in advance of his arrival. "One of the most important 'oil executives' in North America is a tall, slim fellow who lives on a small farm, helps with farm chores from cattle feeding to riding a tractor, conducts a weekly religious broadcast and is paid about $15,000 a year by his Provincial Government." Manning used these opportunities to encourage his brethren to take a forceful stand for Christian democracy. "The world situation today is precarious," he proclaimed at the Banff gathering:

> If we are content to sit back and leave to a handful of men in the world councils of today the responsibility of trying to work out some master plan to superimpose on the human race, from the top down, in the hope of solving this tremendous problem confronting all mankind, we may be idealists but, I suggest, we are not being realists. If we are going to make progress in this . . . then we have to recognize that as individual citizens, we have an inescapable responsibility to do our part to that end, and I am convinced that it is only when we as individual citizens assume that responsibility that we will see progress made.

Wildcatters from both sides of the forty-ninth parallel flooded Manning's office with requests for written copies of this speech so that they could spread the word; revival was coming.[19]

Among the friendships strengthened during Manning's sojourns was that which he shared with R. G. LeTourneau, someone whose labor bridged evangelicalism and oil, and whose drive for revivalism was unceasing. An advocate of the New Evangelical movement, LeTourneau was from a Canadian family who shared Manning's Prairie-populist sensibilities. Born in the 1880s, he achieved his success in the 1930s while turning his company into one of the nation's leading manufacturers of heavy machinery, and his expansive philanthropic work into a cause célèbre among evangelicals. While outside his factory he spoke on behalf of the National Association of Manufacturers and free enterprise (and against the New Deal), with the Christian Business Men's Committee International (CBMCI) he championed bootstrap initiative in the boardroom as well as church pew. Inside his factory, meanwhile, he trained workers in a technical institute. There they learned how Scripture was technologically sound; how the laws of traction and torque applied to evangelism, and grades of steel illustrated stages of Christian growth.[20]

Like Manning, LeTourneau gained international recognition in the 1940s. During World War II, his factories in Illinois, Georgia, and Mississippi buzzed with activity, and turned out seventy-eight new inventions, machinery that carried men ashore at Normandy and carved roads out of jungles in the South Pacific and deserts in North Africa. At war's end 70 percent of all heavy earthmoving equipment used by the allies had been built in his plants.

Already producing land-moving machines for subterranean extraction, in the late 1940s he expanded his reach by building offshore platforms that could offer any oil company access to the sea. His first platform, the industry's first mobile offshore apparatus of its kind, was commissioned for George H. W. Bush, president of the Zapata Off-Shore Company. LeTourneau unveiled the 4,000-ton apparatus in 1954, then a few months later, at a ribbon-cutting ceremony attended by Bush and a young George W. Bush, handed control of it to Zapata for service in the Gulf of Mexico.[21]

LeTourneau's second launch to wider influence came by relocating his operation to Longview, Texas. The Longview plant allowed him proximity both to the area's flourishing oil companies and to the expanding international market they sought to capture. In his 88,000 square-foot steel mill, workers produced 25 tons of molten steel every three hours, and then transported it to the factory where behemoth machines were built for use in the world's largest mines and oil fields. Before being shipped to South America and the Middle East, each piece of equipment was tested on the 12,000 acres of proving grounds. The impressive operation was not strictly business-related; for LeTourneau the massive production promised a massive payoff in religious terms as well. Indeed, as he articulated it while speaking at the 1951 World Trade Conference, the testing he carried out in Texas and the machines he exported promised a new order. "God gave us the raw materials to work with for nothing, and there is plenty to be had if we go to work and produce the things we want." In building machines that could exploit nature's reserves, LeTourneau believed he was acting out God's will for humans to harvest the earth. And as an ardent premillennialist, conversant with Manning in end-times belief, he was certain that the harvesting needed to be expeditious because Christ would surely return soon.[22]

LeTourneau fulfilled this maxim in other contexts, for instance, by expanding LeTourneau Technical Institute and revamping it to meet students' "spiritual requirements of the modern age; educational demands of a scholastic aid; [and] practical needs of a technical age." By the mid-1950s, LeTourneau was sending his graduates to all four corners of the globe. While some stayed on with the company as engineers, others became missionaries with Wycliffe Bible Translators (particularly its transportation wing, Jungle Aviation and Radio Service), and Mission Aviation Fellowship (MAF). LeTourneau was particularly intent on opening up the jungles of South America to evangelism and modernization, initiatives that implicated oil exploration. Wycliffe and MAF's use of Shell Oil camps to reach the isolated Huaorani tribes of eastern Ecuador was but one example of this collaboration. The resulting murder by Huaroani warriors of five missionaries in 1956 stunned LeTourneau and his peers, yet reaffirmed their resolve to draw the world's "lost" peoples and their hidden riches into God's divine plan.[23]

In some cases, LeTourneau's students helped populate missionary bases that he himself established on the Amazon fringe as a model of Christian capitalism for the world to embrace. Here too he displayed the same willingness as his brethren to fuse a crusade for lost souls with a campaign for minerals. His most successful venture transpired in Peru. There, in the late 1950s, he reached an agreement with Peruvian President Manuel Odria and Peruvian oilmen, whereby he would complete thirty-one miles of the Trans-Andean Highway, linking the Amazonian hinterland with the Pacific, in exchange for a million acres of uncultivated land. For Odria, the plan promised to prepare the hinterland for Mobil and Gulf's Peruvian subsidiaries. Land secured, the engineer-evangelist began leveling forests for Tournavista, a community of natives and missionaries that implemented his plan for a free Christian economy, not unlike Manning and Social Credit's, that might be deemed a blueprint for Third World societies and buttress against the encroaching influences of Soviet communism.[24]

Even as he looked to the Global South for opportunities, LeTourneau found more reason to turn north to his family's native land. The manufacturer had always been active in Canada, using ties with friends in government to generate construction contracts, but Manning's presence there meant something more for him. While Manning's sermons and travels through terrain with which he was familiar sparked LeTourneau's interest in the premier, LeTourneau's sense of familiarity with the Canadian province and its leader intensified through his own sojourns as well. The manufacturer's visit to Edmonton in the late 1940s was typical, in this regard: besides allowing him a chance to speak to the city's Christian industrialists about his vocational aspirations, it also afforded him time with Manning, who guaranteed a warm, friendly welcome. Through subsequent visits, and their sustained co-activism within the New Evangelical movement, Manning and LeTourneau nurtured a relationship that would affect all Albertans.[25]

Albertans began feeling its effects in the late 1950s and early 1960s. Bolstered by his friendships with LeTourneau and other American industrialists, concerned about his province's need to grow, not simply sustain, its oil sector, yet always determined to protect his citizenry's best interests, Manning tried to anticipate next steps. Karl Clark, longtime chief metallurgist and proponent of the Athabasca oil sands, helped nudge Manning along in the new direction. After further perfecting his hot water process that facilitated development of the sands, Clark announced in 1953 that the time had definitely come for a move "by big oil companies." Big money and major players were desperately needed. Wanting to extend Alberta's international profile, yet wary of spending the exorbitant funds needed to extract usable oil from the Athabasca tar sands, Manning agreed with Clark and started soliciting the corporate sector.[26]

Sunoco soon appeared, checkbook in hand. The Pew's family-owned, Philadelphia-based company, with operations centered in the Southwest, was in fact already making its move, acquiring patents and leases and sending geologists into the Athabasca area. Under the guidance of Sunoco vice president and future GCOS president Clarence Thayer, Sunoco's interest in Alberta had already become tangible. Besides demonstrating a command of oil frontiers, Thayer had helped commercialize the Houdry catalytic cracking process, which placed Sunoco at the forefront of oil manufacturing in the 1930s, so his high opinions of the Alberta prospects were respected at headquarters. There, company chief J. Howard Pew organized his own fascinations with Alberta's oil sands in a thick file labeled "Athabasca Tar Sands," which he would excitedly show to anyone who would oblige him. Urged on by Thayer and his own obsession, Pew decided to take the biggest gamble in company history by committing a quarter of a billion dollars to Clark's technology and the creation of GCOS in 1952. Besides breaking company records, this payout represented the "largest single private investment" ever made in Canada. As one Sunoco insider noted, this "was a daring venture into an un-known field," one that "jolted Wall Street's appraisal of Sun Oil as a conservative company." Pew and Manning would manage this investment together over the coming years, as business partners and fellow believers.[27]

Pew's willingness to take such a heavy risk was not so out of character, especially considering his family's long ties to wildcatting. Pew was born to Joseph Newton (J.N.) Pew, a "farm boy from Pennsylvania" who grew up in a Presbyterian family that taught him to "pray unashamedly" and weigh his "behavior against the Ten Commandments." At the age of eleven, Pew Sr. grew fascinated with oil speculation in Titusville, just 40 miles away, and at the age of twenty he moved to the boomtown to start a gas business. For the next three decades, he and his company floundered in the "oligopolistic environment" ruled by Standard Oil, but in 1901 Sun Company, as it was then known, achieved its breakthrough. Within days of Lucas 1's geyser at Spindletop, in Beaumont, Texas, which thrust American oil to the forefront of global production, J. Edgar Pew, Joseph's nephew, joined the human deluge of this Gulf town, and through the acquisition of numerous drill sites, guaranteed Sun a foothold in this Southwestern hub. Over the next two decades, Edgar continued to expand Sun's holdings throughout the region, making it competitive even against corporate heavyweights like Texaco and Gulf.[28]

J. Howard Pew was the man responsible for Sun's competitive edge. The young, Cornell-trained engineer assumed head executive responsibilities in 1912. Joining Howard in the head office was his younger brother, Joseph Pew Jr., who would serve as his right hand for the next fifty years. For most of Howard's presidency, the renamed Sun Oil Company remained a family-run operation, something his father decreed. Pew Sr. also set Sunoco on a conservative fiscal path by resisting debt financing and high-risk ventures. While keeping the company in the black, this strategy prevented it from expanding. Under Howard, Sunoco became slightly more daring in its outlook. Between the 1910s and late 1940s, he shaped it into a mid-major oil company whose combination of fiscal responsibility, savvy marketing, and creative manufacturing made it a vital player in the industry. Sunoco's most dramatic growth came during World War II when it used its new catalytic refining process to make aviation gasoline, which proved crucial to the US war effort. Its net crude production increased 143 percent during the war years, and by 1947 Sunoco boasted it had grown by "40 times" since Howard became CEO thirty-five years earlier.[29]

Although resigning as president in 1947, ceding control to Robert Dunlop, the first non-family member to hold the post, Howard maintained his authority as Director of the Board. In many ways, his power increased with the flexibility of his new post, and he used it to broaden his company's reach. Pew worried about an American oil shortage, as well as about smaller companies losing their ability to compete with majors in far-flung frontiers like the Middle East. Although self-identifying with the Southwestern independent oil companies, Pew and Sunoco enjoyed more resources at their disposal than the average Texas wildcat operation, so he pushed boundaries on behalf of his peers. He instructed Sunoco to investigate foreign fields, send geologists into remote regions, and aggressively pursue a sphere of international influence. By the 1960s, Sunoco was refining in Canada and Venezuela, marketing its products well beyond the US border, carrying a payroll of 20,000 persons worldwide, and operating in every area of the industry, "from drilling and producing through transportation and manufacturing to distribution," making it one of the most successful mid-majors in the "Free World."[30]

Pew also extended his company's reach into politics, once again on behalf of the interests of small producers. Because of his family's deep antipathy toward Standard Oil and its ingrained suspicions of centralized government, a young Howard had internalized the politics of the wildcatter. In the 1930s and 1940s, in a tone that matched his father's in the 1880s and 1890s, he railed against the oil industry's majors that wanted to increase regulations in order to temper fluctuations in pricing that came with overproduction. Fearful that small companies would succumb to large ones, which enjoyed economy of scale and price-setting abilities, Pew set out to democratize petroleum by helping a number of independent oil associations lobby for deregulated markets and local control. In this same vein, he, along with his brother, Joseph, a powerbroker in the Republican Party, played active roles in opposing the New Deal state. Willing, in this instance, to join hands with monopolistic types they opposed in the oil sector, the Pews helped populate the American Liberty League and stir up anti–New Deal sentiment.[31]

Meanwhile, thanks to Sunoco's inestimable role in national defense during World War II, Pew gained an official voice in Washington, which he used to champion independent oil's political interests abroad. Between 1943 and 1952, as US oil companies looked to the Middle East for new supplies, the federal government and US oil's majors tried to iron out an Anglo-American Petroleum Agreement that would minimize the ability of British oil companies "to exclude American interests" from their territories and bring an "end to the restrictive provisions of the Red Line Agreement of 1928." Through international cooperation, American and British leaders and oil officials hoped to stabilize process of exploration, extraction, and production in petroleum's hot zones. For smaller companies, the agreement smacked of collusion, something Pew stressed. He let Senate Foreign Relations Committee members know that the Anglo-American agreement was a "first step in . . . [a] plan for a super-state control covering the petroleum industry in all parts of the world." Pew played no small part in killing this agreement—it would flounder in the late 1940s and die in 1952—nor in ensuring that an aggressively nationalist foreign policy, which in his mind best protected the interests of all oil companies, would become ensconced in the American Cold War outlook.[32]

In all of these political endeavors, Pew welcomed the role of watchdog on behalf of the bootstrap, laissez-faire, evangelical-minded wildcatter, whom he believed embodied American values' purest form. "Nature has been bountiful in the supply of this resource, and we have barely scratched the surface," he charged when speaking out against stricter regulation of petroleum at home and abroad. Why quell individual drive in the present by "preserving supplies of petroleum for the use of generations yet unborn[?]" Echoing independent's nonconformist pleas, he announced that he "didn't want a nurse for his business, nor did he want anyone else to have one." Pew did not want a "nurse" for his church either. Even as he joined forces with independent oilmen to fight centralizing forces in business and government, Pew also enlisted in conservative Protestantism's fight against the progressive tendencies of their liberal counterparts. He saw these fights in parallel terms: in his eyes, preserving the purity of the Protestant church and the purity of oil's founding spirit were the same, since both sought preservation of the uncompromising, pioneering individualism that centered American Christianity and capitalism.[33]

Here too he followed his father's lead by donating to evangelical causes. Pew Sr. had linked Sun to fundamentalist Protestantism by sending company profits to Dwight L. Moody, the face of orthodoxy in his day, and his employees via company train to Billy Sunday's revivals. In the post–World War II years, the junior Pew followed the example by becoming the chief financial backer of the New Evangelicalism. Internally, he continued his father's pattern of imposing Christian orthodoxy on Sunoco's corporate culture. When addressing company gatherings, Pew practiced exegesis: sermons on the origins of the King James Bible or modernist theological trends were staples in his repertoire. His hand in drafting a company creed that championed Christian patriotism in the context of Cold War petroleum was obvious as well:

> We Believe in America as a land able under God to enrich its people,
> both materially and spiritually. . . . We believe our Company's
> principal role in America's future will be to develop petroleum . . .
> into high quality products for sale at competitive prices and to
> provide such services as will help us to accomplish these ends most
> effectively. We believe that the competitive system of free markets
> is the only effective regulator of economic enterprise, the only
> guarantor of efficient public service, and the indispensable protector
> not only of economic freedom but of all American freedom and
> opportunity. With these principles as our guides, we shall strive to
> manage our affairs so as to reflect credit upon our Company, our
> Industry, and our Country.

Thanks to Howard, such providential assurances colored Sunoco's global vision as well. Although shaped by an increasingly sophisticated science of oil exploration, Sunoco's globalization in the mid-twentieth century never shunned the religious sensibilities of an earlier age. Calling on their geologists to be "present-day Jeremiahs," prophets willing to sacrifice for oil's advance, the Pew brethren blended biblical requisites of evangelism with requirements of the multinational corporation. They sent their "Jeremiahs" into South America's jungles and told them to spread Christian democracy and capitalism even as they searched for the next untapped pool.[34]

In his determination for religious outreach, Pew found a key ally of singular stature, the "D. L. Moody" of his day: Billy Graham. With fewer company responsibilities holding him back, Howard determined to funnel his energy into conservative causes through the Pew family's new charitable trust. Wanting to match the more liberal Rockefeller Foundation's every move, he nurtured economic ties with the nation's leading conservative seminaries (including Fuller Seminary), missionary agencies (such as Wycliffe), and ecumenical organizations, most notably the National Association of Evangelicals (NAE). A cog in these New Evangelical machines, Graham saw Pew as vital to the success of a reengaged orthodoxy. His courting of the petro-capitalist was in keeping with his own enchantment with black gold. At the moment of his breakthrough during the early Cold War, Graham counted on numerous oilmen for help. While in his ecumenism he networked with Herbert Taylor, a former executive with Sinclair Oil who helped guide the NAE, in his home church (First Baptist in Dallas, Texas) he worshiped with members of the Hunt family and mingled with the Murchisons. Meanwhile, he conversed frequently with Sid Richardson, whose clout ties gave him inside access to halls of power.

Graham gave as much as he received in this reciprocity. His access to the hearts and minds of Americans helped oil as it sought to redeem itself in the court of public opinion. Since the 1920s, average Americans had questioned the "Hobbesian" excesses of the oil industry, pointing to corporate scandals and oil titans' lavish lifestyles as proof. Graham's ability to accentuate the positives in this industry—its throwback values of individual initiative and capitalist drive—proved invaluable. In this formative moment, he counseled "titans" like Richardson into conversion experiences, then produced movies that told their salvation stories, two of which were called *Mr. Texas* (1951) and *Oil Town, U.S.A* (1953). Thanks to Graham's deft use of popular media, New Evangelicals were thus able to recast petroleum's life story as a redemptive narrative of Christian America reclaiming it roots, which, amid an intensifying Cold War against "godless communism," carried immediate weight in wider public opinion.[35]

Graham changed more than American hearts and minds, however; his efforts affected oil diplomacy as well. In the early 1960s, as Sunoco looked more intently at the Athabasca region, Graham helped Pew and Manning find more reason and common ground for friendship. GCOS benefited from the strengthening ties. This is because the strengthening bonds developed at a vulnerable time in its development. In the fall of 1963 and spring of 1964, Sunoco officials pressed the Alberta government for permission to mine the oil sands. By now, Canada was central to American oil's foreign outlook. Even as the Middle East captured ever-increasing attention, US imports from Canadian oil sources rose dramatically, from 4.9 percent of total US oil imports in 1958 to 11.7 percent in 1962. By 1967, US imports from Canada would be 18.7 percent, compared to 8.3 percent from the Middle East. Within this unfolding reality, Alberta's oil sands became ever more appealing. The region's "potential to match Saudi Arabia in volume, if not cost of recovery," and the added benefit "of being more secure politically and strategically" were widely appreciated.[36]

Pew knew, then, that it was time to step up his company's commitment to the Athabasca experiment. In 1963, he and Sunoco officials visited Fort McMurray to forge a plan whereby GCOS could become fully operational; the anticipation that had been building since GCOS' creation in 1952 now had its outlet. A critical next step involved formal government approval for the project and its untested procedures of drawing oil wealth from the land. In November 1963, Sunoco executives testified before the Alberta Oil and Gas Conservation Board to secure all necessary permissions. After promising that the oil sands would not hinder the province's conventional oil production, which had continued to expand since the late 1940s and remained primary to government interests, Robert Dunlop highlighted the scale of corporate funds already committed to the project and outlined the terms of purchasing: while Sunoco would purchase 75 percent of the oil sands' production, Shell Canada Limited would purchase the other 25 percent.[37]

Sunoco received the desired approval then moved on to the next round of negotiations with Alberta's Premier. Throughout the first months of 1964, Ernest Manning's office wrestled with Sunoco over the terms of the GCOS venture. Though enthusiastic, Manning was nervous about how an American company would be received by rank-and-file Albertans. In one of several letters sent from the Office of the Premier, Manning insisted that Sunoco's "commercial development of the Athabasca Oil Sands" had to come with concessions: at the very least, a commitment to build a pipeline that suited Alberta's economic and environmental interests, a pledge to hire "local labor ... as far as it is reasonable and practicable to do so," and most important, an agreement that Alberta residents "be accorded an opportunity to purchase up to 15 percent of the initial equity stock of the Company at the same price and on the same terms as those applying to the purchase of such stock by the Sun Oil Company." Albertans, Manning asserted, were not going to give American business a free pass. Although a realist who knew that some degree of cooperation with larger corporations was inevitable, his Social Credit antipathies toward Wall Street and compulsion to protect the common good against excesses of capitalism were feelings he could not abandon, even at this critical juncture.[38]

Sunoco hedged in response, expressing worry that government enjoyed the upper hand. Besides imposing the extra burden of public investors, which added additional risk to an already risky enterprise, the Manning plan also seemed to reduce "Sun's ownership position" and "introduced dangers" by "compromising principles of free enterprise." In his summary dismissal of

Manning's demands, one Sunoco official clearly enunciated what his colleagues were feeling:

> Government is . . . involving themselves in affairs of private
> enterprise to a peculiar degree in suggesting rearrangement of
> issued equity that a corporation might consider fits its corporate
> circumstances. GCOS has authorized 9 million shares, the public
> knows this, and present shareholders approve. To subscribe to
> this particular Government observation might imply that GCOS
> directors would need to check with the Province of Alberta on future
> issues of shares even now authorized by shareholders.

The commentator hoped that his allies could still "impress the free enterprise atmosphere . . . as the project proceeds," but he did not question that the Pews' way clashed with the province's way. Although appreciative of Manning's sustained lobbying on behalf of the Southwestern oil agenda and in defense of the region's small producers, the Pews were not so willing to let such appreciation override their company's bottom-line.[39]

Between 1964 and early 1965, Sunoco and Alberta officials continued to negotiate, even as the project moved forward, but relations remained a bit tense. As developments in the corporate world evolved, exchanges in the church world intensified. With Graham serving as mediator, Pew and Manning began exchanging letters, and soon the correspondence assumed a friendliness that was strengthened by talk about the Bible. In his missives, Pew told of upcoming church conferences, forwarded favorite books (*Calvin*, by Francois Wendel, *The Man God Mastered*, by Jean Cadier), and asked if he could use Manning's sermons (no doubt in company settings). Manning responded by sending the sermons, along with thanks for the books, which his son (Preston) was "now perusing with great interest." In another letter the politician encouraged the oilman to continue fighting for the fundamentals. "The need for aroused Christian laymen to take an uncompromising stand for the faith once delivered was never greater than at the present time, particularly in view of the fact that so many pulpits have become mouth-pieces for liberalism and even the outright denial of the divine authorship of Scripture."[40]

Finding that their theology was similar, even if their politics varied in areas, Pew and Manning grew close. In 1964 they shook hands on the shores of the Athabasca River linked not just by business interests but also by "common commitment to Jesus Christ." These two diplomats met again just a few months later, in the more leisurely setting of Jasper, Alberta, a resort town nestled in the Rocky Mountains. This time Graham, who kept track of the Pew–Manning accord, joined them. Manning had first met Graham while the latter worked with Youth for Christ in the 1940s, and throughout the 1950s and early 1960s the politician remained well connected to the star evangelist. When congregating in Jasper, Manning and Graham surely reminisced even as they schemed a near future when, following Manning's lead, the American would hold revivals in each Canadian city. It is safe to say that in between golf rounds (Pew scored his age—82—a highlight of his trip), meanwhile, Manning and Pew talked through theology and tar sands, and by all accounts the talks went well. Whatever differences they held politically, Pew and Manning's soft diplomacy seemed to work. As their connections deepened it became apparent to Pew that Manning's populist emphases served as protective cover for what was at its core an ideology of individualism and free enterprise, an ideology in other words that was shared. Manning, for his part, seemed to grow more inclined to shed or at least soften some of the populist defensiveness he had inherited from the his Social Credit mentors and champion more forcefully a form of free market economy that Pew and his American corporate cousins vigorously upheld. As Manning and Pew's relationship rapidly warmed, so too did GCOS' dealings with Alberta's government.[41]

So much so, that by the summer of 1965, it was all-systems-go for the oil sands initiative. Following Manning and Pew's political, theological, and personal back-and-forths, Sunoco and Alberta officials, and the multitude of workers already congregated in the province's northern reaches, once again looked optimistically to a future of full-on operation. Anticipating it, R. G. LeTourneau's equipment made the trip to Alberta in the mid-1960s. By 1965 his scrapers, road tampers, electric shovels, and over-sized dump trucks, were carving out the "muskeg and scrub timber" lining GCOS's plant site. By 1966, these same machines, along with hulking bucketwheel excavators, were burrowing even deeper, into 100 feet below the muskeg, glacial boulders, and clay to reach pay dirt. By GCOS's opening in 1967, LeTourneau had quite literally stamped his presence on Alberta's bleakest but richest terrain. So had his evangelical allies. Through their executive leadership, evangelical ecumenism, and political power, Manning and Pew had shaped a world enterprise from beginning to end. Is it any wonder that the GCOS's opening ceremonies in 1967 pulsated to a Protestant beat? When assessing the GCOS for its stockholders, Sunoco proclaimed, "This venture combines drama (man against nature), daring (the risk of large financial resources), and science (the technology of the operation is itself a fascinating story). It is a pioneering undertaking ... in more than one respect." LeTourneau could not have said it any better to his students in Longview, Texas, nor Pew to his employees in Philadelphia, nor Manning to his voters in Calgary and curious fans worldwide.[42]

The GCOS's sense of evangelical assurance would eventually falter, but never completely. By the time it entered its third year, GCOS was slumping under the weight of heavy costs due to production difficulties, financial strains, and Albertans who demanded their share of the profits. Still, Sunoco's relations with Alberta's government would remain steady through the 1970s, thanks in part to their continued claims to shared religion. After Manning's retirement in 1968, Sunoco struck a rapport with Harry Strom, Manning's successor. A Prairie-populist in Manning's mold, Strom was also a New Evangelical who endorsed Graham's ministry and the Pew worldview. One of his first trips after accepting the premiership was to Washington, DC, where he attended Richard Nixon's Presidential Prayer Breakfast, an event helped along by Graham and Pew. Strom returned home determined to make his religion count in the political realm. Alberta citizens who continued to hold firm to the Social Credit's political and religious heritage hailed his devotion: "in its new leader the province of Alberta has a man for whom the word 'honor' carries a deeper meaning. The Honorable Harry Edwin Strom, Premier of Alberta, seeks also to honor Jesus Christ." Strom stayed loyal to Sunoco. In 1970, he reduced the level of royalties it was required to pay, easing the company's burdens but stirring the wrath of political opponents, who said that Strom's act was an "outrageous concession to a subsidiary of a giant multinational corporation." Sunoco officials monitored the backlash, which they attributed to labor unions, and, behind the scenes, negotiated all the more urgently with Strom. In one of the last meetings of his life, Pew convened with Strom in May 1970 at which time Strom stressed he would continue to help GCOS, despite the political heat.[43]

Even with Strom's aid, GCOS limped forward, suffering from its inability to counter rising production costs and charges from environmentalists that the tar sands project caused ecological harm. By the 1980s, GCOS would give way to government ownership, and with the added stability would come another era of fits and starts but also significant growth and success. Despite the most recent decline in world oil prices, which has diminished its profitability, the project is more viable today than ever in its past. But worries over the oil's sand's environmental impact persist, so much so that President Barack Obama, pressured by green activists in his Democratic Party, has cited their "destructive" nature as reason for withholding final approval of the Keystone XL Pipeline, a major intercontinental effort to transport Athabasca's crude south from Alberta to the Texas Gulf Coast. In the wake of the 2014 elections, a Republican-led Congress is promising to make the pipeline happen and essentially solidify with steel a religious and political relationship that Ernest Manning did so much to initiate a half-century ago. Even if the pipeline meets final approval—which is almost inevitable—not all is consistent in the networks that Manning helped build during the Cold War years. Among the large, American lobbies that have joined the fight against Alberta's oil sands is the Pew Foundation; one Pew creation is now fighting the other. Even though he is still celebrated in Fort McMurray (one of the city's parks bears his name), J. Howard Pew would surely voice some frustration were he alive and able to revisit his corporate boardroom and this familiar terrain.[44]

Despite GCOS's undulating trajectories after 1970, its striking ascent prior to this point should remind historians that the relationship between God and black gold was a vital force in twentieth-century America's global encounter. It should also prompt them to write of this encounter with an eye to the manifold patterns of impact, by which America's interests and influence were exported, reciprocated, and returned in altered form from foreign fields. Offered abundant power in Alberta and the American Southwest, analogous hinterlands where the "Petroleum Belt" and "Bible Belt" met, oil-patch evangelicals inhabiting these economic and eschatological spaces synchronized their theologies of salvation and stewardship with a politics of entrepreneurialism and easy access to nature's resources. Although national distinctions persisted, they thought and acted about their material well-being and millennial promises in ways that transcended their citizenship. Together, with clear intent, they found creases of authority in the "cascade of social, technological, economic, cultural, and political revolutions" that was redefining life in the Cold War years and tapped common corporate and state channels to further their Christian values. Contrary to common renderings of modern evangelical politics, however, which tend to focus on narrow culture-war concerns, these values encompassed much more than diktats about home and hearth. For Pew, Manning, LeTourneau, and their brethren, the quest was always about something bigger on a larger stage: the right to extract all of the bountiful gifts of the great Creator in ways that affirmed their authority over the earth in its boundless entirety.[45]

NOTES

1. Ernest C. Manning, "Christian Statesmanship," *Decision Magazine* (February 1962), 6.

2. "Alberta Premier Lauds Athabasca Oil Project," *Sunoco News* (August 1964), Folder 18, Box 641, Sun Oil Collection, Hagley Museum and Library, Wilmington, Delaware (hereinafter SOC).

3. "Athabasca Special Report: One Year to Completion," *Canadian Petroleum* (September 1966), 43–45, Folder 16, Box 641; "Tar Sand and Oil Mining," *Engineering and Mining Journal* (December 1967), Folder 16, Box 641, both in SOC.

4. "GCOS: The Way It Works," *Our Sun* (Autumn 1967), 30, Box 34, SOC.

5. Ibid.; "Film Tells Athabasca Story," untitled clipping in Folder 18, Box 641, SOC. This prayer was offered at a company celebration years before GCOS opened its plant, but its same sentiments were heard during Pew's addresses to company in the months surrounding GCOS's opening. See Sun Oil—Anniversaries—1951—Marcus Hook, Folder 5, Box 639, SOC.

6. Sven Beckert, *Empire of Cotton: A Global History* (New York: Alfred A. Knopf, 2014).

7. This chapter draws from a book-length account of religion and oil, related parts of which have appeared in other venues. For further study related to the post–World War II manifestation of this relationship, see Darren Dochuk, "Blessed by Oil, Cursed with Crude; God and Black Gold in the Modern Southwest," *Journal of American History* 99 (June 2012): 51–61; Darren Dochuk, "Prairie Fire: The New Evangelicalism and the Politics of Oil, Money, and Moral Geography," in *Talkin 'Bout a Revolution? Evangelicals in 1960s Society and Culture*, ed. Axel R. Schäfer (Madison: University of Wisconsin Press, 2013), 39–60; Darren Dochuk, "There Will Be Oil: Presidents, Wildcat Religion, and the Culture Wars of Pipeline Politics," in *Recapturing the Oval Office: New Historical Approaches to the American Presidency*, ed. Brian Balogh and Bruce Schulman (Ithaca, NY: Cornell University Press, 2015), 93–107.

8. Mark Humphries, "North American Oil Sands: History of Development, Prospects for the Future," *CRS Report for Congress*, January 17, 2008, 8–9; Paul Chastko, *Developing Alberta's Oil Sands: From Karl Clark to Kyoto* (Calgary, AB: University of Calgary Press, 2005), 87, 105.

9. Malcolm Gordon Taylor, "The Social Credit Movement in Alberta" (MA thesis, University of California, n.d.), 6–7, 82.

10. Ibid., 82. For further insight, see William E. Akin, *Technocracy and the American Dream: The Technocrat Movement, 1900–1941* (Berkeley: University of California Press, 1977).

11. On American migration and its influence on Alberta, and insight into Social Credit politics forged out of Alberta's distinctive demographics, politics, and Protestantism, see Nelson Wiseman, "The American Imprint on Alberta Politics," paper prepared for the Annual Meeting of the Canadian Political Science Association, Montreal, Quebec, 2010, copy in author's possession. On Aberhart and Manning, see Lloyd Mackey, *Like Father, Like Son: Ernest Manning and Preston Manning* (Toronto, ON: ECW Press, 1997), 20.

12. Ernest Manning biographical profile (untitled), 2–3, File 1821, Premiers William Aberhart and Ernest C. Manning Papers, Provincial Archives of Alberta, Edmonton, Alberta (hereinafter cited as ECM). See Harry Roye to Ernest Manning, September 5, 1946, File 1179, ECM. Manning was a close associate of Fuller's. The two men co-chaired the "Christ for America" campaign of 1951. See Horace F. Dean to Peter Elliott, November 20, 1951, File 1828, ECM. On the New Evangelicalism, see George Marsden, *Reforming Fundamentalism: Fuller Seminary and the New Evangelicalism* (Grand Rapids, MI: William B. Eerdmans, 1988).

13. Taylor, "The Social Credit Movement in Alberta," 6–7. On Manning's popularity with evangelicals and in the United States, see Bob Jones to Ernest Manning, July 5, 1946, File 1179; "Hon. Ernest Charles Manning—Edmonton Constituency," File 1821; "Address of Ernest C. Manning, 39th National Gideon Convention, Montreal, June 15th to 18th, 1950," File 1826, ECM.

14. Mark Lisac, "Leduc First Gush of Alberta Oil Wealth," *Ottawa Citizen*, February 7, 1987, A22. See also David H. Breen, *Alberta's Petroleum Industry and the Conservation* Board (Edmonton, AB: University of Alberta Press, 1993), 245–46. Ted Byfield, *Alberta in the 20th Century: Leduc, Manning, and the Age of Prosperity, 1946–1963* (Edmonton, AB: United Western Communications, 2001), 8–9, 13–14. Earle Gray, *The Great Canadian Oil Patch*, 2d ed. (Edmonton, AB: June Warren Publishing, 2004), 140.

15. Bob Jones to Ernest Manning, July 5, 1946, File 1179, ECM.

16. "Broadcast on Provincial Affairs, by Ernest C. Manning, Alberta Series No. 7: Our Minerals and Forests," File 1824, ECM.

17. "Broadcast on Provincial Affairs, by Ernest C. Manning, Premier of Alberta: Alberta Series No. 14, Government Insurance: Breaking Monopoly—Not Creating Monopoly," File 1824; Remarks by J. R. White, Association of Professional Engineers of Alberta, Annual Meeting, Calgary, Alberta, Marcy 27, 1954, File 1826; Ernest Manning speech, undated, File 1825, ECM.

18. On Hubbert and peak oil, see Kenneth S. Deffeyes, *Hubbert's Peak: The Impending World Oil Shortage* (Princeton: Princeton University Press, 2008).

19. Ernest Manning speech to Interstate Oil Compact Commission, September 1–3, 1952, File 1825; Charles E. Simons to Ernest Manning, August 20, 1954, File 1821; Peter Elliott to John W. Wagner, September 3, 1954, file 1821, ECM. See, for instance, Olin Culberson, Railroad Commission of Texas, Austin, to Ernest Manning, September 30, 1952, File 1825, ECM.

20. LeTourneau's biographical information gleaned from R. G. LeTourneau, *Mover of Men and Mountains: The Autobiography of R. G. LeTourneau* (Upper Saddle River, NJ: Prentice Hall, 1960). Examples drawn from "Shifting of Load from Traction," *NOW* (February 1, 1962), 2; "Steel to Illustrate a Spiritual Truth," reprinted in *NOW* (September 1971), 1. Issues of *NOW* accessed at the LeTourneau University Archives, Longview, Texas (hereinafter cited as LUA).

21. "Invasion," *NOW* (December 8, 1944), 1; "R.G. Talks," *NOW* (September 15, 1961), 2; "The Wildcat and the Black Dog," *NOW* (September 15, 1961), 2–3.

22. LeTourneau, *Mover of Men and Mountains*, 242; 245; "The Wildcat and the Black Dog," *NOW* (September 15, 1961), 2–3.

23. "LeTourneau College," *NOW* (May 1, 1962), 1. The relationship of oil to evangelical missionary efforts in Ecuador is charted in Kathryn Long, "God in the Rainforest: Missionaries among the Waorani in Amazonian Ecuador," working book manuscript in author's possession.

24. Details of this arrangement are charted in LeTourneau's correspondence. See James C. LeTourneau to Mr. M. C. Gleter, August 24, 1961, Mobile Oil Company

Del Peru, 1961 Folder, Box JFE; Roy LeTourneau to Mr. R. G. LeTourneau, December 21, 1959, Letters from Roy LeTourneau—1959 Folder, Box B5G; Roy LeTourneau to Sterling Stephens, July 1, 1960, Letters from Peru—1960 Folder, Box B5G, LUA. For summary of the project see also "Peru," *NOW* (February 1, 1962), 3; "Feeding the Billions," *NOW* (September 15, 1961), 1.

25. See, for instance, correspondence between R. G. LeTourneau and P. A. Gaglardi, British Columbia's Minister of Highways, in Mr. P. A. Gaglardi Folder, Box FIT, LUA. Ernest Manning to R. G. LeTourneau, April 18, 1945, Premier Correspondence, ECM.

26. Humphries, "North American Oil Sands," 8; "Profiles in Pioneering," *Our Sun* (Autumn 1967), 2, Box 34, SOC.

27. Ibid.; Chastko, *Developing Alberta's Oil Sands*, 87, 105.

28. "J.N. Pew: A Biographical Sketch," *Our Sun: 75th Anniversary Issue* (1961), 11, Sun Oil—75th Anniversary, 1961 Folder, Box 55; "1901–1912: Spindletop and the Rise of Sun," *Our Sun: 75th Anniversary Issue* (1961), 20, Sun Oil—75th Anniversary, 1961 Folder, Box 55, SOC. August W. Giebelhaus, *Business and Government in the Oil Industry: A Case Study of Sun Oil, 1876–1945* (Greenwich, CT: JAI Press, 1980), 6–8.

29. Ibid., 59–61. "The Story of Sun," *Our Sun, 75th Anniversary Issue* (1961), 30–31, Sun Oil—75th Anniversary, 1961 Folder, Box 55, SOC.

30. "Suncor, Inc.: An Account of the First Seventy Years," 7–8, 32–33, in "Subsidiaries, 1987" Folder, Box 605, SOC.

31. On Pews' and business's assault on the New Deal, see Kim Phillips-Fein, *Invisible Hands: The Making of the Conservative Movement from the New Deal to Reagan* (New York: Norton, 2009).

32. Quoted and referenced in Stephen J. Randall, *United States Foreign Oil Policy since World War II: For Profits and Security* (Montreal and Kingston: McGill-Queen's University Press, 2005), 172–3, 197.

33. Quoted in Giebelhaus, *Business and Government in the Oil Industry*, 218; "The Creed We Work By: A Statement of Principles," *Our Sun: 75th Anniversary Issue* (1961), 20, Sun Oil—75th Anniversary, 1961 Folder, Box 55, SOC; J. Howard Pew, "Management and the Free Market," May 17, 1950, in Binder marked Speeches & Remarks by J. Howard Pew, #54-89, SOC; Roger M. Olien and Diana Davids Olien, *Oil and Ideology: The Cultural Creation of the American Petroleum Industry* (Chapel Hill: University of North Carolina Press, 2000), 204; Receipt for Pew donation in Box 1, Pew Family Collection, Hagley Museum and Library, Wilmington, Delaware (hereinafter cited as PFC); "An Album of Sun Memories," *Our Sun, 75th Anniversary Issue*, 34, Sun Oil—75th Anniversary, 1961 Folder, Box 55, SOC.

34. "The Creed We Work By: A Statement of Principles," *Our Sun, 75th Anniversary Issue*, 51; J. Edgar Pew, "The Fifth Dimension in the Oil Industry," Speech to A.A.P.G. Annual Meeting, Houston, Texas, April 3, 1941, J. Edgar Pew's Speeches—A.P.I. Folder, Box 18, SOC.

35. For more on Graham's relationship to Texas oilmen, see Dochuk, "There Will Be Oil."

36. Randall, *United States Foreign Oil Policy since World War II*, 282, 320.

37. See logbook for "Sunoco Trip #2, Sept. 18–19, 1963, Loose File, Box 35, Series 6, SOC; "New Oil Sands Project May Have Fast Start," *The Albertan*, November 26, 1963.

38. Premier Ernest Manning to Mr. D. J. Wilkins, March 9, 1964, Athabasca Tar Sands Project, Great Canadian Oil Sands Correspondence, 1963–1964 Folder, Box 35, SOC.

39. W. H. Rea to Robert G. Dunlop, September 2, 1964, and Sun Memo titled "Investment in GCOS by Albertans," March 30, 1964, Athabasca Tar Sands Project, Great Canadian Oil Sands Correspondence, 1963–1964 Folder, Box 35; "Memorandum," March 1964, Athabasca Tar Sands Project, Great Canadian Oil Sands Correspondence, 1963–1964 Folder, Box 35, SOC.

40. "Notes Re Meeting in Sun Aircraft—Quebec City on April 2, 1964—Athabasca Project," Athabasca Tar Sands Project, Great Canadian Oil Sands Correspondence, 1963–1964 Folder, Box 35, Series 6, SOC. Key letters between the two men, referenced here, include J. Howard Pew to Ernest C. Manning, January 4, 1965, J. Howard Pew to Ernest C. Manning, February 23, 1965, J. Howard Pew to Ernest Manning, March 15, 1965, Ernest Manning to J. Howard Pew (via Miss Pauline M. Baker), March 29, 1965, Ernest Manning to J. Howard Pew, April 2, 1965, all in C-P 1965 Folder, Box 231, JHP.

41. Mackey, *Ernest Manning*, 126, 130–131; "Memorandum," Premier of Alberta—Honorable Ernest C. Manning, December 21, 1964, C-P 1965 Folder, Box 231, JHP. Ernest Manning to J. Howard Pew, April 2, 1965, C-P 1965 Folder, Box 231 and June 11, 1965, G 1965 Folder, Box 231, JHP.

42. "Athabasca Press Conference Proposal," Athabasca Tar Sands Project Great Canadian Oil Sands, 1963–1964 Folder, Box 35, SOC. "Athabasca: One Year to Completion," *Canadian Petroleum* (September 1966), 43–45.

43. On Strom and Sunoco, see Robert Dunlop to Harry Strom, June 12, 1970, and F. O'Sullivan to Robert Dunlop, July 9, 1970, Great Canadian Oil Sands, Ltd., 1970 Folder, Box 36, SOC. See also "Notley Raps Royalty Reduction," July 2, 1970, untitled clipping, in Great Canadian Oil Sands, Ltd., 1970 Folder, Box 36; "Meet Alberta's New Premier," *Power for Living* (May 3, 1970), 7, attached to correspondence between W. S. Woods Jr. and Robert Dunlop, July 21, 1970, Great Canadian Oil Sands, Ltd., 1970 Folder, Box 36; and Memorandum of Meeting, April 28, 1970, labeled "Confidential," Great Canadian Oil Sands, Ltd., 1971 Folder, Box 36, SOC.

44. Humphries, "North American Oil Sands." See Sheldon Alberts, "U.S. President Obama Cites 'Destructive' Canadian Oilsands, Hints at Withholding Approval of Keystone Pipeline," *Vancouver Sun*, April 7, 2011, 1. On recent developments in the Keystone and oil sands debate, including the Pew Foundation's opposition, see Coral Davenport, "Senate Fails to Override Obama's Keystone Pipeline Veto, *New York Times*, March 4, 2015, http://www.nytimes.com/2015/03/05/us/senate-fails-to-override-obamas-keystone-pipeline-veto.html; Peter Foster, "Peter Foster: Green Billionaires Undermining Canada," *Financial Post*, August 8,

2014, http://business.financialpost.com/2014/08/08/peter-foster-green-billionaires-undermining-canada/.

45. Kevin Phillips, *American Theocracy: The Peril and Politics of Radical Religion, Oil, and Borrowed Money in the 21st Century* (New York: Penguin Books, 2006), xiv–xv, 42; Walter Russell Mead, *God and Gold: Britain, America, and the Making of the Modern World* (New York: Alfred A. Knopf, 2007), 274; Dochuk, "Moving Mountains," 81.

8

An Incessant Struggle against White Supremacy

The International Congress against Imperialism and the International Circuits of Black Radicalism

Minkah Makalani

In July 1929, three black radicals from the United States, Williana Burroughs, William Patterson, and James Ford, boarded a train in Moscow heading for Frankfurt, Germany, where they would attend the Second International Congress against Imperialism. Each had become Communists in the United States: Burroughs and Patterson had joined in Harlem, while Ford, at the time the most prominent black Communist in America, had joined its Chicago branch. Whatever their personal motivations, they considered the Communist International (Comintern), headquartered in Moscow, a global movement in which they could pursue their long-standing belief that struggles in Asia, Latin America, Ireland, and Europe were essential to black liberation and world revolution. Indeed, as Patterson recalls, they left Moscow "hoping and expecting to speak with as many delegates as possible," particularly "the Black delegates from Africa and the Americas, North and South."[1]

The congress in Frankfurt appeared to offer black radicals within the international communist movement their first opportunity to pursue a program for African diasporic liberation. One goal of the 1927 International Congress against Colonial Oppression and Imperialism that met in Brussels, Belgium, had been to establish a "permanent international organisation [linking] all forces combating international imperialism" and supporting national liberation struggles.[2] While the Comintern viewed the League against Imperialism (LAI) that emerged out of Brussels as a means of influencing anticolonial struggles, black radicals, Communists and non-Communist alike, saw in this new organization an opportunity to build the kinds of ties they believed essential to pan-African liberation. Immediately after the Frankfurt Congress, Patterson, Burroughs, and Ford met with such figures as Jomo Kenyatta and the Paris-based Sudanese radical Garan Kouyaté to outline a program that would become the International Trade Union Committee for Negro Workers (ITUCNW). Within a year, the Trinidadian George Padmore, who also came to Moscow through the American party's Harlem branch, assumed leadership of the group and built an international network of diasporic contacts, many of whom went on to work in African national liberation movements, anticolonial organizations in Europe, Caribbean independence, and American antiracist organizations. Patterson captured the mood of that meeting when he explained that it represented the "gathering of Black men from all parts of the world [that] was necessary if a united anti-imperialist position was to be taken."[3]

The rise of a black international through organized communism marked a critical moment in black radical organizing, as it provided a global formation within which to challenge US racial politics through an anticolonial frame. In their efforts to link domestic US political struggles to African diasporic liberation, black Communists reflected a habit of thought among black intellectuals of viewing US political history in global terms. Yet believing that world affairs bore on black citizenship did not always produce a radical politics. Many black intellectuals saw in American involvement in Puerto Rico and the Philippines, for example, an opportunity to demonstrate black people's racial manhood. Many others approached Liberia as if the historical ties between African Americans and the small African nation rendered it a natural launching pad for enlightened New World black leadership of African redemption.[4] As such, black radicals in the international communist movement did not so much introduce a global framework for thinking about black freedom, as they centered a critique of an ever-expanding US empire in their attempts to understand race as a colonial issue that one could hardly adequately address if seen as a domestic political question. In refusing to limit their notion of freedom to mere inclusion in American society, these radicals often approached the United States as an imperial power, responding to their exclusion as the "other" from the reciprocal engagements of modern governmentalities that, as Richard Iton reminds us, positions black people against the citizen.[5] While there exists a wealth of historical scholarship detailing how black intellectuals have pursued civil rights through a politics attuned to global concerns, generally within the framing narrative of the Cold War,[6] my focus here follows a growing historiographical approach that asks whether anticolonial black radicals in fact viewed the nation-state as a normative goal of anticolonial struggles, suggesting that calls for self-determination often entailed a more capacious critique of the nation-state and modern forms of governance than previously assumed.[7] It thus seems reasonable to question what we might gain by contemplating the history of black radicalism in terms of the nexus of American and world politics.

What does it mean to approach this nexus through a story whose narrative arc issues from multiple settings—the Caribbean, Harlem, Paris, Brussels—only to settle in yet even more diverse locales—colonial West Africa, Hamburg, Guadeloupe, London, Moscow? Is it significant that the history of radical black internationalism, always incomplete when told as a national narrative, continuously routed itself through such global networks and institutions like W. E. B. Du Bois's Pan-African Congresses, Marcus Garvey's Universal Negro Improvement Association, and the Comintern? Is it merely coincidental that the political horizon of such formations always exceeded the conceptual and teleological norms of the nation-state? It may well be that interrogating the relationship between world politics and US political history is demanded by the contemporary moment. Still, it strikes me that as a frame for studying black radicalism, it privileges a sense of national belonging for a group whose exclusion has been constitutive of the American citizen.

If the nation proves inadequate, transnationalism and internationalism are not entirely satisfying alternatives. Transnationalism reflects an intellectual preoccupation with how events, actors, and even state policies exceed national boundaries. When done well, it brings into focus the global dimensions of any story by resisting the tendency to delimit its analytical range to the nation-state, yet heeds Antoinette Burton's warning not to dismiss "the continued vigor of the nation" as geopolitical reality and political project.[8] Internationalism denotes social movements, institutions, and political exchanges that occur across multiple national contexts.[9] Chronicling a given political approach to a global system of exploitation and oppression, internationalism's attention to the imbrication of European and US workers' struggle with anticolonial movements for self-determination retains distinctions between their constitutive localities. As narrative approaches, both internationalism and transnationalism guard against the filial historiographical tendency to identify streams of influence from one location to another, where the United States might be taken as shaping anticolonial struggles, or anticolonial struggles influencing US black struggles. Both frames underscore a sense of historical time and geopolitical currents more as a latticework, an intricate weave that draws multiple locations into a whole for which it becomes almost futile to attempt to pinpoint a given origin, the national boundaries of a given movement. Still, as frames, the nation remains the key referent that transnationalism and internationalism seek to transcend yet never displace, the condition of their very conceptual possibility that simultaneously marks their political horizon.

The African diaspora offers the possibility of disarticulating black political history from any necessary invocation of the nation. As a social formation, the African diaspora does not emerge from a national homeland, nor is the nation-state necessarily a goal. Nationalist anticolonial projects have played an undeniable role in the African diaspora, and its constituent vernaculars of blackness reflect the internal dynamics of the nations that peoples of African descent inhabit. Analytically it involves a response to European and American empire in Africa, Asia, and the Americas, its import resting in the potential it allows for bringing forth alternative modes of being and affiliation, the possibility of a refracted and non-national project that resists the nationalist impulses that often dominate anticolonial projects.

The black radicals considered here highlight just such a possibility, and underscore the shortcomings in continuing to view US political history as either simply a domestic story or necessarily one of the Cold War. The story of their pursuit of a black international through Brussels and the ITUCNW did not begin at the nexus of world and US political history. Rather, it places the US alongside European empires, the Caribbean, West Africa, and possibly most important black political thought, in a uniquely diasporic story. This creates a historiographical opening in which it becomes possible to break from the Cold War frame that has dominated a good deal of the scholarship on black internationalism. Yet while "the Cold War is the central discourse in the international history of the late twentieth century," Odd Arne Westad reminds us "it is by no means the full story." Even for the early twentieth century, the key conflict focuses on the emergence of an "international system based on two opposing versions of European modernist thought," for which the key global conflict is the future of modernity.[10]

The "Wilsonian moment" that historian Erez Manela argues framed and ignited anticolonial rhetoric and organizing following World War I is suggestive, though it obscures how, at the precise moment US President Woodrow Wilson proclaimed self-determination a universal right, Asian and African diasporic radicals noted the hypocrisy given Wilson's place at the helm of an ever-expanding US empire. Cyril Briggs, a Harlem-based journalist from Nevis, argued that unless England and France were "prepared to give up their millions of square miles of African territory" and America to end its occupation of Haiti and the Dominican Republic, grant Filipinos independence, and "apply self-determination" to southern Negroes, Wilson's League of Nations would do little more than strengthen the "thieves and tyrants" whose interests lay in "the exploitation of the darker races."[11] The Vietnamese revolutionary Nguyen Ai Quoc, who gained world renown as Ho Chi Minh, saw in V. I. Lenin's position on self-determination adopted by the Comintern "the path to our liberation" and helped found the Parti Communiste Français (PCF) in December 1920. As Briggs would put it, it was "the anti-imperialist orientation of the Soviet State" that proved compelling to many anticolonial radicals.[12]

Black radicals in the United States and Europe who first entered organized communist formations did so as committed activist-intellectuals willing to stretch the boundaries of a political theory so that it might address racial oppression and colonialism. Thus, as appealing as it may be to replace Wilson's League with Lenin's Comintern, greater attention to the long-standing anticolonial currents among black radicals reveals a far more complex history. The Comintern, along with being perhaps "the era's sole international white-led movement ... formally dedicated to a revolutionary transformation of the global political *and* radical order,"[13] had the potential to facilitate a black international among African diasporic populations. But because membership was funneled through national communist parties, black Communists often encountered frustrating setbacks and roadblocks from their local party leadership. The Comintern had backed the 1925 founding of the American Negro Labor Congress (ANLC), which it considered a potential international organization; tepid support (if not hostility) from American party officials rendered the group dysfunctional and, within a year, deep in debt. For their part, French Communist Party officials had refused the request of the Paris-based Senegalese Communist Lamine Senghor to attend the ANLC's founding convention. This slight, along with the PCF's general neglect of black people, led Senghor to establish the independent Comité de Defense de la Race Nègre (Committee for the Defense of the Black Race, CDRN).

Where frustrations with local national parties were routine, the Comintern itself often proved littler better. Lenin's position on self-determination owed a good deal of its appeal to the arguments of Indian Communist M. N. Roy on the centrality of African and Asian anticolonial struggles to world revolution— a notion initially stridently resisted by many Comintern officials. The shift in Comintern policy on national liberation was only for a time, and failed to carry thoroughgoing theoretical or programmatic change, especially when considering Africa and black people worldwide. When the Guadeloupian radical Joseph Gothon-Lunion, also in the CDRN, proposed that the Comintern support Senghor's group, reasoning that it could build an international socialist movement among colonized peoples, the Comintern never responded. For US black radicals, the American party had never seriously pursued Negro work and remained dismissive of its black comrades. Black radicals in both the American and French Communist parties hoped to build institutional ties with one another, but were constantly frustrated by their local party leadership. By 1927, many of the black radicals who had gravitated to the Comintern were so disgruntled with their local parties that they began to question the international body's efficacy for pan-African liberation. That is, until Brussels.

Brussels

When the German Communist Willi Münzenberg announced the convening of the International Congress against Colonial Oppression and Imperialism in Brussels, Belgium, anticolonial radicals worldwide responded enthusiastically. The Indian radicals Jawaharlal Nehru and the US-based Ghadar Party's Maulavi Barkatullah were in contact with congress officials and planned to attend, as did long-time Communist M. N. Roy and Indonesia's Mohammad Hatta. Messali Hadj, founder of the Paris-based Étoile Nord Africaine (North African Star) would come with fellow Étoile members Chedi Ben Mustapha and Ahmed Hassan Mattar. Even Albert Einstein, an honorary president of the congress, considered Brussels a "solidly united endeavour of the oppressed to achieve independence."[14]

Black radicals were similarly enthusiastic. When NAACP field secretary William Pickens proposed to that group's board of directors that he attend as its delegate, he argued that the future of the race lay in a worldwide struggle for freedom, a view with which nearly every board member agreed.[15] Members of the National Congress of British West Africa (NCBWA) and other Africans were involved in planning the congress, with Gold Coast lawyer Joseph Casely-Hayford informing organizers that the NCBWA would send delegates. Senghor sent word that his Comité would send six delegates to work with the congress and all Negroes under French imperialism. The African National Congress sent its president, Josiah T. Gumede, to Brussels, while Carlos Deambrosis Martins came from Haiti to represent the nationalist Union Patriotique (Patriotic Union).[16] US black Communists were equally eager, hoping to send Richard B. Moore along with Hubert Harrison and several others to Brussels, even proposing to create an organization to help get Asian and Latin American radicals in America to Brussels.[17]

Moore would be the sole US black radical to attend, but he interacted with an impressive array of anticolonial radicals. Most important, Brussels provided Moore and other black radicals in the international communist movement their first opportunity to meet on a scale that approached that of either Du Bois's

Pan-African Congresses or the UNIA's international conventions. In particular, the Comintern possessed the infrastructure to have real time translation between French and English, not to mention as well Russian, German, Dutch, Mandarin, Cantonese, and Spanish. Indeed, anticolonial radicals more generally considered it an opportunity to dialogue and coordinate their struggles, something they could do, quite literally, for the first time. Nehru echoed the hopes of many when he declared that out of the congress "a new 'Association of Oppressed Nations' will come about, if not right away then in the not-too-distant future."[18]

When the congress opened at the Egmont Palace in Brussels on February 10, 1927, it welcomed 174 delegates from 37 countries. The French novelist and Communist Henri Barbusse opened the congress by striking a chord that resonated with those who had come to vindicate the "oppressed races and peoples" of the world. He decried colonialism, racism, and imperialism, insisting that colonial peoples themselves "must take ... the right to self-determination," and called on those in the Caribbean, China, India, and Africa to join their struggles with the struggles attacking "colonization behind closed doors, such as that of the Negroes in the United States."[19] To many in attendance, the major anti-imperialist struggle was unfolding in China. The Japanese Communist Sen Katayama applauded China for having already "struck a blow against the strongest imperialism of the world—England," while Nehru hoped India would soon follow the "noble example of the Chinese nationalists."[20] But apart from Barbusse's opening comments, Africa and black people received little attention at Brussels until the Negro question came up for full discussion.

The speeches of the black delegates suggest that they were intent on outlining the global contours of the Negro question and inserting race into any conception of imperialism. The ANC's Gumede characterized antiracist struggles in South Africa as part of a larger struggle against European imperialism and openly questioned how congress organizers could display a map of the colonial world that portrayed South Africa "as if imperialism does not operate there." South Africa's troubled history, he explained, was the responsibility of "the whole of Europe."[21] Francophone Caribbean radicals turned their attention to France and the United States. Martins highlighted brutal American practices during its ongoing occupation of Haiti, including "the murder of more than three thousand Haitians." The Guadeloupian Max Bloncourt detailed French atrocities in the Caribbean as well as the horrors of US imperialism, telling the congress that in Guadeloupe and Martinique black people were revolting against their limited freedoms and inequality.[22]

The highlight, however, came when Senghor addressed the congress. Senghor had come to Paris after World War I as a decommissioned colonial soldier whose wartime injuries left him with an increasingly worsening pulmonary condition. When he arrived in Brussels, his health was so poor that he avoided going out into the cold. Still, many remembered his intensity, intelligence, and unmatched oratorical skills. Those skills were on full display as Senghor began his speech by referencing reports that the United States would purchase French Caribbean colonies, to which he remarked that colonial oppressors "don't sell us nowadays individually. They trade us wholesale, passing entire peoples from one to another."[23] Senghor urged a joint struggle between the colonized and those in the metropole to destroy "world imperialism." But in the middle of his speech, he singled out the Chinese delegates as providing "a good revolutionary example to all the peoples suppressed under the colonizers' yoke. I only hope," he added, in an important rhetorical turn, that Africans "will all take inspiration from your revolutionary spirit." With this gesture, Senghor removed Russia from the center of revolutionary struggle by drawing a line from China to Africa. Rather than taking the "advanced" proletariat as their example, he hoped Africans would come to see other anticolonial struggles, like China's, but also in Morocco, Syria, and Indochina, as essential to their own liberation. In a final flourish highlighting the importance of Africa, he admitted that "the blacks have slept too long," but warned those present, "beware! He who has slept long and soundly, once he has awakened will not fall asleep again."[24]

Senghor's gesture to the Chinese delegation reflected a general tone of coalition building that in the League against Imperialism seemed poised to build a truly global anticolonial movement. Many of the resolutions drafted at Brussels called for united struggles. Delegates from Britain, India, and China drafted a resolution calling on workers in England to support Indian and Chinese liberation, and for all to commit to "unity and cooperative action." James La Guma and Daniel Colraine, the colored and white delegates, respectively, of the South African Communist Party, worked with Gumede on a resolution demanding "the right of self-determination, by the complete overthrow of capitalist and imperialist domination" in South Africa. They also proposed establishing an LAI branch for black, white, and Indian radicals to work together against all forms of racial oppression and colonialism and capitalist exploitation.[25]

Yet it was the black delegates, with their far-ranging "Common Resolution on the Negro Question," who brought race fully into the discussion of imperialism. One of the more geographically diverse groupings at Brussels, the Committee on the Negro Question, chaired by Senghor and with Moore as secretary, also included Gumede, Bloncourt, Martins, Danae Narcisse, and St. Jacques Camille. This diasporic grouping drew on their global biographies and corresponding conceptions of race to draft a resolution touching on several national groups and colonial empires, race providing them an idiom through which to imagine a global struggle centered on the "emancipation of the Negro peoples of the world."[26] The resolution struck a balance between the histories of racial and colonial oppression in Africa, the Caribbean, and the United States while framing struggles in these places as contingent battles central to proletarian revolution.

Moore captured the crux of the committee's approach to imperialism when he introduced the resolution to the congress by announcing, rather provocatively, that "the fight against imperialism is first of all an incessant struggle against imperialistic ideology," which entailed a struggle against "fascism, the Ku-Klux-Klan, chauvinism and the doctrine of the supremacy of the white race." This required that white workers understand black workers' reluctance to join their struggles, especially when "even in the more progressive groups of the labor movement we are treated as inferiors." Anti-imperialists had to "work harder to organize the Negro masses," he added, since it was "conceivable that the despised Negro peoples will be instrumental in tipping the scale of freedom in favor of the oppressed classes."[27]

The committee's resolution thus situated race at the center of anti-imperialist struggle in order to envision a more capacious notion of liberation. In the pan-African parlance of the time, it demanded the complete freedom of Africa and black people, African control of Africa, and racial equality. Alongside such familiar refrains, the committee advocated unionizing Negro workers, forming consumer cooperatives, and in a turn that broke from the general concern with anticolonial struggles in a given empire, called for unifying all oppressed peoples and classes for world liberation. The resolution therefore brought US empire into its purview by demanding independence for Haiti, Cuba, Dominican Republic, Puerto Rico, and the Virgin Islands, and called for the "confederation of the British West Indies," which would help bring about "the Union of all these peoples." Along these lines, Moore also worked with US, Latin American, and Chinese delegations on a declaration supporting "nationalists and national liberation movements [in] countries under the heel of U.S. imperialist domination" and calling for the unification of liberation struggles in Latin America with nationalist movements in the Philippines and China.[28]

Delegates left Brussels excited about the possibilities for a global movement, convinced that they had fostered meaningful ties to one another for a struggle against Europe.[29] Senghor was elected to the LAI's executive branch, the only black delegate to hold such a position. But his pulmonary condition worsened after returning to Paris, precipitating his untimely death later that year. Nonetheless, many saw in his post an indication of the role the LAI would play in African diasporic struggles. Moore traveled from Brussels throughout France with the CDRN delegation, which afforded him the opportunity to meet and converse with its members and other black radicals in Paris and Marseilles, and to gain a better sense of the possibility for a black international independent of the white Left.[30]

A Black International beyond the Party

When Richard Moore returned to Harlem with news of the Brussels Congress and stories of his exchanges with black radicals from throughout the diaspora, black communists seemed to sense that the Comintern might have finally realized its potential, and that they could finally build a black international capable of independent political organizing. Moore disseminated copies of the congress's various resolutions and its *Manifesto of the Brussels Congress against Imperialism*, as well as told audiences across the country that the LAI had drafted "a basic program for joint action to forward the struggle for world emancipation." W. E. B. Du Bois, who described Brussels as an asset to the American Negro, reprinted Moore's address, along with the Negro Committee's resolution in *Crisis*. He also published a passage from yet another *Manifesto to All Oppressed Peoples*, which claimed that African, Asian, Caribbean, Latin American, and working-class struggles would "abolish international capitalism and civilize the whole world."[31] At the fourth Pan-African Congress held in Harlem, the NAACP's Pickens gave a report on Brussels that highlighted the diverse groups of black radicals who had gathered there, calling it the "first league of the economically, politically and socially oppressed" that had forcefully "called for complete racial equality throughout the world."[32] Pickens even maneuvered to have Moore and fellow black Communist Otto Huiswoud work on a resolution calling for Egyptian, Chinese, and Indian national independence and urging national liberation struggles in the West Indies.[33]

Black Communists rode the momentum from Brussels and increased their role in New Negro political circles, as well as branching out to organize black working-class communities. On February 12, 1928, Elizabeth Hendrickson, Captain Ely, and Victor Gasper organized the Harlem Tenants League (HTL), which focused on combating exploitative landlords and soaring housing costs, as well as detailing how discriminatory rents and poor housing conditions created disproportionately high death rates for black families.[34] Alongside Moore, the tenants league's president, Grace Campbell, urged Harlem tenants to "organize militant, fighting tenants leagues" that could work at the state and local levels "for the protection of the welfare and lives of the masses of the people."[35] Campbell and Moore helped established tenants' committees throughout Harlem to pressure landlords to make basic repairs, lower rents, and address overcrowding, and worked to stem the tide of evictions as well as gain residents much needed relief. The HTL soon claimed more than five hundred members and organized new committees in buildings across Harlem,[36] and party leaders soon viewed its community organizing approach as a model for organizing black communities elsewhere. This would seem to have been the view of Otto Huiswoud, when he urged the party to "develop similar leagues in other large cities where Negroes are segregated and forced to pay exorbitant rents." Indeed, the HTL not only provided the model for the party's Unemployed Councils of the 1930s,[37] it was the initial organization through which Malcolm Nurse, a young Trinidadian student who studied law in New York, came into the party.

Nurse, who would achieve world renown as George Padmore, had worked as a journalist in his native Port of Spain, Trinidad, before coming to the United States in 1924 to study at Fisk University in Nashville. A voracious reader and keen intellect, Nurse seems to have arrived with a burgeoning internationalist vision. At Fisk, he worked with an organization of foreign black students that in part sought to prepare black people worldwide for revolutionary struggle and replicated elements of China's Kuomintang Party.[38] Padmore became a Communist in New York, where he helped organize local residents in Harlem. Party leaders soon assigned him to organize students at Howard University in Washington, DC, where he developed a knack for drawing both Caribbean and African students into the party's sphere of influence. Padmore also distinguished himself as a journalist, serving on the editorial board of *Negro Champion* and writing articles for the *Daily Worker*. Even while organizing for the party, he drew connections between black liberation and Asia, at one point imploring a crowd in Brooklyn to aid their "African brothers when they, taking courage from the heroic revolution of the Chinese workers, launch the inevitable revolution against white capitalist domination and exploitation." It is not coincidental, then, that he also saw in organized communism the possibility for a black international.[39]

For black radicals in the international communist movement, the years from 1926 to 1933 seemed the most promising for an international organization of black people. By 1926, several black Communists, like ABB member Otto Hall, his younger brother Harry Haywood, Patterson, and Maude White, were at the University of the Toilers of the East studying alongside African, Asian, and Indian anticolonial radicals. As the Comintern prepared for its now famous Sixth Congress, these students were joined by Ford and Burroughs and charged with developing a new position on the American Negro question.

As it turned out, black Communists had little positive to say about their party's record on race. For years they had urged the party to notice the international appeal of Negro work. At one party convention, Padmore had urged the party to move beyond its narrow understanding of Negro work as solely organizing American black people, suggesting that if the party considered the "millions of colonial blacks who have come from various . . . sections of the world," the more than "5 million Mexican workers" along with the "millions of Chinese, Japanese, Koreans, Philipinos [sic] and Hindus in the United States," it would realize in the United States a powerful international force.[40] Yet as Hall noted, the American party generally refused to work in "close cooperation" with its "Negro comrades."[41] Even Comintern directives had proven ineffective. Ford pointed out that Moscow had sent the American party "no less than 19 resolutions and documents upon the Negro question," yet "not a single one of them had been carried into effect." The problem was bigger than just the American party, however. The British and French parties, too, needed to alter their approach to race in colonial territories and realize that black workers globally represented the "next great revolutionary wave" in the fight "for the overthrow of capitalism and the downfall of imperialism throughout the world." Black Communists recognized in "the racial movement . . . a revolutionary anti-imperialist struggle" that related to "the general question of the Negroes throughout the world." In hopes of realizing this potential, Ford urged the Comintern to organize "trade unions among the Negro peoples of the world."[42] Where various national parties generally dismissed the proposals of its black comrades, the Comintern appeared to listen.

In the midst of the Sixth Congress, South African party delegates and the Comintern official Alexander Losovsky joined Ford, Patterson, Hall, Haywood, and Burroughs in proposing the establishment of an International Bureau of Negro Workers (IBNW). Patterson believed such a bureau would resolve the inability of European parties to deal with the Negro question and help them recruit black members. Ford was selected to chair the Bureau and pull together a conference that would draw black workers from around the world into a global organization.[43] To black Communists from the United States, France, and West Africa, the proposed Bureau answered more than a decade of calls for a world meeting of black people.

Despite the high expectations that followed Brussels, the LAI had done little to realize a global anticolonial struggle. After Senghor's death, the League showed little interests in diasporic struggle, a viable group or international network of anticolonial activists never materialized, and few LAI locals took colonial work seriously.[44] In a January 1929 report, Ford recounted various missed opportunities that had left many black radicals to question the LAI. Black radicals in Paris like Garan Kouyaté, whose Ligue de Defense de la Race Nègre (League for the Defense of the Black Race, LDRN) had succeeded Senghor's CDRN, and Stéphane Rosso noted the French party's failures to adequately organize in French colonial Africa. While the LDRN claimed branches throughout France and in Africa, the French party had no such contacts. Similarly, German Communists could report no inroads among African seamen who routinely came into port in Hamburg. All of this led Ford to insist that the LAI embark on a "second period" of an "organised, systematic campaign against imperialism," assist in organizing the Bureau's conference, and set up LAI branches in the United States, South Africa, and Caribbean. Moreover, he convinced the LAI to hold informal meetings with Negro delegates at its Frankfurt Congress, where he would outline the Bureau's program.[45]

As the LAI prepared for its Frankfurt Congress, the effects of the Comintern's rigid Third Period, "class-against-class" policies were beginning to take their toll. Moscow sought to tightly control the congress and pressured LAI branches to assume greater ties with Moscow. Nehru, who refused to take orders from Communists or to subordinate his work in the Indian National Congress to the dictates of Moscow, was soon marginalized. Even when the Comintern could not remove all "social reformists" from the Frankfurt Congress program, it still sought to dictate policy. When Münzenberg included the NAACP's Pickens among those to address the Negro question, the secretariat considered reprimanding him, and ultimately ordered that he replace Pickens with Ford and James La Guma.[46] So heavy-handed was Comintern control that rather than have black delegates draft their own resolution, that resolution and similar ones on India, China, and Latin America were drafted months before in Moscow.[47]

It is no small irony that the black delegates to Frankfurt were far more diverse than those at Brussels. Pickens, who was able to attend the Brussels Congress, now joined Ford, Kouyaté, Patterson, Burroughs, US-based Haitian Communist Henry Rosemond, and a young Jomo Kenyatta, then studying at the London School of Economics. Although Comintern mandates foreclosed the kinds of deliberations that had led to the innovative Brussels resolution, the speeches by black delegates still conveyed a sense of their independence of thought. Burroughs criticized the LAI for its inadequate work among African Americans and in the Caribbean, while Kouyaté stressed the primacy of diasporic liberation. Echoing Senghor's Brussels speech, Kouyaté told the congress that the LDRN would "do everything to coordinate, centralize, [and] unify the national emancipation movements of the Negroes of black Africa [les Nègres de l'Afrique noire]." Far from simply a continental struggle, however, he insisted that the "national emancipation movement of the Negroes of Africa and the Negro movement for political and social emancipation in America ... will mutually support each other."[48]

The mood among black delegates was certainly buoyed by Kouyaté's remarks. In a series of meetings in Frankfurt, they outlined plans for the International Conference of Negro Workers. The potential global reach of the conference and the proposed ITUCNW suggested a new turn in international communism's approach to the Negro. Patterson captured the feeling best when he described it as the "internationalisation of the Negro problem" with a program that would stress to black workers globally "the commonality of interests between their struggle and those of the oppressed toiling masses of other colonies" and of European workers.[49] The call to the conference conveyed this internationalist impulse by requesting that "all sympathizing organisations of all nationalities ... send their fraternal delegates," suggesting a much broader scope than just black workers. Indeed, not only were Sen Katayama, a Chinese Workers Union representative, and a member of the Indian National Congress in the meetings at Frankfurt, the organizational participants listed for the conference included the Indian National Congress and the All-China Trade Union Federation.[50]

Over the next year, as work on the ICNW proceeded at a dizzying pace, Padmore was selected to work on the organizing committee, a decision that helped catapult him onto the world stage. Padmore's expansive intellect and uncanny grasp of world events as they related to Africa made up for any inexperience he had as an organizer. Ford found him so impressive, he assured those in Europe that they were getting "a good, energetic and capable comrade." By year's end, he was well known in Moscow, meeting students at KUTV and occasionally lecturing on Africa and the world proletarian struggle.[51] Yet whatever enthusiasm Padmore may have brought to this new position, work in the international arena soon proved far more difficult than he could have imagined.

Patterson, who remained in Europe following Frankfurt, wore a path between Hamburg and Paris, meeting with black Communists and establishing contacts with seamen in Hamburg, London, Cardiff, and Marseilles. During a brief stay in Paris with Kouyaté, he witnessed firsthand the French party's "very unsatisfactory Negro work," noting in particular that it had no contacts with any LDRN branch outside Paris, let alone in Africa. He also recognized this pattern of neglect in the British party's colonial work and its lack of progress among black seamen.[52]

At the beginning of 1930, Padmore and Patterson intensified their organizing activities, preparing materials for work in the Caribbean and building ties with African radicals in Europe and Africa. Their efforts were aided by Kouyaté who, following the Frankfurt Congress, accompanied Münzenberg to Berlin where he met a small group of Cameroonian radicals centered on their compatriot Joseph Bilé, who had formed the German branch of the LDRN. Having spoken with Kouyaté, when Padmore arrived in Berlin that April, he immediately contacted Bilé and the Gambian labor organizer Edward Small; in London he and Patterson met Kenyatta, black seamen from Cardiff, and the Nigerian radical Frank Macaulay.[53] These contacts led many black Communists to see the ICNW's importance resting in its potential to link black working-class movements in Gambia, Nigeria, Kenya, the Caribbean, and the United States. Their efforts were so promising that when Padmore traveled with Edward Small to West Africa to recruit delegates, he felt he had found "good prospects for future work" and a "strong anti-imperialist sentiment everywhere." He returned to Europe convinced that the conference could be a huge success "if other sectors responded" as had West Africa.[54]

Despite such strides, Padmore and Patterson were beginning to question what might come of their contacts, given the indifference that communist parties in London, Berlin, and Paris had shown toward the conference. For those conference delegates who secured visas for travel to Europe, upon their arrival they found a rather unwelcoming, if not hostile, "advanced" proletariat that was largely uninformed about the conference. As late as April, Small, Bilé, and other African trade union leaders had received no information from any Communist group. In Germany, the LAI and other Comintern groups knew little about the conference and had made no efforts to carry on work among Africans in Berlin or Hamburg.[55] When Padmore arrived in Germany with four West African delegates, German Communists refused to provide support of any kind, even food or housing. Frustrated, hungry, and likely disillusioned, the delegates returned home, leaving an exasperated Padmore to complain to Moscow, "This is a hell of a way of doing things."[56]

Under such circumstances, it was remarkable that nineteen delegates made it to Hamburg. Joined by three fraternal delegates, the small group crowded into the top floor of Hamburg's Seamen's Club and began to hash out a program for international black struggle.[57] The conference entailed the reading of reports on colonial abuses balanced by accounts of trade union organizing, and the outline of the ITUCNW's future agenda. Helen McClain, a Philadelphia Needle Trade Workers organizer, insisted that the group pay "special attention to the position of women workers everywhere," while Small urged support for the struggle in Cameroon and for the "rights and the independence that belongs to Man and to all races."

While official Comintern observers considered the conference only a mod-est success, black Communists responded quite differently.[58] In his report, Ford claimed that those present represented more than twenty thousand workers from different parts of Africa, the United States, and the Caribbean. Although a dubious number, it reflected the sense of possibility that drew those present to Hamburg. The ITUCNW was to be an organization encompassing a diverse range of radicals and political movements. Rather than a mere cog in the Comintern machinery, the ITUCNW would foreground questions of race and colonialism in building diasporic anticolonial movements.[59]

When Burroughs, Patterson, and Ford arrived in Frankfurt, they could hardly have imagined that they would help build a movement uniting black workers around the world. The ITUCNW surpassed anything that had come before it in its reach and appeal to diasporic radicals. This was the context in which George Padmore assumed control of the ITUCNW and rapidly emerged as the most powerful black person in the international communist movement. In this position, Padmore cultivated a network of more than a thousand black activist-intellectuals throughout the diaspora, with ITUCNW chapters in Guadeloupe, Haiti, Senegal, Cameroon, Liberia, Panama, St. Lucia, and Madagascar.[60] It was not surprising, then, that when Padmore resigned from the Comintern in 1933 over what he considered its abandonment of anticolonial struggles in Africa and Asia, he would help build one of the more important anticolonial movements in the European metropole—the London-based International African Services Bureau. In this group, where he worked closely with C. L. R. James, Amy Ashwood Garvey, and several former ITUCNW members, Padmore helped build a group that focused on anticolonial struggle in Africa, the Caribbean, China, and India.[61]

I remain uncertain about the place of US political history in this dia-sporic story. Not because I believe there is nothing to gain from attending to the many political histories of the United States (maybe my unease is in the implied singularity), but because of the easy slippage that accompanies a given field or frame, which, to borrow from anthropologist Michel Rolph-Trouillot, often silences as much as it reveals.[62] Padmore's international career took off in the United States, but hardly began there. Nor did it end in Europe (if an end place must be named, Ghana, as advisor to Kwame Nkrumah). Yet those in the ITUCNW, and later the International African Service Bureau, played key roles in global anticolonial struggles. Padmore's Pan-African Federation, the group he established after dissolving the IASB in 1944, had organized the pivotal Fifth Pan-African Congress that met in Manchester, England, in 1945. Out of these formations would come key figures in African national liberation movements, Caribbean independence and the West Indies Federation, and even in American political formations like the Council on African Affairs and the National Negro Congress, groups that were important precursors to the Civil Rights and Black Power Movements, possibly even foils to the general tendency to see these as national movements. Indeed, William Patterson played a key role, alongside such figures as W. E. B. Du Bois and Paul Robeson, in the Civil Rights Congress that would draft a sorely understudied document on US racial violence against its own citizens, *We Charge Genocide*.[63] If one were to take the LAI as a precursor to Bandung, we are necessarily drawn out of any sort of national frame for thinking the political, especially when we consider that such a capacious formation as the ITUCNW—itself something of a collateral formation to Brussels, Frankfurt, and even Moscow—could have such wide-ranging ramifications around the globe, it may prove necessary to begin taking US political history as the issue of other stories, especially the African diaspora.

NOTES

1. William L. Patterson, *Man Who Cried Genocide: An Autobiography* (New York: International, 1971), 44–9, 81, 92–3, 109–11.

2. Jean Jones, *The League against Imperialism*, Socialist History Society Occasional Papers Series 4 (London: Socialist History Society, 1996), esp. 14–15, 24–30; Item 1: "Invitation to the International Congress against Colonial Oppression and Imperialism," Berlin, December 15, 1926, League Against Imperialism Archives, International Institute of Social History, Amsterdam, Netherlands (hereinafter LAI Archives); Russian State Archive of Socio-Political History (RGASPI) 515/1/720/11–12. RGASPI citations follow the archival organizational structure, which gives *fond* (collection), *opis* (index), *delo* (file), and *listok* (page).

3. Patterson, *Man Who Cried Genocide*, 111.

4. Michele Mitchell, *Righteous Propagation: African American and the Politics of Racial Destiny after Reconstruction* (Chapel Hill: University of North Carolina Press, 2004), 53–75; Ibrahim Sundiata, *Brothers and Strangers: Black Zion, Black Slavery, 1914–1940* (Durham, NC: Duke University Press, 2003).

5. Richard Iton, *In Search of the Black Fantastic: Politics & Popular Culture in the Post–Civil Rights Era* (New York: Oxford University Press, 2010), 135.

6. See Mary Dudziak, *Cold War Civil Rights: Race and the Image of American Democracy* (Princeton: Princeton University Press, 2000); Brenda Gayle Plummer, *Rising Wind: Black Americans and U.S. Foreign Affairs, 1935–1960* (Chapel Hill: University of North Carolina Press, 1996); Penny Von Eschen, *Race against Empire: Black Americans and Anticolonialism, 1937–1957* (Ithaca, NY: Cornell University Press, 1997); Carol Anderson, *Eyes Off the Prize: African Americans, the United Nations, and the Struggle for Human Rights, 1944–1955* (Cambridge: Cambridge University Press, 2003); Carol Anderson, *Bourgeois Radicals: The NAACP and the Struggle for Colonial Liberation, 1941–1960* (Cambridge: Cambridge University Press, 2014).

7. See Robin D. G. Kelley, "'But a Local Phase of a World Problem': Black History's Global Vision, 1883–1950," *Journal of American History* (December 1999): 1045–77; Brent Hayes Edwards, *The Practice of Diaspora: Literature, Translation, and the Rise of Black Internationalism* (Cambridge, MA: Harvard University Press, 2003); Dayo Gore, *Radicalism at the Crossroads: African American Women Activists in the Cold War* (New York: New York University Press, 2011); Gary Wilder, *Freedom Time: Negritude, Decolonization, and the Future of the World* (Durham, NC: Duke University Press, 2015).

8. Antoinette Burton, "Introduction: On the Inadequacy and the Indispensability of the Nation," in *After the Imperial Turn: Thinking with and through the Nation*, ed. Antoinette Burton (Durham, NC: Duke University Press, 2003), 1. See also Daniel T. Rogers, *Atlantic Crossings: Social Politics in a Progressive Age* (Cambridge, MA: Harvard University Press, 1998); Harvey R. Neptune, *Caliban and the Yankees: Trinidad and the United States Occupation* (Chapel Hill: University of North Carolina Press, 2007); Ian Tyrrell, *Transnational Nation: United States History in Global Perspective since 1789* (New York: Palgrave Macmillan, 2007).

9. For new scholarship in this vein, see Michelle Stephens, *Black Empire: The Masculine Global Imaginary of Caribbean Intellectuals in the United States, 1919–1962* (Durham, NC: Duke University Press, 2005); Erik McDuffie, *Sojourning for Freedom: Black Women, American Communism, and the Making of Black Left Feminism* (Durham, NC: Duke University Press, 2010); Nico Slate, *Colored Cosmopolitanism: The Shared Struggle for Freedom in the United States and India* (Cambridge, MA: Harvard University Press, 2012); Cheryl Higashida, *Black Internationalist Feminism: Women Writers of the Black Left, 1945–1995* (Urbana: University of Illinois Press, 2011); Lara Putnam, *Radical Moves: Caribbean Migrants and the Politics of Race in the Jazz Age* (Chapel Hill: University of North Carolina Press, 2013); Gerald Horne, *Black Liberation/Red Scare: Ben Davis and the Communist Party* (Newark, NJ: University of Delaware Press, 1994); Erik S. Gellman, *Death Blow to Jim Crow: The National Negro Congress and the Rise of Militant Civil Rights* (Chapel Hill: University of North Carolina Press, 2012).

10. Odd Arne Westad, *The Global Cold War* (Cambridge: Cambridge University Press, 2005), 4. Westad's argument corresponds with a central claim about the dominance of European modernity as found in the modernity/(de)coloniality school, reflected most prominently by Walter Mignolo, *The Darker Side of Western Modernity* (Durham, NC: Duke University Press, 2011).

11. Erez Manela, *The Wilsonian Moment: Self-Determination and the International Origins of Anticolonial Nationalism* (New York: Oxford University Press, 2007); "If It Were Only True," *Crusader*, March 1919, 10; Cyril Briggs, "The American Race Problem," *Crusader*, September 1918, 12; "League of Nations," *Crusader*, February 1919, 6.

12. Cyril Briggs to Theodore Draper, March 17, 1958, box 31, folder Briggs, Theodore Draper Collection, Hoover Institute of War, Revolution, and Peace, Stanford University, Stanford, CA (hereinafter Draper Collection). Ho Chi Minh quoted in William J. Duiker, *Ho Chi Minh: A Life* (New York: Hyperion, 2000), 64.

13. Hakim Adi, "The Negro Question: The Communist International and Black Liberation in the Interwar Years," in *From Toussaint to Tupac: The Black International since the Age of Revolution*, ed. Michael West, William Martin, and Fanon Che Wilkins (Chapel Hill: University of North Carolina Press, 2009), 155.

14. RGASPI 542/1/7/27; RGASPI 542/1/7/61–61bp; RGASPI 515/1/917/42; Item 2: "List of Organizations and Delegates attending the Congress against Colonial Oppression and Imperialism," Brussels, February 10, 1927, Egmont Palace, LAI Archives; Item 6: "Adressen an den Kongress gegen Kolonialunterdrückung und Imperialismus," February 10, 1927, Brussels, LAI Archives. Einstein, George Lansbury, and China's Madame Sun Yat-sen were all listed as honorary presidents.

15. Joel E. Spingarn to William Pickens, October 1, 1926, William Pickens, "Conference of Colonial, Semi-Colonial, and Repressed Peoples, in Belgium," September 23, 1926, and untitled memo, n.d., in box 11, folder 1, reel 11, William Pickens Papers (Additions), Schomburg Center for Research in Black Culture, Manuscript, Archives, and Rare Books Division, New York Public Library, New York (hereinafter Pickens Papers).

16. CDRN delegates included Narcisse Danae, Max Bloncourt, and Eli Bloncourt from Guadeloupe and the Haitian Camille St. Jacques, a former Communist. Item 1: "Invitation to the International Congress against Colonial Oppression and Imperialism," Berlin, December 15, 1926, Item 2: "List of Organizations and Delegates," Item 6: "Adressen an den Kongress gegen Kolonialunterdrückung und Imperialismus," February 10, 1927, Brussels, LAI Archives; J. A. Langley, "Pan-Africanism in Paris, 1924–1936," *Journal of Modern African Studies* 7, no. 1 (1969): 84–85.

17. RGASPI 515/1/917/43, 54, 62.

18. Item 44: "Interview par Daniele Martini avec Jawahar Lal Nehru," LAI Archives; Jawaharlal Nehru, *Toward Freedom: The Autobiography of Jawaharlal Nehru* (Boston: Beacon, 1967).

19. Item 9: "Texte du Discours d'Ouverture par Henri Barbusse," LAI Archives.

20. RGASPI 542/1/77/75–81; RGASPI 542/1/69/62–4.

21. J. T. Gumede speech to International Congress against Imperialism, Brussels, February 10–15, 1927, http://www.anc.org.za/ancdocs/speeches/1920s/gumedesp.htm; RGASPI 542/1/69/28–30.

22. Item 53: "Discours de Max Bloncourt, Délégué des Antilles" (stenographic copy), LAI Archives.

23. J. S. Spiegler, "Aspects of Nationalist Thought among French-Speaking West Africans, 1921–1939" (D.Phil. diss., Nuffield College, Oxford University, 1968), 118; Roger N. Baldwin, "The Capital of the Men without a Country," *Survey Graphic*, August 1927, 446.

24. Lamine Senghor, "Au Congrès de Bruxelles du 10 au 15 Février 1927: Condamnation de l'impérialisme et de la colonisation," *Voix des Nègres*, March 1927, 1, reproduced as "Under the Dark Man's Burden," *Living Age*, May 15, 1927, 866–8; Brent Hayes Edwards, "The Shadow of Shadows," *positions* 11, no. 1 (2003): 26–7.

25. Item 24: "Résolution Anglo-Indoue-Chinoise," LAI Archives; Item 19: "Resolution betr. Südafrika von den Delegierten der Südafrikanischen Union, D. Colraine, J. A. La Guma, J. Gumede," LAI Archives; "Pandit Nehru and the Unity of the Oppressed People of South Africa," African National Congress, http://www.anc.org.za/ancdocs/history/solidarity/indiasa4.html.

26. Item 54: "Résolutions Communes sur la Question Nègre," 1927, LAI Archives.

27. Richard B. Moore, "Statement at the Congress of the League against Imperialism and for National Independence," in Richard B. Moore, Caribbean Militant in Harlem: Collected Writings, 1920–1972, ed. W. Burghardt Turner and Joyce Moore Turner (Bloomington: Indiana University Press, 1988), 143–46; Item 54: "Résolutions Communes sur la Question Nègre," LAI Archives.

28. Daily Worker, February 11, 1927, 4, March 14, 1927, 3, March 15, 1927, 3, March 16, 1927, 3.

29. Josephine Fowler, Japanese and Chinese Immigrant Activists: Organizing in American and International Communist Movements, 1919–1933 (New Brunswick, NJ: Rutgers University Press, 2007), 2; Nehru, Toward Freedom, 123–7.

30. Joyce Moore Turner, "Richard B. Moore and His Works," in Richard B. Moore, 54.

31. Flyer announcing rally, Sunday, April 10, 1927, RGASPI 515/1/1212; Flyer announcing rally, February 14, 1927, RGASPI 515/1/1213; "The Colonial Congress and the Negro," Crisis, July 1927, 165–6; "To All Oppressed Peoples and Classes," Crisis, October 1927, 273; "Postscript," Crisis, January 1928, 23.

32. William Pickens, "The Brussels Congress," address to the Fourth Pan-African Congress, New York, August 21, 1927, box 11, folder 1, reel 11, Pickens Papers; "Pan-Africa," Crisis, October 1927, 263; RGASPI 515/1/1067/13–14; RGASPI 542/1/18/28; Joyce Moore Turner, Caribbean Crusaders and the Harlem Renaissance (Urbana: University of Illinois Press, 2005), 147–58.

33. "The Pan-African Congresses," Crisis, October 1927, 264.

34. Elizabeth Hendrickson, "Man in the Street," Amsterdam News, January 8, 1930, 20.

35. Liberator, December 7, 1929, 2; CB, "High Rents and the Death Rate," Liberator, December 7, 1929, 3; Richard B. Moore, "Housing and the Negro Masses," Negro Champion, September 8, 1928, 1, 5; Mark Solomon, Cry Was Unity: Communism and African Americans, 1917–1936 (Jackson: University Press of Mississippi, 1998), 97, 99.

36. Daily Worker, August 5, 1929, 1, August 6, 1929, 3; Amsterdam News, January 1, 1930, 20, June 5, 1929, 1, 2, June 12, 1929, 3, November 27, 1929, 3; Chicago Defender, August 3, 1929, 11; Pittsburgh Courier, December 21, 1929, 19; Liberator, December 7, 1929, 1, 2, 3, December 14, 1929, 1, December 28, 1929, 1.

37. W. Foster, "Draft Report: The 4th Convention of the Trade Union Unity League," November 28, 1929, RGASPI 515/1/1565; "Program of Action," n.d., 515/1/3356.

38. James R. Hooker, *Black Revolutionary: George Padmore's Path from Communism to Pan-Africanism* (New York: Praeger, 1967), 2, 5–7; Nnamdi Azikiwe, *My Odyssey: An Autobiography* (New York: Praeger, 1970), 138–9.

39. Minutes of the Negro Commission, January 3, 1929, RGASPI 515/1/1685; RGASPI 515/1/1366/7, 8–10, 12–13; RGASPI 515/1/1535/42; 515/1/1688/25–7; *Liberator*, May 10, 1930, 1.

40. RGASPI 515/1/1579/165–8; RGASPI 515/1/1580/166–75; RGASPI 515/1/1583/110–12; *Negro Champion*, March 23, 1929, 2; Cyril Briggs, "Our Negro Work," *The Communist*, September 1929, 494, 501; Solomon, *Cry Was Unity*, 60, 96–8.

41. *International Press Correspondence*, August 8, 1928, 812.

42. Ibid., August 3, 1928, 772–3, 781–2, August 8, 1928, 811–12, August 11, 1928, 856, August 13, 1928, 872, October 25, 1928, 1345–6, October 30, 1928, 1392.

43. Hakim Adi, "Pan-Africanism and Communism: The Comintern, the 'Negro Question' and the First International Conference of Negro Workers, Hamburg 1930," *African and Black Diaspora Journal* 1, no. 2 (2008): 240–1.

44. RGASPI 542/1/16/26/32; RGASPI 542/1/18/22–4; RGASPI 542/1/20/17–19.

45. RGASPI 542/1/32/34–5; RGASPI 495/155/70/62–8; RGASPI 495/155/70/69–71, 72–3, 74–6; RGASPI 495/155/87/350–5; RGASPI 542/1/30/48, 70; RGASPI 542/1/79/48.

46. RGASPI 542/1/88/5–6bp; RGASPI 542/1/79/20–2, 26–7, 41; RGASPI 542/1/32/50.

47. RGASPI 542/1/79/45; RGASPI 495/155/72/59–62.

48. RGASPI 495/155/77/184; Kouyaté quoted in Edwards, *Practice of Diaspora*, 354.

49. RGASPI 495/155/87/28–31.

50. "An Appeal to Negro Workers of the World," *Negro Worker*, January–February 1930, 1; RGASPI 495/155/77/184–6; Adi, "Pan-Africanism," 242.

51. RGASPI 534/3/450/89–90; Hooker, *Black Revolutionary*, 13–14.

52. RGASPI 495/155/80/54–7; RGASPI 495/155/70/57–8, 59; RGASPI 495/155/77/306.

53. Adi, "Pan-Africanism," 243; Holger Weiss, *Framing a Radical African Atlantic: African American Agency, West African Intellectuals and the International Trade Union Committee of Negro Workers* (Leiden: Koninklijke Brill NV, 2014), 443–50.

54. *Amsterdam News*, February 26, 1930, 20; RGASPI 495/155/89/22/27; RGASPI 534/4/330/24–5; Adi, "Pan-Africanism," 243–44; Robbie Aitken, "From Cameroon to Germany and Back via Moscow and Paris: The Political Career of Joseph Bile (1892–1959), Performer, 'Negerarbeiter' and Comintern Activist," *Journal of Contemporary History* 43, no. 4 (2008): 597, 601, 603.

55. RGASPI 495/155/87/246–7, 250; RGASPI 495/155/83/96–7; Weiss, *Framing*, 216.

56. Adi, "Pan-Africanism," 245–6; RGASPI 495/155/87/246–7, 250; RGASPI 495/155/83/96–7; Weiss, *Framing*, 265.

57. *Report of the Proceedings and Decisions of the First International Conference of Negro Workers* (Hamburg, Ger.: International Trade Union Committee of Negro

Workers, 1932), 1, 40; RGASPI 495/155/87/247, 295. ICNW delegates included Bilé, Macaulay, Small, Padmore, Ford, Burroughs, Patterson, E. A. Richards (Sierra Leone), T. S. Morton (Gold Coast), J. A. Akrong (Gold Coast), M. De Leon (Jamaica), Helen McClain (United States), and four other African Americans. Fraternal delegates included A. Green (South Africa), Willi Budich (Germany), Budich's stenographer, and Berlin-based Indian Communist Virendranath Chattopadhyaya.

58. *International Press Correspondence*, July 24, 1930, 635; Adi, "Pan-Africanism," 248–50; Weiss, *Framing*.

59. RGASPI 495/155/87/243–51, 290–6; Weiss, *Road*, 112, 116. The ITUCNW Executive included Ford, I. Hawkins, McClain, and Padmore (United States); Kouyaté, Macaulay, Small, and South African Albert Nzula (Africa); and E. Reid (Caribbean).

60. RGASPI 495/155/100/29–31; RGASPI 542/1/54/92; Turner, *Caribbean Crusaders*, 197.

61. On the International African Service Bureau, see Minkah Makalani, *In the Cause of Freedom: Radical Black Internationalism from Harlem to London, 1917–1939* (Chapel Hill: University of North Carolina Press, 2011), 195–224.

62. Michel Rolph-Trouillot, *Silencing the Past: Power and the Production of History* (Boston: Beacon, 1995).

63. In addition to my own work suggesting such connections, see Penny von Eschen, *Race against Empire*; Gellman, *Death Blow to Jim Crow*. For scholars of Civil Rights and Black Power charting the international dimensions of these movements, see Fanon Che Wilkins, "Beyond Bandung: The Critical Nationalism of Lorraine Hansberry, 1950–1965," *Radical History Review Spring* 95 (2006): 191–210; Joshua Guild, "You Can't go Home Again: Migration, Citizenship, and Black Communist in Postwar New York and London" (PhD diss., Yale University, 2007); David Austin, "All Roads Led to Montreal: Black Power, the Caribbean, and the Black Radical Tradition in Canada," *Journal of African American History* 92 (Autumn 2007): 516–39; Dayo F. Gore, "From Communist Politics to Black Power: The Visionary Politics and Transnational Solidarities of Victoria 'Vicki' Ama Garvin," 72–94, in *Want to Start a Revolution? Radical Women in the Black Freedom Movement*, ed. Dayo F. Gore, Jeanne Theoharris, and Komozi Woodard (New York: New York University Press, 2009); Anne-Marie Angelo, "The Black Panthers in London, 1967–1972: A Diasporic Struggle Navigates the Black Atlantic," *Radical History Review* 103 (Winter 2009): 17–35; Seth Markle, " 'We Are Not Tourists': The Black Power Movement and the Making of 'Socialist' Tanzania, 1960–1974" (PhD diss., New York University, 2011); and Stephen Tuck, "Malcolm X's Visit to Oxford University: U.S. Civil Rights, Black Britain, and the Special Relationship on Race," *American Historical Review* (February 2013): 76–103.

9

"The South's No. 1 Salesman"

Luther Hodges and the Nuevo South's
Transatlantic Circuitry

Elizabeth Tandy Shermer

"We've Become Sweden's Mexico," an organizer lamented during a 2011 battle to unionize a Danville Ikea factory. This impoverished Virginia hamlet certainly seems to have more in common with Juarez than the Research Triangle Park (RTP), which sprawls 50 miles away in land between Duke University, the University of North Carolina, Chapel Hill, and North Carolina State University. Unlike Danville, the Triangle exemplifies the lucrative potential of the postindustrial knowledge economy. Yet Durham, Raleigh, and Chapel Hill only appear a century removed from their tobacco-centric past. Only recently have developers turned the Lucky Strike cigarette factory into luxury lofts for lawyers, bankers, and engineers. The latter, as more than a few quip, are often Indians, not Native Americans but South Asians rapidly bettering communication, security, and medical technologies.[1]

Lucrative Triangle opportunities and low-wage Ikea jobs are emblematic of the South's twentieth-century transformation from the "Nation's No. 1 Economic Problem," as FDR described it in 1938, into the millennial center of American manufacturing. Nuevo South scholarship largely attributes its metamorphosis to defense contracts and American auto and electronics manufacturers relocating to nonunion Dixie, a generation before a new wave of Mexican migrants arrived for factory work well-away from the US–Mexico border. The globalization of the 1970s has generally been explored separately and often credited to economists associated with the Mont Pelerin Society and other postwar academic refuges from Keynesianism. Their early cautious defenses of the market inspired a new generation of economists to prescribe aggressive free-trade policies. The resultant multipolar world order became shockingly apparent during the oil crisis, which symbolized the apogee of the Western allegiances to the Fordism and social-welfare guarantees that had made a generation of European and North American trade unionists into blue-collar consumers with middle-class tastes.[2]

Economists and policymakers were not the only ones responsible for North Atlantic manufacturing's crumbling. Major executives, mid-level managers, and small business owners made the business deals, supply chains, and organizations behind capital's flight to underdeveloped areas around the world, where taxes, regulations, and labor costs were lower. Entrepreneurial efforts were as much about profits as politics. Many involved loathed social democracy and had important connections to think tanks and official diplomatic channels. Entrepreneurial executives also expanded and strengthened business networks, like the Rotary International, to arrange the foreign investment that undermined North Atlantic postwar prosperity.

Wheeler-dealers interacted at local, regional, national, and international levels to create the circuitry for the coming hyper-competitive, interdependent, postindustrial world order. Luther Hodges operated in all of these overlapping castes to aggressively recruit industry to impoverished mid-century North Carolina. This Tar Heel rose through the ranks of Marshall Field & Company textile operations, had deep connections with the Rotary, and served liberals who trusted this Southern Democrat to set prices at home during World War II and then help oversee postwar recovery efforts abroad. Like many small-town Southerners and high-ranking executives, Hodges distrusted New Dealers. His federal service cemented his distaste for their statecraft and inspired him to become the South's first self-proclaimed "businessman in the statehouse." The governor skillfully vied for investment through policies antithetical to liberal social democracy. He was also the first promoter to systematically court Europeans. His foreign and Rotary service had introduced him to many who shared his managerial worldview and had already explained their business needs and constraints. He hence already knew how to market the South for international investors, who needed incentives that complemented the concurrent calls for trade liberalization coming out of international think tanks.

He Profits Most Who Serves Best

"I was shocked," Hodges reflected in 1962, "to receive a report . . . that listed North Carolina as forty-fourth among the then forty-eight states in per capita income." He should not have been astonished: rural poverty had been Hodges's birthright. This tenant farmer's son (born just 20 miles from Danville in 1898 but raised a Tar Heel) had grown up well outside the South's agricultural aristocracy and the coterie of urban businessmen, the ones convinced that northern industry and investment would dethrone the rural planter class. Hodges spent his youth working in the Piedmont mill world, the low-wage province of northeastern investors. He became an office boy at age twelve in a Spray factory near the Virginia border. The teenager proved himself an eager, education-oriented politician. This senior-class president matriculated at UNC-Chapel Hill. His 1919 degree still did not offer him entry into the Raleigh, Durham, or Charlotte business elite. Hodges instead returned to the Spray-Leaksville area, where he assisted the general manager of a Marshall Field's mill.[3]

The Rotary International did the most to shape Hodges's managerial style. Rotarianism differed sharply from the boosterism practiced within southern Chambers of Commerce, where small-town and big-city promoters bought payroll for their communities with giveaways and guarantees. In contrast, white Protestant entrepreneurs had started the Rotary in 1905, a sheltered Chicago fraternity to mix business with the collegiality needed to face the Second City's ruthless financial elites and uncooperative white-ethnic ward bosses. Prosperity and fellowship also inspired businessmen outside Chicago. The organization became a symbol of small-town America but also progressive internationalism. In the 1910s, Los Angeles, Winnipeg, Dublin, and Dresden Rotarians made "world peace" their rallying cry. The interwar Rotary then emphasized "Service above Self" because "He profits most who serves best." Even small-town Rotarians deemed their local good works a part of something bigger. For example, Leaksville members considered mundane issues, such as the structure of local law enforcement agencies, as vital as committees dedicated to club, vocational, and international service. American Rotarians hence tended to welcome voluntarism, Herbert Hoover's associationalism, and even early New Deal liberalism, which offered to nationalize private interwar experiments for economic stability.[4]

Yet Hodges's service to the Rotary and his employer inadvertently brought him into elite anti-Roosevelt circles. He presided over the Leaksville affiliate, chaired its vocational service committee, and became district governor in the late 1920s. That ascent occurred alongside the mill boy's move through the personnel, production, and general manager offices, which culminated in Marshall Field and Company making him a New York-based vice president. This promotion inducted him into Gotham's Rotary and the expanding circle of major executives rebelling against the New Deal.[5]

Sectors of American capitalism had always been wary of the Roosevelt administration but business obstinacy soared after 1935. That year's landmark union and social-welfare legislation alienated progressive businessmen who considered these measures dangerously excessive. Tensions escalated during the war. Industrialists defied FDR's demand that the interior house war production plants and military installations (a dictum justified in the name of defense but intended to fulfill liberal desires) to direct money, people, and manufacturing into the South and West. CEOs ignored these directives because industry-friendly officials, many "dollar-a-year men" still on their companies' payroll, staffed warfare-state bureaucracies. Those on the War Production Board favored the corporate status quo when it came to awarding contracts, as did military leaders. Large, established Steelbelt and Pacific Coast corporations became prime contractors and bristled at opening plants outside these areas, only conceding once their existing facilities could not fulfill demand.[6]

Dollar-a-year men had help thwarting liberalism's victory at home. Their allies were not to be found in the rural textile hamlets where Hodges had come of age but among the local booster organizations dedicated to reviving southern cities. Urban promoters lobbied policymakers for wartime investment and also promised contractors that their towns would put business needs first, an implicit promise to keep unions out, taxes low, and regulations minimal. Installations nonetheless transformed destitute whistle-stops into defense boomtowns. "[T]his whole draft business is just a Southern trick," one officer joked, "something put over by Southern merchants to hold the big trade they get from the training camps." Corporate profits also soared in this high-tax period because administrators signed generous contracts with suppliers and embraced "cost-plus" clauses to ensure defense would be lucrative to manufacturers still rebounding from the Depression. Even cancellation generated record after-tax earnings. The government paid up to 90 percent of nullified agreements, sold surplus inventory and factories well below cost, and provided large tax breaks on new or retooled plants and equipment.[7]

Defense also helped anti-New Deal businessmen recapture the prestige and political influence lost to liberalism. Hostile industrialists assailed strikers, labor rights, and, by extension, New Dealers. All represented obstacles to victory abroad. Groups opposed to labor liberalism, chiefly the National Association of Manufacturers, became far more active during the war. Jingoistic, free-enterprise appeals masked the anti-liberal bent to business activism, especially the hostility found outside the leadership circles that had advised Roosevelt and profited the most from Depression and wartime spending.[8]

Similar dissension could be found within international and local business circles. The Rotary, for example, may have publicly proclaimed itself dedicated to the democratic principles of peace, stability, and social welfare but Chicago leaders could hardly enforce diktats in far-flung affiliates (over three hundred in Europe). More than a few Rotarians proved mistrustful of industrial unionism, shopfloor democracy, and expansive social insurance schemes. Hodges, for one, outlined comparisons between New Dealers and Nazis, who outlawed the Rotary in 1937. Contemporaries often shared his conviction that they could not "properly operate" with "all the regulations . . . on us." "I don't like [the] attitude toward Company profits," Hodges admitted, "control of [railroad] and Utilities because of fear of rates and monopoly," or "War Labor Board policies" that had a "Company make a crooked deal with a union." "Diplomats, Ambassadors (so called statesman), Presidents, Politicians, Soldiers, Labor Leaders, Some Preachers, [and] University Presidents," he warned, "are not helping the World." "Ethical standards in business" were surely something "the world will learn and has learned from us—the USA," he told Carolina Rotarians in 1942. Evangelizing this entrepreneurial gospel had to be "a job for the future years of prosperity and activity."[9]

Autocracy, Nepotism, and the Office of Price Administration

Liberals ignored this hostility. Hodges's climb up Rotary ranks and within Marshall Field's made him an easy choice for a dollar-a-year man. He oversaw all of his employer's foreign and domestic textile mills and even chaired the Committee on Participation of Rotarians in the Post-War World, whose inaugural Chapel Hill meeting included American, Canadian, Swiss, English, Mexican, and South African members. The Tar Heel also looked to be the kind of grassroots Southerner whom New Dealers considered likely to support their efforts. He even had important connections to the elite networks of businessmen mobilizing for war and preparing for peace.[10]

Hodges nonetheless ignored federal officials' overtures until 1944, when he agreed to oversee textile costs for the Office of Price Administration (OPA). Marshall Field's managers deemed this task "the most pressing." This agency figured heavily in Board members' and Rotarians' postwar plans because it set prices. Many considered this practice at odds with free enterprise, a rallying cry among the anti-liberal businessmen who later funded America's postwar conservative movement. Hodges certainly doubted controls. He arrived in this controversial bureaucracy after many liberals had been ousted. Like other dollar-a-year men, he hardly seemed "on loan." He spent Mondays in his

New York office, commuted to Washington via airplane, and conducted mill inspections every few weeks.[11]

Hodges proved an undercover agent on the frontlines of policymaking. His opposition to liberalism hardened while in the Consumer Goods Price Division's Primary Products Branch. "I am in favor of Price Control," Hodges proclaimed a month into his service. He still did not hesitate to issue a litany of complaints to his business associates against "our economists and law-yers," liberals who had overruled his attempt to raise prices. "[They] shouldn't assume powers of policy or decisions," he complained. The Rotarian consid-ered his business sense and values ignored. "I cannot," he fumed, "get busi-ness men [sic] into OPA" because we cannot "assure them we have a business organization run on business lines, not subject to snooping and stalling and attempt to throttle industry."[12]

This last lament shaped Hodges's conduct during his postwar work for the federal government. He readily consulted with Department of Agriculture appointees, advising them to weaken, consolidate, or dismantle federal pro-grams. But business competition motivated Hodges to advise the military gov-ernment's Joint Export Import Agency, which asked him in 1948 "to analyze the textile situation and make recommendation as to both the policy and the operation of the textile branch." Service and profit led Hodges to accept this invitation. Many of his peers wanted to stop the Army from reviving the once-mighty German cotton industry. Executives had reason to be proactive: prior to Hodges's arrival, officials had distributed American fibers to German mills and then instituted a policy of permitting German manufacturers to cheaply source supplies from American and Egyptian exporters.[13]

Hodges was not the only anti-liberal American executive undermining social democracy at home and abroad. Recent scholarship underscores that business conservatives' most public counteroffensives against the New Deal order may have waited until the early 1950s but many had always been hos-tile to liberalism or had grown increasingly dissatisfied during World War II. This literature excludes dollar-a-year men like Hodges, who undermined Roosevelt, the liberal warfare state, and European economic recovery from within Democratic administrations. Historians have largely overlooked the entrepreneurial backgrounds of these lower-level policymakers, instead focus-ing on divisions between unionists and appointees or assuming that all con-sultants shared the business creed of Paul Hoffman, the liberal Studebaker executive heading the Marshall Plan. These assumptions have led scholars to conclude that Americans only successfully distributed the "politics of pro-ductivity" because aid was scattershot, lacking, and unnecessary for rebound-ing countries. Yankees better distributed consumerism and a labor-liberalism built on power-sharing between businesses, unions, and government agencies. As in America, these so-called "corporatist" or "tri-partite" arrangements secured continental industrial peace and economic growth through contract negotiations. This routinized collective bargaining undermined the kind of labor alliances that had previously formed a Popular Front against Fascism and then seemed poised to have an outsized role in reconstructing postwar Western Europe. With American and European labor sated on roast beef and apple pie, historian Charles Maier noted, "Western leaders recovered more of their prosperity and ... retained more of their privileges and prerogatives, than they would have dared predict."[14]

Hodges had not wanted the world to learn American labor-liberalism or union militancy. He was hardly alone. Bitter divisions existed between military leaders, liberal bureaucrats, business advisors, and politicians even before the Marshall Plan formally began. Generals envisioned small businesses leading a Jeffersonian rebuilding of the German economy, whereas Truman Administration officials sought to take apart the conglomerations behind the Nazi war machine. New York executives considered both plans an affront to American corporate capitalism and maneuvered themselves to redirect key divisions in the American military government. Staunch Republican critic of the New Deal Senator Arthur Vandenberg then ensured the Marshall Plan would not be overseen by the State Department, whose New Deal holdovers faced congressional and public scrutiny over their loyalty. Vandenberg demanded an administrator "from the outside business world with strong industrial credentials." Hoffman fit the bill. So did enlistees from the Committee for Economic Development, a group formed at Commerce Secretary Jesse Jones's behest. This Texas Democrat had never been a New Dealer. His hand-picked appointees publicly proclaimed themselves Keynesians but actually spread a free-enterprise, anti-New Deal gospel when they traveled to the wartime boomtowns devastated by closing military bases and shuttered defense plants.

Hodges and other executive conscripts need not have worried about their ability to proselytize for free enterprise. The decentralized Marshall Plan enabled them to empower like-minded Europeans. In Germany, for example, American officials embraced Freiburg School economists, even though their prewar assertions that interventionism, cartelization, and protectionism were akin to political authoritarianism had made them intellectual outcasts. These ordoliberals found themselves back in power far sooner than Hayek and other social-welfare skeptics on the fringes of mainstream economic thought. American officials embraced Germany's free-market advocates, even though these academics' laissez-faire reasoning troubled continental manufacturers and policymakers and also stood outside the confines of New and Fair Deal liberalism. German businessmen eventually accepted these experts. These scholars remained decision-makers while industrialists reestablished their old export markets and embraced the postwar organizations that oversaw 1970s trade liberalization.[15]

American executives benefited a great deal from meeting their European counterparts while in government service. For example, during a 1948 two-week trip to Western Europe, Hodges and other on-loan executives met fellow Rotarians eager to rebuild enterprises dedicated to textiles, woolens, lathes, tractors, shoes, presses, cameras, cars, tools, toys, jewelry, chemicals, and pharmaceuticals. But these like-minded businessmen showed Hodges the threat a revived Germany posed. "It will be a number of years before the German textile industry will export textiles in quantity to the USA," he confided to his colleagues back home, but Germans "do not have . . . the same standards of living as that of our workmen," "wages in the textile plants generally over there will run around 30¢ whereas ours will be approximately four times that amount."[16]

Hodges's whirlwind tour convinced him that businessmen needed to govern. In his personal notes, he described the provisional government as "Autocracy. Nepotism. OPA, W[ar] P[roduction] B[oard], N[ational] R[ecovery] A[dministration] rolled into one plus. Got to ask for permission to go to the toilet." He had little faith in bureaucrats, servicemen, and politicians, especially the military officers who paid "No attention . . . to deliveries, printing orders, dye orders, bleaching orders, or any other detail of the business." He eagerly shared these observances with his elite friends at home, proudly recounting his recommendations to drastically reduce the textile division's size and align it "with the overall policy of the economic government." Yet his employers had him rebuff Army overtures to stay on to help implement the recently passed Marshall Plan. They needed him at home to oversee the firm's internal reconversion but accepted his retirement two years later so that he could head the Economic Cooperation Administration's (ECA) West German industry division. Marshall Field higher-ups "pray[ed] that your efforts will result in creating a greater appreciation for the American way of life in Western Germany than has existed before."[17] Hodges met many industrialists already envious of American business conditions during a two-year tour-of-duty that vastly expanded his Rolodex. Officially, he helped oversee ECA and advised State Department officials involved in a top-level technical assistance program for European corporations. These duties quickly embroiled him in one of the flash points between liberal policymakers and executive recruits in the US military government: decartelization. Liberals were dedicated to preventing the creation of another German war machine, which they blamed on the cartels that limited competition and centralized capital within a few firms. Their solution: break up these enterprises. Wall Street recruits (many with prewar connections to German manufacturers) resisted dismembering corporations, much as they did at home. Businessmen nonetheless disdained cartelization for exactly the reason many trade unionists embraced it: concentration tended to stabilize and even raise wages. That effect also pleased select progressive economists, who hoped this form of horizontal integration would lead to the nationalization of "natural monopolies."[18]

Executives, like Hodges, had grounds to fear cartelization's persistence abroad because of their experiences at home. The New Deal's landmark Tennessee Valley Authority had been just such an experiment in managing competition, a project that had quickly transformed the entire nation's public and private utilities. Plus, American steel, auto, and light-electronics industries seemed on the precipice of cartelization in the early postwar period, just a few years after the Congress of Industrial Organizations had legally organized these sectors' principal firms. The CIO also seemed poised to gain such a powerful advantage over Hodges and his colleagues. By the late 1940s, Textile Workers Union of America (TWUA) leaders had increased members' power, militancy, and pay, the victories that Hodges had interpreted as keeping American labor costs well above those expenses in war-ravaged Europe. TWUA campaigns had also occurred in Hodges's backyard. He returned to Europe after Yonkers, Manhattan's "Sixth Borough," had become a TWUA stronghold. TWUA was also a driving force in the CIO's attempt to unionize southern industry. This effort included a 1951 general strike, during which 40,000 laborers across North Carolina and six other southern states walked off the job.[19]

Such domestic turmoil no doubt colored Hodge's displeasure at cartelization's international popularity. Hodges feared that "[t]he German mind runs to controls and combines," which could lead to the "nationalization of steel and coal," not free-market competition. Other American officials were equally frustrated. American magnates resistant to this sort of business arrangement had already forced some liberal administrators to resign from the Marshall Plan but former executives still spared no expense to "indoctrinate" German industrialists and lawyers in the principles of American antitrust legislation, which penalized trade restraints (not bigness).[20]

Hodges also chipped away at the liberal American warfare state's remnants. He immediately set guidelines to fully define jobs and responsibilities, reduce staff numbers, and make periodic personnel and policy reviews. These priorities fell in line with his previous frustrations with liberal bureaucracies. Hodges happily reduced expenditures and consolidated branches dedicated to fuel, power, and production. "I've changed [them] to 'Industrial Progress,'" he explained, "and cut out useless functions at [other] offices and saved 14 people out of 80."[21]

Hodges's official duties also gave him the chance to establish connections between like-minded European and American businessmen. The Rotary provided an entry with those Europeans who had remained in business during Depression, war, and recovery. Accommodation, collaboration, and cooption had enabled these industrialists' survival and their willingness to cooperate with postwar policymakers undertaking the task of reconstructing European states and economies. Hodges resisted replicating the tripartite arrangements behind the American warfare state. He left bureaucrats and laborites out of the meetings he arranged between his former superiors at Marshall Field's and the European manufacturers eager to venture into continental recovery. Hodges's previous employers thanked Hodges for acquainting them with German CEOs. American investors also considered his recommendations invaluable because he had met extensively with Europeans and taken part in economic reconstruction. He had not availed himself out of self-interest. He was living up to the Rotary's principles of service, community, and internationalism. He said as much in reports back to family and friends, many of them anti-liberal businessmen who shared Hodges's commitment to preventing a social-democratic rebirth of Western Europe.[22]

Businessman in the Statehouse

ECA had embedded Hodges within an international contingent of anti-liberal businessmen but largely removed him from goings-on at home. He had transferred his offices to Spray in 1947 but constantly flew back to New York to supervise merchandising and sales. When he returned from Europe in 1952, the persistence of postwar poverty alarmed the retiree. North Carolina ranked near the bottom in per capita income in the early 1950s, when investment was transforming other nascent Sunbelt cities. In these emergent metropolises, promoters had already built sophisticated industrial recruitment programs and ensconced themselves in local, state, and national politics.[23]

Hodges hence found himself in what journalists at the time called the "Second War between the States." Outside investment triggered this conflict, which first began between western and southern states long starved of credit but ravaged during demobilization when abandoned war-production plants and military bases left boosters scrambling to find jobs for thousands of unemployed workers and veterans. Local drastic measures to "buy payroll" developed into more systematic efforts to attract continued Yankee investment in the 1950s, when corporations fatted on demobilization policies had the money to flee unions, regulations, and taxes. Local and national business-men embraced government power and planning because the policies that they hammered out in boardrooms, country clubs, and Chambers of Commerce reconstructed southern and western towns into metropolitan oases from the Steelbelt's labor liberalism. Together, anti-liberal boosterism and corporate cost-cutting undermined electoral politics, limited unionization, undermined regulation, and curbed profit redistribution. Interregional competition for lucrative, high-skill, high-tech investment enabled manufacturers to demand publicly financed factories, roads, utilities, parks, subdivisions, and schools, all of which became a part of a conservative, anti-Fordist "business climate" designed to limit corporate responsibility for living, work, and managerial standards.[24]

Hodges too embraced politics to run Carolina as he had managed ECA's textile division: like a competitive business. Hodges's 1952 campaign for lieu-tenant governor alarmed the state's agriculturally rooted political elite, those who benefited most from Jim Crow laws and the legislative malapportionment that kept commodities (like cotton and tobacco) king. Hodges had emerged from well outside their ranks and did not have their support. So he conducted what he later called a grassroots campaign, which entailed traversing the state to meet voters. His success relied more on Tar Heel businessmen than the common folk. His business background thrilled these boosters. Many hoped a 1952 victory would be the beginning of Hodges's political career and subse-quently did much to promote his candidacy locally.[25]

Hodges's victory gave him a chance to direct industrialization from within the state government, more than a decade after Atlanta, Dallas, and Phoenix promoters had made their way into legislatures and statehouses. Hodges faced fierce opposition from assemblymen and Governor William Umstead, who had refused to tie his election run to Hodges's campaign and kept the textile executive out of his dealings with the state senate. Nonetheless, the lieutenant governor promoted growth and even cited his experience in Europe as evi-dence of a need for cut-throat promotion, sowing the seeds for the kind of busi-ness-climate politics already predominant in the sprawling South and West. "We need competition between states to keep us active," the Rotarian told southeastern Chamber of Commerce leaders in 1953, "but we need coopera-tion to keep us growing and healthy." He cited his first-hand experience with German industrialists as proof that complacency threatened free enterprise: "Many of the European countries, including Germany the most advanced industrially, are inclined to perpetuate old ideas and to make the same mis-takes." Hodges's boosterism and business renown proved vital to his nascent promotional efforts. Outsiders, for example, took it upon themselves to contact him personally about possible branch plant locations.[26]

Hodges did not launch a full-scale industrialization initiative until Umstead's sudden 1954 death. Hodges initially faced resistance from agriculturalists, liberals, and unionists. Like other boosters, he wanted Yankee manufacturing investment to raise wages. But tobacco farmers relied on a cheap, desperate labor force. These rural elites also bristled at his efforts to expand the executive branch, which required more spending and increased taxation in the name of outside investment. Hodges hardly helped the trade unionists or civil rights activists who detested the planter classes. He famously used his authority to crush a strike at a Henderson textile mill. His "sworn duty to maintain law and order" inspired him to send in highway patrolmen and the national guard after 1,000 TWUA members walked off the job. Hodges never turned to reservists to suppress civil rights, as Arkansas's Orval Faubus did. Hodges instead allowed local communities to close schools, funded private options for children whose parents did not want them integrated, and created an advisory board to navigate demands for massive resistance.[27]

Hodges also embraced state power to construct the kind of business-friendly government necessary to compete for and support lucrative manufacturing. Like other booster governors, he expanded bureaus dedicated to economic growth. His appointees to the Department of Conservation and Development (C&D) were fellow textile barons who followed the lead of other southern, state-employed "bird dogs" to pursue investment across the country. The governor, as his principles dictated and his competitors ensured, resisted raising taxes on manufacturing to pay for recruiters or the modern roads, utilities, and schools that potential investors demanded. Legislators, especially those beholden to agriculturalists, balked at Hodges's proposal to make levies on tobacco and alcohol sales (not production) comparable to duties in forty-one other states. Lawmakers only passed taxes on beer and wine. So Hodges endeavored to improve collection methods. He mandated that employers withhold and forward state income taxes directly to the government, which, the governor later noted, "added to the tax rolls many thousands of people who for some reason or another had never before made a tax return." All total, this revenue revolution gave the state an additional $27.5 million and helped pay for improving Carolina's business climate.[28]

These receipts could not offset Hodges's higher education overhaul. The governor had initially targeted the state's colleges and universities as impediments to business governance until "new or expanding industries . . . asked about the quality as well as the quantity of the labor supply." Hodges confessed, "The answer we had to give was not satisfactory." He brazenly used the governor's mansion to expand K–12 schooling, technical training, and higher education. University expansion was integral to the Research Triangle Park, a fantasy that had circulated among university officials and boosters throughout the mid-1950s. The governor welcomed the plan as a shared venture between state officials, school administrators, and industrialists, which he united under the Governor's Research Triangle Committee. Two years of surveys resulted in a 1957 directive to build and promote RTP, whose development relied on expanding the science curriculum at North Carolina State College and UNC-Chapel Hill. The money came from state funds, private investments, and public shareholders, which Hodges considered proof that "[e]ducation is the chief business of the State of North Carolina."[29]

European Reinvestment

Hodges's enthusiasm for education's entrepreneurial potential did not make him unique; his long-standing Rotarianism and previous service abroad did. He was the first Sunbelt booster-statesman to aggressively, systematically court foreign industrialists. He realized early in his governorship that North Carolinians had to go abroad: well-heeled Steelbelt manufacturers already had hordes of promoters visiting their offices or inviting them out to inspect mushrooming cities. Tar-Heel recruiters, like all southern birddogs, also labored to attract the urban North's investors because of national attention to Dixie civil rights conflicts. Steelbelt executives may have been willing to uproot but their educated staff resisted moving South at the moment when reporters more readily covered Southerners' eagerness to close schools rather than Hodges's more covert resistance to integration and massive resistance.[30]

Hodges began to direct his energies eastward in the midst of this turmoil. Revitalized, unionized European manufacturers were primed for expansion. German industrialists, for example, had endeavored to reestablish themselves as world exporters at World War II's end. Just before Americans installed Freiburg School economists in West German government, these scholars had reasoned "initiative of private enterprise has to be employed on as large a scale as possible" because "merchants of the world have to resume their old business connections if the catastrophe of the war is to be overcome." Germans sent goods to North Africa and Eastern Europe before Latin America where Ferrostaal executives reported "a scarcity of dollars . . . had led to a stagnation of American private business there." By 1949 English presence had also declined "because of 'their very long deliver times' and . . . the frequent poor quality of goods." Three years later, a consortium of German companies negotiated with

Juan Peron to deliver 700 trolley buses to Buenos Aires, a niche that roadsters and station wagons from Detroit's Big Three could not fill. Germans started selling more wares in the United States in the mid-1950s, when advertisers marketed their goods (automobiles in particular) as well-crafted alternatives to mass-produced American merchandise. This overall reinvestment in the Americas in turn prompted new arrangements between German manufacturers and New York bankers to finance large-scale exports but also set up Gotham offices for firms' international operations, all of which Ferrostaal higher-ups considered a means "to reckon with heightened American efforts at export."[31]

Moving production stood to benefit many European CEOs. Shipping goods to American markets was expensive. Plus, Hodges had wrongly assumed that continental wage levels would undercut American manufacturers' labor costs. By the late 1950s, Steelbelt and Western European workers received more pay, enjoyed the middle-class purchasing power that routinized bargaining provided, and remained politically potent, especially in comparison to their brethren in the American South and West. In these states, labor restrictions and state interventions, akin to Hodges's response to the Henderson strike, had suppressed earnings, stoppages, and political campaigns during a period of remarkable economic growth.[32]

Most European industrialists were unaware of Carolina's competitive business climate until Hodges's 1959 industrial-recruitment expedition. British and continental Rotarians certainly knew of this retired businessman. He had remained in active service to the International. Months into his lieutenant governorship, he attended a Paris gathering of 10,000 businessmen from seventy-five different countries. There, he was overwhelmingly elected to the Rotary's Board of Directors. Yet European manufacturers had to seek out the then-lieutenant governor. Shortly after his return from France, he put C&D officials in contact with and authorized them to give site tours to Dutch manufacturers who had asked Hodges's advice on establishing a cement processing facility.[33]

Hodges eventually became the one ferreting out investment opportunities. European overtures and Rotary service had shown him the lucrative potential of a state-sponsored international investment initiative. Between October 31 and November 15, sixty-eight men covered six countries and ten cities and met 1,600 European businessmen in the 1959 "Trade and Industry Mission to Europe." "We know that European capital is looking for investment opportunities in the U.S.," a C&D official explained to *Wall Street Journal* reporters, "some businessmen from over there already have visited our state to look things over." Over one hundred Tar Heels wanted to sell North Carolina to Europeans. The sixty slots went to those at the helm of brokerage, insurance, law, transportation, utility, lumber, textile, building, supermarket, bottling, wholesaling, furniture, accounting, and oil firms. Four journalists and several state representatives from C&D as well as the state's port authority and Farm Bureau joined these boosters.[34]

Hodges's years of international experience led him to set realistically ambitious goals. He told both Europeans and Tar Heels that the mission sought investors eager to send raw materials and manufactured goods through North Carolina's two ports (effectively rerouting European access to American markets through North Carolina, not unionized New York, ports), entice investors with franchise arrangements that left Europeans in control of plants that trained Tar Heels would staff, and "obtain assembly or repackaging operations for North Carolina that would serve the American market." These aspirations were intended to make the state a commercial hub with the ability to cheaply refabricate well-made European goods, a postwar upgrade to the South's historic role as a commodity producer.[35]

Hodges's government and Rotary service eased this expedition's planning. Scouts arriving just weeks before to finalize events relied heavily on the Department of Commerce, State Department, and Embassies, whose staff welcomed this free-enterprise crusade. Stuttgart's Consul General proved especially devoted to recruitment, coordinating forty face-to-face meetings with potential investors, putting together a 250-person luncheon that still could not accommodate everyone interested, arranging a private dinner at the Minister President's home, and telling the press that this trip and German enthusiasm was just the step toward trade liberalization that Europeans had seemed reluctant to embrace (particularly with the United States).[36]

Scouts covered much ground. They landed in London and split into three groups. Some went through Hamburg on their way to Amsterdam. Others went to Rotterdam and Stuttgart before a side trip to Frankfurt on the way to Munich. They had but one day of rest before they moved on to Zurich and then reunited with the others in Paris. A few split off for a special envoy to Brussels, where they called on investors and heads of the recently formed European Common Market, an institution dedicated to continental trade liberalization. Hodges's personal itinerary included both these formal events and press appearances. He also made more personal transatlantic reconnections. He reacquainted himself with Germans he knew from ECA, checked in with past business associates at the helm of corporations or working as international consultants, and conferred with fellow Rotarians, including those heading the International. [37]

Raids unfolded in a remarkably similar manner. American embassy personnel, United Press journalists, and American Express representatives always greeted promoters, who had financiers at their disposal as a favor to Hodges from the firm's president (and perhaps because New York bankers had already begun aiding European investors eyeing US markets). Every visit included press events, a formal luncheon, time for individual meetings with interested manufacturers, and a private function with local luminaries. Guest lists were impressive. Stuttgart's roster included major bankers, textile magnates, Daimler-Benz and Porsche managers, farm machinery manufacturers, textile and home furnishing producers, machine-tool makers, turbine industrialists, builders, architects, shippers, airline tycoons, pharmaceutical and medical equipment specialists, plus representatives from the Common Market.[38]

Hodges even gave the same pitch for the greatest "product" he ever peddled: North Carolina. Tar Heels were his "Secret Weapon." Their "spirit of cooperation" pleased Steelbelt investors who employed the former farmhands trained in the state programs for "skilled trade and technician areas." These "honest, hard-working people with a deep rooted spirit of independence" were "unafraid of a real day's work." They personified his "conservative-progressive State's" overall "business climate" built on "sound and effective government," a "balanced budget," and "*equitable* and *fair* [sic]" business taxation, best evidenced by "several reductions" in corporate taxes. The governor prided himself on refusing "spending commitments until we feel the expenditure is really justified" but continually "gearing our policies to the changing spirit of the times and needs of our people."[39]

"Nothing I sold touches North Carolina as a 'product,'" he proclaimed. Yet Hodges admitted Europeans were most familiar with Yankee might and "school integration problems in the South." He even told British reporters that he encountered a textile machinery manufacturer who shipped wares to New York City even though 75 percent of his haul went to North Carolina ("This man didn't even know we had ports in North Carolina"). That was why he had crossed the Atlantic: to "develop stronger trade with Europe through North Carolina State Ports," "express our appreciation ... with whom our ports now do business," "seek added industrial development," and "to create a better understanding and good will between our nations." This expression of Rotarian internationalism was also an excuse to change European perceptions of southern schools and race relations. Tar Heels were hardly backwards. They were trained and ready for any "research minded" enterprise that might find the nascent Triangle alluring. "Racial problems," he also emphasized, "are not confined to the Southern region of the United States nor indeed the United States." But his "moderation has operated satisfactorily"; indeed "cities have voluntarily accepted Negro applicants to White schools although the vast majority of the Negro children are voluntarily attending their own public schools."⁴⁰

This salesman also tailored his spiel. Promoters had specific booklets that presented specific "historical reference to the relations with North Carolina," which Hodges always repeated to audiences (often listing the raw materials and goods that the country previously or already exported to or imported from North Carolina). He even laid a wreath at the statute of Sir Walter Raleigh to draw the British press's attention to the state capital's eponym. He also offered local charm befitting his early years as a Leaksville Rotarian gift-giving. He proudly presented Stuttgart's Minister President with a Carolina-made musical lighter during a morning press conference. This present proved embarrassing at the official's house later that evening, when an empty-handed Hodges received "a medal of their Poet Schiller." The governor quickly "took off the Tar Heel pin that I had and put it on him and told him that now he was a good Tar Heel." The former mill boy was proud of every offering, including a GE electric blanket (made in Asheboro) that the governor gave former West German president Theodor Heuss. Hodges hoped Heuss "could rest in peace and comfort" since a Carolina covering "would bring him most comfort in his retirement days."⁴¹

Hodges recalled Heuss's response as "humorous and heart-warming." Journalists seemed less enchanted but boosters still enthralled Europeans. True, Hodges found continental perceptions of southern racism frustrating. "We have not gotten the truth [out]," he opined after medical students in a Munich beer house regaled him with their interpretation of Little Rock's school desegregation. He was astounded to learn that the Oxford-trained chairman of the foreign trade committee of the Federation of German Industries "knew nothing whatever about North Carolina," just New York City (even though their sons were Harvard classmates). "In the only encyclopedia where I could find any reference to North Carolina, I found just two items," Hans Boden admitted, "the area in square miles and the percentage of Negroes in the state." But the "wonderful story" Hodges told during an intimate two-and-a-half-hour luncheon made Boden eager to help the governor with his mission, warning that it would be years before factories could begin operations.⁴²

European reporters repeated this message in coverage that indicated Hodges had sold them on North Carolina. *Deutsches Volksblatt* correspondents lauded him for the "melting" of blacks and whites, who worked together, had equal rights, and received an excellent professional education in a state that prioritized scientific research. Papers often did not catch the threat Hodges posed to social democracy. The *Esslinger Zeitung* proclaimed Hodges in search of international understanding and an exchange of personnel, whereas

Stuttgarter Zeitung columnists asserted that "scientists and technicians" visiting Europe promoted business expansion, not capital flight. This press fantasized about outfitting Carolina cigarette factories with German machinery, accessing American markets, and training Tar Heels whose salaries kept labor costs lower than elsewhere in the United States.[43]

European leaders clearly understood scouts' intentions. Baden-Württemberg Prime Minister Kurt Georg Kiesinger lauded the expedition as a beginning to solving joint economic problems through cooperation. This former Nazi official and future Chancellor praised the mission's entrepreneurial zeal, which he considered American in spirit and vital for industrialization. Others shared Kiesinger's enthusiasm. For example, Hodges so impressed Common Market representatives that they made him an honorary member during his Brussels' sojourn.[44]

European excitement thrilled Hodges. "The Common Market," Hodges conjectured, "created great interest and change in the attitudes and outlook of the European businessmen we met. The rapid growth of competition from other areas of the world is causing Europeans to re-examine and analyze their own present operations as well as their plans for the future." He based this prediction on the nearly three hundred industrialists indicating definite interest in Carolina ports, research park, manufacturing capacity, and distribution potential. But Hodges never expected capital to flee instantly. New facilities required time, money, and manpower to plan, much less build or assume operations. He asked Tar Heels for the same kind of patience European investors had requested of him, telling voters "this Mission will result in stronger trade with Europe for our two State ports, will in time provide added industrial development for North Carolina through European-financed plants or European-controlled franchise agreements, and certainly will bring about better and deeper understanding between our nations."[45]

American news coverage ensured that Hodges received a hero's welcome in and outside Carolina. His response to *Brown* and the Henderson strike had already made him a national figure. Reporters also watched him in Europe because *Time* had profiled him twice, once as "the South's No. 1 salesman" and then as the man responsible for doubling Carolina's industrial investment. *Business Abroad, Wall Street Journal,* and *U.S. News & World Report* journalists now lauded him for dazzling European investors, "breaking new ground in the search for investment capital" "far off the beaten path," and likely convincing "Three big European exporters, including West Germany's Daimler-Benz, . . . to shift some of their business from New York to North Carolina's two seaports." Carolina papers also praised this venture. Although Greensboro reporters warned that Amsterdam cigarette makers preferred to use cheaper, inferior Rhodesian and Indonesian tobacco, their admission only underscored the need for Tar Heels to industrialize through a competitive business climate. Luckily, "Attilla the Hun had nothing on this crowd," who had "established a beachhead in the land of Swiss cheese and the Matterhorn." These dispatches also excited voters. "Going abroad to get new industry," a Thomasville banker enthused, was "one of the best things you have done for our State." The governor's competitors agreed and soon began their own coordinated missions.[46]

Transatlantic acclaim also aided Hodges's career. His business renown, moderate response to *Brown*, and party loyalty appealed to Democratic Party heads, who needed Southerners to fill out the Kennedy administration. Commerce Secretary Hodges used his office to promote the kind of conservative free-enterprise politics that had inspired him to run ECA's textile division and North Carolina like a business. Hodges, for example, asked Congress to allocate resources for an Assistant Secretary devoted to science and technology, which he considered a "good investment." He also continued to promote "competition and challenge" as "spurs that make us try to do our best today and try to do still better tomorrow." He had little patience for continued economic "security and stability," principles at odds with cutthroat competition to build the best business climate. He also promoted the same anti-liberal politics that he had espoused during the Depression and World War II to businessmen in Ottawa, Tokyo, Manila, Hong Kong, Sydney, New Delhi, Athens, and Paris. By then, these principles were embedded within the modern American conservative movement but also complementary to the more high-minded theories coming out of economics departments or European and American think tanks then releasing manifestos more strident than Hayek's *Road to Serfdom*.[47]

Hodges hardly abandoned the Triangle, boosterism, or Rotarianism. He watched for opportunities from Washington because the Park had struggled to find investors, especially in lucrative manufacturing. He predicted that Medicare and Medicaid would make medicine profitable (a forecast that prompted Park heads to lobby for passage). Hodges left Washington, DC, in 1965 to oversee the Triangle's reorientation around the emergent postindustrial knowledge economy's medical, communication, and financial sectors. His executive contacts provided him entrée into IBM boardrooms. Landing this giant led to a marked increase in corporate interest. Hodges nonetheless traveled overseas to recruit investors, who could hardly doubt this mill boy's business credentials: he served as the International's president in 1967. He then took ready advantage of finance reforms facilitating the rise of international conglomerates and universal banks. A new side business invested profits in overseas tax shelters (often in the Middle East). This outfit enticed investors so much that RTP heads could turn away mundane manufacturers

by 1970. Struggling nearby townships embraced such enterprises, which profited from wages far lower than national and RTP averages. Two decades later
experts could quip that European car plants south of the Triangle on I-85 south
represented a nonunion "American autobahn."[48]

Hodges did not live to see the fruits of his international ambitions. He
died in 1974, when his investment firm was reaping the rewards of Carolina's
postwar reconstruction and the Triangle's postindustrial future. He had
helped orchestrate both during World War II, European recovery, and Cold
War industrialization. He only succeeded because a growing international cast
of boosters and executives also spread free-enterprise ideals and policies. Their
business deals and associations created the circuitry necessary for draining
the North Atlantic of good manufacturing jobs. International capital flight
and global reintegration nevertheless left the so-called Global South impoverished and in service to North Atlantic financial capitals, whose tycoons
now head enterprises best described as multinationals. Select areas, like the
Triangle, have prospered after their rebirth as free-enterprise oases. Yet the
politics behind these sanctuaries have also produced chronic crises in global
production, finance, and consumption, which are most felt in communities
in the shadow of places like the Triangle. After all, towns like Danville—just
north of RTP on I-85—remain as much a precarious low-wage desert as far-
away Mexico.

NOTES

1. Nathaniel Popper, "Ikea's U.S. Factory Churns Out Unhappy Workers,"
Los Angeles Times, April 10, 2011, http://articles.latimes.com/print/2011/apr/10/
business/la-fi-ikea-union-20110410; Josh Eidelson, "Union Victory at Ikea Plant,"
Alternet.org, http://www.alternet.org/story/151909/union_victory_at_virginia_
ikea_plant%3A_resistance_grows_against_race-to-bottom_wages; William Graves
and Heather A. Smith, eds., *Charlotte, NC: The Global Evolution of a New South
City* (Athens: University of Georgia Press, 2010); Marko Maunula, *Guten Tag,
Y'all: Globalization and the Southern Piedmont, 1950–2000* (Athens: University of
Georgia Press, 2010); Carl L. Bankston, "New People in the New South: An Overview
of Southern Immigration," *Southern Cultures* (Winter 2007): 24–44.

2. Quoted in National Emergency Council, *Report on Economic Conditions of
the South* (Washington, DC: Government Printing Office, 1938), 1; Gavin Wright,
Old South, New South: Revolutions in the Southern Economy since the Civil War
(New York: Basic Books, 1986); Bruce Schulman, *From Cotton Belt to Sunbelt: Federal
Policy, Economic Development, and the Transformation of the South, 1938–1990*
(New York: Oxford University Press, 1991); James Cobb, *The Selling of the South: The
Southern Crusade for Industrial Development, 1936–1990* (Urbana: University of
Illinois Press, 1993); Elizabeth Tandy Shermer, *Sunbelt Capitalism: Phoenix and*

the Transformation of American Politics (Philadelphia: University of Pennsylvania Press, 2013); Peter A. Cochlanis and Louis M. Kyriakoudes, "Selling Which South?: Economic Change in Rural and Small-Town North Carolina," *Southern Cultures* (Winter 2007): 86–103; Maunula, *Guten Tag Y'All!*; A. G. Hopkins, ed., *Globalization in World History* (New York: W. W. Norton, 2002); Charles S. Maier, "The Politics of Productivity: Foundations of American International Economic Policy after World War II," *International Organization* 31 (Autumn 1977): 607–33; Niall Ferguson et al., eds., *The Shock of the Global: The 1970s in Perspective* (Cambridge: Belknap Press of Harvard University Press, 2010); Angus Burgin, *The Great Persuasion: Re-Inventing Free Markets since the Depression* (Cambridge, MA: Harvard University Press, 2012).

3. Luther H. Hodges, *Businessman in the Statehouse: Six Years as Governor of North Carolina* (Chapel Hill: University of North Carolina Press, 1962), 3–7, esp. 29; for background on southern agriculture, industrial, and booster hierarchy, see Shermer, *Sunbelt Capitalism*, 17–38; Paul Luebke, *Tar Heel Politics 2000* (Chapel Hill: University of North Carolina Press, 1998).

4. For southern "buy payroll" traditions, see Cochlanis and Kyriakoudes, "Selling Which South?"; on the Rotary, see Victoria de Grazia, *Irresistible Empire: America's Advance through Twentieth-Century Europe* (Cambridge, MA: Belknap Press of Harvard University Press, 2005), 15–74, quoted 33; Report of Rotary Committee to Leaksville-Spray Rotary Club, July 19, 1932, Folder 2, Luther Hartwell Hodges Papers, The Southern Historical Collection at the Louis Round Wilson Special Collections Library (University of North Carolina, Chapel Hill) [NB: The Hodges's papers are solely organized by folder number. His papers are hereinafter cited as Hodges]; "Leaksville-Spray Rotary Club Committee Appointments, July 1, 1937–June 30, 1938," undated, Folder 1272, Hodges.

5. Hodges, *Businessman in the Statehouse*, 6–8.

6. Shermer, *Sunbelt Capitalism*, 71–92.

7. Ibid.; Schulman, *From Cotton Belt to Sunbelt*, 92–100, quoted 95.

8. Andrew Workman, "Manufacturing Power: The Organizational Revival of the National Association of Manufacturers, 1941–1945," *Business History Review* 72 (Summer 1998): 279–317; Shermer, *Sunbelt Capitalism*, 71–92; Robert M. Collins, *The Business Response to Keynes, 1929–1964* (New York: Columbia University Press, 1981).

9. De Grazia, *Irresistible Empire*, 15–74; Luther Hodges, Speech Notes for "Rotary Is Needed Now," undated [1926–1941], Folder 1272, Hodges; Luther Hodges, "A Vocational Talk on 'Employer–employee Relationships,'" June 23, 1936, pp. 1–2, Folder 1973, Hodges; Luther Hodges, Notes for "Talk at Pinehurst on May 7, 1942," April 22, 1942, pp. 1–2, Folder 1973, Hodges.

10. Hodges, *Businessman in the Statehouse*, 6–9; "Former Tar Heel Leading Post-War Activities" and "Post-War Committee Will Meet in Chapel Hill," *Governor's Monthly Newsletter* 7 (August 1944): 1; Schulman, *From Cotton Belt to Sunbelt*, 3–62.

11. Meg Jacobs, "'How about Some Meat?': The Office of Price Administration, Consumption Politics, and State Building from the Bottom Up, 1941–1946," *Journal of American History* 84 (December 1997): 910–41; Kim Phillips-Fein, *Invisible Hands: The Making of the Conservative Movement from the New Deal to Reagan*

(New York: W. W. Norton, 2009), 26–52; Luther Hodges to Clint [Anderson], May 30, 1945, Folder 6, Hodges; "Luther Hodges O.P.A. Executive," *Secretary's Letter to R.I. Officials*, August 14, 1944, p. 2; "Mr. Hodges with O.P.A.," *Mill Whistle* 3 (August 14, 1944): 1.

12. Luther Hodges to James Rogers Jr., September 5, 1944, p. 4, Folder 6, Hodges.

13. Luther Hodges to Clint [Anderson], May 30, 1945, Folder 6, Hodges; Clinton Anderson to Luther Hodges, June 7, 1945, Folder 6, Hodges; Clinton Anderson to Luther Hodges, July 12, 1945, Folder 6; Hodges; Luther Hodges to Clinton Anderson, with enclosure "Report to the Secretary of Agriculture on Inventory Situation, Commodity Credit Corporation," July 31, 1945, Folder 6, Hodges; William H. Draper Jr. to Luther Hodges, telegram [October 13, 1948], Folder 7, Hodges.

14. Nelson Lichtenstein, *Labor's War at Home: The CIO in World War II* (Philadelphia: Temple University Press, 2003); Collins, *Business Response to Keynes*; Workman, "Manufacturing Power"; Phillips-Fein, *Invisible Hands*; Charles S. Maier, ed., *The Cold War in Europe* (New York: Markus Wiener, 1991); Michael Hogan, *The Marshall Plan: America, Britain and the Reconstruction of Western Europe, 1947–1952* (Cambridge: Cambridge University Press, 1989); Michael Bernstein, "American Economic Expertise from the Great War to the Cold War; Some Initial Observations," *Journal of Economic History* 50 (June 1990): 407–16; Federico Romero, *The United States and the European Trade Union Movement, 1944–1951* (Chapel Hill: University of North Carolina Press, 1992); Anthony Carew, *Labour and the Marshall Plan: The Politics of Productivity and the Marketing of Management Science* (Manchester: Manchester University Press, 1987); de Grazia, *Irresistible Empire*, 336–75; Charles S. Maier, "The Two Postwar Eras and the Conditions for Stability in Twentieth-Century Western Europe," *American Historical Review* 86 (April 1981): 327–52, esp. 347.

15. Phillips-Fein, *Invisible Hands*; Burgin, *Great Persuasion*, 85 and 134; Stedman Jones, *Masters of the Universe*, 87–88, 122–24; Taylor C. Boas and Jordan Gans-Morse, "Neoliberalism: From New Liberal Philosophy to Anti-Liberal Slogan," *Studies in Comparative International Development* 44 (Summer 2009): 137–61; Marie-Laure Djelic, *Exporting the American Model: The Postwar Transformation of European Business* (Oxford: Oxford University Press, 1998), 103–11; Shermer, *Sunbelt Capitalism*, 71–92; Jordon A. Schwarz, *The New Dealers: Power Politics in the Age of Roosevelt* (New York: Alfred A. Knopf, 1993), 59–95, esp. 73; Reinhard Neebe, "German Big Business and the Return to the World Market after World War II," in *Quest for Economic Empire: European Strategies of German Big Business in the Twentieth Century*, ed. Volker R. Berghahn (Oxford: Berghahn Books, 1996), 95–121; Alan M. Taylor, "The Global 1970s and the Echo of the Great Depression," in *Shock of the Global*, 97–112; Timothy Smith, *France in Crisis: Welfare, Inequality and Globalization since 1980* (Cambridge: Cambridge University Press, 2004); David Harvey, *A Brief History of Neoliberalism* (Oxford: Oxford University Press, 2005).

16. W. Ray Bill to Luther Hodges, October 13, 1948, with enclosures, Folder 7, Hodges; Luther Hodges, "Answers to Questions submitted by WLOE," December 1, 1948, pp. 1–2, Folder 7, Hodges; Luther to Martha, Betsy, Nancy, and Luther, October

26, 1948, Folder 2089, Hodges; Luther to Folks, October letter retyped November 1948, Folder 2089, Hodges.

17. [Hodges], Typescript notes entitled "Conversation with Mr. Gus Anderson, Cotton Import," October 27, 1948, Folder 7, Hodges; Luther to Martha, Betsy, Nancy, and Luther, October 26, 1948, Folder 2089, Hodges; Luther to Folks, October letter retyped November 1948, Folder 2089, Hodges; Hodges, Typescript Notes titled "Organized Confusion," October 16, 1948, Folder 7, Hodges; W. Ray Bell to Hodges, with enclosures, October 13, 1948, Folder 8, Hodges; Management Confidential Bulletin, "Mr. Hodges Completes Army Mission," December 7, 1948, pp. 1–2, Folder 9, Hodges; Luther Hodges to William Foster, February 14, 1950, Folder 11, Hodges; R. T. Graham to Luther Hodges, March 21, 1950, Folder 12, Hodges; [Illegible signature] to Luther Hodges, March 21, 1950, Folder 12, Hodges.

18. Djelic, *Exporting the American Model*, 82–6, 104–7; Jordan Schwarz, *New Dealers: Power Politics in the Age of Roosevelt* (New York: Alfred A. Knopf, 1993), 195–248.

19. Schwarz, *New Dealers*, 195–248; Nelson Lichtenstein, *State of the Union: A Century of American Labor* (Princeton: Princeton University Press, 2003), 54–97; Tami Friedman, "Exploiting the North–South Differential: Corporate Power, Southern Politics, and the Decline of Organized Labor after World War II," *Journal of American History* 95 (September 2008): 323–48; Timothy J. Minchin, *What Do We Need a Union For? The TWUA in the South, 1945–1955* (Chapel Hill: University of North Carolina Press, 1997).

20. Djelic, *Exporting the American Model*, 82–6, 104–7, esp. 107; Hodges, "Personal Notes of Luther H. Hodges," May 29, 1950, Folder 17, Hodges.

21. Hodges to Friends, May 3, 1950, pp. 1–3, Folder 2091, Hodges; Hughston McBain to Luther Hodges, November 6, 1951, Folder 19, Hodges; Hodges, *Businessman in the Statehouse*, 1–17, 65–78; Luther Hodges to Clinton Anderson, May 30, 1945, Folder 6, Hodges; W. Ray Bell to Hodges, with enclosures, October 13, 1948, Folder 8, Hodges; Management Confidential Bulletin, "Mr. Hodges Completes Army Mission," December 7, 1948, pp. 1–2, Folder 9, Hodges; Hodges, "Personal Notes of Luther H. Hodges," May 29, 1950, Folder 17, Hodges; Office of Economic Affairs Industry Division Memo, "Mr. Hodges' Itineraries, Firms and People Visited from His Arrival April 6, 1950 to June 6, 1950," undated, Folder 17, Hodges; Hughston M. McBain to Hodges, November 16, 1951, Folder 19, Hodges; Paul Kelly to George Santry, June 24, 1953, Folder 51, Hodges.

22. Roland Sarti, *Fascism and the Industrial Leadership in Italy, 1919–1940: A Study in the Expansion of Private Power under Fascism* (Berkeley: University of California Press, 1971); Richard Vinen, *The Politics of French Business, 1936–1945* (Cambridge: Cambridge University Press, 1991); Robert O. Paxton, "Five Stages of Fascism," *Journal of Modern History* 70, no. 1 (March 1998): 1–23; Bernard P. Bellon, *Mercedes in Peace and War: German Automobile Workers, 1903–1945* (New York: Columbia University Press, 1990); Harold James and Jakob Tanner, eds., *Enterprise in the Period of Fascism in Europe* (London: Ashgate, 2002); Office of Economic Affairs Industry Division Memo, "Mr. Hodges' Itineraries, Firms and

People Visited from His Arrival April 6, 1950 to June 6, 1950," undated, Folder 17, Hodges; Houhgston M. McBain to Hodges, November 16, 1951, Folder 19, Hodges; Office of Economic Affairs Industry Division Memo, "Mr. Hodges' Itineraries, Firms and People Visited from His Arrival April 6, 1950 to June 6, 1950," undated, Folder 17, Hodges.

23. Untitled insert, *The State*, September 13, 1947, Folder 7, Hodges; Hodges, *Businessman in the Statehouse.*

24. Shermer, *Sunbelt Capitalism.*

25. Hodges, *Businessman in the Statehouse*, 9–16; R. B. Terry to Luther Hodges, January 28, 1952, Folder 1868, Hodges; Bill [Dowd] to Luther Hodges, February 6, 1952, Folder 1868, Hodges; John M. Hough to Luther Hodges, February 7, 1952, Folder 1868, Hodges [with enclosed letter to friends on Hodges's behalf].

26. Hodges, *Businessman in the Statehouse*, 18–20; Hodges, Untitled Talk, June 22, 1953, typescript, pp. 1–2, Folder 51, Hodges; Edward "Ted" S. Jamison to Luther [Hodges], July 6, 1953, Folder 51, Hodges.

27. Hodges, *Businessman in the Statehouse*, 10–46, esp. 224–5; Daniel J. Clark, *Like Night and Day: Unionization in a Southern Mill Town* (Chapel Hill: University of North Carolina Press, 1997); Anders Walker, *Ghost of Jim Crow: How Southern Whites Used* Brown v. Board of Education *to Stall Civil Rights* (Oxford: Oxford University Press, 2009), 49–84.

28. Sylvia Altman, "CC's Story—Through the Years," *Metropolitan Miamian* 49, no. 3 (April 1957): 7; Cobb, *Industrialization and Southern Society*, 102–4; Hodges, *Businessman in the Statehouse*, 30–46, 157–60, esp. 30–1, 43, and 160; Shermer, *Sunbelt Capitalism*, 173, 179, 212–14, 218, 243, 244, 259, 286.

29. Hodges, *Businessman in the Statehouse*, 6–19, 156–225, esp. 156, 177, 187, 189–90, 196–7, 203–4, quoted on 198; Michael I. Luger and Harvey Goldstein, *Technology in the Garden: Research Parks and Regional Economic Development* (Chapel Hill: University of North Carolina, 1991), 76–99; Margaret Pugh O'Mara, *Cities of Knowledge: Cold War Science and the Search for the Next Silicon Valley* (Princeton: Princeton University Press, 2004), 216–17; Cobb, *Industrialization and Southern Society*, 108.

30. Shermer, *Sunbelt Capitalism*, 229–30, 243–5, 266.

31. Djelic, *Exporting the American Model*, 107–10; Reinhard Neebe, "German Big Business and the Return to the World Market after World War II," in *Quest for Economic Empire: European Strategies of German Big Business in the Twentieth Century*, ed. Volker R. Berghahn (Oxford: Berghahn Books, 1996), 95–121, quoted 97, 109, 114.

32. Lichtenstein, *State of the Union*, 98–140; Maier, "Politics of Productivity"; Maier, "The Two Postwar Eras and the Conditions for Stability in Twentieth-Century Western Europe"; de Grazia, *Irresistible Empire*, 336–75.

33. Luther H. Hodges, "Letter No. 2" in "Trip to Europe May–June, 1953," pp. 1–2, Folder 2092, Hodges; Paul Kelly to George Santry, June 24, 1953, pp. 1–2, Folder 51, Hodges.

34. Hodges, *Businessman in the Statehouse*, 65–78; quoted in Cal Brumley, "North Carolina Turns to Europe as Luring Industry Gets Harder," *Wall Street*

Journal, November 5, 1959, clipping in "North Carolina Trade and Industry Mission to Europe, October 31–November 15, 1959" booklet stamped Governor Luther H. Hodges [hereinafter called Trip Booklet], [December 1959], Folder 1802, Hodges; Luther Hodges, "Report from Europe (1)," November 8, 1959, Folder 2102, Hodges; Hodges, Address at Fall Meeting of Board of Conservation and Development with Charlotte Civic Leaders, October 26, 1959, Folder 2078, Hodges.

35. Trip Booklet, p. 3.

36. Hodges, "Report from Europe (1); Trip Booklet; "Hodges: Enger Kontakt mit Europa angestrebt," *Esslinger Zeitungen*, [November 6, 1959], n.p., clipping found Folder 1803, Hodges.

37. Hodges, Address at Fall Meeting of Board of Conservation and Development with Charlotte Civic Leaders, October 26, 1959, Folder 2078, Hodges; Hodges, "Report from Europe (1)," esp. pp. 5–7, 11; Luther Hodges, "Report from Europe (2)," November 15, 1959, pp. 4 and 6, Folder 2102, Hodges.

38. "Trip Booklet"; "Report from Europe (1)," pp. 2–3.

39. Hodges, "North Carolina Story of Economic Opportunity," November 2, 1959 [London], pp. 5, 6, 7, 9, 8, Folder 1802, Hodges.

40. Ibid., 1, 2, 3, 6, 7; "Carolina Woos the Rich European," *Business Abroad*, undated clipping, included in Trip Booklet.

41. "Report from Europe (1)," p. 5; "68 Ambassadors of Good Will," *The Times*, November 3, 1959, clipping in Trip Booklet; "Report from Europe (1), pp. 11 and 12; specific introductions for speeches given in Amsterdam, Stuttgart, Zurich, and Paris are in Folder 2078, Hodges.

42. "Report from Europe (1)," pp. 12, 13,16; "Hodges: Enger Kontakt mit Europa angestrebt"; quoted in Hodges, *Businessman in the Statehouse*, 70.

43. "Hodges: Enger Kontakt mit Europa angestrebt"; "North Carolina sucht deutsche Fabriken," *Stuttgarter Nachrichten*, November 6, 1959, Folder 1803, Hodges; "North Carolina Sucht Kontakte," *Stuttgarter Zeitung*, November 6, 1959, Folder 1803, Hodges; "Dieser Kontakt ist tür beide Teile von Vorteil," *Deutsches Volksblatt*, November 6, 1959, Folder 1803, Hodges.

44. "Dieser Kontakt ist tür beide Teile von Vorteil"; "North Carolina Sucht Kontakte"; Hodges, "Report from Europe (2)," p. 7.

45. R. Aleigh [Hodges dictated this letter] to Members of the North Carolina Trade and Industry Mission, December 4, 1959, pp. 1–3 of Trip Booklet; Hodges, *Businessman in the Statehouse*, 75.

46. Cobb, *Selling of the South*, 171–6; Maunula, *Guten Tag Y'all*, 57–75; "North Carolina: The South's New Leader," *Time*, May 4, 1959, Hodges; "How to Woo New Business," *Time*, October 20, 1958, reprint, Folder 205, Hodges; Wilson Wyatt to Luther Hodges, November 3, 1958, Folder 207, Hodges; George Hunbley to Luther Hodges, September 19, 1959, p. 1, Folder 223, Hodges; Guy Munger, "Caravan Takes Stock of Trip," *Greensboro Daily News*, November 13, 1959, 1 and 14; "Carolina Woos the Rich European"; Brumley, "North Carolina Turns to Europe as Luring Industry Gets Harder," in Trip Booklet; title not clipped from *U.S. News & World Report*, November 16, 1959, in Trip Booklet.

47. Hodges, *Businessman in the Statehouse*, 65–78; Cobb, *Selling of the South*, 171–6; Burgin, *Great Persuasion*; Harvey, *Short History of Neoliberalism*; Phillips-Fein, *Invisible Hands*; Hodges, Untitled speech at Commercial Officer Convention in New Delhi, India, November 28, 1962, Folder 1980, Hodges; Ned [Huffman] to Hodges, October 29, 1966, Folder 1634, Hodges; Elizabeth Aycock to Mr. Haden, June 23, 1970, Folder 2107, Hodges; Luther H. Hodges, Remarks at Meeting of Congressional Staff Personnel, typescript, pp. 2–3, January 26, 1962, Folder 1976, Hodges; Luther Hodges, "A World in Competition," typescript, p. 3, February 11, 1962, Folder 1976, Hodges; see Folder 1981 ("Speeches and Public Appearances by Sec. Hodges – 1962," Hodges.

48. Hodges, *Businessman in the Statehouse*, 65–78; Cobb, *Selling of the South*, 171–6; Maunula, *Guten Tag Y'all*, 93–120; Albert Link, *A Generosity of Spirit: The Early History of the Research Triangle Park* (Research Triangle Park: Research Triangle Foundation of North Carolina, 1995); Albert N. Link, *From Seed to Harvest: The Growth of the Research Triangle Park* (Research Triangle Park: Research Triangle Foundation of North Carolina, 2002); Correspondence and Reports on Overseas Travel: Folders 2106–7, Hodges; Correspondence and Reports on Financial Consulting: Folders 1639–1698, Hodges; Correspondence and speeches in regards to Medicare/Medicaid: Folders 2051, Hodges; Folders 305, 821, and 1599, Research Triangle Park Papers, Louis Round Wilson Special Collections Library (University of North Carolina, Chapel Hill) and Folder 1706, UNC Board Of Trustees Papers, Louis Round Wilson Special Collections Library (University of North Carolina, Chapel Hill).

10

The Dirty War Network

Right-Wing Internationalism through Cold War America

Doug Rossinow

We Have Always Been at War with the Terrorists

"The basic weapon of *modern warfare*, particularly in the cities, is terrorism. . . . The goal of the guerrilla . . . is not so much to obtain local successes as it is to create a climate of insecurity."[1] Insurgents "will frequently institute terrorist tactics to bring the mass of people under control."[2] "A terrorist is not just someone with a gun or a bomb, but someone who spreads ideas that are contrary to Western and Christian civilization."[3] Do these characterizations of terrorism issue from the decade following September 11, 2001?

In fact, these are statements from the heart of the Cold War. The first was written by Roger Trinquier, one of the French fathers of "modern" counterinsurgency thought, in a book published in France in 1961 and in the United States in 1964. The second statement comes from a 1966 publication, *The Police and Internal Security*, produced at the US government's International Police Academy (IPA) in Washington, DC, established in 1963 to conduct training for security personnel from other, mainly Latin American, nations. The third and most extravagant comment was offered in 1976 by General Jorge Rafael Videla, the lead figure in the Argentine junta that seized power in Buenos Aires in that year. They all called their countries' enemies terrorists. To the US government, the enemy throughout the Cold War was international communism, and "wars of national liberation" often seemed to be cat's-paws of Moscow and Beijing. To the French, like the British trying to keep hold of pieces of their dying empire in the 1950s and 1960s, the enemy was a set of national liberation movements, but the French and British sometimes discerned a sinister linkage tying the world Communist conspiracy to independence movements not only in Vietnam and Malaya but in Algeria as well. Latin American rightists like Videla drew the curtain of counterterrorism across all enemies—and even merely potential enemies—of the dictatorship. To him and his ilk, not only armed revolutionaries of the Left but also human rights activists were fair game for murder and torture. The latter were guilty of what George Orwell, in *Nineteen Eighty-Four*, called *thoughtcrime*, and supposedly provided respectable cover for those who wielded bombs and submachine guns.[4]

French, US, and Latin American thinkers and government officials, whatever their regionally distinctive description of the Cold War enemy, found it useful to call their antagonists terrorists. Throughout the US–Vietnam War (1961–1975), the United States emphasized the National Liberation Front's (NLF) use of "terror" and "terrorism" in the Republic of Vietnam (RVN, i.e., South Vietnam).[5] In the Malayan "Emergency" (1948–1960), the British came to call the insurgents "Communist terrorists," using the designation "CT" for short.[6] A US Department of Defense directive of the early 1980s defined terrorism as "the unlawful use or threatened use of force or violence *by a revolutionary organization*."[7] Terrorism has always been hard to define; or rather it is hard to define it, when at war, in a way that quarantines the violence of one's enemy from one's own. Equating terror with the forces of revolution was one solution. "*La terreur*" first came into usage as a name claimed by the French Revolutionary regime in the 1790s; Maximilien Robespierrre said, "Terror is nothing but justice, prompt, severe, and inflexible."[8] The Russian Bolsheviks, seeing themselves as latter-day Jacobins, did not shrink from the concept of terror.[9] But this described methods of rule by a revolutionary state. The American Cold War–era concept of revolutionary terror pointed straight at rebels, generally insisting that terrorists were insurgents, even in a case like that of the NLF, which bore a strong claim to governmental legitimacy. Counterinsurgency in emerging postcolonial zones was the US concern.[10]

US counterinsurgency (COIN) thought and policy during the Cold War was part of a broader political and intellectual latticework, a long and wide tradition of violence. This tradition did not begin or end with the Cold War, but the Cold War is an important part of its history. This is why I say this network operated through Cold War America. It did so in space and in time.

Rightist activists and US government officials during the Cold War saw themselves as part of a larger geographic alliance of anti-communist stalwarts. Internationalism did not exist only on the Left, and an adequate understanding of "the profound international connections of modern American society," to quote Ian Tyrrell, must include a consideration of the transnational Right.[11] While French and British precedents and contemporaries were important influences on those who favored "dirty war"—a term first used to condemn the methods of COIN and terror/counterterror, then embraced, mainly by Latin American practitioners—the tightest transnational links forged by US rightists during the Cold War were those that stretched west across the Pacific and south to Central and South America.

It is important to distinguish between distinct levels of the transnational circuitry I am describing, and the different degrees of involvement by officials of the American state in each level. US officials often kept at arm's length those rightist elements in the United States who commingled personally with neofascist and other far-right groups abroad. However, such transnational far-right networks, which sometimes included officials of other governments, shared personnel with the direct military-to-military relationships in which the United States and other governments transferred knowledge and practices across borders. White House officials did not usually participate in what I am calling the dirty war network, but general staff officers in the Pentagon, and in the field, sometimes did. Also highly important was the transnational discursive terrain of COIN knowledge, some of it highly practical and mundane and some of it strongly rhetorical and, in its violent way, idealistic. North Americans participated in those transnational conversations. Officials of the US state tended mainly to absorb and deploy the tactical insights from the transnational COIN discourse while holding in abeyance the extreme political justifications—whether explicitly imperialist or overtly fascist—that circulated in those communicative circuits. Those justifications, nonetheless, helped to constitute the networks that sustained and extended COIN practice and thought alike, and there is no reason for us to omit this ideological stratum from the story of America's appropriation and application of late-imperial methods and reasoning.

In terms of time, the methods of COIN and "pacification" stretch far back into the history of imperialism. The call by colonial powers to defeat terrorist insurgents (i.e., to repress native uprisings in the "Global South") antedated the Cold War. But during the Cold War, it proved not difficult to adapt the "expertise" gained through "small wars" and pacification campaigns to a new environment. In 1965 the journalist Robert Taber, in his book *The War of the Flea*, saw his way around what Matthew Connelly called "the Cold War lens" rather easily. Describing what he termed "guerrilla warfare," Taber wrote: "In its total effect, it is creating new alignments and a new confrontation of powers that vitally relates to and yet transcends the Cold War. It is a confrontation, in its essence, of the world's *haves* and the world's *have-nots*, of the rich nations and the poor nations."[12]

Advocates of guerrilla warfare against the United States and its allies during the Cold War viewed things similarly. Whether they were Maoist champions of rural insurgency or, following Ernesto Guevara, believers in the outsized power that a small group of urban *focos* could leverage, revolutionaries conceded that terror was an essential tool for them. However, the logic of insurgent terrorism, as expounded, for example, in the Brazilian Communist Carlos Marighella's 1969 *Minimanual of the Urban Guerrilla*, differed from the way the United States usually described it. During the Cold War, the 1966 comment related above was typical: revolutionaries supposedly used terror to coerce naturally indifferent villagers into joining up with them. This view of peasants in particular as essentially apolitical but shrewdly calculating as to which side in a civil war was stronger was painted consistently by social scientists and US government officials in explaining the danger posed by Communist terror. Occasionally a different note came through. "Mass terror is used to demonstrate the weakness of the government, its inability to protect its people, *or to incite blind and brutal reprisals by government forces which may drive the uncommitted to the side of the insurgents*," stated a US Army publication on *Civil Affairs Operations* in 1969 (emphasis mine). This last possibility, that insurgent terror tactics might excite a disproportionate response by a more powerful state, thus winning support for the insurgents, was exactly the chain of events Marighella outlined. But such concessions to revolutionary thinking were rare among Americans. Far more common was the comment by Franklin Lindsay, in a *Foreign Affairs* article in 1962, that "the side which uses violent reprisals most aggressively will dominate most of the people, even though their sympathies may lie in the other direction."[13] Despite the counsels of restraint that sometimes issued from the pens of COIN experts, the temptation to justify mass violence as counterterror proved often irresistible to Americans in practice, just as the use of overwhelming firepower proved impossible to renounce in the face of refractory peoples.

Rising Empire and Dying Empires

In the 1940s, 1950s, and 1960s, some on both sides of the divide between the dying and rising powers in the Western alliance were interested to transmit knowledge acquired in the era's European COIN operations for America's use.

The United States had produced some knowledge of its own already. The US Marine Corps had produced a *Small Wars Manual* in 1940. The marines gleaned "lessons" from their many forays into the Caribbean Basin in the early twentieth century; they also looked to the army's wars against Filipino nationalists and Moro rebels between 1899 and 1913. US military historians have shown more awareness than others of the long roots of COIN in US military tradition, going back to warfare against Native Americans.[14] But this body of knowledge always has had a slight underground quality.

This store of military learning is represented today by COIN experts like the Australian David Kilcullen, who continue to reprise the "lessons learned" mode of advice offered to policymakers.[15] Repetitive articles fill the pages of journals like *Military Review, Survival, Parameters,* and *Small Wars and Insurgencies,* sometimes taking on an unintentionally comic aspect, as in one that offers COIN "best practices," as if proffering tips to schoolteachers.[16] Kilcullen is in the same military-advice-dispensing lineage as the Frenchmen Trinquier and David Galula and the British officer Sir Robert Thompson. He emphasizes the need for restraint by an outside occupying force, placing himself squarely in the "hearts and minds" camp. At first glance Galula and Trinquier appear to be on the other side of the debate, advocates for the efficacy of fearsome violence. But appearances can be deceiving; debates between different camps among COIN thinkers can divert attention from the large common ground they share. All these men, both English- and French-speakers, have seen themselves as part of an international brotherhood of warriors for the West, sometimes, as with Thompson and Kilcullen, loaned by their home countries' militaries to the United States. They have been not mercenaries precisely, but still Great White Hunters tracking their dark quarry and beating back the tide of revolution on a hot frontier girdling the globe.

For fifty years, the great touchstone for COIN advocates has been the British war in Malaya, the good news of which Thompson brought to interested Americans. The success enjoyed by the US-backed Filipino regime in deflating the Hukbalahap uprising and the victory of Greek rightists over their leftist enemies in that country's civil war, both in the 1940s, also have come in for honorable mention. But the direct involvement of the US military in those wars was quite modest. Therefore they have not formed as inviting a template for large-scale intervention as has the British "success" in Malaya. As one historian of British COIN efforts noted, after reviewing a series of British failures, "The one bright spot in the disappointing list of counterinsurgencies was Malaya, where from 1948 to 1960 the British conducted a model campaign."[17]

This judgment, with its clear indication of the author's identification with the British viewpoint, is merely typical of those offered in the United States ever since the mid-1960s, when the United States was embarked on its most ambitious COIN effort ever, not so far from Kuala Lumpur. Some Americans were aware that the ethnic specificity of the Communist-led Malayan revolution, basically confined to the large Chinese minority in the country, made the qualified victory the British extracted from the situation (Malaysia won independence, but it did not become a left-wing state) not easily replicable in Vietnam. Nonetheless, interested Americans from the late 1950s onward viewed the mass forced relocation of ethnic Chinese in Malaya and their "rehabilitation" under confinement in "New Villages" as an enlightened and successful example of grinding toward victory against an insurgency.[18] In South Vietnam, champions of the "agrovilles" of the late 1950s and the Strategic Hamlet program of the early 1960s, where villagers were supposedly protected from the NLF but were in fact imprisoned, uprooted from their homes which had become part of the NLF's support system, referred constantly to the model of Malaya. Thompson, fresh from Malaya, in 1961 headed a British Advisory Mission to the US/RVN war in Vietnam, and is often credited with urging on the Strategic Hamlet initiative.[19]

But Christopher Bayly and Tim Harper, in their splendid history *Forgotten Wars*, caution against viewing the Malayan campaign as a clean war. They arrive at a mixed verdict regarding the level of sheer cruelty involved, seeing the British campaign lessen in violence after an initial fearsome period in 1948–1949. But there is no denying, as they say, that "[t]he end of empire is not a pretty thing if examined too closely." They conclude that "the wild and unchecked fury of white terror in the first years; the extra-judicial killings of young men and women; the grotesque atrocity exhibitions of the mutilated slain; the violence to family life and livelihoods of hundreds of thousands of farmers and labourers during resettlement; the insidious small tyrannies of a vast and largely unaccountable bureaucracy; the racism and arrogance of empire—all this must be set in the balance."[20] Such elements in the Malayan "success" story never reached the eyes and ears of the American public.

While the chain of influence from British COIN efforts to America's is clear, more curious has been the wide interest in the wisdom of those who fought the losing French counterinsurgencies in Indochina (1946–1954) and Algeria (1954–1962). Many were persuaded that even losers had valuable, hard-earned lessons to impart. During the heyday of American COIN, during the Vietnam War, the French influence was uncertain on US thinking. In the 1960s, the French impact was more evident in Latin America, whence many countries had sent officers to Paris for advanced training beginning in the 1950s.[21]

Yet ultimately the ideas of the French experts filtered through to American thinking. The two major phrases associated with the French thinkers were, first, *la tache d'huile* or oil stain, and later *la guerre révolutionnaire*. *La tache*

d'huile was a metaphor coined in the early twentieth century by French commanders working to repress that era's rebellions in Indochina and North
Africa. Joseph-Simon Galliéni wrote to his more famous brother-in-arms
Louis-Hubert-Gonzalve Lyautey in 1903 that French victory would come "not
by mighty blows, but as a patch of oil spreads, through step by step progres-
sion."[22] In this conception, the Europeans would slowly expand pacified zones,
within which they would illuminate for the natives the superiority of life
under colonial rule. Essentially the same idea has been prominent in recent
US thought, usually under the rubric of "clear and hold."[23] *La guerre révolutionnaire*, born of the post-1945 experience, suggested something more dramatically innovative, but this doctrine's original features can be hard to pin down.
In fact, it is often unclear whether the thinkers associated with this phrase
meant it to denote novel COIN methods or only to describe the supposedly
new character of Third World insurgencies. The French military established
a Centre d'Instruction de Pacification et de Contre-Guérilla near Arzew, in
Algeria, in 1956. In its five years of existence, it emphasized understanding the
specific character of the Algerian revolt, the concepts and techniques of revolutionary war as practiced by the Algerian rebels, and methods of psychological
warfare that might help the French prevail.[24] According to at least one account
the Centre also taught the wisdom of forced relocation and the fortification of
barriers between resettled "pacified" areas and enemy-held zones.[25]

Marnia Lazreg argues that French writers of the Indochina-Algeria generation who found a political home to the right of President de Gaulle, some of
whose comrades eventually plotted his overthrow (following in the footsteps
of Lyautey, who was attracted to French fascism in the 1930s), envisioned an
"alliance of international communism and Pan-Islamism" at work in a world
of insurgencies.[26] They painted a vision of Europe's encirclement. One French
general officer stated in 1958 that communism's "primary thrust is not a direct
assault, but a wide encircling movement passing by China, the Far East, India,
the Middle East, Egypt and North Africa, finally to strangle Europe."[27] This
picture of a combined communist-Islamist conquest of Europe retains currency on today's US Right, its Cold War element neatly excised. Some of today's
American conservatives believe that the Islamic penetration of European society is far advanced, that Europe is a lost cause.[28]

For many, the signal insight of French COIN thought of the 1950s and
1960s was conveyed in the 1965 film *The Battle of Algiers* by the character
Colonel Mathieu. In a famous scene from this film (which got a new audience among Americans when the Directorate for Special Operations and Low-
Intensity Conflict in the Pentagon held a screening for its personnel in 2003 to
help them think about the Iraq War), Mathieu explains that if the French want

to keep Algeria, they are going to have to sanction torture and other atrocities. There was no clean path to victory.[29] The term *"la sale guerre"* had gained currency among leftist opponents of the Indochina War. During the Algerian War, the idea of using "dirty" methods came out of the closet partway, hinted at and implied by French commanders. Not until later, in another part of the world, did military leaders and political rulers explicitly state that they were engaged in *"la guerra sucia."*

Comrades: Building the Cold War Network

The US government did not set out to augment its COIN capabilities at the Cold War's outset. It did so haltingly and in some confusion about what COIN really was. By the time US COIN policy was in full swing, in the 1960s, it had become intertwined with policy emanating from US allies in the Western Pacific. From there, the network of COIN advocates spread into Latin America. Knitting all these areas together were not only government officials but also private citizens and nongovernment organizations, catalyzed by the Cold War into a new form of right-wing internationalism.

Before there was a formal COIN apparatus, there was "unconventional warfare." This term denoted a set of methods for infiltrating and destabilizing hostile nations, not for helping allies to repress rebellions or win civil wars. The Central Intelligence Agency (CIA) first got the brief for conducting unconventional warfare operations in the early Cold War, drawing on the experience of behind-the-lines World War II operations. The army got into the game with the establishment of a Psychological Warfare Center at Fort Bragg, North Carolina, and the formation of the first Special Forces unit, both in 1952. In 1956–1957, the Special Forces started exporting their training to US allies around the Pacific Rim, sending small Mobile Training Teams to Vietnam, the Republic of China (ROC, i.e., Taiwan), and Thailand and basing a substantial unit permanently in Okinawa, Japan.

When John F. Kennedy became president in 1961, within days he established a top-level Special Group, Counterinsurgency and ordered military commanders to turn existing unconventional warfare methods toward a new mission: defeating, not instigating, rebellions. In some ways this always was an awkward fit, since it was not clear that effective counter-guerrilla methods would mirror guerrilla tactics themselves, even though that was the message often conveyed in the Kennedy years concerning the army's newly expanded Special Forces (the Green Berets). Even decades later, army General Joseph Lutz complained in 1983 that he was "amazed at the lack of understanding

... of what it is we are actually talking about. ... special forces, special operations, special warfare, unconventional warfare, guerrilla warfare, partisan warfare, paramilitary operations, revolutionary warfare, proxies, surrogates, low-intensity conflict. ... We have really serious problems with definitions."[30] Despite this conceptual haze the United States continued building up Special Operations units, based partly on a COIN justification.[31] The other pieces of the growing COIN picture were the Office of Public Safety, established within the Agency for International Development in 1962 and working closely with CIA to train national police forces, and US military training schools that hosted foreign officers, including the US Army Caribbean School at Fort Gulick, inside the Panama Canal Zone (renamed the School of the Americas in 1963), and the IPA, already mentioned.[32]

The Seoul and Taipei regimes became the key centers in the Western Pacific cooperating with US unconventional warfare and COIN training organs. The ROC established a Political Warfare Cadres Academy (PWCA) in the 1950s, taking inspiration from the famed Whampoa Military Academy in Guangzhou, where military leaders on both sides of China's civil war had been schooled. Those in the Guomindang, led by Jiang Jieshi, particularly the Blue Shirt organization, developed an interest in fascism in the 1930s. Leninist and fascist states shared a commitment to a highly politicized officer corps, and political education was central to the training and doctrines promulgated at Whampoa and at the PWCA.[33] The PWCA would become a destination for a swelling stream of international trainees, particularly from Latin America.

In 1966 a meeting in Taiwan established the World Anti-Communist League (WACL). The WACL was conceived as a coalition of the Asian People's Anti-Communist League, formed earlier by Jiang, with other planned regional counterparts. These were cockpits of the high-level Asian Right, with scant respect paid to distinctions between governments and private citizens. Others involved in the Asian League were Park Chung Hee, who led the ROK following a coup d'état in 1961, and prominent figures in the Japanese Right, including Ryoichi Sasakawa, a billionaire self-identified "fascist," and Osami Kuboki, later the leader of the Unification Church of the Korean Sun Myung Moon in Japan. Sasakawa had been tried but acquitted of war-crimes charges after World War II.[34] The affiliates of the WACL would come to include the *Confederación Anti-Comunisto Latinoamericana* (CAL) and, in the United States, the American Council for World Freedom (ACWF), founded in 1970. In the 1970s Taiwan went scouting for new allies, as the United States and others seemed to be in the process of throwing them over in favor of improved ties with the People's Republic. The Taiwanese established a high profile in various right-wing Latin American states and provided expenses-paid training courses at the PWCA to Latin American army officers.

The Unification Church, although it was based in Korea, worked closely with the ROC in establishing Latin American operations to promote the idea of a global militant anti-communist alliance against the political Left. The Unification Church often acted through a group it established in Latin America, CAUSA International, established in 1980.[35] CAUSA was on friendly terms with a number of governments, notably the Guatemalan regime led by Efraín Ríos Montt, an evangelical Protestant, after a *golpe de estado* in 1982 that intensified a genocidal campaign by state forces against the country's Mayan population.[36] Taiwan's presence in Guatemala first had become pronounced during the period between 1974 and 1978 when death squad killings spiked upward. In those years the country's vice president was Mario Sandoval Alarcón, often called the "godfather" of the death squads. One former Guatemalan official said, "Sandoval went to Taiwan while he was vice-president, and he brought them in. If you want to trace the Taiwanese presence here, you can begin in 1974."[37]

CAUSA and the American Council became venues for cooperation between US rightists and counterparts to the south and west (although many US evangelicals remained leery of the Unification Church, seeing it as an unchristian organization bent on converting true Christians[38]), but US associations with the figures involved in this network of anti-communist militancy went back to the so-called China Lobby, the individuals and groups who had striven to keep Taiwanese interests well represented in US politics since 1949. A key China Lobby group was the Committee of One Million (Against the Admission of Red China to the United Nations), whose secretary was Lee Edwards, a protégé of US Congressman Walter Judd (Republican of Minnesota), a former medical missionary in China who was a leading pro-Jiang voice in the US Congress. Edwards went on to help organize Young Americans for Freedom, the main new right youth group of the 1960s, and many other important conservative movement initiatives, including the ACWF.[39] Edwards and his comrades on the Right saw themselves as a global movement for freedom—defined as extreme anti-communism, capitalist economics, and Christian faith—who would remain mobilized to keep pro-freedom governments from relenting in the fight against the Left. In the late 1970s, scandal hit the ACWF when the leading involvement of scientific racists as well as the American Council's ties to other WACL associates filled with neofascists received unwelcome publicity. The ACWF went through a partial housecleaning and reemerged in 1981 as the US Council for World Freedom, with retired generals John Singlaub and Daniel Graham as chairman and vice chairman, and an advisory board and board of directors including Fred Schlafly, Howard Phillips, and Anthony Kubek, a historian of East Asian communism involved in the Institute for Historical Review, a notorious hotbed of Holocaust deniers.[40]

Official Washington saw a potential laboratory for the refinement of dirty war methods in Latin America, where rightist dictatorships in the 1970s and 1980s joined forces to cleanse their societies of subversion. During the Nixon and Ford administrations, the United States approved dirty war methods used by "Southern Cone" regimes, coordinated through Operation Condor, an international effort, organized by Augusto Pinochet's Chile, to find both revolutionaries and opposition leaders and kill them wherever they were. An internal US State Department report explained that these governments saw themselves fighting a "Third World War" against the Left and were "joining forces to eradicate 'subversion,' a word which increasingly translates into non-violent dissent from the left and center left."[41] Secretary of State Henry Kissinger in 1976 told Argentina's foreign minister, "We are aware you are in a difficult period. It's a curious time, when political, criminal and terrorist activities tend to merge without any clear separation. We understand you need to establish your authority."[42] In the 1980s, Ronald Reagan's government looked to Central America, particularly to El Salvador, as a showcase for COIN methods.[43] In Latin America, COIN enthusiasts in the United States found their greatest opportunity to support a no-holds-barred fight for a right-wing version of freedom. This was also the region where the political justifications for scorched-earth COIN methods became garish, featuring occasional nods to fascist influence.

The fascist legacy long had bobbed above the surface of discussion in COIN and extreme anti-communist circles. Trinquier told a newspaper in 1958, when discussing the tactics he recommended in Algeria, "Call me a fascist if you like, but we must make the population docile and manageable; everybody's acts must be controlled."[44] Perhaps he was merely mocking his leftist critics with his mention of fascism, but perhaps not. If it was inconceivable to North Americans that fascism could have had a lingering influence anywhere outside fringe political elements after 1945, in other parts of the world fascism was viewed, while extreme, as a serious tradition with many adherents. Americans were shocked when one of their Saigon protégés, Premier Nguyen Cao Ky, said in 1965, "People ask me who my heroes are. I have only one—Hitler. I admire Hitler because he pulled his country together when it was in a terrible state."[45] The American public did not grasp the currency of fascism, as an intense and militarized form of nationalism, in the rightist circles where the United States found many of its Asian allies during the Cold War. This was also true in Latin America. In the 1984 presidential election campaign in El Salvador, the

US-supported candidate, José Napoleón Duarte, denounced ARENA, the party of his rival, Roberto D'Aubuisson—a graduate of the School of the Americas and the IPA as well as the PWCA in Taiwan, and the inspirational leader of his country's death-squad apparatus—as "ARE–Nazis" and "Nazi fascists."[46] Before discounting this as overheated election rhetoric, we should note that in Guatemala, Sandoval Alarcón said in 1981, "I could perhaps accept the label of Fascist, in the historical sense of the word were it not for the fact that it refers to a type of socialism, albeit national socialism."[47]

"[O]f course we understand that this is a dirty war," said Sandoval Alarcón.[48] This was the basic truth that undergirded all the extremism of Latin American COIN practice. Rightist regimes there were not at war merely with guerrillas in the 1970s and 1980s. As they presented matters, they were at war with a global communist conspiracy; they were at war with the revolutionaries' fellow travelers—human-rights and democracy activists; they were at war with all potential subversives, not only with those in whom the virus of rebellion was already palpable. As D'Aubuisson put it, "You can be a Communist even if you personally don't believe you are a Communist."[49] The governor of Buenos Aires province once said during the period of Argentine dictatorship (1976–1983), "First we will kill all the subversives, then we will kill their collaborators, then ... their sympathizers, then ... those who remain indifferent; and finally we will kill the timid."[50] Also in Argentina, a 1981 army document included a three-branched organizational chart of "Marxist subversion." One branch was labeled "Terrorist groups," the second "Political-military organization," and the third "Advocacy groups." This last category was merely a list of human-rights organizations.[51] As Gustavo Alvarez, a Honduran military officer favored by Washington in the 1980s put it, "Everything you do to destroy a Marxist regime is moral."[52] All enemies of the state, actual and potential, were "Marxists" and "subversives." Alvarez was not actually at war with a "Marxist" regime. He was justifying repression by a rightist state. But without the repression, might not a "Marxist" regime come to power through an insurgency? And might not human-rights groups assist in this process by tying the state's hands? This logic underwrote the terror of the dirty wars. This concept of a preventive white terror was indeed in the fascist tradition.

The flow of influence between transnational political networks on the far right and international state networks waging dirty wars ran in multiple directions during the Cold War. Movement conservatives forged ties across oceans and continents, linking up with like-minded comrades, some of them on the front lines of the "Third World War." This dirty war network was not neatly sealed off from state power. In many places, forces in and out of government worked together seamlessly. Meanwhile, the awareness that at least some states around the world openly embraced the scorched-earth tactics of dirty war and the rightist politics that the US government kept at arm's length sustained the morale of rightists in the United States. The US government was involved in international dirty war efforts and networks throughout the Cold War and consciously sought to carry forward the most effective repressive methods of the old colonial powers, belying the notion that COIN was merely a product of the Cold War. While not all US political leaders were enthusiastic about the far-right ideas and networks in which international dirty war was enmeshed, those ideas and networks were connected to the capabilities, political and military, that the United States used to uphold its vision of world order and win the unceasing war on terror from the 1940s until today.

NOTES

1. Roger Trinquier, *Modern Warfare: A French View of Counterinsurgency*, trans. Daniel Lee (London: Pall Mall Press, 1964), 52.

2. D. Michael Shafer, *Deadly Paradigms: The Failure of U.S. Counterinsurgency Policy* (Princeton: Princeton University Press, 1988), 106.

3. Grace Livingstone, *America's Backyard: The United States and Latin America from the Monroe Doctrine to the War on Terror* (London: Latin America Bureau/Zed Books, 2009), 67.

4. George Orwell, *Nineteen Eighty-Four* (London: Martin Secker and Warburg, 1949).

5. See, e.g., US Department of State, *Aggression from the North: The Record of North Vietnam's Campaign to Conquer South Vietnam*, Publication 7839, Far Eastern Series 130 (Washington, DC: US Government Printing Office, 1965), excerpted as reading 35, "Rationale for Escalation: The US Government 'White Paper' of 1965," in *Vietnam and America: A Documented History*, rev. ed., ed. Marvin Gettleman et al. (New York: Grove Press, 1995), 266–7; or Douglas Pike, *The Viet Cong Strategy of Terror* (Saigon: US Information Agency, 1970), in general.

6. Christopher Bayly and Tim Harper, *Forgotten Wars: Freedom and Revolution in Southeast Asia* (Cambridge, MA: Belknap Press of Harvard University Press, 2007), 436, note that this term was in use as of 1952. See Phillip Deery, "The Terminology of Terrorism: Malaya, 1948–52," *Journal of Southeast Asian Studies* 34, no. 2 (June 2003): 231–47.

7. Michael McClintock, *Instruments of Statecraft: U.S. Guerrilla Warfare, Counterinsurgency, and Counterterrorism, 1940–1990* (New York: Pantheon Books, 1992), 370, emphasis added.

8. Bruce Hoffman, "What Is Terrorism?" in *The Global History Reader*, ed. Bruce Mazlish and Akira Iriye (New York: Routledge, 2005), 256.

9. See John Gray, *Black Mass: Apocalyptic Religion and the Death of Utopia* (New York: Farrar, Straus and Giroux, 2007), 40–54.

10. Late in the Cold War the United States labeled certain regimes "terrorist states," mainly in the Middle East (e.g., Iran, Libya). But this was unusual.

11. Ian Tyrrell, "American Exceptionalism in an Age of International History," *American Historical Review* 96, no. 4 (October 1991): 1050.

12. Robert Taber, *The War of the Flea: A Study of Guerrilla Warfare Theory and Practice* (New York: Lyle Stuart, 1965), 11. Matthew Connelly, "Taking Off the Cold War Lens: Visions of North–South Conflict during the Algerian War for Independence," *American Historical Review* 105, no. 3 (June 2000): 739–69.

13. Carlos Marighella, *Minimanual of the Urban Guerrilla* (1969; St. Petersburg, FL: Red and Black Publishers, 2008); McClintock, *Instruments of Statecraft*, 237; Franklin A. Lindsay, "Unconventional Warfare," *Foreign Affairs* 40, no. 2 (January 1962): 268. Lindsay allowed in passing, "The strategy of the Communists may be to use acts of terror and sabotage to goad the government into repressive counter-measures and thereby widen the split between the population and the government" (268–9). But this was an aside, not central to his analysis.

14. For examples, see Claude G. Sturgill, *Low-Intensity Conflict in American History* (Westport, CT: Praeger Publishers, 1993); Anthony James Joes, *America and Guerrilla Warfare* (Lexington: University Press of Kentucky, 2000); and John J. Tierney, *Chasing Ghosts: Unconventional Warfare in American History* (Washington, DC: Potomac Books, 2006). "Low-intensity conflict" was a term for COIN current in the 1980s and 1990s. Praeger was long a major publishing outlet for COIN experts, having brought Trinquier, David Galula, and Robert Thompson, mentioned below, into print in the United States in the 1960s. David Galula, *Counterinsurgency Warfare: Theory and Practice* (New York: Frederick A. Praeger, 1964); Sir Robert Thompson, *Defeating Communist Insurgency: The Lessons of Malaya and Vietnam* (New York: Frederick A. Praeger, 1966).

15. Kilcullen has established an unusually high profile. For his ideas, see David Kilcullen, *The Accidental Terrorist: Fighting Small Wars Inside of a Big One* (New York: Oxford University Press, 2009) and David Kilcullen, *Counterinsurgency* (New York: Oxford University Press, 2010), which begins by dispensing twenty-eight bite-sized "articles" of "company-level" COIN tactics.

16. Kalev I. Sepp, "Best Practices in Counterinsurgency," *Military Review*, May–June 2005, 8–12.

17. Thomas R. Mockaitis, *British Counterinsurgency, 1919–60* (New York: St. Martin's Press, 1990), 8.

18. See the discussion in Karl Hack, "'Iron Claws on Malaya': The Historiography of the Malayan Emergency," *Journal of Southeast Asian Studies* 30, no. 1 (March 1999): 99–125.

19. Things ended badly. Eric M. Bergerud, *The Dynamics of Defeat: The Vietnam War in Hau Nghia Province* (Boulder, CO: Westview Press, 1991) provides a detailed critique of COIN efforts in South Vietnam. Bernd Greiner, *War Without Fronts: The USA in Vietnam*, trans. Anne Wyburd with Victoria Fern (New Haven: Yale University Press, 2009) offers an unflinching look at dirty war methods between 1967 and 1971.

20. Bayly and Harper, *Forgotten Wars*, 532, 500.

21. Marnia Lazreg, *Torture and the Twilight of Empire: From Algiers to Baghdad* (Princeton: Princeton University Press, 2008), 19.

22. Ian F. W. Beckett, *Modern Insurgencies and Counter-Insurgencies: Guerrillas and their Opponents since 1750* (London: Routledge, 2001), 40.

23. Andrew Krepinevich, another military intellectual, has associated himself with this concept. Andrew Krepinevich, "How to Win in Iraq," *Foreign Affairs* 84, no. 5 (September–October 2005): 87–104.

24. Lt. Colonel Frédéric Guelton, "The French Army 'Centre for Training and Preparation in Counter-Guerrilla Warfare' (CIPCG) at Arzew," in *France and the Algerian War, 1954–62: Strategy, Operations, and Diplomacy*, ed. Martin S. Alexander and J. F. V. Keiger (Portland, OR: Frank Cass Publishers, 2002), 35–53.

25. Beckett, *Modern Insurgencies and Counter-Insurgencies*, 159–60.

26. Lazreg, *Torture and the Twilight of Empire*, 32.

27. Shafer, *Deadly Paradigms*, 150.

28. See Johann Hari, "Ship of Fools," *Independent* (London), July 13, 2007.

29. *The Battle of Algiers* (1965; dir. Gillo Pontecorvo). This film followed several popular books published in France justifying torture by the French in their late-colonial wars. Darius Rejali, *Torture and Democracy* (Princeton: Princeton University Press, 2007), 533–6, 545–8, discusses the gap between fiction and reality.

30. McClintock, *Instruments of Statecraft*, 35.

31. Following the army, the other service branches got on board during the Kennedy years. The navy formed the SEALs (Sea, Air, and Land units) and the air force formed a Special Air Warfare Center at Eglin Air Force Base to train members of a new First Air Commando Group. McClintock, *Instruments of Statecraft*, 183. Today the US military contains numerous Special Operations (the generic term) units. In 1987 the US government formed a unified US Special Operations Command (USSOCOM), located at MacDill Air Force Base in Florida, with authority over Special Operations units in all the service branches.

32. On the Office of Public Safety and its role in torture abroad, see Alfred W. McCoy, *A Question of Torture: CIA Interrogation, from the Cold War to the War on Terror* (New York: Metropolitan Books, 2006), 60–2, 71–4. Following a public scandal concerning dirty war methods used by the US government, the Congress abolished the Office in 1975.

33. See Lloyd E. Eastman, "Fascism in Kuomintang China: The Blue Shirts," *China Quarterly* 49 (January–March 1972): 1–31, as well as the critique in Maria Hsia Chang, "'Fascism' and Modern China," *China Quarterly* 79 (September 1979): 553–67, and Lloyd E. Eastman, "Fascism and Modern China: A Rejoinder," ibid., 838–42. Also see Hans van de Ven, "The Military in the Republic," *China Quarterly* 150 (June 1997): 352–74.

34. On Sasakawa, see "Japan: The Godfather-san," *Time*, August 26, 1974, http://www.time.com/time/magazine/article/0,9171,944948,00.html.

35. CAUSA stood for the Confederation of the Associations for the Unification of Societies of Latin America. One suspects this awkward name was concocted in order to explain an attractive acronym. "La Causa," or the cause, is a common Spanish-language term for grassroots movements for social justice.

36. Scott Anderson and Jon Lee Anderson, *Inside the League: The Shocking Expose of How Terrorists, Nazis, and Latin American Death Squads Have Infiltrated*

the World Anti-Communist League (New York: Dodd, Mead, 1986), 181. In 1996 a UN-brokered set of peace accords ended the country's civil conflict and established a Commission for Historical Clarification, whose report concluded that the Guatemalan state committed acts of genocide against the Mayan people specifically between 1981 and 1983. The report, *Guatemala: Memory of Silence*, concluded that government forces committed 93 percent of atrocities in the country during the period considered. The report is available at the website of Yale University's Genocide Studies Program, http://shr.aaas.org/guatemala/ceh/report/english/toc.html.

37. Anderson and Anderson, *Inside the League*, 170.

38. See Beth Spring, "Sun Myung Moon's Followers Recruit Christians to Assist in Battle against Communism," *Christianity Today*, June 14, 1985, http://www.christianitytoday.com/ct/2001/augustweb-only/8-6-37.0.html. Also see Michael Isikoff, "Church Spends Millions on Its Image," *Washington Post*, September 17, 1984, A1.

39. Lee Edwards, *Missionary for Freedom: The Life and Times of Walter Judd* (New York: Paragon House, 1990), a hagiographic account, is the only biography of Judd.

40. Anderson and Anderson, *Inside the League*, 152. On the Institute for Historical Review, see Deborah Lipstadt, *Denying the Holocaust: The Growing Assault on Truth and Memory* (New York: Free Press, 1992), ch. 8.

41. John Dinges, *The Condor Years: How Pinochet and His Allies Brought Terror to Three Continents* (New York: New Press, 2004), 171.

42. Livingstone, *America's Backyard*, 68.

43. On El Salvador, see Benjamin Schwarz, "Dirty Hands," *Atlantic Monthly*, December 1998: 106–16.

44. Shafer, *Deadly Paradigms*, 156.

45. Ky made his statement to the London *Sunday Mirror*. After criticism by British Members of Parliament over his reported remarks, Ky denied he had given the interview, but through a spokesman he said, "When I referred to Hitler incidentally during one of my conversations with journalists, I had in mind the idea that Vietnam needed above all leadership and a sense of discipline in order to face the criminal aggression of Communism."

"The idea is far from me of praising Hitler or adopting his view, especially when here in Vietnam nobody can forget the inhuman methods he used during the Second World War, methods which the Communists are using right now on our land." "Premier Ky, in Saigon, Denies That He Called Hitler His Hero," *New York Times* July 16, 1965, 3.

46. William M. LeoGrande, *Our Own Backyard: The United States in Central America, 1977–1992* (Chapel Hill: University of North Carolina Press, 1998), 248. The Reagan administration badly wanted to keep D'Aubuisson in the shadows, and heavily backed the Christian Democratic Duarte (who prevailed), outraging conservatives like Senator Jesse Helms (Republican of North Carolina).

47. Anderson and Anderson, *Inside the League*, 163.

48. Christopher Dickey, *With the Contras: A Reporter in the Wilds of Nicaragua* (New York: Simon and Schuster, 1985), 87.

49. Anderson and Anderson, *Inside the League*, 194.

50. Ceclilia Menjívar and Néstor Rodríguez, "State Terror in the U.S.–Latin American Interstate Regime," in *When States Kill: Latin America, the U.S., and Technologies of Terror*, ed. Ceclilia Menjívar and Néstor Rodríguez (Austin: University of Texas Press, 2005), 15. Emphasis in original.

51. This chart is reproduced as figure 1.2 in Ariel C. Armony, *Argentina, the United States, and the Anti-Communist Crusade in Central America, 1977–1984* (Athens: Center for International Studies, Ohio University, 1997), 24.

52. Dickey, *With the Contras*, 115.

11

American Internationalists in France and the Politics of Travel Control in the Era of Vietnam

Moshik Temkin

In June 1966, the French National Police delivered a report to the Minister of the Interior, generically entitled "Les Américains en France." The report, which was prepared by Renseignements Generaux (RG), the state's principal internal intelligence service, was a fairly routine affair; the government regularly commissioned such classified reports on foreign national communities residing in or visiting the country. There was little in it that might worry government officials. It provided some basic numbers: it estimated, for example, that as of December 1965 there were approximately 80,000 Americans living in France. (Their numbers had declined since 1960, when there had been at least 100,000.) Of these, 45,267 were American citizens included in the official census; approximately 26,000 were members of the US military; and between 7,000 and 8,000 were Americans living "irregularly" in the country, particularly in and around Paris. A majority of the American civilians were retirees in the south of France or businesspeople living mostly in Paris.[1]

In a sense, the 1966 RG report confirmed a long-standing, commonplace perception of Americans in France. It characterized most of these expatriates as indulging in a lively club life, and their ties to France as primarily sensual and sentimental. The most prominent among them were former captains of industry spending their golden years in pleasant surroundings. With some exceptions, the Americans in France kept their distance from the surrounding society—and that, presumably, was a good thing.[2]

But the report also made clear that not all was completely tranquil when it came to some of the Americans. A number of them were active or former CIA agents; others (mentioned by name) were CIA contacts and informers. (Most of them had arrived in France during World War II and cut their teeth fighting fascism.) Others engaged in moderate political activity, much of which mirrored civil rights activism in the United States. On August 21, 1963—one week before the March on Washington in the United States—about 150 Americans, led by what RG called "a few black public figures passing through Paris," participated in what the police called an "anti-segregation demonstration" outside the US embassy (the report, following French intelligence policy, distinguished between white and black people, counting 40 of the 150 among the latter). The report noted that the demonstration did not attract the attention of most American expatriates in the city, who, at that time, took little interest in the civil rights movement. Few French citizens participated.

Also, by the mid-1960s the American military campaign in Vietnam was beginning to stir more protest, though full-blown antiwar activism was still a way's off. On November 27, 1965, a few dozen people, most of them American, protested the escalation of the war by the Johnson administration by marching in front of the American embassy. There were also growing protests in 1966. But despite the reference to what RG called "quelques éléments communisants" within the American community, including one group based in the International Quaker Center (informally led by the novelist and actor Henry Pillsbury, heir to the food fortune, who had been living in Paris since the 1950s) by and large the report concluded that the Americans in France did not present major concerns to the government. RG and other intelligence services, the Minister was assured, would continue monitoring the American community, as they did all foreigners in France.

Four years later, in June 1970, RG delivered another report to the government on the Americans in France, whose very different title—"Revolutionary Activism within the American Colony in France"—made clear just how much had changed, politically and otherwise, in a few short years. Gone was RG's prior emphasis on retired bankers living placidly in pastoral surroundings. The overall number of Americans in France had precipitously dropped from 45,267 in 1966 to around 17,000 in 1970, mostly as a result of the ongoing departure from France of American military servicemen and their families, a trend that had been going on since the end of World War II. But the Americans who remained in France now presented an entirely different sort of challenge for the authorities. One significant change was that, increasingly, officials saw the Americans in France as itinerant rather than resident. As American military families left the country, American students, for example, began to arrive in higher numbers. Intelligence reports on Americans now reflected as much an interest in the political nature of their travel to the country as in the conditions of their residency. The French authorities shifted from primarily seeing the Americans as expatriates to primarily seeing them as political travelers, though the boundary between these two groups would remain blurry.[3]

Students of American, French, and international history will not be surprised that RG reports delivered in 1966 and 1970 differed so starkly. Historians have abundantly documented the dramatic transformations in the international politics of those intervening five years. In particular, the escalation of the war in Vietnam brought about an increasingly vocal antiwar movement, in the United States and worldwide; and out of the more radical elements of the civil rights movement came the rise of the black power movement, with ambitions and activity not only in the United States but also abroad. In France, decolonization and the birth of independent African nations in the former French colonies had created new considerable social, economic, and geopolitical challenges for the government as well as a richer and more combustible context for the growth of radical politics. And right between the two RG reports came the events of Spring–Summer 1968, with uprisings in France, the United States, Eastern Europe, Latin America, and other parts of the world.[4] The Americans in France not only reflected these political developments but also, in the eyes of French officials, heavily contributed to them.

The authors of the 1970 RG report saw three "themes" to the so-called revolutionary activity of the Americans in France: (1) opposition to the Vietnam War, (2) support for US military deserters, and (3) participation in (or support for) the black power movement. These "themes" overlapped (especially themes one and two), but what they most had in common, as far as the government was concerned, was their explicit internationalism. Their American counterparts, as we will see, shared this concern.

RG's main message in 1970 to its overseers in the government was that foreigners, including and especially Americans, had seen fit to get involved in political goings-on in France and that their general approach to politics was international (i.e., that what concerned protesters and activists in the United States should concern their counterparts in France, and that what happened in France or anywhere else, for that matter, should matter to American and other foreigners). Two years after the events of May 1968, RG was still convinced that "American agitators" had, along with other foreigners, played an outsize role in what was, for the governments of President Charles de Gaulle and his successor Georges Pompidou, a deeply disturbing event. What particularly troubled the authorities was the way in which, in their perception, internal political issues had become entangled in unsavory and dangerous ways with external, international politics. (For the Minister of the Interior Raymond Marcellin, for example, May 1968 was more or less a sinister international plot, perhaps concocted in Havana or Beijing but certainly instigated by foreigners).[5] The inevitable and unwelcome result of this, from the government's perspective, was that French people were involving themselves in global political causes, and they did not even have to leave France to do so. They were simply incited by foreigners in their midst.

The French government's response to all this was swift and decisive. Beginning in 1967, but especially after the events of 1968, state authorities tracked foreigners visiting the country, in particular Americans, with increasing vigor and attention. Many Americans and other foreigners were barred from entering France, or deported if they had already entered France. As the government took its revenge against foreigners generally, and American specifically, who were either actively or even seemingly involved in the events of 1968, it made its position on international politics clear: it would not abide by it.

We do not have full data on how many Americans (or non-Americans) experienced French travel control in its various forms, but the archival evidence from this period is abundant, and the individual cases in the French archives range from obscure students to celebrities such as actress Jane Fonda and singer Joan Baez, who were allowed to enter France under certain conditions and then closely tracked while in the country. There are also long lists of people not let into the country, either in advance or upon their arrival at the border. It was sometimes enough that the authorities received word of someone merely planning to travel or considering traveling to France for the travel restriction be come into play, even if the person in question did not actually travel and did not have a concrete plan to do so.

Still other travelers were let in but expressly warned not to engage in any political activity. Jane Fonda had a film about Vietnam seized at the airport and the French police kept tabs on her as well as on her Parisian friends. SDECE, the External Documentation and Counter-Espionage Service (which can be seen as the French equivalent of the CIA) had a file on her as well, which included an exhaustive list of her contacts in Paris that reads like a who's who of the city's cinematic and intellectual bon ton: Jean Genet, Alain Delon, Roger Vadim (Fonda's ex-husband), Simone Signoret, Jean-Louis Trintignant, Jean-Luc Godard, Mary McCarthy, and Agnès Varda, among others. (One typical report labeled Fonda "an unremitting militant of the extreme left").[6]

Baez—who was also labeled "an unremitting extremist" ("Une militante acharnée") by the French authorities—was asked, upon her arrival in France, not to talk about the Vietnam War while giving a live performance on French television; when she did anyway (she later stated that she had refused the French request in advance), the national television channel cut her off, leaving her fuming and refusing to leave the stage.[7] And some American travelers wound up deported, or not let in again, when they failed to heed the warnings about political activity to the government's satisfaction.

Some clarifications are in order. First, by international or internationalist politics I do not mean the way that people on the Left had been identifying themselves since the nineteenth century as members of an International. Nor do I mean global or supranational governance, or state-to-state and international relations, or diplomacy. Rather, I use the terms "international politics" and "internationalist politics" interchangeably and generically to describe political activity that involved the physical crossing of borders and connections between people and groups—of the sort that social scientists like to call non-state actors—from different parts of the world, who took an interest or even developed a stake in each other's political causes, often fusing them together.[8]

It is true that most of the subjects of this essay were on the political Left, which tends to be "international," even in the general way I have described above, in a way that the nationalist Right, whose politics are usually not for export, is not. But for the French state this was not merely a matter of combating the Left specifically; extreme right-wing groups and separatist movements also came under surveillance and opprobrium, even though the government, in this period, clearly felt more threatened by the Left.[9] What mattered in this context, rather, was the separation of national from international affairs, along with the maintenance of what the authorities consistently referred to as L'ordre public.

Looking at border control and surveillance policies in the context of political travel allows us to understand the general dynamics of American engagement with the wider world in new ways. The contact between American political travelers, in particular, with the agents and security institutions of the French state created, in effect, a transnational zone of political activity that has remained unexplored by scholars. As opposed to the study of migration and immigration and their political impacts and meanings, focusing on travelers—who were often literally in physical and legal spaces that were "in between" their home countries and their destinations—shows that, in addition to the influence of Americans on the outside world, or the influence of the outside world on Americans, the meeting point between Americans and the outside world generated a diffuse transnational dynamic and new forms of radical discourse and political action, on both the Left and the Right, and from both the side of the travelers and that of the authorities. American political travelers and French state authorities together created a unique political space that further illuminates the "transnational circuitry" of this book's title.

In the late 1960s and early 1970s, the Vietnam War served as the sort of umbrella cause that united activists of different stripes and drove the sort of international activity that in turn threw state surveillance and travel control, in France as elsewhere, into high gear. Still, for all of Vietnam's motivating power, international politics of the sort I describe above was by no means an innovation of these years, and neither was the French state's attempt to keep apart what it considered domestic and foreign politics: the French had already been practicing forms of border and travel control that were meant to keep specific foreign activists—and thus promoters of international politics—out of the country and its politics. One earlier high-profile victim of this policy was the African American activist Malcolm X, who was turned back at the border when he traveled to France—for what would have been his second trip—in February 1965.[10] The longer-term history of French surveillance of foreigners, and control of its borders, is beyond the scope of this essay.[11] This chapter focuses on political travelers as a category separate from migrants, traders, tourists, and others who crossed borders and also encountered border control. In doing so, I hope to open up scholarly discussion of the concept and the history of "travel control" as an important component and driving force of American and international politics during the Cold War and beyond.[12]

Nor for that matter did the French have a monopoly on the use of travel control and surveillance for political purposes. Michel Foucault and other scholars have shown in different ways that surveillance and "knowledge" went hand in hand with the evolution of the modern state and its goal of social and political control.[13] In the period I cover here, France was not alone in practicing travel control of this sort (when one activist was rejected from entry into France, she was often also not allowed into West Germany or Britain, for example). Indeed, travel control as a policy entailed considerable state-to-state contact; in a sense, one sort of internationalism (cooperation between different national authorities) worked to curtail, or defeat, another kind of internationalism.

But some states practiced travel control with greater zeal and know-how than others, and despite the prevalence of the policy over space and time, it was in France during the Cold War years that this policy arguably reached its zenith and was carried out most systematically. This was due both to outside factors—the global scale of the political events of these years—but also to internal political considerations, and in particular the government's interpretation of the 1968 events, on the one hand, and France's new place in the postcolonial world, on the other. The French state is famously centralized, and internally powerful, with a well-organized bureaucracy and watchful police. These means were turned in their full force toward international political activists in the long 1960s.

There were also a few more prosaic reasons for the increase in political travel to France, on the one hand, and the control of that political travel, on the other. Paris had long been a highly attractive destination for politically, culturally, and intellectually driven travelers. It could serve both as a meeting or transit point for foreign nationals interested in making political connections and promoting causes. (For example, Paris was the primary gateway in the late 1960s and early 1970s for American activists who went to Vietnam, thus heightening both American attention to its own citizens passing through the city en route to Hanoi or Saigon and French attention to foreigners on their way there.)[14] In addition, in the 1960s the growing ease and availability of air travel made political travel more accessible, especially for young people.[15] But with the increase in travel came an increase, or at least a growing effort, at travel control. The state (in this case, France) grew increasingly sophisticated at finding ways to combat what it considered the undesirable internationalization of its national politics.

Yet another crucial factor in this development was the ongoing concern of American policymakers and officials over the politics US citizens espoused and promoted abroad.[16] As both Vietnam and black power gained political traction, so the attention paid to American activists abroad increased. The surveillance, border and travel control techniques, and policy of separation between supposedly national and international politics were transatlantic phenomena, the product of cooperation between different national bureaucracies (in this case, American and French) that may have had competing geopolitical interests but also overlapping concerns and interests when it came to international politics. Different national governments (in this case, the American and the French) worried about the exportation of its own political problems into the global arena, as well as the importation of what they considered external political problems into their own national political arenas. The Americans focused more on export (i.e., American political travelers abroad), whereas Europeans tended to worry about import (i.e., foreign political travelers entering into their territory). But the commonality outweighed the difference, and this can be seen in the ways the intelligence services from the different countries collaborated in monitoring and controlling political travelers in these years.

Although travel control of Americans began earlier, and the events of May–June 1968 came later, we can consider 1967 to be a turning point in this history.

In late March and early April of that year, near the height of the American military involvement in Vietnam, US Vice President Hubert Humphrey undertook what may have been one of the most thankless trips in the history of his office. At Lyndon Johnson's request, Humphrey traveled for a series of meetings with the leaders of America's allies in Europe, with whom Johnson wished to shore up troubled relations. (Johnson himself then similarly toured Latin America.) The tour took Humphrey to Geneva, the Hague, Bonn, Rome, Florence, London, West Berlin, Paris, and Brussels, in that order. The meetings were tense, but that was not what made the trip difficult. At nearly all these stops, and as the press in the communist bloc watched with glee, antiwar protesters harassed Humphrey in various ways; in Berlin, perhaps most memorably, he "survived" a faux-attack by anarchist communards, an episode later dubbed the "pudding assassination."[17] Humphrey spent two days, April 7–8, in Paris. It was probably the toughest leg of a tough journey.[18]

Vietnam did not suddenly burst as an issue upon the French political scene in 1967. There had been previous antiwar demonstrations in France (as elsewhere in Europe) in previous years, and the memory of the country's own disastrous fight against Indochinese independence was still fresh and painful for many.[19] But although the authorities had received some prior warning as to the extent of the protest to come (including from their American intelligence counterparts, some of whom were dispatched to Paris for the occasion), and also knew that Humphrey had encountered noisy protest in his other European stops, the scale of Parisian anger directed at the US vice president still seems to have taken them by surprise. This would have significant political implications.

The protests, spread out over two days, included demonstrations—which turned into riots—outside the embassies of the United States and the Republic of Vietnam; a public burning of the American flag outside the American Church; and an attack on the American Express office. Protesters threw tomatoes and cans of paint in Humphrey's direction, narrowly missing the vice president but hitting some members of his entourage. They were able, briefly, to drape a banner on the Eiffel Tower with the words "USA go home." Riot crews from the Compagnies Républicaines de Sécurité (CRS) responded by pushing into the crowds and, as a result, injuring several protesters. With the possible exception of the so-called "Ridgway riots" of May 28, 1952 (organized by the then-more powerful Communist Party to protest the appointment of General Matthew Ridgway—whom the communists accused of having ordered the use of bacterial weapons during the Korean War—as Supreme NATO Europe commander in place of Dwight Eisenhower), Paris had not seen such violent anti-American street protests since forty years before, on the occasion of the executions of the Italian anarchists Nicola Sacco and Bartolomeo Vanzetti in Massachusetts in August 1927.[20]

In terms of the authorities' response, one crucial difference between prior antiwar (or generally anti-American) protests and the one that took place in April 1967 was the presence of a senior American official whom the state needed to protect. When officials got the impression that the protests presented an actual physical danger to Humphrey, they sprung into action and, indeed, overreaction. After confrontations with demonstrators outside the US embassy and at Place d'Iena, the police reported 59 injured officials, including one who needed to be hospitalized, and 36 whose injuries were bad enough that they were then granted leaves of absence. The press reported even larger numbers: 20 hospitalized protesters, police, and journalists, and 156 arrests.[21]

The anti-Humphrey violence was deeply embarrassing to the police, the city of Paris, and the French government. Many of journalists who were at Place d'Iena to cover Humphrey's visit turned their attention to the actions of the riot police, which meant that they too became part of the confrontation, and their subsequent coverage of the police's behavior was scathing. In the course of the altercations, the police also brutally beat four newspapermen, two of them British and two French. Internal police and government correspondence in the aftermath of Humphrey's visit reveals a high degree of institutional recrimination. The police prefect, Maurice Grimard, was criticized for not having anticipated the scale of protest. City officials had also set up some of the logistics in ways that set themselves up for embarrassment (e.g., members of Les Anciens Combattants et Victimes de Guerre, a group for veterans and families of deceased soldiers, were invited to participate in the ceremony in front of the statue of George Washington at Place d'Iena, with both Pompidou and Humphrey in attendance; that ceremony, thanks in large part to the zealousness of the riot police, turned into the most violent part of the protests). The local *Maire* of the 16th arrondissement deplored the "lack of courtesy toward a nation [the United States] that helped us enormously in the two world wars."[22]

One police report on the incident outside the US embassy included the names of 59 arrested protesters. Worryingly, for the authorities, 46 of these were French nationals (the others included ten Americans, and one each from Britain, Sweden, Tunisia, and Spain). The master list of all the arrested was even more alarming for the authorities: 156 people, of whom 126 were French. Of the 30 foreigners, 18 were Americans, and of those 18, 11 were students. Officials would want in due course to deal with these foreigners, but the most urgent question before them was: Why would French citizens participate in a demonstration against the American war in Vietnam, on which the French government's official position was one of strict neutrality? The authorities would soon come up with an answer: evidently, these local innocents had become mixed up with foreign political elements.

The police files from Humphrey's visit portend the state's forthcoming response to this perceived development. The list of arrested Americans and other foreigners feature names of individuals who would soon star in government documents, as well as the name of an organization, Paris American Committee to Stop War (PACS), that would become menacing enough, fast enough, that the authorities saw fit to outlaw it and deport two of its main activists from France within the year. Humphrey's visit and its aftermath signaled a turning point not only for Americans' political activity in France but also for the state's response to it. This would be the last time that officials were caught, in a sense, unawares. From that point onward, the authorities' attitude toward the Americans in France—and American-related politics in France—would be not one of reaction, but of preemption.

To the French authorities monitoring foreigners' political activity in this period, three American (or American-dominated) groups stood out: PACS, Friends of Resistance Inside the Army (FRITA), and the black power movement, which did not coalesce around any particular group, at least until the Black Panther Party came on the European scene in 1969. There was overlap between these groups, and certainly the state tended to see them all as being in cahoots, even if each group had its own distinct history, goals, membership, and identity. What they had in common that was perhaps most alarming to the authorities (and thus interesting from the perspective of international politics) was that they all tried to establish roots in, or at least contact with, the surrounding French society.

Here I focus on only one of these groups, PACS, as its experience in promoting international politics and facing travel control policies was representative in several ways. In its earliest days, PACS, which was formed in 1966 as a French branch of the American organization "Committee for a SANE Nuclear Policy" (aka SANE), had a reputation for moderation; at least until 1967 the authorities considered its members primarily "peace activists" or pacifists.[23] At the outset of PACS's activity, its founders defined themselves as "non-denominational and politically unaffiliated" and their role as "getting as many Americans in Paris to be aware of what's going on as possible."[24] They did this by bringing in speakers both American and French, hosting American public figures and activists passing through the city, and organizing various cultural and literary events.

But PACS was not spared the general radicalization of left-wing politics in the late 1960s. By the time of the events of Humphrey's April 1967 visit PACS was part of an international network of antiwar activity sometimes called American Opposition Abroad; sister branches of this movement existed, under different names, in Japan, Sweden, Canada, and Britain, among other places. This put the group, which was already closely monitored by French intelligence, even more squarely on the state's radar. As with all such foreigner-dominated groups (i.e., from the French official perspective, groups whose foreign membership exceeded 25 percent), PACS's activities were restricted by the interdiction to engage in direct political protest, including demonstrations.[25] Once the group became identified with the events of April 1967—perhaps unfairly, since while some of the group's individual members were arrested, PACS did not officially endorse the anti-Humphrey demonstrations, and did not make an appearance as a group—its days as an active and tolerated organization in France became numbered. But the state's actions toward PACS exceeded anything that American activists in France had previously experienced and in the way the government approached the issue of foreigners' political activity in France harked back to the years of the Algerian War.[26]

Government files from the period reveal that while the French annoyance with PACS began in the aftermath of Humphrey's visit, its patience with the group ended definitively in 1968 when PACS became associated with two causes that it tried to bring together: the international deserters' network, which supported US army deserters from the Vietnam War, and the student and worker uprising of that year. Two of PACS's leaders would anger the authorities in particular and pay the ultimate price of the government's anti-internationalist policies—deportation.[27]

One of these two leaders was not actually an American, but rather an Austrian national who had been living in France since the 1950s. Thomas (Tomi) Schwaetzer, a man of many aliases, was the (probably unaware) subject of one of the thickest files the French intelligence community may have accumulated on an individual never convicted of a crime on its territory. Schwaetzer was the son of Jewish World War II refugees who had escaped Austria for London in 1938; after sojourns in Palestine and the United States, he finally settled in France, where he became a graduate student of nuclear physics at the Centre National de la Recherche Scientifique (CNRS), France's most important research compendium. This was a station that, in the eyes of the authorities, was not compatible with his role as one of the most dedicated and creative antiwar activists operating in Europe.

The other PACS leader was Schofield Coryell, an American journalist who had also been living in France since the 1950s and eked out a living as a freelancer for left-wing newspapers abroad. Like Schwaetzer, he was arrested during the anti-Humphrey protests. By 1968, Coryell was featuring in reports not only of RG, but also Direction de la surveillance du territoire (DST), the state's principal counterespionage agency—an even higher level of surveillance. The state officials did not like that in Paris Coryell was allegedly establishing political friendships with the North Vietnamese delegates in the country, as well as other Vietnamese communists, especially students. According to RG, Coryell was the primary person responsible for the widening and radicalizing of PACS's activity, including participation in a "Che Guevara week" and public screenings of films about the Vietnam War.

But the downfalls of both Schwaetzer and Coryell would be their involvement—as the government saw it—in the tumultuous events of spring 1968. The 1970 RG report made clear that although Coryell had been politically active since the 1950s, "it was really the events of May–June 1968 that gave free expression to his revolutionary ambitions ... he thought the bell had rung for great changes in our society and that a revolution in France would have incalculable repercussions in the USA."[28] The RG report was particularly vexed over Coryell's writing of solidarity messages for "French revolutionaries" of 1968 and his extensive contacts with American military deserters who, contrary to explicit warnings that they were given by the authorities when they began to arrive in France, had engaged in political activity, most notably the street protests of May 1968. It is worth noting that Coryell himself was not known as a firebrand, never gave speeches, and indeed was and remains unknown to many of the more prominent participants in the political protest of the period. Rather, his political sin, the act that landed him in hot water with French officialdom, was playing the role of a facilitator who brought disparate groups together, in ways that most worried the government. The breaking point for the authorities came when Coryell and his PACS colleagues, in tandem with black power activists, planned to host a public event at the Sorbonne on "the American conduct of war in Vietnam," with North Vietnamese delegates to feature as speakers. The police did not allow this event to take place, and the Ministry of the Interior followed suit, issuing an "expulsion measure" from the country for Coryell on August 10, 1968, and banning PACS as a group outright on August 19, 1968.[29]

An important part of the backdrop was that as of 1968 (and until 1973) the French government offered Paris as a neutral site for hosting the complex peace talks between the United States and the North Vietnamese. French fear of radical activity, and the particular opposition to foreigners taking part in local or national protest, had multiple sources. One was geopolitical and transatlantic: namely, pressure from both the American and French authorities, to avoid the embarrassment of the peace talks taking place with noisy violent protests in the background. Indeed, the official reason that the government gave for banning PACS was that the group's activities "caused harm to the climate of calm and total neutrality that needed to reign in Paris around the negotiations over [Vietnam]."[30]

That, at any rate, was the formal reason given for Coryell's expulsion; internal government correspondence gives a clearer picture of the real threat that this one fairly obscure American presented to the local authorities. The RG director explained in a report to the government that it was necessary to rid the country of Coryell's presence in order to put an end to the "illusions" of some of the deserters, and their French and American friends in Paris, that they would be able to make "political use" of the French state's agreement to let them stay in the country. But the deserters, according to RG's leadership, incited and encouraged by Coryell and others, ignored the restrictions placed on their residency and became involved in the events of 1968. Nor did the authorities in charge of keeping an eye on this group like its members' lifestyles or their famous left-wing French friends, many of who had been thorns in the side of the government for years.[31]

If anything, Schwaetzer was an even greater annoyance than Coryell for the French authorities. Although not an American, it was his constant involvement in American radical politics, and specifically his activity connecting the army deserters to the events of 1968, that got him in trouble with the state. The charismatic and energetic Schwaetzer (known to his friends as Max Watts) was a PACS activist, but his main engagement was with RITA (Resistance Inside the Army), an antiwar group consisting of US soldiers or former soldiers, and its global network of support, FRITA (Friends of Resistance Inside the Army). These groups, RG noted with apprehension, benefited from the political and financial support of a variety of French celebrity intellectuals, including Pierre Vidal-Naquet, Jean-Paul Sartre, and Jean-Marie Domenach.[32]

One of the events that Schwaetzer organized seemed, in particular, to unnerve the authorities. In a mansion on the western outskirts of Paris, owned by an anonymous aristocrat and former general, Schwaetzer, calling himself Monsieur Cook, held a press conference in which he introduced several US army deserters. These deserters told their stories and why they were opposed to the war. Schwaetzer himself, much to the chagrin of the RG agent in attendance, hid and spoke from behind a curtain. The effect, as the agent saw it, was both eerie and politically menacing, making the mysterious "Cook" appear like the puppet master of a movement that was unsettling the political equilibrium in Paris.[33]

Schwaetzer also helped connect the army deserters in Paris to the black power movement, a combination that was anathema to authorities in both Washington, DC, and Paris. (One note sent by American intelligence to French counterparts, asking for information on Schwaetzer's activities, referred to him as "the *eminence grise* of US army deserters in France."[34]) When the radical black activist James Forman spoke at the Maison de la Mutualité (a large hall in the fifth arrondissement), on April 29, 1968, the RG agent in attendance noted that the audience included at least a dozen American deserters, accompanied by Schwaetzer. They came to hear Forman give what the agent described as a "violent diatribe" on the "imperial and colonialist politics of France and the USA."[35] On May 28, at the height of the uprising, the Schwaetzer-led group of deserters sent to the major newspapers a "message of solidarity" with "the struggle of the French students and workers."[36] It was at this point that the French government, specifically the Ministry of the Interior, decided that it had had enough of Schwaetzer/Watts. In September 1968, the Ministry sent down the expulsion order. After some legal wrangling, in June 1969 Schwaetzer, like Coryell before him, was "escorted" out of the country. The protest of his friends, and of his colleagues in the science community, as well as the outrage in the left-wing press, did not prevent the deportation. A Paris Tribunal Court ordered the government to let Schwaetzer back in the country for two days in late 1969 so that he could defend his PhD thesis; but after that, he was gone for good.[37]

The expulsions of Schwaetzer and Coryell, along with the banning of PACS, had a perhaps unintended double effect. On the one hand, it forced the remnants of the group (to the extent that they could or chose to stay in France) to look for other outlets for their political activism and growing outrage over the Vietnam War. On the other hand, it splintered what had been a movement with moderate origins and tendencies into increasingly radical smaller groups. As of early 1969, the new American-led Parisian antiwar group was the euphemistically named "Comité de Langue anglaise" (CLA). In order to avoid being classified as a foreigner-dominated group, a status that in a way had been at the origin of PACS's undoing, CLA attached itself to "Le movement pour le désarmement, la paix et la liberté," a French group led by the journalist and former World War II resistance fighter and anticolonial and antinuclear activist, Claude Bourdet. The authorities, having banned PACS, found themselves facing a new and trickier phenomenon: Americans and other foreigners who now blended their radical political activity with that of French counterparts, including writers, activists, and prominent fellow-traveling intellectuals such as Sartre, Simone de Beauvoir, Domenach, and Vidal-Naquet.

In the fall of 1969, in a sign of growing radicalism, CLA announced that its struggle was not merely against the Vietnam War, as had been the case for PACS, but also against the ensemble of American global politics: nuclear power, policy toward China, and racism in the United States and in the rest of the world. RG would come to classify CLA as part of the wave of New Left groups that, as they saw it, were attempting to subvert society (in America and France) as a whole. Overall, however, the government's overall policy of preventing the importation of the antiwar mass movement into France, and more broadly, preventing the importation of American radical politics into the French national political arena, was successful. In banning PACS, deporting some of its most active and committed leaders, and preventing numerous activists from traveling to the country to forge alliances and continue the radical political struggle of previous years, the authorities were in effect able to marginalize these foreigners, keep them away from the center of political attention, and make sure that the antiwar protests never became a mass protest movement in France in the way that it did in the United States. It would be simplistic to claim that travel control, in this case, defeated internationalism, or international politics. But it clearly served to contain or blunt it.

Among other reasons, the expulsions of Schwaetzer and Coryell were extraordinary, and got a fair amount of attention, because neither of the two was an itinerant traveler in France. Both men had been living in the country for several years, which makes them atypical for a study on political travel; but they were foreigners nonetheless, and their cases reveal how the French state acted to keep separate what it considered external, international politics from what it considered internal national politics.

Both Schwaetzer and Coryell were guilty, as the expulsion orders put it, of "disturbing the public order." When I first encountered this term (*troubler l'ordre public*) at the outset of my research on travel control, and in the context of Malcolm X's *réfoulement* at Orly airport in February 1965, I understood it literally—as a fear of demonstrations or actual violence. Over time I came to see its real meaning, which is figurative—reflecting the way in which state authorities wished to keep the political sphere organized.[38] Coryell and Schwaetzer, and many others who were barred from entering the country or deported with less fanfare, had dared, as foreigners, to involve themselves in political goings on in France, and even more alarmingly, had tried to connect politics in France to politics at the global level. These were grave disturbances to the so-called *ordre public*.

But this is also a story that is specific to American political travelers. The effort to keep internationalism, and specifically American-related politics, from crossing borders, was not a one-sided French effort. When examining specific dossiers in the French archives, very often one comes across notes in English, apparently written by American intelligence operatives and transmitted from the US embassy, asking their French intelligence counterparts to keep an eye or someone or other, to pass on information on certain people's activities, or sometimes to help locate someone of interest who had slipped the US authorities and was suspected to be somewhere in Europe. This was true of both a famous person like Fonda or a more obscure person like Schwaetzer. Similarly, one can find documents in the State Department's records in the National Archives, from the American side, on some of the same people who turn up in the French files, in connection with their politically motivated travels abroad. In this sense, travel control, which was designed to contain the spread of internationalist politics, or its importation into a tightly monitored national public sphere, entailed in itself a distinct form of internationalism. State bureaucracies (in this case, American and French, but others as well) cooperated closely in order to make the policy of travel control work most effectively. In other words, one form of transnationalism worked to curtail, or stop, another.

What makes this history important for students of American foreign relations (or generally, America's presence in the world) is that in this period we see a contest, as it were, that in my view has been dramatically understudied: between accelerated, increased internationalism, on the one hand, and travel control, on the other hand, which represented the state's interest in keeping international politics, and diplomatic relations, in the exclusive domain of sovereign nation-states and their official, sanctioned representatives on the global stage. American political travelers of the unsanctioned sort, the ones who represented themselves, or informal groups, and were oppositional or dissenting in nature, represented a particular menace to this interest—that, in essence, is what the French officials referred to as "disturbing the public order" when they gave the order to keep someone out.

We can see here what the "transnational circuitry of US history" actually meant in practice—American political travelers, encountering travel control and surveillance in a figurative (and sometimes actual) transit zone, reshaped the meanings of their own activism and their understanding of the politics of the day. And the state authorities, in dealing with the menace that they believed travelers represented, were forced to define, and react to, the threat to their geopolitical and domestic interests by marking the borders of that transit zone as clearly—and as aggressively—as they could. In these senses, the history of travel control also points to the ultimate limits of internationalism as well as to the enduring power of the state. Simply put, when it comes to political travel, as in all international travel, the nation-state holds the cards. Its representatives can reject a passport, deny a visa, refuse entry at the border, deport a foreigner, spy on people and groups, and keep its citizens separate from noncitizens. Even in an era of the supposed globalization of politics, of border crossings, of transnationalism, all of which have captivated the imagination of scholars, the nation-state still has the means to contain and even stop these phenomena—and in the era of Vietnam it clearly did.

NOTES

1. Directions des Renseignements Generaux (hereinafter RG), "Les Américains en France," June 1966, Archives Nationales de France, Centre des Archives Contemporaines (hereinafter AN-CAC), 19850087/60.

2. Ibid. There is an abundant literature on Americans in France; the pre–World War II period has received far more attention than the postwar years. See, e.g., Nancy L. Green, "Americans Abroad and the Uses of Citizenship: Paris, 1914–1940," *Journal of American Ethnic History* 31, no. 3 (Spring 2012): 5–32; Warren Irving Susman, "Pilgrimage to Paris: The Backgrounds of American Expatriation, 1920–1934" (PhD diss., University of Wisconsin, 1957); Harvey Levenstein, *Seductive Journey: American Tourists in France from Jefferson to the Jazz Age* (Chicago: University of Chicago Press, 1998); Harvey Levenstein, *We'll Always Have Paris: American Tourists in France since 1930* (Chicago: University of Chicago Press, 2004); Moshik Temkin, *The Sacco-Vanzetti Affair: America on Trial* (New Haven: Yale University Press, 2009), ch. 3 ("The Transatlantic Affair"); Brooke Blower, *Becoming Americans in Paris: Transatlantic Politics and Culture between the World Wars* (New York: Oxford University Press, 2011); Nancy F. Cott, "Revisiting the Transatlantic 1920s: Vincent Sheean vs. Malcolm Cowley," *American Historical Review* 118, no. 1 (February 2013): 46–75.

3. RG, "Les Menées révolutionnaires au sein de la colonie américaine en France," June 1970, AN-CAC, 19850087/64. For background on "expats," see Green, "Expatriation, Expatriates, and Expats: The American Transformation of a Concept," *American Historical Review* 114, no. 2 (April 2009), 307–28.

4. The vast literature on the 1968 political and cultural moment, on the global 1960s, and on the global dimensions of the Vietnam War includes Odd Arne Westad, *The Global Cold War: Third World Interventions and the Making of Our Times* (Cambridge: Cambridge University Press, 2005); Jeremi Suri, *Power and Protest: Global Revolution and the Rise of Détente* (Cambridge, MA: Harvard University Press, 2003); Martin Klimke, *The Other Alliance: Student Protest in West Germany and the United States in the Global Sixties* (Princeton: Princeton University Press, 2010); Andrew W. Daum, Lloyd C. Gardner, and Wilfred Mausbach, eds., *America, the Vietnam War, and the World: Comparative and International Perspectives* (Cambridge: Cambridge University Press, 2003); Gerard J. de Groot, *The Sixties Unplugged: A Kaleidoscopic History of a Disorderly Decade* (Cambridge, MA: Harvard University Press, 2008); Tony Judt, *Postwar: A History of Europe since 1945* (New York: Penguin Press, 2006), 390–449; Arthur Marwick, *The Sixties: Cultural Revolution in Britain, France, Italy, and the United States* (Oxford: Oxford University Press, 1998).

5. Raymond Marcellin, *L'Ordre public et les groups révolutionnaires* (Paris, 1969). For background, see the essays in the two-part forum on "The International 1968" hosted by the *American Historical Review* in 2009. For the parallel process occurring

in West Germany, see Quinn Slobodian, *Foreign Front: Third World Politics in Sixties West Germany* (Durham, NC: Duke University Press, 2012).

6. AN-CAC 19850087/62. Fonda's file at the police prefecture in Paris contains several notes from American intelligence asking their French counterparts for information on Fonda's activities in Europe. "Jane Fonda," PPP. The RG agent who attended one of her press conferences noted worryingly that Fonda spoke "nearly perfect French, with a very light accent."

7. RG began tracking Baez upon her first professional visit to France in 1966. AN/CAC, 19850087/64. For (partial) media coverage of the censorship incident, see "Joan Baez interrompue a 'Tele-Dimanche': Elle voulait lire un message politique," *France Soir*, June 1, 1971; "Joan Baez: Comment j'ai été censurée," *L'Humanité*, June 2, 1971.

8. There is no definitive historical work on the topic of internationalism. For a good introduction to definitions, see Giuliana Chamedes, "Internationalism," in *The Routledge Encyclopedia of Modernism*, ed. Vincent Pecora (New York: Routledge, 2014). See also Martin H. Geyer and Johannes Paulmann, eds., *The Mechanics of Internationalism: Culture, Society and Politics from the 1840s to the First World War* (Oxford: Oxford University Press, 2001); and Akira Iriye, *Cultural Internationalism and World Order* (Baltimore: The Johns Hopkins University Press, 1997). For internationalism as global governance, see Mark Mazower, *Governing the World: The History of an Idea* (New York: Penguin Books, 2012).

9. Marcellin's Ministry of the Interior also banned the right-wing group Occident in 1968, though this was primarily because, as he claimed in his memoir, they had served as a "catalyst" for revolutionary left-wing activity in Paris. See Marcellin, *L'Ordre public*, 54.

10. See Moshik Temkin, "Malcolm X in France, 1964–1965: Anti-Imperialism and the Politics of Border Control in the Cold War Era," in *Decolonization and the Cold War: Negotiating Independence* (London: Bloomsbury, 2015), ed. Leslie James and Elisabeth Leake. See also Temkin, "From Black Revolution to 'Radical Humanism': Malcolm X between Biography and International History," *Humanity: An International Journal of Human Rights, Humanitarianism, and Development* 3, no. 2 (Summer 2012): 267–88.

11. The surveillance and monitoring of Americans in France is but one, albeit intense, chapter in the longer history of surveillance and monitoring of foreigners by the French state. The topic has not received as much scholarly attention as it merits, but a good starting point is Clifford Rosenberg, *Policing Paris: The Origins of Modern Immigration Control between the Wars* (Ithaca, NY: Cornell University Press, 2006). For background on French intelligence services, SDECE in particular, see Roger Faligot, Jean Guisnel, and Rémi Kauffer, *Histoire politique des services secrets français: De la Seconde Guerre mondiale à nos jours* (Paris: La Découverte, 2012).

12. To my knowledge, there is no definitive study of travel control and international politics in history, particularly in the context of political travel. Border control has been thematized mostly in relation to migration or immigration—see, e.g., Adam McKeown, *Melancholy Order: Asian Migration and the Globalization*

of Borders (New York: Columbia University Press, 2008)—but political travelers and their encounters with border control policies have not seen the same kind of scholarly attention. For studies of passports, see John Torpey, *The Invention of the Passport: Surveillance, Citizenship, and the State* (Cambridge: Cambridge University Press, 1999); and Craig Robertson, *The Passport in America: The History of a Document* (New York: Oxford University Press, 2010). Foreigners in democracies have been of interest to political theorists. Saskia Sassen has written about the connections between the nation-state, migrations, and different forms of globalization—see, e.g., *Guests and Aliens* (New York: New Press, 2000). See also Bonnie Honig, *Democracy and the Foreigner* (Princeton: Princeton University Press, 2001).

13. See, e.g., Michel Foucault, *The History of Sexuality*, vol. 1: *The Will to Knowledge* (New York: Vintage, 1990).

14. For American travelers to Vietnam (especially those less well-known than Fonda), see Mary Hershberger, *Traveling to Vietnam: American Peace Activists and the War* (Syracuse, NY: Syarcuse University Press, 1998).

15. On this point, see Richard Ivan Jobs, "Youth Movements: Travel, Protest, and Europe in 1968," *American Historical Review* 114, no. 2 (April 2009): 376–404.

16. For American political travelers in an earlier era and the concerns of the US government, with an emphasis on black activists and the civil rights struggle in a global context, see, e.g., Mary L. Dudziak, *Cold War Civil Rights: Race and the Image of American Democracy* (Princeton: Princeton University Press, 2000); Penny M. Von Eschen, *Race Against Empire: Black Americans and Anticolonialism, 1937–1957* (Ithaca, NY: Cornell University Press, 1997); Thomas Borstelmann, *The Cold War and the Color Line: American Race Relations in the Global Arena* (Cambridge, MA: Harvard University Press, 2003); Carol Anderson, *Eyes Off the Prize: The United Nations and the African American Struggle for Human Rights, 1944–1955* (New York: Cambridge University Press, 2003); Brenda Gayle Plummer, *Rising Wind: Black Americans and U.S. Foreign Affairs, 1935–1960* (Chapel Hill: University of North Carolina Press, 1996); Kevin K. Gaines, *American Africans in Ghana: Black Expatriates and the Civil Rights Era* (Chapel Hill: University of North Carolina Press, 2006); and Azza Salama Layton, *International Politics and Civil Rights Policies in the United States, 1941–1960* (Cambridge: Cambridge University Press, 2000).

17. See Klimke, *The Other Alliance*, 155–7.

18. For Humphrey's visit to Paris, I draw on materials in the classified RG file "Humphrey Avril 1967" in the Archives de la Préfecture de Police de Paris (hereinafter APP). I thank Françoise Gicquel, Commissaire Divisonnaire at the Musée des Collections Historiques de la Préfecture de Police de Paris, for her invaluable assistance in obtaining access to these materials.

19. On France's role in the transition from Indochina's struggle for independence to the American military involvement in Vietnam, see the major study by Fredrik Logevall, *Embers of War: The Fall of an Empire and the Making of America's Vietnam* (New York: Random House, 2012). For Charles de Gaulle and the Vietnam War, see, e.g., Pierre Journoud, *De Gaulle et le Vietnam (1945–1969)* (Paris: Tallandier, 2011). Footage of the anti-Humphrey riots features in *Loin du*

Vietnam (1967), an antiwar film co-directed by Alain Resnais, Agnès Varda, Chris Marker, Jean-Luc Godard, Claude Lelouch, William Klein, and Joris Ivens. See also the recollections in H. Bruce Franklin, *Back Where You Came From: A Life in the Death of the Empire* (New York: Harper's Magazine Press, 1975), 182–93. Franklin, then an assistant professor at Stanford University's campus in Tours, was one of the arrested American protesters.

20. For the Paris Sacco-Vanzetti riots of August 23, 1927, provoked by the executions of two men tried and convicted of a 1920 robbery and murder but widely seen as innocents railroaded by Massachusetts authorities because of their radicalism and ethnicity, see Temkin, *The Sacco-Vanzetti Affair*, 127–33; and Blower, *Becoming Americans in Paris*, 93–5, 114–28. On the Ridgway riots, see, e.g., Rosemary Wakeman, *The Heroic City: Paris, 1945–1958* (Chicago: University of Chicago Press, 2009), 124–7.

21. Some of the press reports include "Concorde envahie par les manifestants," *France Soir,* April 9, 1967; "Plusieurs milliers de manifestants ont participé à Paris aux demonstrations organisées contre la politique américaine au Vietnam," *Le Monde,* April 9, 1967; "Plusieurs manifestations anti-américaines ont ponctué le programme de la visite," *Le Figaro,* April 8, 1967; "Violents incident hier à Paris," *Populaire,* April 8 1967; "Rogne et Grogne Contre Humphrey," *Paris Jour,* April 9, 1967; "Quel Malheur, c'etait un drapeau tout neuf," *Paris Presse,* April 9, 1967. The latter article, about the burning of the American flag outside the American Church, quoted the Dean of the American Church (formally the American Episcopal Cathedral of the Holy Trinity), Sturgis Riddle: "These young people [the demonstrators outside the church] do not represent France. They are a gang of irresponsible beatniks."

22. "Le Préfet de police interrogé sur les incidents qui ont marqué la visite de M. Humphrey," *La Croix*, April 13, 1967.

23. For the organizational history of PACS, based on the group's archives, see Bethany S. Keenan, "'At the Crossroads of World Attitudes and Reaction': The Paris-American Committee to Stopwar and American Antiwar Activism in France, 1966–1968," *Journal of Transatlantic Studies* 11, no. 1 (2013): 62–82.

24. Ibid., 64.

25. Ibid., 80.

26. For earlier French resistance to the internationalization of its major conflict of the post–World War II period, see Matthew Connelly, *A Diplomatic Revolution: Algeria's Fight for Independence and the Origins of the Post-Cold War Era* (New York: Oxford University Press, 2002). For African Americans in France in the 1950s and their stances on Algeria, see Tyler Stovall, "The Fire This Time: Black American Expatriates and the Algerian War," *Yale French Studies* 98 (2000): 182–200; and Michel Fabre, *The Unfinished Quest of Richard Wright* (Urbana: University of Illinois Press, 1993), 461–5, 471–2.

27. Unless otherwise indicated, for my account of the disbanding of PACS and the deportation of its activists I draw on materials in AN-CAC, 19850087/60–4, and on the files "Schofield Coryell" and "Thomas (Tomi) Schwaetzer" in APP.

28. "Les Menées révolutionnaires," AN-CAC 19850087/64.

29. Ibid.
30. AN-CAC, 19850087/62.
31. RG report, January 23, 1970, AN-CAC 19850087/63.
32. "Les Menées révolutionnaires," AN-CAC 19850087/64.
33. Ibid.
34. AN-CAC, 19850087/62.
35. "Les Menées révolutionnaires," AN-CAC 19850087/64.
36. Ibid.
37. Ibid.
38. In this, to be sure, the French are not alone, nor is the phenomenon unique either to Western democracies or to the long 1960s. Most recently, the Chinese government detained Xu Zhiyong, the human-rights activist and transparency advocate, on the suspicion of "gathering people to disturb the public order." See the *Economist*, July 20, 2013, 5.

Index

British Empire
American dependency on, 26–28
dominance of, 20
gold standard, 51
Polignac Memorandum, 27
Brockett, L. P., 65–66
Brown v. Board (1954), 134, 221, 222
Bruere, Robert, 86
Bryan, William Jennings, 41
Buddhism, 104, 105
Bunting v. Oregon (1915), 86–87
Burroughs, Williana, 182–183, 193, 194, 197
Burton, Antoinette, 184
Bush, George H. W., 165
Bush, George W., 165
Bushnell, Horace, 64–66
Butler, Josephine, 102

Cairnes, John Elliott, 67
Calgary Prophetic Bible Institute, 158
Calhoun, John C., 22
Cambridge Seven, 103
Campaign of Action for Equal Pay (Australia), 91
Campbell, Grace, 191–192
Campbell, James T., 107
Canada. *See also* Hodges and neoliberal developmentalism
Social Credit movement, 157–159, 172, 174, 175
Canning, George, 26–27
capitalism reform. *See* neoliberal religionists, and oil industry in Alberta, Canada
Caribbean
Americanization of, 27–28
debt repayment, 31
French imperialism in, 188
Carlson, Paul, 123–126, 128, 141–143
Carlyle, Thomas, 61–62
Carter, Jimmy, 48–49
Carter Bonds, 49
Casely-Hayford, Joseph, 187
Catholic missionaries, 127–128
CAUSA International, 239

CBFMS. *See* Conservative Baptist Foreign Missions Society (CBFMS)
CBMCI. *See* Christian Business Men's Committee International (CBMCI)
CDRN. *See* Comité de Defense de la Race Nègre (Committee for the Defense of the Black Race) (CDRN)
Ceylon
Hindu revivalism, 104
Chamberlain, Jacob, 105–106
Chamberlain, Mary, 85
Chile
applicability of Monroe Doctrine for, 29–30
China
anti-colonialism in, 189
applicability of Monroe Doctrine for, 29
Boxer Rebellion, 106
Protestant missionaries and, 106, 109
Taiping Rebellion, 104
trade interdependence, 41, 45
China Inland Mission, 103, 110–111
Chinese Question, The (Baldwin), 103–104
Chinese Workers Union, 195
Christian Business Men's Committee International (CBMCI), 164
Christian internationalists. *See* Congo and evangelical internationalism (1960-1965); neoliberal religionists, and oil industry in Alberta, Canada; Protestant missionary expansion (1870s)
Church of God in Christ, 132
CIA. *See* US Central Intelligence Agency (CIA)
CIO. *See* Congress of Industrial Organizations (CIO)
Civil Rights Congress, 198
Civil War
global significance of, 57
Monroe Doctrine and, 22–23
post-war cross-national connections, 100–102
CLA. *See* Comité de Langue anglaise (CLA)